PREFACE

This is the first volume of a new verse translation of Aristophanes. It contains his longest play, *Birds*, his sexiest play, *Lysistrata*, and two works from very near the end of his career, *Assembly-Women* and *Wealth*. Volume ii will contain the 'political' plays from the 420s, *Acharnians*, *Knights*, *Wasps*, and *Peace*; Volume iii the comedies on more 'cultural' themes, *Clouds*, *Women at the Thesmophoria*, and *Frogs*, as well as a selection of fragments from the lost plays. The translation is intended to have sufficient clarity and fluency to make it pleasurably readable in its own right, while retaining the historical accuracy necessary for those (not least the large numbers, in both schools and universities, now studying the ancient world in translation) who wish to gain a reasonably authentic feel of the fabric of Aristophanic comedy. The principles on which my translation is based are explained in more detail in the section of the Introduction entitled 'Translating Aristophanes'; see also the Note on the Translation. The Introduction as a whole offers a broad perspective on the plays and their cultural context; it is supplemented by Introductions to the individual plays which are fuller than those which often accompany translations. Taken together with the Notes and Index of Names, I hope these sections provide sufficient information as well as interpretative guidance to enable readers to develop their own appreciation of Aristophanes' work.

In the vexed matter of the spelling of ancient Greek names, I have aimed for reasonable but inevitably less-than-perfect consistency. In particular, I have sometimes kept familiar English spellings where their pronunciation assists the rhythms of the translation. Most dates are BC; the exceptions, especially in the part of the Introduction entitled 'Aristophanes and Posterity', will be obvious. The Index of Names contains only people, places, and institutions mentioned in the translation itself; technical terms relating to theatrical performance are explained in the general Introduction, in the sections 'Formality and Performance' and 'Stage Directions'. Finally, marginal numerals in the translation refer to the lineation of the Greek text.

S.H.

St Andrews,
Spring 1996

OXFORD WORLD'S CLASSICS

BIRDS AND OTHER PLAYS

ARISTOPHANES (*c*.450–385) was the most important poet of Old Comedy, the exuberant, satirical, and often obscene form of festival drama which flourished during the heyday of classical Athenian culture in the fifth century BC. Much of his career fell within the years of the prolonged Peloponnesian War between Athens and Sparta (431–404); three of his plays, *Acharnians* (425), *Peace* (421), and *Lysistrata* (411), draw on the war, though in highly fantastic fashion, for inspiration. The earlier part of his career was dominated by issues from the city's democratic politics and by scurrilous treatment of the demogague Kleon, especially in *Knights* (424) and, more obliquely, in his comedy on the law courts, *Wasps* (422). But Aristophanes also showed a leaning towards cultural themes: hence his caricature of the philosopher Sokrates in *Clouds* (423), and later his burlesque of materials from the tragic stage in both *Women at the Thesmophoria* (411) and *Frogs* (405). A vein of sheer absurdity and dreamlike wish-fulfilment runs through his work, reaching a kind of *ne plus ultra* in the cosmic triumph of Peisetairos, the man–bird–god, in *Birds* (414). His last two surviving plays, *Assembly-Women* (*c*.393) and *Wealth* (388), partly represent a change of direction for the genre, moving away from a biting, uninhibited ethos towards the gentler humour of character and situation which was eventually to generate the New Comedy of Menander.

STEPHEN HALLIWELL is Professor of Greek in the University of St Andrews. He has taught previously in the Universities of Oxford, London, Cambridge, and Birmingham, and has held visiting posts in the Universities of Chicago and California (at Riverside). His many publications cover the fields of Greek literature (especially Aristophanes and Greek tragedy), philosophy, and rhetoric, and his books include *Aristotle's Poetics* (1986), *Plato Republic 10* (1988), and *Plato Republic 5* (1993). He is currently writing a book on *Aristophanic Satire*.

OXFORD WORLD'S CLASSICS

For over 100 years Oxford World's Classics have brought readers closer to the world's great literature. Now with over 700 titles—from the 4,000-year-old myths of Mesopotamia to the twentieth century's greatest novels—the series makes available lesser-known as well as celebrated writing.

The pocket-sized hardbacks of the early years contained introductions by Virginia Woolf, T. S. Eliot, Graham Greene, and other literary figures which enriched the experience of reading. Today the series is recognized for its fine scholarship and reliability in texts that span world literature, drama and poetry, religion, philosophy and politics. Each edition includes perceptive commentary and essential background information to meet the changing needs of readers.

OXFORD WORLD'S CLASSICS

ARISTOPHANES

Birds · Lysistrata Assembly–Women · Wealth

Translated with an Introduction and Notes by
STEPHEN HALLIWELL

OXFORD
UNIVERSITY PRESS

OXFORD

UNIVERSITY PRESS

Great Clarendon Street, Oxford OX2 6DP

Oxford University Press is a department of the University of Oxford.
It furthers the University's objective of excellence in research, scholarship,
and education by publishing worldwide in

Oxford New York

Athens Auckland Bangkok Bogotá Buenos Aires Calcutta
Cape Town Chennai Dar es Salaam Delhi Florence Hong Kong Istanbul
Karachi Kuala Lumpur Madrid Melbourne Mexico City Mumbai
Nairobi Paris São Paulo Singapore Taipei Tokyo Toronto Warsaw

with associated companies in Berlin Ibadan

Oxford is a registered trade mark of Oxford University Press
in the UK and in certain other countries

Published in the United States
by Oxford University Press Inc., New York

First published as a World's Classics paperback 1997
Reissued as an Oxford World's Classics paperback 1998
Reissued 2008

British Library Cataloguing in Publication Data

Data available

Library of Congress Cataloging in Publication Data

Data available

ISBN 978-0-19-955567-3

18

Printed in Great Britain by
Clays Ltd, Elcograf S.p.A.

CONTENTS

INTRODUCTION

Psychologically as well as culturally, the workings of comedy and humour are notoriously resistant to analysis. This is because they involve, to varying degrees, the distortion, confusion, and subversion of expectations which settle what counts as 'serious' within a given framework of behaviour. Yet, despite this intrinsic fluidity, it is possible to identify within the Western traditions of drama two major types of humour which define the opposite ends of a comic spectrum. These two types first emerged in ancient Athenian culture, and they came to be known in antiquity itself by the basic labels of 'Old' and 'New' Comedy. Old Comedy, whose roots, as I shall shortly explain, lay partly in the 'folk' traditions of popular festivity, had its heyday in the second half of the fifth century. Its ethos, as we see from the surviving plays of Aristophanes, is quintessentially zany, fantastic, scurrilous, and larger-than-life; its treatment of characters and actions shows slight concern for consistency, plausibility, or coherence; and it tends to rely on a mentality which is physically reductive and crudely cynical. New Comedy, by contrast, which flourished in the time of Menander and other playwrights during the later fourth and third centuries, is marked by semi-realistic though somewhat stylized characterization, integrated and neatly resolved plots, benign sentimentality, and an underlying tolerance; its central interest is in recurrent tensions in human relationships, both within the family and on a larger social scale; and it is the ancestor, via the Roman adaptations of Plautus and Terence, of later European comedy of manners. The history of ancient Greek comedy was a process of evolution from the first to the second of these species of theatrical entertainment. Although we cannot any longer chart the whole of this process in detail, it is possible to see in the last two of Aristophanes' eleven extant plays—*Assembly-Women* and *Wealth*—indications of a transitional stage which was subsequently termed Middle Comedy and which roughly occupied the first half of the fourth century.[1]

In a career which stretched from 427 to the mid-380s,

---

[1] For further information on Middle Comedy, see the Introductions to the two plays concerned.

Aristophanes wrote more than forty plays for the Athenian theatre. The eleven which remain demonstrate that the dominant traits of his comic style were unrestrained exuberance, irreverence, and indecency, as well as a repertoire of dramatic techniques which revels in the topsy-turvy mixing and jumbling of categories (mythical and actual, human and animal, male and female, abstract and concrete, real and pretended, public and private), as well as the juxtaposing of many disparate registers of language and poetry. To have a chance of appreciating something of this vein of comedy at a distance of two-and-a-half millennia, we certainly need to open our imaginations to an exceptionally multifarious class of theatrical performance, in which vulgarity and sophistication, far-fetched extravagance and down-to-earth grossness, constantly rub shoulders. But we also need a historical framework of understanding, without which the cultural specificity of Old Comedy will elude us.

At the time of Aristophanes' birth, probably somewhere around 450–445, comedy had been part of the official programme at the City or Great Dionysia festival, celebrated around late March or early April each year, for something close to two generations (since 487/486, to be precise). It was added to the events of the Lenaia (late January), another festival of Dionysos, not long before 440, when Aristophanes was a boy or adolescent. For comedy as for tragedy, inclusion in these festivals meant, by the second half of the fifth century at least, performance by professional actors (though amateur choruses) at technically high standards of production which comported with the status of major state-organized celebrations. But Attic comedy had had a long prehistory in a range of improvised and popular entertainments performed by 'volunteers'. That last term is Aristotle's (*Poetics* 4.1449a2), in a passage where he also picks out traditional phallic songs as the most obvious forerunner of the poetic genre of comedy (ibid. 4.1449a10–13). As it happens, Aristophanes himself incorporates a phallic procession into one of his plays, at *Acharnians* 241–279, where we can catch the composite atmosphere of festive ceremonial, bawdy revels, and personal scurrility which might mark such occasions.[2] Here the

---

[2] A comparable example is the Eleusinian procession in the parodos of *Frogs* (316–459), which refers to a mixture of earnestness and mirth at 389–90 and culminates in a representation of communal, festive abuse at 416–30: choral satire is particularly well adapted for evoking the spirit of collective merry-making of this kind.

setting is the carefree and egotistical hedonism of the Rural Dionysia (a local not a centralized festival), as celebrated by the protagonist Dikaiopolis. The scene is in one sense a symbol of Old Comedy's own Dionysiac spirit, but the fact that Aristophanes can dramatize a phallic procession of this type in semi-parodic fashion is itself a sign (albeit a nicely ambiguous one) of how far Athenian comedy had acquired a status above its earthy origins. Beginning from the sub-literary level of folk humour and festival side-shows, comedy had by the mid-fifth century developed into a self-consciously poetic and theatrical genre that was able to sustain a coexistence alongside tragedy at two major civic festivals. In the Rural Dionysia scene of *Acharnians*, we see Aristophanes taking a wry glance at Old Comedy's local roots from the elevation of a state-sponsored dramatic competition at the Lenaia.

Aristophanes reveals his awareness of an established comic tradition above all in the parabasis of *Knights* (514-44),[3] where he surveys a trio of important predecessors from the history of the genre: Magnes, whose career went back close to the official beginnings of comedy at the Dionysia (his first victory occurred *c*.480); Kratinos, whose early plays were staged in the mid-450s but who was still active at this time, and actually competing against *Knights* in 424; and Krates, whose career fell largely in the 440s, and perhaps the early 430s, at a time when Aristophanes is likely to have attended the theatre as a boy. Although the references to these three figures are coloured and embroidered with fictional freedom, they do give us some valuable hints about the features which might have seemed salient to a playwright of Aristophanes' generation in the development of fifth-century comedy. The passage highlights for one thing the visual and musico-choreographic elements which had become so fundamental to comedy's theatrical style, and in which it is reasonable to accept that Magnes had been a pioneer.[4] It mentions also the highly 'urbane' type of wit supposedly characteristic of Krates, whose plays may well have been notable for a less scurrilous seam of humour than was practised by most of his contemporaries.[5] Yet above all it foregrounds, and mock-heroically

---

[3] On the nature of the parabasis, see below, 'Formality and Performance'.

[4] It is not insignificant for Aristophanes himself that Magnes' titles include a *Birds* and a *Frogs*.

[5] In the *Poetics*, 5.1449[b]7-9, Aristotle claims that Krates was the first comic poet at Athens to abandon the 'mode of abuse'—i.e. scurrilous personal satire—and to concentrate on coherent plot-construction.

burlesques, the satirical power of Kratinos, who had dominated the comic theatre of the 440s and 430s (winning a total of nine first prizes) and had specialized in a vehement type of topical ridicule whose targets included Athens's greatest politician, Perikles himself. For all its rhetorical contrivance, then, this part of *Knights* conveys an underlying artistic self-consciousness which recognized the wide range of comic resources made available by the history of the genre in Athens.

The ostensible purpose of Aristophanes' comments in *Knights* on some of his predecessors is to explain why he had not until that date (424) taken personal responsibility for the staging of his own plays. The explanation takes the form of emphasizing, with the colourful elaboration which I have already mentioned, what a complicated and hazardous business it is to produce a comedy in front of a mass festival audience of Athenians. It is plausible that this was the chief reason why Aristophanes, who may have been as young as 18 in 427, turned in the early years of his career to a specialist, professional director-cum-producer, Kallistratos (who may have had qualifications as an actor too). Since Old Comedy employed a chorus of twenty-four dancers (compared to fifteen in tragedy), who needed months of vocal and choreographic training for their substantial and intricate routines,[6] the duties of the producer (*didaskalos*, lit. '(chorus-)trainer') must have been onerous. Inexperience alone makes Aristophanes' early use of Kallistratos understandable; but the fact that several of his later plays as well were produced by others (see the Chronology) suggests that the technical sophistication of theatrical production was by this date giving playwrights increasing grounds for handing over the practicalities of rehearsal and staging to professionals. The old convention of the combined poet-producer, which had almost certainly been the norm for both tragedy and comedy in the first half of the fifth century, was by now well on the wane.

It would be fascinating if we could reconstruct in more general terms how the career of a new, young playwright was launched in classical Athens. Unfortunately our evidence hardly allows us to do so in any detail; but in Aristophanes' case we do have tantalizing hints of some relevant conditions. *Clouds* 528 refers, in connection with his first play, *Banqueters* (427), to a group of people whom the

---

[6] For details of the chorus's main contributions to Old Comedy, see below, 'Formality and Performance'.

author finds it 'a pleasure to mention': we are probably entitled to infer that these were backers or patrons, people of influence who had helped to support his entry into the official world of festival drama.[7] In this same passage Aristophanes talks of himself as an 'unmarried girl' whose baby had to be 'exposed' and reared by another. The reality behind this ironically coy imagery is best interpreted, I think, as a situation in which a gifted but inexperienced young playwright needed extensive help in turning his text into a successful, large-scale performance before an audience of many thousands. Aristophanes is none the less likely to have been involved in theatrical preparations even for his early plays, and *Knights* 541-4 (with its analogy to a hierarchy of functions on board a ship) suggests that he was steadily acquiring familiarity with the arts of production during the period 427-424. As for the ability to write complex texts which were *suitable* for production, Aristophanes must have benefited both from a particularly thorough version of the education in poetry and music which was available to well-to-do Athenian sons,[8] and from many experiences, starting as a boy (cf. *Clouds* 539, *Peace* 50, 766, for the presence of boys), in the theatre itself. But it is also possible that the preparations for, and even the early stages of, his career involved some element of poetic collaboration (of the kind known from other theatrical traditions, including Elizabethan-Jacobean England). The phenomenon of collaboration is, at any rate, apparently assumed at *Wasps* 1018-20, where there is a reference to secret assistance supposedly given by Aristophanes himself to other poets. This is yet another parabatic claim that is no doubt distorted by the rhetorical braggadocio expected of comic poets, but it does receive some support from other pieces of available evidence.[9] No one can now be confident about the circumstances of Aristophanes' 'apprenticeship' in the early to mid-420s, but, given the nature of Athenian theatrical culture, it is a reasonable supposition that they will have been many-stranded.

If, as we earlier glimpsed from the parabasis of *Knights*, a sense of comedy's own history was a factor which helped to shape

[7] On the official procedures involved in gaining selection for a play, see below, 'Old Comedy and Dionysiac Festivity'.

[8] See esp. Plato, *Protagoras* 325d-6c, for a description of this.

[9] See my article, 'Authorial Collaboration in the Athenian Comic Theatre', *Greek, Roman and Byzantine Studies*, 30 (1989), 515-28.

Aristophanes' early development, so too, though in a much more diffuse way, must have been his awareness of working in the largest and most self-confident polis in Greece. Aristophanes grew up at a time when Athens was close to the zenith of its power and authority in the Greek world, during an era of political and cultural life dominated by the leadership of Perikles. The 440s and 430s saw, among much else, the building of the Parthenon as a monument to the imperial leadership and wealth of Athens, and the establishment of the city as a cosmopolitan centre which attracted artists, intellectuals, traders, tourists, and others from all round the Mediterranean and beyond. It was in large part, however, Athens's very success as the head of an alliance[10] of Greek cities gradually transformed into a *de facto* empire which caused in the latter half of this same period a steady deterioration in relations with her main rival, and leader of an alternative power bloc, Sparta. Conflict came to a head in 431 with the outbreak of hostilities which were to run, with only short interruptions, till Athens's final defeat in 404, and which we now know (following Thucydides' conception of it) as the Peloponnesian War. Most of Aristophanes' career, including probably some three-quarters of his output, fell within the years of the war, as can readily be seen from the details of his extant plays given in the Chronology.[11]

The poet's career thus encompassed the years in which Athenian imperial hegemony was challenged and eventually defeated by Sparta and her allies; its latter part saw the rebuilding of Athens's position, and the emergence of new power relations between the leading Greek city states, in the early years of the fourth century. Old Comedy of the kind which Aristophanes practised had been formed in most essential respects in the generation before him, not least under the influence of Kratinos' politically and topically satirical mode of humour. The comic spirit found in Aristophanes' plays therefore presupposes, in its exuberance, its freedom, and its outrageousness, the democratic and cultural self-confidence which had been established in Athens, on the basis of imperial power and the economic prosperity which flowed from it, between 470 and 430. At the same time, his work was produced in a period when this self-

[10] The so-called Delian League, founded in 478/477 in the aftermath of the second Persian invasion: see Thucydides 1.96–7.

[11] The chronology of the lost plays will be separately discussed in vol. iii of the translation.

confidence was being tested and threatened in a war which came to assume unprecedented proportions. Although we cannot precisely correlate the themes and emphases of Aristophanic comedy with the upheavals of the war years, we can at any rate see that without this context much that we find in his plays would not have taken the form that it does. The war itself became a recurrent starting-point for his plots, and three of the extant works (*Acharnians, Peace, Lysistrata*) are in that basic sense 'war plays', though it is important in each case to recognize how very selective, and even unreal, his comic treatment of the war actually is. Other features of Athens's particular historical situation find their echoes in Aristophanes' choice of subjects, among them the supposed workings of the democratic Assembly (*Acharnians, Assembly-Women*), the law courts (*Wasps*), and demagogic leadership of the city in the years after Perikles' death (*Knights*), as well as the officialdom of Athenian imperialism (*Birds*). But it would be difficult to chart a consistent relationship between Aristophanes' themes and the changing currents of Athenian politics and society, especially once sufficient allowance is made for the uneven representation of the different phases of his career in the plays available to us.

The concentration of surviving works from the 420s probably leaves us with a rather unbalanced impression of the playwright's output; but it is none the less far from accidental. This was an intense stretch of Aristophanes' career; between 427, the date of his first play, and the end of the decade he wrote a comedy for each of the major festivals, the City Dionysia and the Lenaia, in most years, and won several first prizes. As a result he became established, alongside his close contemporary Eupolis, as outstanding among a new generation of comic playwrights. During these years he acquired an especially pungent satirical style which owed something to his most successful predecessor, Kratinos. While several playwrights in the 420s fell under the influence of Kratinos, it was Aristophanes who made the most creative and distinctive use of this influence by satirizing the prominent politician Kleon, the most potent figure in the democracy since the death of Perikles. Although Kleon himself may not have been a target in the *Babylonians* of 426, it was that play which provoked him into taking the unusual step of making an official complaint about the comic poet's treatment of Athens's relations with her allies: the gravamen of his complaint was probably that a subject of sensitive importance for the war had been mocked in a performance staged at the City Dionysia when ambassadors from the allied cities themselves were present.[12] This led in turn to the elaborately and scabrously allegorical attack on Kleon in *Knights*, and may have helped, in a way which the dramatist himself could never have designed, to lend a *frisson* of controversy to the early years of Aristophanes' career.

Despite the nature of his clash with Kleon, the extent to which Aristophanes' choice of topics and satirical targets can be interpreted as politically motivated in a thoroughgoing sense remains a keenly disputed issue to which I shall return later in this Introduction (see 'Satire and Seriousness'). But it is worth pointing out here that the 420s witnessed a configuration of factors in Aristophanes' career—not only in terms of his recurrent concern with war and democratic politics, but also in his special attention to a single political leader—which was never subsequently repeated. After the Peace of Nikias in 421, which ended the first phase of the Peloponnesian War, Aristophanes appears to have deliberately moved in a rather different direction. Although we cannot take at face value the account which he gives of this change at *Clouds* 545-62 (a passage revised a number of years after the first performance of 423), it is not meaningless that he there mocks his rivals for continuing to write plays about individual politicians, and boasts, with flamboyant aplomb, about his own perpetual search for comic originality. That passage is entertainingly tendentious, in the usual manner of the poet's parabatic pronouncements, but it contains elements which, in a less rhetorical form, seem to be borne out by our other evidence for his career. In particular, after 420 Aristophanes appears never again to have devoted a play to a single political figure,[13] in the way in which, for example, Plato comicus did on several occasions (with his *Peisandros*, *Hyperbolos*, and *Kleophon*), or Eupolis seems to have done once more around 415, when his *Baptai* ('Bathers') made Alkibiades its major butt. On the other hand, Aristophanes turned repeatedly after this date to mythological burlesque (some ten titles at least apparently belong

---

[12] Interpretation of this episode and its implications can be found in S. Halliwell, 'Comic Satire and Freedom of Speech in Classical Athens', *Journal of Hellenic Studies*, 11 (1991), 48-70; cf. also my Introductions to *Acharnians* and *Knights*.

[13] This includes *Triphalēs*, which was once thought to have been about Alkibiades; see my discussion of this lost play in the Appendix to volume iii of this translation.

in this category), and to themes that were literary or broadly social in comic character. Of course substantial political elements of a kind do appear in some of his post-420 plays, though in the two most obvious cases, *Lysistrata* and *Assembly-Women*, politics is transmuted into the extreme fantasy of 'women-on-top' plots, and there is relatively limited direct satire of contemporary individuals or political issues. So we do have some grounds for supposing that in the rather intense early years of his career Aristophanes had, so to speak, sated his appetite for bitingly political work, and thereafter sought to exploit different possibilities in the repertoire of Old Comedy.

OLD COMEDY AND DIONYSIAC FESTIVITY

Comedy, like tragedy, was not available all year round at Athens in regular performances, but was staged only at a small number of festivals, of which the two main ones, the Lenaia and the City or Great Dionysia, have already been mentioned. The Lenaia took place in mid-winter, the Dionysia in late winter or early spring; but plays for both were selected by major magistrates (Archons) months in advance. In submitting what was presumably an outline and/or provisional extracts, the poet was officially 'requesting a chorus' (cf. *Knights* 513), and in choosing a play the Archon 'granted a chorus', even though the costs of the twenty-four-man chorus, unlike the fees of the individual actors, were defrayed not by the state but by a choregos (a kind of sponsor or impresario) appointed for the purpose on criteria of personal wealth. The long period between selection and performance involved not only rehearsals and the making of costumes (including masks), but also completion and revision of the text. Traces of ongoing revision can be seen, for example, in the case of *Knights*, where gibes about Kleon's 'stolen' victory at Pylos cannot have been inserted before around late August 425, or in that of *Frogs*, where references to the death of Sophokles probably represent a fairly late addition to the text.

The festive context is crucially important for the nature of Old Comedy. The Greek word *kômôdia* means 'revel-song'; a *kômos*, which would frequently form part of a larger festival, typically consisted of a celebratory, exuberant (even inebriated) procession accompanied by song and dance. The ethos of the *kômos* can be sensed at many points in Aristophanes' plays, but perhaps especially in the rumbustious endings of works like _Acharnians_, _Wasps_, _Peace_, and _Birds_: it is no accident that in such cases the opportunity for a _kômos_ arises from, or becomes in some way associated with, the occasion of a symposium (_Wasps_), a drinking contest (_Acharnians_), or a wedding (_Peace_, _Birds_). The generic vitality and freedom of comedy stemmed, as we earlier saw that Aristotle suggested, from the improvisatory spirit of such practices as the _kômos_ and phallic processional-songs. The greater 'respectability' which comedy had achieved by 487/486, when it was first given official status alongside tragedy in the Dionysia, must have reflected a perception of increasingly proficient standards—poetic, dramatic, and theatrical—in practitioners of the genre. But this cultural elevation did not erase the underlying comic impulse towards carnivalesque absurdity, indecency, and vulgarity, all of which preserved a link with the genre's 'folk' origins.

That tragedies and comedies were performed during the same Dionysiac festivals, perhaps even sometimes on the same day,[14] itself epitomizes the double-headed nature of Greek, especially Athenian, festivity. These festivals were both deeply serious, as contexts affirming the collective identity and communal involvement of the democratic polis, and yet at the same time opportunities for a kind of liberated and liberating licence. We can observe these opposed yet complementary forces particularly clearly in the case of the City Dionysia. The festival, which usually lasted for five or six days, was an occasion in part for an exceptionally ostentatious display of Athenian pride and self-confidence. It took place in the presence of visitors from all over the Greek world, including, as earlier mentioned, ambassadors from Athens' allied cities, who brought with them the tribute that embodied their subservience to Athenian hegemony.[15] Its framework, like that of many festivals, was provided by ceremonial processions, prayers, sacrifices, and rituals, and among its oldest elements was the performance of dithyrambs, choral hymns to Dionysos. In addition, the Dionysia contained important public proclamations, such as the bestowal of crowns on public benefactors. Yet amidst all this solemnity there was also a prevailing air of abandon and a heady release from quotidian routine. Much civic business, including that of the courts, was sus-

---

[14] The point is disputed: see my n. on _Birds_ 789.
[15] Aristophanes mentions these aspects of the Dionysia, when making a contrast with the Lenaia, at _Acharnians_ 502–8.

pended for the festival's duration, and prisoners were bailed from the city's prisons. Feasting and revelling of various kinds took place, and it was this side of the festivities which gave great play to the celebratory, *kômos*-conducive traditions from which comedy itself came into existence. If the serious dimension of the Dionysia was typified by ceremonies involving the city's war-orphans in the theatre itself,[16] comedy's inversion of civic seriousness is equally typified by a scene such as *Peace* 1270 ff., where the idea of preparing the young for the acceptance of patriotic–military values is exposed to the scorn of a protagonist bent on festive self-gratification.

The two features of Aristophanes' plays, and of Old Comedy more generally, which most conspicuously express this hedonistic aspect of the Dionysia (and, to a considerable extent, of the Lenaia too) are obscenity and satirical freedom from restraint. Both features could be loosely covered by the Greek term *aischrologia*, which means 'speaking what is shameful'. Comedy, that is to say, incorporated an extreme but temporary escape from the norms of shame and inhibition which were a vital force in Athenian and Greek society. Sexual explicitness, matching the traditional practice of phallic songs, was built into the very fabric of comic performances in the shape of the phalluses and the padding, especially around buttocks and belly, which the actors commonly wore and which gave great scope for physical grotesqueness (cf. 'Stage Directions', below). It was further developed in frequent verbal and physical bawdy (including scatological crudity), such as the scenes between Philokleon and the prostitute in *Wasps* (1341 ff.) or Kinesias and Myrrhine in *Lysistrata* (845 ff.). The extent of this component of Old Comedy should be read as a direct symptom of festive intensity and even of a kind of collective psychological regression—a sign of the genre's charter to throw off the standardly severe inhibitions on sexual language and action in the public sphere.

The same is broadly true of comedy's satirical freedom, which gave it a special privilege to lampoon and denigrate even the most prominent of citizens, including not only leading politicians such as Perikles and Kleon but also the city's major military officers, the generals, during their tenure of office. (See further in 'Satire and Seriousness', below.) While the making of certain serious

[16] The orphans were presented with suits of armour in the theatre, and some were given front seats for the dramatic performances: Isokrates, *On the Peace* 82; Aischines, *Against Ktesiphon* 154.

allegations in public life—such as that of being a 'shield-discarder' or military deserter—was prohibited by law, and would in any case have brought with it the direct risk of political or legal reprisals, comedy appears to have enjoyed a largely unlimited licence to ridicule and abuse, protected as it was by a traditionally sanctioned exemption from the common conditions of public speech. This generalization is not substantially undermined by the fact that on certain occasions the freedom of comedy led to political tensions, as when Kleon reacted adversely to Aristophanes' *Babylonians* in 426 (as mentioned above), and even to attempts, always short-lived, to impose formal limits on what comic poets should be permitted to say. The extreme autonomy which comedy had acquired by the mid-fifth century both reflected and required a buoyant Athenian culture to sustain it. When the city's affairs were under acute pressure, especially during war, even the liberty of comedy could be questioned. And in a longer historical overview we can see that the indulgence allowed to comic poets by Athenian democracy in the fifth century was an extraordinary cultural experiment which gradually gave way, in the fourth, to the more measured type of entertainment which eventually produced the inoffensive urbanity of New Comedy.

In the earlier part of this section I emphasized that Old Comedy was performed in precisely the same cultural context as tragedy. The two genres shared many basic theatrical and dramatic conventions, such as the combination of actors and chorus, the use of masks, multiple role-playing by actors, and some of the same metres and verse forms. It is plausible to suppose that comic poets were influenced by the desire to produce plays that could match tragedy for poetic and dramatic quality, while at the same time creating a variety of entertainment that was in ethos the polar opposite of tragedy. We cannot now confidently reconstruct the lines of comedy's relationship to tragedy before the time of Aristophanes, though the fragments of earlier plays suggest that none of Aristophanes' predecessors manifested quite his degree of interest in the detailed parody and burlesquing of tragic materials. This would help to explain why Kratinos, who seems himself to have turned more readily to epic and lyric poetry for parodic possibilities, made one of his characters refer to someone as a 'Euripid-aristophanizer' (fr. 342), thereby jibing at Aristophanes' particular penchant, well illustrated for us now by *Acharnians* 393–488 and the whole of *Women at the Thesmophoria*, as well as by an abundance of shorter paratragic passages, for extracting comedy out of Euripidean plays and motifs.

Aristophanes was certainly not alone in exploiting a kind of comic 'parasitism' on tragic plays, but he does appear to have made a distinctive trait out of humour which relies on a feeling for destabilizing shifts and overlaps between the disparate voices of the two genres. The modern reader of his plays needs to bear this constantly in mind, since it is so often basic to both his conception of situations and to the fine texture of his writing. The first of these two aspects is easier to appreciate, since it involves overtly marked borrowing from one or more tragic models, as in the *Telephos* parody of *Acharnians* 496ff., where Dikaiopolis moves intricately in and out of the persona of a Euripidean hero. Rather harder to appreciate is Aristophanes' habit of allowing the language and tone of tragedy to infect virtually any context, as when, to take a characteristically unannounced instance, Blepyros inserts two (doctored) lines from Aischylos when lamenting the loss of his Assembly pay:

BLEPYROS [*like a tragic actor*]. O alack alas!
  'Antilochos, lament your fill for me
  And not for my—three obols. The loss is mine.'
  [*Normally*] But what was going on, to make this throng
  Turn up in such good time?

(*Assembly-Women* 391–5)

Without warning we have to adjust to the old Athenian's momentary and partial assumption of the voice of Achilles, from Aischylos' *Myrmidons*, lamenting the death of his companion Patroklos; and then to switch back to his ordinary citizen voice. Literary historians continue to argue about just how precise a knowledge of his tragic 'models' Aristophanes assumed in his audience. What is beyond doubt is that he takes for granted, and comically titillates, a finely tuned ear for the incongruities of blended tragic and comic timbres. That he was able to do so is a reflection on the hybrid cultural conditions of Athenian festive theatre, where the two genres embodied an imaginative range of experience defined by starkly opposed yet equally extreme divergences from the mundane.

THE DYNAMICS OF FANTASY

Although it is hazardous to generalize about Old Comedy on the basis of just eleven plays (out of several hundred staged at Athens

in the course of the fifth century), our appreciation of Aristophanes'
comic artistry can benefit from a critical perspective which sets the
specific features of individual works against the backcloth of generic
characteristics. In this and the following section I shall explore in
turn both aspects of a central and paradoxical feature of the genre:
its combination of imaginative fluidity with theatrical formality.

The fluidity of Old Comedy derives most obviously from the freedom with which it selects and develops its materials, and from the
consequently wide range of humorous modes (satire, parody, caricature, burlesque, bawdy, farce, irony, wit) which it encompasses.
Unlike tragedy, which with rare exceptions such as Aischylos'
Persians came to be circumscribed by the myths of what might be
called 'heroic sufferings' (Aischines 3.153), comedy could and did
take its subjects from virtually any and every source. The stuff of
Athenian life, both high and low; figures and events from earlier
Greek history; the stories of myth, fable, and folk-tale; life on
Olympos and in Hades; the subject matter and styles of other
genres of poetry, including epic, tragedy, and lyric—these and other
spheres were used, in assorted and unpredictable ways, to create the
scenarios of comedy, though more often than not (always, in our
eleven plays) with a dominant focus on the notional 'present'
shared by author and audience. Athenians attending the theatre to
watch tragedies could have clearly anticipated the kinds of story
they would be likely to see. The same people turning up for comic
performances in the fifth century would have had no way of knowing what sort of characters or action they would be treated to, and
their expectations would probably have been limited to, on the one
hand, certain formal theatrical conventions (see 'Formality and
Performance'), and, on the other, the typical ethos of scurrility
and festive indecency whose context I sketched in the previous section.

At the heart of Aristophanes' and Old Comedy's unpredictability
lies the exercise of fantasy, which in this context might be defined
as the unfettered manipulation of materials furnished by the full
gamut of both experience and imagination. One way of gaining a
preliminary sense of how Aristophanic fantasy operates is to consider a characteristic opening from one of his plays. Let us take as
our example *Birds*, which starts in a rural setting (probably indicated, but only sketchily, in the original staging) where two elderly
Athenians, their age and apparently rather ordinary social status

indicated by their masks and costumes, are staggering around with birds on their wrists and with a variety of baggage and paraphernalia. They appear bewildered and lost, and so too, though with more amusement, might an audience be. For what are these old men doing? Their baggage probably suggests a long journey, perhaps even 'emigration', as well as the possibility of a sacrifice. But why are they using chained birds for orientation? As soon as Euelpides tells us that these are birds bought from a named Athenian market-trader, yet purchased with a view to finding Tereus (13–15), we are faced by a binary frame of reference that is quintessentially Aristophanic. We are required not only to accept simultaneously, but also to allow to merge into one another, the real-life logic of the contemporary polis, where ordinary birds are for sale every day on market stalls, and the world of Greek myth, within which metamorphosis from man to bird is possible. We are invited, in other words, into a special comic universe, which both is and is not continuous with the Athens of the audience.

The nature of this comic universe is gradually revealed in more detail when Euelpides eventually turns to the audience at 27 ff. (an extra-dramatic gesture itself characteristic of comic freedom) to explain the situation. Euelpides and Peisetairos are ageing Athenians looking for an escape from the oppressive reality of the city, especially its culture of litigation. That they are so old and yet prepared to turn to such a far-fetched means of release from their frustrations is itself significantly improbable. Aristophanes repeatedly associates the transformations effected by comic fantasy with elderly protagonists who become symbols of prodigious daring and/or rejuvenation (cf. *Acharnians, Knights, Clouds, Wasps, Peace, Wealth*). Moreover, as characters these people are thoroughly adapted to the absurdity of the setting. They do not speak as consistent individuals with whom reasonably predictable dealings would be possible, but as figures whose voices constantly shift tone and level, now reflecting elements of social reality (concern over debts, and so on), now engaging in the artificial joke exchanges of a comic double act (e.g. 54–60), and generally displaying a capacity to tolerate incongruity in themselves as well as around them. This quality, which is familiar to us from the behaviour of stand-up comedians and clowns, and which is a defining characteristic of Aristophanic characterization, can best be described as quasi-*improvisatory*. It leaves the impression that, to invert a principle of

Aristotle's,[17] the figures often say what the playwright wants and not what (in realistic terms) the situation plausibly calls for. It is the freedom of Aristophanic fantasy which gives rise to this malleability of persona (as of plot), so that many of the leading characters in the plays are constructed more by aggregation than integration. We cannot coherently connect the world-weary Peisetairos who opens *Birds* with the world-ruling 'hero' who ends it, at any rate beyond the level at which all his behaviour issues from an underlying pursuit of the pleasure principle (see below).

Already, then, within the first fifty lines of *Birds*, Aristophanes has teased his audience with hints of quirky peculiarity, and then opened up for them a scenario which fuses the possible with the impossible, the real with the mythological, in a manner which can be carried further (with a whole sequence of unforeseen twists) by the rest of the plot. Comparable observations could be made about the openings of virtually all the extant plays. What is salient about the germinal conception of the fantasy fluctuates from case to case. In *Birds* it includes, for example, the cardinal use—as a link between the human and the ornithological—of a figure whose story was one of the most gruesome in Greek myth, involving as it did a combination of incest, rape, murder, and cannibalism. This provides, therefore, a particularly telling example of comedy's ability to convert and travesty tragic material for its own purposes, and something analogous occurs with Trygaios's Bellerophon-like journey to Olympos in *Peace*. In other instances the hinge of the plot's fantasy is a complete transmutation of social and political conditions, as in *Acharnians*, where Dikaiopolis opposes the Assembly and democratic officialdom single-handed; or *Knights*, where a Sausage-Seller, the crudest of tradesmen, challenges the city's leading politician; or *Lysistrata* and *Assembly-Women*, where the wives of Athens conspire to invert the normal relations of power and subservience between male and female in the city. In *Wasps*, on the other hand, as in parts of other plays too, it is a superimposition of the public (the polis) upon the domestic (the oikos), or vice versa, which lies at the core of the action. In yet other cases, especially *Women at the*

---

[17] Aristotle, *Poetics* 16.1454[b]34–5: his principle applies, of course, to the serious genres of epic and tragedy. It would be instructive to see how far Aristophanic characterization could be effectively read as an inversion of Aristotle's own principles of characterization in *Poetics* 15.

Thesmophoria and *Frogs*, it is an interplay between life and theatricality which provides the central mechanism of the plot's development. These rudimentary and partial observations ideally need much fuller refinement, and some of them will be picked up in the introductions to individual plays. But they usefully draw attention to the diversity of ways in which Aristophanes freely manipulates ideas and situations, and in the process creates a field of play for the confusion of those very categories and distinctions whose maintenance is a general prerequisite of the social world.

In terms of what might be called its narrative logic, the type of fantasy characteristic of Old Comedy has broad affinities with both mythology, from which we have seen that it often borrows (and distorts) materials, and dreaming.[18] In all three realms, the impossible becomes not only thinkable but capable of attainment. The mundane impediments which have to be faced in the real social world can be imaginatively ignored in the interests of some grand goal, whether this involves—to oversimplify—the creation of deep and lasting significance (myth), the enactment of basic fears and desires (dreaming), or the pleasure derived from allowing the imagination to blur and dissolve the normally accepted categories of experience (comic fantasy). Equally, and for much the same reason, Aristophanic comedy, dreams, and (perhaps to a lesser extent) myth all share a tendency towards dislocation, discontinuity, and the temporal telescoping of events, so that selective attention to key moments can override the need for detailed sequential cohesion. Finally, these three modes of thought commonly show interest in the concrete, sensuous, or personified representation of abstract and general ideas. In Aristophanes' case, we find, for instance, the chef-like figure of War with his pestle and mortar, at *Peace* 236 ff., as well as Peace herself, the statuesquely symbolic female, in the same play; the caricature of the Athenian people as a semi-senile householder, Demos, in *Knights*; the girl Princess, in *Birds*, who is a symbolic incarnation of the cosmic power which passes from Zeus to Peisetairos; and the blind god Wealth, in the play of the same name, whose entry into a house is tantamount to its acquisition of

---

[18] On the particular relevance of dreaming to the plot of *Birds*, see my Introduction to that play. Note also the start of *Wasps* (13 ff.), where the two slaves narrate dreams which exhibit, in miniature, characteristic elements of Aristophanic comedy itself: narrative discontinuity, the blurring of identities, and confusion of categories (especially human and animal).

material prosperity.[19] Realization of the impossible, narrative discontinuity, and concrete embodiment of the abstract, are recurrent, defining features of Aristophanic fantasy which lend its creations, intermittently at least, an air of comic mythologization and dreamlike transcendence.

I have already stressed how the figures who participate in this world of fantasy tend, though with many gradations, towards a semi-improvised, aggregrative form of behaviour. But there is another essential component of Aristophanic characterization which deserves to be highlighted, and that is the adventurous energy, and sometimes the egotism, of his protagonists.[20] This is a feature which critics have often analysed in terms of wishfulfilment. On this reading, individual characters give embodiment to strong psychological cravings, whether for material goods, power, sexual fulfilment, or a more generalized relief from the problems and pressures of reality. It is easy to find a prima facie justification in the surviving plays for this type of analysis. Most Aristophanic protagonists display a vitality which leads to the breaching of boundaries and the transgression of norms, whether those of class (e.g. with the peasant-farmers of *Acharnians* and *Peace*, or the Sausage-Seller in *Knights*, all of whom discover an improbable political prowess), of age (as with the elderly males of *Acharnians*, *Wasps*, *Peace*, and *Birds*, who experience a rejuvenation in their vigour, sexuality, capacities of persuasion, and so on), of gender (as with the active heroines of *Lysistrata* and *Assembly-Women*), or even of 'biology' (as with the god-defying Trygaios in *Peace* or the semi-metamorphosed Peisetairos in *Birds*).

Yet wish-fulfilment in its most self-centred forms is a far from invariable trait of these figures. In most plays the action of the central character(s) involves the exercise of a radical, problem-solving ingenuity, whether individual or collective; and in every case but one (the exception being *Clouds*[21]) the end result is the gratification of fundamental desires or the harmonization of previously conflict-

---

[19] The idea of a domestic visit from Wealth, as a metaphor for prosperity, occurs in a fragment of the sixth-century iambic poet Hipponax (M. L. West (ed.), *Iambi et Elegi Graeci* (2nd edn., Oxford, 1989–92), fr. 36).

[20] It is no coincidence, in view of the previous paragraph, that these are features, respectively, of many myths and dreams.

[21] Strepsiades is ultimately left with the pleasure of revenge, but that does nothing to mitigate the outright failure of his original and driving desire to escape his creditors: see the Introduction to the play.

ing forces. In the broadest terms, power is a salient goal and/or achievement in *Knights*, *Birds*, *Lysistrata*, and *Assembly-Women*, though in all of these but *Knights*[22] it is coupled with some variety of sexual fulfilment, which is also an achievement of the protagonists of *Acharnians*, *Wasps* (briefly, at least: 1341 ff.), and *Peace*. The attainment of wealth, and escape from the conditions which threaten or diminish it, is the aim that drives the protagonists of *Clouds* and *Wealth* itself, and a benefit that accrues to Dikaiopolis in *Acharnians* and to everyone in *Assembly-Women*. The desire for peace, with the wider potential for prosperity (including wealth and sexual fertility) which it represents and presumptively creates, is the central goal of *Acharnians*, *Peace*, and *Lysistrata*, and plays a subordinate part in *Knights* (1388 ff.) and *Birds* as well. *Women at the Thesmophoria* and *Frogs* are less easy to categorize in such basic terms, but both construct a solution to difficulties and conflicts: the former resolves the male/female and poetry/life tensions between Euripides and the city's women, while the latter celebrates a triumphant finale that equates Athenian 'salvation' with the recovery, via Aischylos, of ancestral wisdom, strength, and peace.

As even this schematic survey of the plays indicates, the model of comic fantasy as wish-fulfilment needs to be qualified by a recognition of the complexities and peculiarities of individual figures and their situations. Although egotism *qua* bold self-assertion is a recurrent characteristic, Aristophanic protagonists are certainly not uniform manifestations of a Freudian id or of purely selfish instincts. Peisetairos in *Birds* comes closest to this status: his original desire, shared with Euelpides, for a decadently sybaritic life (128–42) is eventually fulfilled in a blaze of cosmic glory in which, as mentioned, power and sexuality coalesce. Philokleon in *Wasps* is Peisetairos's nearest neighbour in terms of a craving for pleasure without responsibility, and this is equally true of him both in his role as juryman and in the rechannelled energies of the later scenes: what he loses by way of power over others in the courts he more than makes up for in the rampant and irrepressible sensuality of his new social life. But other protagonists, with the exception of Strepsiades in *Clouds* (whose immoral ambitions remain finally unfulfilled), are impelled by mixed impulses. Dikaiopolis in *Acharnians* initially wants the city as a whole to make peace; the

---

[22] Even there we have the sexual symbolism/incarnation of the peace libations at 1388 ff.

fantasy of his exclusive peace treaty stems from a thwarted political desire, not from sheer selfishness. What Dikaiopolis originally craves is what Trygaios actually brings about in *Peace*, with the help of the farmers whose class he belongs to: both the internal dynamics of the plot and the contemporary context of an imminent peace treaty between Athens and Sparta make the protagonist's achievement, like his marriage to Harvest, an emblem of something more-than-individual. In the cases of *Lysistrata*, *Assembly-Women*, and *Wealth* the communal concerns of the main character are unequivocal. Chremylos, in *Wealth*, is troubled by a decline in moral behaviour and social justice; what he goes on to accomplish is restored prosperity not just for himself but for all 'decent' people. Lysistrata and Praxagora are patently motivated by the interests not only of all women but of all Athenians (even, in Lysistrata's case, all Greece). The former is prepared to use the containment of female libido, paradoxically combined with the arousal of men's, for the higher goals of peace and marital concord; Praxagora goes further still, planning a female seizure of power in pursuit of permanent utopia for the entire polis. Different again is the Sausage-Seller of *Knights*, whose initial role (foisted on him by others: an unusual pattern[23]) as the *ne plus ultra* in political depravity is subsequently overtaken by the function of saviour of the democracy. Finally, even the 'effeminately' sensualist Dionysos of *Frogs*, for whom the idea of bringing back Euripides from the dead has an almost physical intensity (52–66), turns out, in a typically late twist to the plot, to have a public-spirited interest in bringing back from Hades a poet who can help to 'save' the city (1419).

Aristophanic protagonists, then, typically possess a determination, inventiveness, and confidence which make them suitable agents for the achievement of fantastic ends. But their specific motivations vary considerably, and may well change, without much regard for plausible consistency of character, in the course of the play. Furthermore, the success and hedonistic gratification which usually come their way are not necessarily accompanied by outright self-centredness: to judge by the eleven plays we have, these characters are, or aspire to be, 'saviours' as often as they are egotists. One important implication of these claims is that there are no

---

[23] The nearest parallel is *Women at the Thesmophoria*, where Euripides tries to enlist Agathon's services and then falls back on those of the Kinsman.

straightforward conclusions to be drawn about the relationship between the protagonists of Old Comedy and the allegiances of the mass audiences which gathered for the Dionysiac festivals at Athens.

In the past critics have too often attempted to construct or detect correlations between Aristophanes' choice of characters and particular sections of Athenian society, especially the smallholder farmers who made up a substantial portion of the demos. Sociological hypotheses have led to critical judgements about the intrinsically 'sympathetic' nature of certain protagonists. But there are too many variables in the configurations of plot and protagonist to yield useful generalizations of this kind; each case needs considering on its merits. For example, Dikaiopolis in *Acharnians* and Trygaios in *Peace* both belong to the same broad class of peasant-farmers, yet the question of how 'sympathetic' either of them might have been to an Athenian audience at large cannot be treated independently of their specific contexts: above all, it makes a big difference that Dikaiopolis' opponents, the Acharnians themselves, are also farmers. Strepsiades in *Clouds* is also from a rural background, but both his utter immorality and the distinctive nature of his marriage to an aristocratic woman give his case a special slant. In *Knights*, on the other hand, the 'hero' is a sausage-seller who can only represent a class of low urban workers, if he represents anything at all; yet the momentum of the allegorical satire, particularly in the later stages, makes him apparently a figure with whom the audience is invited to 'sympathize'. It is arguable that in another case again, that of *Birds*, the protagonist is sociologically somewhat indeterminate, though conceivably thought of at one point (33, where there is reference to the characters' clear 'ancestry') as from a well-to-do family which has fallen on hard times.[24] But his salient features are old age and disillusionment with Athenian litigiousness; it is hard to see that this makes him 'identifiable' in class terms for an audience. These examples bear out the difficulty of assimilating Aristophanic protagonists to a uniform model. They also indicate the danger of assuming that the kinds of fantasy in which the protagonists become involved can be interpreted so as to yield a consistent pleasure or satisfaction, other than that of rather primitive psychological

[24] It is possible that costume was used to mark him as a rustic, but if so the text gives no clue to this. His companion Euelpides is apparently given a rural deme at 496 (but a different one at 645!).

urges, for the large and mixed audiences of Athenian citizens who watched the plays.

FORMALITY AND PERFORMANCE

Old Comedy is remarkable, as we have seen, for its festive freedom and the imaginative plasticity of its plots and protagonists. But it was also, and just as significantly, a genre which exhibited a high degree of formality and structural patterning—more so, perhaps surprisingly, than tragedy. The origins of this formality have been often but inconclusively investigated. For our purposes it is enough to register the fact that the fragments of Old Comedy establish that the types of structure found in Aristophanes' surviving plays were well established before his time and were, in the second half of the fifth century, the common property of all comic poets. That is not, however, to suggest that the formality of the genre was static. Aristophanes' own works clearly show otherwise, and it was change and experiment in this area which contributed greatly to the evolution of the new phase of comedy, Middle Comedy, which we see in the last two extant plays, *Assembly-Women* and *Wealth*.

The formal conventions and structures of interest for us in this section have to be identified, for and by the modern reader, on the printed page.[25] But it is essential to grasp at once that for Aristophanes and his audience they were integral to *performance*— that is, to presentation through verbal/rhythmical shape, musical character, and visual reinforcement (especially dance). To understand something of the theatricality of these elements, then, we need to know that comedy, like tragedy, used three principal 'modes' of performance:[26] first, the spoken verses of the iambic trimeter, a metre whose poetic nature is flexible enough to admit a large range of styles and registers, including the colloquial; secondly, longer verses, in both iambic and other rhythms, which were probably chanted or declaimed (often by the chorus-leader), to the accompaniment of the reed pipe (*aulos*), in a way which is now cus-

---

[25] My translation marks the major formal sections of each play, in order to keep the reader alert to this aspect of comic theatricality.

[26] Cf. my further comments on these modes in 'Translating Aristophanes' below. Comedy also occasionally admits short portions of prose, such as the Herald's announcements at *Acharnians* 43, 61, 123, the Decree-Seller's utterances at *Birds* 1036 ff., or the Woman's instructions at *Women at the Thesmophoria* 295 ff.

tomarily termed 'recitative';[27] and, finally, the full-blown song of lyric sections, again accompanied by the *aulos*, which make use of a very wide selection of rhythms but are frequently constructed in matching strophic pairs (strophe + antistrophe). Of these modes, the first and second depend on stichic metres—that is, those involving the repetition of regular 'lines'—whereas the lyrics comprise units of varying length. Both the second, when employed by the chorus, and (virtually always) the third mode were delivered and supported with choreographed movements.

In our surviving fifth-century tragedies the recitative mode is put to more limited use than in comedy, being predominantly limited to (part of) the entrance, or parodos, of the chorus in certain plays. For the most part, tragedy is constructed from scenes of iambic speech/dialogue, alternating with the lyric songs or odes of the chorus (and sometimes of individual characters too). Old Comedy, too, employs iambic speech and free-standing choral songs, but it also makes much more extensive use than tragedy of recitative, which it incorporates into large-scale structures of a strikingly formal, often symmetrical, type. This is all part and parcel of comedy's interest in a theatrically flamboyant and showy style of entertainment which maximizes the resources of both actors and singers/dancers. In this connection it is helpful to keep in mind two attributes of the comic chorus which differentiate it from the tragic variety: first, its size, namely twenty-four dancers as opposed to tragedy's fifteen (originally twelve); secondly, its characteristically colourful and elaborate costuming, often involving animal forms (wasps, birds, frogs, and so on) or the distinctive accoutrements of special groups such as the charcoal-burners of *Acharnians*, the cavalry of *Knights*, or the old men (with logs, and so on) and women (carrying buckets of water) in *Lysistrata*. These features contribute to, and can be illuminated by, the three major formal units or sequences of Old Comedy—the parodos, agon, and parabasis—which I shall now consider in turn.

The parodos is the section of a play built around the entrance of the chorus.[28] Aristophanes always treats it as a dramatic event or

---

[27] Since this term has been borrowed from musical usage, it is worth remembering that early Italian opera, which invented the practice, was influenced by the belief (largely mistaken) that *all* parts of classical tragedy were musically accompanied.

[28] An exception, which reflects the development of Middle Comedy, is *Assembly-Women*, where the chorus exits at 285 ff. (and returns at 478 ff.): see the

episode in its own right, not just a juncture in the performance; he uses the organization of the parodos, which was clearly a formal convention long before his time, to create a specific and usually extravagant effect. The chorus's movements are always choreographed to represent a particular kind of action, condition, or mood, ranging from the eager animosity of the charcoal-burners in *Acharnians* to the pathetic sluggishness of the old jurors in *Wasps*,[29] from the earthy robustness of the farmers in *Peace* (complete with spades, crowbars, and ropes) to the ethereal remoteness of the cloud-deities in *Clouds*. No two parodoi are identical in form;[30] each one manifests a variable amalgam of the three modes of delivery, but especially recitative and song, moulded so as to express the dramatic interaction between chorus and characters. In *Knights*, for example, the choral entry comes in response to the request from one of the slaves for assistance in the fight against the Paphlagonian (242–6). It is entirely in recitative mode, whose rhythms here convey the mimicry of a galloping cavalry attack (247 ff.). Whether on pantomime horses or in piggy-back fashion, the dancers manœuvre themselves in quasi-equestrian formation, circling round, cornering, and eventually assaulting the Paphlagonian with—among other gestures—kicks to the belly (273). The sight of cavalry drill would have been familiar to most Athenians from training-grounds in the city, but this parodos is of course a burlesque version of the practice, in which the model of equestrian exercises is comically suffused with the ethos of crude brawling, wrestling imagery, and political polemics.[31] Taken as a whole, from 247 to 302, the parodos of *Knights* constitutes a gradual crescendo of verbal and physical hostility: the effect of the Knights' onslaught is to embolden the Sausage-Seller, who gradually takes over the momentum of the campaign against the Paphlagonian.

In *Birds* the parodos is different in a number of respects. For one

---

Introduction to the play. More complex is the case of *Frogs*, where 209 ff. serves as a sort of 'false' parodos (whether or not the frogs are actually visible), to be followed in due course by the arrival of the main chorus at 316 ff.

[29] After the warning of waspishness at 223 ff., the parodos brings a humorous defeat of expectations; 404 ff. subsequently functions as a kind of deferred or postponed parodos of the chorus *qua* wasps.

[30] In fact, there is legitimate disagreement about precisely how to delimit the parodos of a comedy; but this technicality does not affect my general observations.

[31] See my Introduction to *Knights* on the different levels of significance in the play's allegory.

thing it is unusually preceded, or initiated, by the appearance of four extra dancers in specially ostentatious bird costumes on the roof of the stage building (267–93). Aristophanes teases the audience at this point, raising the possibility that the whole chorus may enter individually on the roof (i.e. 'in the air'). But at 294, as the human characters look into the sky for further birds, the real chorus suddenly enters on ground level in a flurry of running, wing-flapping, and screaming cries. All this multiform ornithological commotion is going on for sixteen lines (294–309) before the chorus-leader starts to chant, in recitative, on behalf of the group. Uniquely as far as the surviving plays go (but there were precedents and parallels in lost works), the twenty-four dancers are individually costumed to represent different species. Unlike the announced cavalry attack in *Knights*, this parodos initially projects a confusion of colour, movement, and sound, and it is a crucial part of the comic effect that only gradually, at least to the humans themselves, does it become apparent that the birds are collecting with menacing intentions. Also, whereas in *Knights* the chorus's hostility is a burlesque version of an obvious model—real-life cavalry man-œuvres—the birds' aggression incongruously endows the animal-chorus with a type of behaviour not naturally characteristic of it. At any rate, it seems likely, in view of the military language later in the encounter at 352 ff., that the birds' parodos made use of choreography which included not only feathery agitation but also movements and gestures reminiscent of warfare. Here, as elsewhere in the play, the comedy engenders a deliberate confusion of the ornithological and the human.

After the preliminary information provided by the prologue of a comedy, the parodos usually carries with it a grand expansion of the play's scenario through a rich array of poetry, dance, and music. It sets up an interplay, whether of alliance or hostility, between characters and chorus, or even within the chorus itself, where, as in *Lysistrata*, it is divided into two opposed halves. The parodos typically initiates or prepares for a drama of confrontation, which brings us to the second of the three major forms with which we are concerned. This is the agon, the 'contest' or 'debate'. Formal competition was a pervasive feature of Greek culture, and the term *agôn* was applied to the adversarial contexts of speeches in law courts and political assemblies, to athletic events, to military conflicts, as well as to dramatic competitions themselves. Although

military associations regularly attach themselves to the larger setting of a comic agon, it is the first of these areas—the sphere of verbal and argumentative contests—which lends the convention its
predominant tone of keen dialectic. Moreover, the agon not only
provides the framework for a specific dramatic clash; it also allows
for the opening-up of general issues—political, educational, artistic,
and so on—which go beyond the immediate situation in the play.

In its full form, the agon is a substantially symmetrical structure,[32] each half of which comprises (i) a lyric section, in which the
chorus elaborates on its expectations of the speaker; (ii) a long
stretch of recitative, introduced by an exhortation to the partici-
pants by the chorus, and containing the arguments themselves; (iii)
a climactic conclusion and tailpiece to the recitative, consisting of
shorter lines and more rapid rhythm—a kind of accelerando flour-
ish. This is the form which occurs, for example, at *Clouds*
949–1104, *Wasps* 526–724, *Lysistrata* 476–607. The symmetry of
the full agon thus constitutes a combination of songs and declama-
tions, technically known as a syzygy, which we shall shortly meet
again in the parabasis and whose main components can be set out
in diagrammatic form as in Table 1.[33] The importance of this symmetry is that it represents the harnessing of poetry, music, and (for
the lyrics) dance, to create a theatrical design which in performance
would be simultaneously aural and visual. Although the parodos

TABLE 1. *Symmetrical structure of the Aristophanic agon*

	First half	Second half
SONG/DANCE	(1) strophe: choral expectations	(1) antistrophe
RECITATIVE	(2) arguments (introduced by choral exhortation)	(2) counter-arguments (with second exhortation)
	(3) accelerando conclusion ('pnigos')	(3) accelerando conclusion

[32] The agon proper is sometimes preceded by a preparatory recitative or proagon
(e.g. *Clouds* 889–948, *Lysistrata* 467–75): I ignore this for present purposes.
[33] The technical terms normally used for the components are: ode/antode
(songs); epirrhema/antepirrhema (arguments); katakeleusmos/antikatakeleusmos
(exhortations); pnigos/antipnigos (conclusions).

and the agon both use a combination of song and recitative, it is easy to see why the agon but not the parodos should usually be symmetrical. Where the parodos forms a dynamic juncture, connecting the prologue to what follows (often the agon itself) and moving the action forward into a new phase, the agon supplies a framework in which the issues of a conflict can be squarely faced up to and, more often than not, resolved. Theatrical patterns mirror dramatic functions.

Just as in the parodos, however, the precise deployment and function of the agon vary from play to play. It is sometimes argued that the norm is a single complete agon occurring in the first half of the drama, i.e. before the main parabasis, and producing an outcome whose consequences are then explored (typically through a sequence of 'intruder-scenes', as in e.g. *Acharnians* or *Birds*) after the parabasis. But, as with so many aspects of Old Comedy, talk of norms can be misplaced: the scheme just indicated is strictly found in only two of the surviving works, *Wasps* and *Birds*, though in a third, *Lysistrata*, there is something close to it.[34] *Frogs*, by contrast, has an agon in the second half of the play, for it is only there that a contest between Aischylos and Euripides (an element not anticipated in the earlier scenes) is staged. In *Knights* and *Clouds* there are actually two full agons.[35] In *Knights* this reflects the fact that most of the drama is an ongoing, serial conflict between the Sausage-Seller and the Paphlagonian, and is not settled until the latter's final defeat at 1263. In *Clouds*, on the other hand, the second agon serves a comically ironic function, by marking the reversal which Strepsiades suffers when his son uses against him the very sophistic education which he had originally so much wanted him to obtain.

Several plays (*Peace*, *Women at the Thesmophoria*, *Assembly-Women*, and *Wealth*), on the other hand, possess only a half-agon, where formality of structure is retained but without the symmetry. In *Peace* (582–656), at least, this scaling-down probably arises from the agon's special function as explanation (of Peace's absence from

[34] The victory won by the women at *Lysistrata* 607 is only over the Commissioner; resolution of the larger male/female conflict has to wait till much later in the play.

[35] Passages such as *Wasps* 334–402 and *Birds* 327–99 are also sometimes counted as preliminary agons: what is certainly germane is that these passages do display, on a smaller scale, the theatrical symmetry which gives the agon its distinctive shape.

Greece) rather than debate. In *Assembly-Women* and *Wealth* it is more likely a symptom of the overall decline in theatrical formality and in the chorus's role which characterizes the period of Middle Comedy. Finally, Aristophanes' earliest surviving play, *Acharnians*, has no formal agon at all, in the sense considered, even though it does involve a scene of quasi-forensic confrontation in which Dikaiopolis has to defend himself against the chorus's aggressive allegation of treason. Here the omission of a structured agon seems to be motivated by the desire to give the protagonist a parody of the great speech of self-defence made by Telephos in Euripides' play of that name. There are other variables too in Aristophanes' manipulation of the agon, such as the difference between genuinely two-sided debates (e.g. *Clouds*, *Wasps*) and those which are dominated by a single party (e.g. *Birds* and *Lysistrata*). But enough has been said already to indicate that the agon is at the same time a structure of elaborately theatrical formality, and yet a dramatic unit which can be tailored in diverse ways to suit the particular character of any plot in which it finds a place.

Whereas the agon, like the parodos which I considered earlier, is always causally integrated into the plot, the last of the major formal sequences of Old Comedy, the parabasis (*parábasis*, plural *parábases*) functions above all as a major interlude. The parabasis has often been thought to be a very old formal sequence, though there is no agreement whether it might originally have been placed before or after the dramatic action. In the surviving comedies it is typically positioned somewhere towards the middle of the plot, the limiting cases being *Clouds* (510 ff.), where only a third of the play precedes it, and *Wasps* (1009 ff.), where it occurs two-thirds through the work. The parabasis, whose Greek meaning is 'stepping forward', is definable as a section of performance in which the chorus, normally alone on stage,[36] goes through a routine which is addressed directly to the audience and therefore stands outside the structure of the plot. The full form of that routine is introduced by a short linking comment (song or recitative) on the preceding scene, continues with the parabasis proper (a substantial recitative section of audience-address, sometimes called the 'anapaests'), and is completed by a symmetrical pattern or syzygy—song, recitative; match-

---

[36] *Women at the Thesmophoria* 785–845 is an exception: the Kinsman is on stage too, trapped at the altar of the Thesmophoreion.

TABLE 2. *Formal structure of the Aristophanic parabasis*

SONG/RECITATIVE	Linking comment, usually addressed by the chorus to departing character(s)
RECITATIVE	Parabasis proper ('anapaests'), addressed by the chorus to the audience
SONG	Strophe (typically a prayer/hymn)
RECITATIVE	Declamation ('epirrhema'), usually delivered in the chorus's dramatic identity
SONG	Antistrophe
RECITATIVE	Matching declamation ('antepirrhema')

ing song and recitative—which is parallel to that of an agon. The structure thus takes the form indicated in Table 2.

This full form is found, with only small variations, in *Acharnians, Knights, Clouds, Wasps,* and *Birds. Peace, Lysistrata, Women at the Thesmophoria,* and *Frogs* all have reduced or reorganized parabases, while by the time of *Assembly-Women* and *Wealth* the convention has disappeared altogether. This distribution tends to suggest that the parabasis exercised a declining appeal for poets and audiences in the later years of the fifth century and beyond. That inference is reinforced by the parallel disappearance of 'second parabases': the plays which have this component, usually a reduced version of the main parabasis, are *Knights, Clouds, Wasps, Peace,* all from the 420s, and *Birds* of 414; but in the last five works the only remaining trace of this convention is the section of audience-address at *Assembly-Women* 1154-62.

Unlike the parodos and agon, where the choral element was interwoven with the world of the dramatic characters, the parabasis was an exclusively choral presentation which exploited to the full the vocal, choreographic, and visual aspects of the dancers. But that general observation fails to do justice to what is the most remarkable feature of the parabasis, namely its fluctuations and flexibility of 'voice'. There are three fundamental personae or points of view which can be adopted, in part or whole, by the chorus of a parabasis. The first is that of the poet, which can be expressed in either the first-person singular, as though the playwright himself were speaking (*Clouds* 518-62), or in the third-person singular, with the chorus(-leader) 'reporting' a message from the poet

(*Acharnians, Knights, Wasps,* and *Peace*): at *Acharnians* 659–64 and
Peace 754 ff., there is a switch from the third to the first person
within the same passage. The second persona is that of the chorus's
dramatic identity, and this is the usual voice in which they deliver
the symmetrical section (the syzygy), both songs and recitatives, as
we see from all the surviving parabases except *Peace* and *Frogs*. But
here too there are variations of emphasis: in *Acharnians*, for example, one song reminds us of the chorus's primary status as charcoal-
burners (665–75), but what follows represents the standpoint of old
men in general. The third stance sometimes assumed in the parabasis—as *Peace* (773 ff.) and *Frogs* (throughout)[37] demonstrate—is
that of a comic, dramatic, or festival chorus pure and simple, without more specific signs of identity.

The availability of these different voices and frames of reference,
often juxtaposed within a single parabasis, yields a particularly rich
vehicle of poetry, humour, and thematic material. Indeed, the
length of the parabasis, together with the fact that it never concretely affects the action of the play proper, makes it—unlike either
the parodos or the agon—a strikingly free-standing form in its own
right, which is the main reason why it has been the subject of so
much speculation regarding its origins. Aristophanes' plays from
the 420s suggest that the independence and the internal complex-
ity of the parabasis gave it, at that stage of comedy's history, attractions for both playwrights and audiences. One of the most
interesting of these attractions can be described as a kind of theatrical self-consciousness, to which I drew attention in a previous
section when discussing the parabasis of *Knights* (see 'Aristophanes'
Career in Context'). It is a related point that Aristophanes uses the
parabases of his early plays to build up an extravagantly rhetorical
image of the poet's own character, standing, and ambitions, as well
as the supposed shortcomings of his rivals.[38] Perhaps his most vir-
tuoso effort in this respect is the section of *Wasps* (1030 ff.) where
he depicts himself as a new Herakles fighting against the terrifying
monstrosity of the politician Kleon. The theatrical appeal of this

---

[37] *Frogs* is actually a little more complex, for two reasons: first, the section of
'advice' (686 ff.) might be thought implicitly reminiscent of the convention of the
poet's own parabatic voice; secondly, the references to 'sacred' choruses (674, 686)
might be treated as reminders of the Initiates' identity, though, taken as a whole,
the parabasis hardly makes this necessary.

[38] The fragments of other poets' works from roughly this period show that comic
boasting and the denigration of rivals were prominent themes in their parabases too.

passage seems to be vouched for by the fact that Aristophanes repeated these lines, almost verbatim, the following year in *Peace* (752 ff.). I shall have more to say in the next section about the nature of such Aristophanic bravado and boasting, but there is no doubt at all that in the earlier part of his career he was able to exploit very effectively the potential of the parabasis for ostensibly extra-dramatic entertainment. On the other hand, it is this particular feature of the parabasis which appears to have faded rather rapidly after the 420s, so that in *Birds*, *Lysistrata*, and *Women at the Thesmophoria* the chorus remains in its dramatic identity throughout the parabasis.[39] Given the more general evidence, already noted, for a decline in the parabasis during the later fifth century, it is a reasonable hypothesis that the intricacies of the form, which had once provided such elaborate scope for musico-poetic, comic, and choreographic effects, had come to seem too cumbersome and old-fashioned for the evolving tastes of dramatists and their public.[40]

I stressed at the outset of this section that we should not allow the technical analysis of compositional forms in Old Comedy to conceal their primarily theatrical character as structures in which meaning, rhythm, music, and dance all came together in a performative synthesis. The parodos, agon, and parabasis helped Aristophanes, as they did other poets, to give shape to his plays in ways which drew on, yet constantly modified (and sometimes defeated), the expectations of his audience. Understanding something about these structural components allows us to form an idea of an important interface between convention and creativity, continuity and change, in Old Comedy.

SATIRE AND SERIOUSNESS

The overwhelming impression left by Aristophanic humour is of an imaginative world that is unlimitedly zany, grotesque, and fluid.

---

[39] *Frogs* (cf. n. 37 above) revives the tradition of parabatic 'advice', but not with overt reference to the supposed views or standing of the poet himself.

[40] It is often suggested that the diminution in choral elements, including the parabasis, seen by the time of *Assembly-Women* and *Wealth* was a result of Athens's impoverishment in the Peloponnesian War. Although economic factors may have played a part, I would prefer to look, in the first instance, for an explanation in terms of theatrical and dramatic evolution.

Despite this, scholars and critics have long been interested in seeking, and have often claimed to discover, a layer of seriousness in the playwright's work. While fantasy, as my earlier sections have emphasized, is the dominant mode of Old Comedy, the materials of fantasy are of course frequently drawn, through all their distortions, from aspects of the contemporary political and social world of Athens. It is, at root, the interplay between fantasy and reality which has given rise to sharply contrasting judgements of Aristophanes' dramatic aims and character. For a long time after the Renaissance the extremes of this disagreement were posed chiefly in moral terms, with Aristophanes regarded either as a shameless, indiscriminate jester or as a moral, didactic chastiser of reprobates. The play most often treated as a test case in this debate was *Clouds*, where the question at issue was whether Aristophanes had wantonly attacked the blameless Sokrates, or had perhaps used the figure of Sokrates as a means of exposing the subversive fraudulence of very different types of intellectuals, especially the Sophists. In eighteenth-century England, when an ideal of benevolent humour prevailed, the case of *Clouds* was cited so regularly in this connection that one literary historian has suggested that the period made the issue 'its peculiar property, by infinite repetition'.[41] Unsurprisingly, given the ethical aesthetics of the time, the standard reaction can be exemplified by Joseph Addison, who saw *Clouds* as a prominent illustration of satire's 'poisoned darts, which not only inflict a wound but make it incurable'.[42]

From the early nineteenth century, however, the focus of debate over Aristophanic satire shifted markedly towards the arena of politics. The central questions, which have tended to dominate scholarship on the playwright ever since, became: was Aristophanes a committed, purposeful satirist, in his treatment both of individual leaders and of the workings of democracy? and, if so, where did he stand in terms of the major political affiliations of late fifth-century Athens? It was first in Germany, and subsequently elsewhere, that the basic interpretative positions were staked out, with the philosopher Hegel, among others, advancing a view of Aristophanes as a patriotically motivated teacher, and the translator Droysen delineating the opposing idea of the pure entertainer. For most of the last 150 years the majority view has been that Aristophanes *was* in

[41] S. M. Tave, *The Amiable Humorist* (Chicago, 1960), 23.
[42] *Spectator*, 23 (27 Mar. 1711).

some degree committed to expressing political judgements in his comedies, especially through the use of satire. But there has been much less agreement about exactly what those judgements were, or from what kind of general stance they were delivered. Commonest is the inference that Aristophanes was a 'conservative', which is defined in this context principally in terms of opposition to the radical democracy of the time and a hankering after an earlier, supposedly more moderate era of Athenian politics.[43] But there have been many variations on and modifications to this inference, with arguments being advanced for Aristophanes the 'oligarch' (opposed to democracy *per se*), Aristophanes the true democrat (opposed above all to the abuse of power by demagogues and others), Aristophanes the champion of the rural classes—and other positions besides. It is not possible to examine each of these possibilities here, nor the ascription of more particular commitments to the poet (such as an acute individual antipathy to the politician Kleon, for example, or passionate opposition to the war with Sparta). One objection to categorical formulations of Aristophanes' putative values or beliefs is that they are inevitably based on, and tend to simplify, a mass of comically and dramatically variegated material which by its very nature might be thought to destabilize the possibility of a consistent reading. It is, therefore, right that some of the more specific issues raised by the sort of views I have mentioned should be addressed in my introductions to individual plays. What I shall attempt in the rest of this section is to offer some general reasons for caution about deducing Aristophanes' personal allegiances from his comedies.

The plays of Aristophanes contain such frank and often extreme satirical elements precisely because they belong to a special genre of festival entertainment. As I indicated earlier (see 'Old Comedy and Dionysiac Festivity'), Old Comedy enjoyed a peculiar freedom, which expresses itself in obscenity as well as (and often at the same time as) satire, to break the taboos and contravene the norms which obtained in the social world at large. This freedom stemmed partly from 'folk' practices of scurrilous jesting and inebriated celebration

---

[43] Aristophanes has also frequently been regarded as a 'cultural' conservative in matters of education, poetry, and music, despite the fact that his boasts about his own dramatic artistry stress originality and innovation (*Clouds* 545–8, *Wasps* 1053–9). For reasons against inferring the poet's own views on topics such as these as well, see my Introductions to *Clouds* and *Frogs*.

of the kind which Aristophanes himself twice incorporates in his
surviving plays.[44] What is so telling about this side of comedy is the
'irresponsibility' of its licence to ridicule, to lampoon, and to vilify.
The playwrights of the genre were exempted from any need to
explain or answer for their choice of satirical targets. Unlike the personal abusiveness which undoubtedly played a part in political life,
comedy was not usually constrained by the possibility of legal
reprisals, nor by the pressures involved in persuading an audience
to take a practical decision (other than the judges' voting of a prize
to the best comedy) on a particular occasion. These differences are
culturally and psychologically fundamental, and without them it
would be impossible to explain why classical Athens permitted comedy a type and degree of freedom which was not available in other
contexts of public life. The broad significance of this point for my
argument lies in the way in which comic satire of the Aristophanic
variety takes on a kind of *gratuitousness*, which is very hard to
translate into the terms of authorial commitments. If a comic playwright was entitled to denigrate and attack with impunity, the conditions do not exist in which his individual attitudes can be readily
identified as such through the medium of unbridled mockery. With
rare exceptions (see 'Aristophanes Career in Context', above), comedy was, so to speak, disconnected from the procedures of challenge, justification, and even reprisal which applied in the life of the
polis in general.

In the case of many victims of satire, comic prominence should
be taken as a reflection not of scandalous notoriety but of the
achievement of status and power within the city. This is most obviously true of leading politicians, generals, and office-holders
(Perikles, Kleon, Hyperbolos, Lamachos, etc.), but while our evidence is often inadequate for certainty, we can be confident that this
was true of many of the lesser targets as well. Kleonymos, for example, is set up as a glutton and coward in several of Aristophanes'
plays, but we know that he was politically prominent on more than
one important occasion and we have some reason to connect him
with Kleon in the 420s.[45] Similarly, the Kinesias who appears as
both a vacuous poetaster and a physical freak, at *Birds* 1372 ff. and
elsewhere, was very probably a much more significant figure, both

---

[44] For the phallic song at *Acharnians* 263 ff. and the Eleusinian mockery at *Frogs*
416 ff., see 'Aristophanes' Career in Context', with n. 2 above.
[45] See the Index of Names in each volume of the translation.

culturally (as composer and chorus-trainer) and even politically, than we would ever guess from a literal-minded reading of his persona in Aristophanes. Naturally not all butts of satire were eminent or influential, but, like many later satirists, Aristophanes did not waste much of his humour on utter social misfits or outcasts. Aristophanic ridicule has an intrinsically debasing and degrading thrust, and therefore an inbuilt tendency to direct itself against targets which permit a satisfying disparity between accepted realities outside the theatre and the grotesque reductiveness of comedy itself. In this respect Old Comedy's mockery of human beings is parallel to its burlesque presentation of the gods. Just as most readers would not now infer Aristophanes' own religious attitudes, nor prevailing currents of religious feeling in Athens, from the treatment of Hermes in *Peace*, *Birds*, or *Wealth*, of Iris and Poseidon in *Birds*, or of Dionysos in *Frogs*, so we should be highly circumspect about translating his satire of individual Athenians into a personal set of political or social convictions.

At this point we need to address a seemingly obvious objection. This amounts to the commonly stated orthodoxy that comic playwrights *did* possess, in their parabases (and occasionally elsewhere too), means of announcing to their audiences the specific points of view from which they observed the life of their polis. It is on the basis of parabatic passages where the chorus can speak either in the voice of the poet or on his behalf (see 'Formality and Performance', above) that Aristophanes has commonly been regarded as a professedly *engagé* dramatist. In *Acharnians*, for example, the chorus explains that Aristophanes believes himself to have been responsible for many benefits to the democracy, especially by drawing to its attention (in his recent play *Babylonians*) the deceitful flattery of foreign ambassadors who come to address the Assembly in Athens (*Acharnians* 633 ff.). The poet, they suggest, is not afraid to speak out in the interests of justice, and thereby to serve his people as adviser and teacher (ibid. 645-58). In similar vein, the chorus of *Wasps* reports Aristophanes' boast that he has not indulged in petty ridicule of ordinary people but has deployed his satire against the biggest of targets, namely the politician Kleon, who is here allegorically described as a monster whom it requires Heraklean powers to overcome (1029-35, cf. *Peace* 751-8). Aristophanes, the chorus claims, has fought and continues to fight on behalf of the Athenian people (*Wasps* 1037).

But it is a naïve error to suppose that any such passage offers us the direct or authentic voice of the poet himself. The parabasis, though always standing outside the progress of the dramatic action, is none the less a full part of the comic performance. Its elaborate formality (rhythmical, musical, and choreographic), which I discussed in the last section, provides a highly stylized interlude which is a theatrical event in its own right. Moreover, the 'voice' of the poet which can be incorporated in a parabasis is a conventional fiction, an opportunity for comedy to burlesque the postures of public discourse which were so familiar to Athenian audiences from the political Assembly, the adversarial contests of the law courts, and other democratic institutions. When in his parabases Aristophanes 'speaks', whether in the first or third person, to the city, he can always be seen to be engaging in a more-or-less parodic rhetoric, an assumed role of adviser, teacher, defendant, or the like. Of the two examples which I mentioned in the previous paragraph, *Acharnians* provides a ripe instance of mock rhetoric in two modes, both that of self-defence (Aristophanes is replying to the complaint made by Kleon about *Babylonians*) and that of political advice: what gives the game away, above all, are the ludicrous claims at 643 ff., that representatives of allied cities will now hurry to Athens with their annual tribute in order to have a chance to see Aristophanes himself; and that even the king of Persia is said to have remarked on the value of the poet to the war effort (and this is *Acharnians*!) of his city. In *Wasps*, similarly, Aristophanes' depiction of himself as a quasi-Heraklean enemy of Kleon is an exercise in extravagantly hyperbolical bluster, the spirit of which matches the comically outrageous terms (briefly anticipated at 35-6) in which Kleon is transmogrified into a physically repulsive mongrel. Finally, and very tellingly, the boast of fighting for the people (1037) is a transparently rhetorical cliché, and as such was twice satirized earlier in the play—ironically through the mouth of Philokleon himself (593), and directly by his son (667)—as a hallmark of slick, exploitative orators.

In short, there is nothing authoritative about anything said in the poet's name in a parabasis, since the poet's voice is part of, not a detached commentary on, the theatrically inflated world of the play.[46] Indeed, the kind of argument I have been criticizing could

---

[46] The same is true of *Acharnians* 497-500, where Dikaiopolis prefaces his 'defence speech' with some remarks about comedy itself: to treat this as

profitably be stood on its head: it is the *mock*-seriousness, the posturing rhetoric, and the pretence of didactic influence found in some parabases which reinforce our grounds for supposing that Old Comedy is a perpetual creator of illusions and fabrications about itself as about everything else. As for the general issue of satirical purpose in Aristophanes, it is practically inevitable that a form of comedy predicated on the licence to abuse, denigrate, and lampoon should give the *impression* of political and other commitments. In most social contexts, forthright mockery is a weapon of aggression, superiority, or contempt. But Athenian democracy had allowed comic drama to develop, however riskily, as a carefully defined festive opportunity for scurrility-without-responsibility. From at least the time of Kratinos, in the generation before Aristophanes, poets had exploited this opportunity to expose leading politicians, generals, and other office-holders, as well as a range of lesser individuals, to the force of collective laughter. If we ask why this should have been so, it is impossible to avoid a culturally and psychologically speculative model of explanation. Two factors of fundamental importance were stressed in my earlier section on 'Old Comedy and Dionysiac Festivity': one, the sub-literary, 'folk' roots of this variety of comic satire; the other, the flourishing of Old Comedy during the period when Athenian democracy was most buoyant and prosperous (as well as 'imperialist'). We are probably dealing, in other words, with a type of collective, festive celebration which is predemocratic in origin, yet quintessentially democratic in its artistically elaborated forms.

The state festivals at which comedy, like tragedy, was performed were occasions on which the city distributed marks and awards of honour to pre-eminent citizens. They were also occasions which, even outside comic drama as such, traditionally made room for the carnivalesque pleasures of ritual mockery and licensed obscenity. It is as if the distinctively intense, heady atmosphere of Dionysiac festivals was thought simultaneously appropriate for the opposing extremes of solemn, civic earnestness and disruptive, topsy-turvy play.[47] More interestingly still, the recipients of honorific and

programmatic of the author's own stance, as has often been done, is to tear it out of the context of parody and metatheatre in which it is teasingly embedded.

[47] The comments of the Spartan Megillos at Plato, *Laws* 1.637a–b, suggest that Dionysiac ribaldry was a particular feature of Athenian culture, though not actually exclusive to it.

satirical attention were in some cases the very same people, as, for example, with the city's generals, who were granted rights of front seating (*prohedria*) in the theatre,[48] but who might then find themselves, as Kleon and others did, the object of vilification in the very plays they were watching. Satirical mockery may, in a psychologically subtle way, have temporarily counterbalanced and inverted the possession of public power or esteem, but it is hard to believe that it could have been allowed to negate or cancel out these things.[49] And indeed our evidence is not, in my view, encouraging to a belief in comedy's potency as an influence upon currents of publicity or public opinion in classical Athens. The famous case of Plato's *Apology*, with its references to Sokrates' treatment in the *Clouds* (18c–19c), has been overworked in this respect. It is far from clear that Plato ascribes real influence to the comedy in dissemination of a false picture of the philosopher's interests; more likely he is citing *Clouds* as a pointed illustration of just how ludicrous the distortions of Sokrates' life could become. Be that as it may, Plato was not actually well placed, still less sufficiently impartial, to be a precise witness of the effect of *Clouds* (a play which flopped, it seems, at its first performance) on Athenian views of Sokrates. In the case of Kleon, Aristophanes' own parabatic boast of having floored the politician, as in a wrestling contest (*Clouds* 549–50), is a self-evident piece of pseudo-political arrogance: if anything, Kleon's power and prestige in Athens grew greater during the very years when Aristophanes was lampooning him in often scabrous style.

Because comic performances were limited to two main festivals in the year, they were not sufficiently embedded in the all-year-round processes of social and political life to make any regular or much practical difference to them. This is not to say that comedy was 'innocent fun'. Its unfettered freedom of speech permitted it to voice feelings of dissatisfaction, exasperation, irreverence, and cynicism which no doubt partially reflected the underside of political consciousness in the city. But we will be prone to considerable self-deception if we think that we now have much chance of picking our

---

[48] See *Knights* 575, 702–4.

[49] Our only fifth-century observation on the satirical practices of Old Comedy is the claim in pseudo-Xenophon (so-called 'Old Oligarch'), *Constitution of the Athenians* 2.18, that the targets of comedy are largely 'the rich, noble, or powerful', not members of the common people: although this passage is hardly a precise formulation, it surely leaves the impression that comedy did not *change* anything in Athenian life.

way through its distortions, its absurdities, its contradictions, and its outrageous transformations of life, and coming out at the end with a coherent or steady sense of the playwright's own point of view. All humour tends to some extent towards the dissolution of sense, and the characteristic modes of Old Comedy do so to an exceptional degree. Aristophanes' theatrical strength lies in the fertility of his inventiveness and the multifariousness of his talent for manipulating images and ideas into surprising yet satisfying scenarios. But anyone who looks to him for deep insights into Athenian society is likely to be ultimately disappointed.

TRANSLATING ARISTOPHANES

The translator of Aristophanes is confronted by a challenge more varied and formidable than that posed by any other ancient author. There are three main sources of difficulty. First, Aristophanic verse encompasses many different forms and registers, and frequently extracts humour from piquant or incongruous combinations of these. All other types of Greek poetry—epic, lyric, and above all tragedy[50]—are echoed, parodied, and exploited by Aristophanes in ways which can involve vocabulary, rhythmical form, or thematic materials. As a result, the stylistic range of Old Comedy constantly moves backwards and forwards between, as well as bringing into stimulating adjacency, the colloquial and the elevated, the informal and the technical, the delicate and the gross. Secondly, large areas of Aristophanic humour are inextricably tied up with verbal details of imagery, puns, and other kinds of wordplay, many of which do not readily lend themselves to effective translation. Finally, Old Comedy is saturated with historically specific references to people, places, institutions, and much besides, of the kind which created problems even for post-classical readers in antiquity and which continue to form a barrier to appreciation for many who are not extensively familiar with fifth-century Athenian culture. The combination of these factors means that issues of fidelity which affect all fields of translation arise in an acute form with Aristophanes' work, where the demands of comic effectiveness and historical accuracy make competing and often irreconcilable demands.

---

[50] Cf. my earlier section, 'Old Comedy and Dionysiac Festivity'.

Translations are by their very nature ambivalent constructions. On the one hand, they implicitly invite us—and the more so, the greater the cultural distance between their originals and ourselves—to extend our experience beyond the bounds of what has been produced within the thought-world of our own language. On the other hand, they inevitably engage in some degree of assimilation by the very act of transference into the translator's and reader's language. Translators strive, according to their inclinations and purposes, either to strike a balance between these contrasting implications, or else to accentuate one at the expense of the other. In the case of comic texts the temptation to prefer assimilation and modernization over the acknowledgement and savouring of historical distance is very considerable, for the simple reason that readers of comedy readily expect to be amused, and amusement is by nature a relatively spontaneous response which does not require special effort of imagination or understanding. But the present translation tries, in the main, to resist this temptation, on the assumption that readers of Aristophanes should be looking for something other than a ready-made entertainment which is directly interchangeable with the kinds available in their own culture.

My translation has accordingly been guided by the conviction that, while it is desirable to make Aristophanes as accessible as possible, accessibility must involve access *to* something that is not our own (rather than a modern substitute for it). The comic pleasure which can still be obtained from these plays by modern readers depends on a willingness to participate in a well-informed experience of a historically different, even alien, mode of drama. What I have tried to provide are versions which approximate as closely to the original texture of Aristophanic poetry, and to the proclivities of Aristophanic humour, as is compatible with reasonable fluency in modern English. This means, for one thing, that I have generally retained as much as possible of the historical fabric of names, references, and allusions, so that readers will not at any rate be badly misled about the kinds of things which Aristophanes wrote and imagined. It also, and equally importantly, means that I have chosen not to translate the plays into prose, since that would involve, in my judgement, too great (and comfortable) an assimilation to the dominant medium of comic drama in our own world, with a corresponding loss of the poetic forms which are so integral to the nature of Old Comedy. Here as elsewhere, however, some compromise is appropriate, as will become clear from further explanation of the verse forms I have adopted.[51]

In my earlier section on 'Formality and Performance' I explained Aristophanes' use of the three basic modes of theatrical delivery: speech (in iambic trimeters), recitative (in longer lines of various rhythms), and lyrics (in often complex metrical units). These three modes pose separate challenges to a translator. The spoken iambic trimeters call for treatment in a way which preserves a sense of verse structure while allowing, as the trimeter did, for a spectrum of registers and effects, including the colloquial,[52] which is not however as dominant a voice as many modern translators of Aristophanes have made it. Here I have used a five-beat line which represents a maximally supple version of blank verse (the so-called 'iambic pentameter'). This has three advantages to recommend it: first, it is not too far in metrical shape from the Greek iambic trimeter (making allowance for the difference between the quantitative rhythms of Greek verse and the dynamic stress patterns of English[53]); secondly, it has a combination of regularity with flexibility which allows it to cope with the gamut of styles which Aristophanes employs, echoes, and parodies in these portions of his comedies; thirdly, it has a historical embeddedness in English verse (particularly in the practice of dramatic and satiric poets) which stretches back to the sixteenth century and which ought to make it conveniently familiar to modern readers. In order to catch something of the racy vigour of Aristophanes' trimeters, I have tried to exploit extensively the capacity of blank verse to keep its defining pattern of five major stresses while permitting rich variation in terms of phrase structure, pauses, and division between speakers (the latter being a particular source of Aristophanic verbal

---

[51] In the case of oracles, which use dactylic hexameters (the metre of epic) in Greek, I have used accentual hexameters, despite the problems of this form in English: see e.g. *Knights* 1015 ff., *Birds* 967 ff., *Lysistrata* 770 ff.

[52] See Aristotle's well-known remark that 'the iambic trimeter, more than any other metre, has the rhythm of speech: an indication of this is that we speak many trimeters in conversation with one another' (*Poetics* 4.1449^24–7; cf. 22.1459^12).

[53] If Greek iambics were assimilated to a stress-patterned metre, the result would be six main 'beats' in the line, as opposed to the five of blank verse. It is thus important to notice the difference between standard terminology for Greek and English metres. An English iambic 'trimeter' would have *three* beats, a 'tetrameter' four, etc.; for Greek units, '-meter' denotes a metron, which roughly corresponds to a pair of feet, hence two beats, in English rhythms. Cf. n. 55 below.

neatness).[54] The nature of the line imposes a discipline which inhibits indulgent improvisation by the translator; unlike many other modern versions, mine are no longer than the originals. At the same time the line can be used with varying degrees of freedom, and this has made it possible for me, I believe, to convey something of the evolution of Aristophanic dialogue from the livelier, less predictable style of the fifth-century plays to the staider, quieter tone of *Assembly-Women* and *Wealth*.

The recitative sections of Aristophanes' comedies use longer lines (tetrameters[55]) of iambic, trochaic, and anapaestic type, and occasionally other rhythms too. Here I have not thought it advisable to match all of these rhythms with their nearest English equivalents. Trochaic rhythms in Greek typically had a springy quality, but it is hard to capture this consistently by English trochees, which cut too much against the grain of the language and tend to sound laboriously mannered. Even so, I have occasionally kept Aristophanes' trochaic tetrameters for shorter passages, as for example at *Lysistrata* 1014-42, where male and female half-choruses move through the cautious steps of their *rapprochement*, or in the choral proclamations of the parabasis and second parabasis of *Birds* (752-68, 785-800, 1071-87, 1101-17). Anapaests are even harder to sustain without either awkwardness or a rolling Gilbertian manner that palls when kept up for the length of passages in which Aristophanes uses this metre. The attempt by Swinburne to translate the parabasis of *Birds* into anapaestic tetrameters shows that even a practised versifier is stretched to carry off the exercise without making a reader stumble;[56] and I give my reasons, in 'Aristophanes and Posterity' (below), for thinking it necessary to avoid assimilation of Aristophanes to W. S. Gilbert. I have, therefore, retained anapaestic rhythms in only a few shorter passages, e.g. *Birds* 209-22, where they well suit the Hoopoe's excited summons to his nightingale wife. Iambic tetrameters, on the other hand, lend themselves in English to a treatment which is accentually stricter than blank verse yet retains

---

[54] *Wealth* 190-2 and 393 provide extreme cases of trimeters divided between speakers: I have tried to preserve such effects whenever possible.

[55] In the Greek context, 'tetrameter' denotes four metra, which roughly correspond to either seven or eight English feet/beats; thus a Greek iambic tetrameter is approximately twice as long as the English line so-called (as e.g. in Marvell's 'To his Coy Mistress'). Cf. n. 53 above.

[56] Swinburne's version was first published in the *Athenaeum*, 30 Oct. 1880. Smoother anapaests, such as those of B. B. Rogers, tend to become trottier.

a fluency that makes the line less awkwardly demanding on the ear than either the trochaic or anapaestic lines just mentioned. I have, therefore, chosen to render most of Aristophanes' recitative metres in this form, sometimes known as the 'fourteener' or heptameter in English verse.[57]

Finally, the lyrics. Here it would be pointless to follow Rogers and several of his Victorian predecessors in aiming for anything like a consistent correlation with Greek rhythms, since too many of the latter, even when turned into stress metres, would make no recognizable pattern to a modern ear. In some passages, however, it is feasible to capture part of the rhythmical ethos in at least an approximate manner, either by the general 'shape' and length of metrical phrases or by some of their dominant rhythms. My strategy in this area has been to employ marked English stress patterns in a few contexts where they can provide an intelligible match for the original (e.g. with the trochaic rhythms of the *faux-naif*, mock-fairy-tale songs at *Birds* 1470-93, 1553-64, 1695-1705, and the predominantly iambic rhythms of the old men's sexist grumbles at *Lysistrata* 256-65/271-80), but often to allow myself a more fluid, free-verse technique. Aristophanic lyrics vary greatly both within and between plays. Some of those in *Assembly-Women* (289 ff., 483 ff.), for example, represent a relatively plain and pedestrian band of a spectrum whose opposite end can be found in, say, the elaborate ornithological melismas of *Birds* 737-52, or the inflated pseudo-elevation of *Clouds* 275 ff. In between lie songs involving a quintessentially Aristophanic mixture of vulgar, ditty-like crudity (or even, on occasion, infantile obviousness[58]) with various twists of comic subtlety: a case in point is *Acharnians* 836-59, whose compact iambic rhythms, borrowed from popular song, are taut yet spry. Formally and linguistically, therefore, translations of the lyrics need to leave room for maximum pliancy. In this connection I should add that I have always avoided structural use of rhyme, despite its recurrent appeal to English translators of Aristophanes:

---

[57] The English metre is sometimes divided into alternating lines of four and three stresses, as in Coleridge's *Rhyme of the Ancient Mariner*. It may be worth adding that my treatment of the end of this line allows both 'masculine' (final syllable stressed) and 'feminine' (final syllable unstressed) cadences (see e.g. *Lysistrata* 254-5 for one of each); the same is true of my occasional trochaic tetrameters.

[58] The best examples of this are the songs at *Lysistrata* 1043 ff., 1189 ff.: the 'feebleness' of the humour is best taken, I think, as tongue-in-cheek frivolity, presumably reinforced by the musico-choreographic style.

in my judgement, rhyme produces a jauntiness which is occasionally but not consistently apt for the song forms of the original.

I referred at the start of this section to three main categories of
difficulty facing any translator of Aristophanes. The problem of
mixed and unexpectedly shifting stylistic registers—above all, the
typical Aristophanic juxtapositioning of 'high' and 'low'—is ubiquitous. In coming to terms with it I have made use, where appropriate, of 'stage directions' (see the next section), as well as
quotation marks, designed to guide the aural imagination. In the
case of puns and wordplay, one is at the mercy of luck and of the
latent verbal potential of English. At *Acharnians* 3, for example,
Dikaiopolis uses a long comic coinage whose main elements can be
represented schematically as sand-hundreds-plenty. My own 'innu-
merabillions' attempts to catch at least the sense of a novelty growing out of something familiar. At *Wealth* 1128–9 Aristophanes
constructs a pun between *kôlê*, 'ham' (an offering to the god
Hermes), and *askôliazein*, whose literal meaning is to dance on a
greasy wine-skin (hence 'hop around' or, as one might say, 'make
a song and dance'). English fortuitously presents the translator with
the possibility of punning on 'ham' in the sense of feeble acting, and
this parallels the ethos, though not the semantics, of the original
joke. But very often nothing like this is feasible. In such cases one
option is to be independently inventive, but I have tried, in keeping
with the general aims of my translation, never to stray too far from
the verbal details of the text, since it is these which cumulatively
create the flavour of Aristophanic humour.[59] As already explained,
the same principle has been largely applied to the historical and topical elements which embed the plays in their time and place.

Yet there remain difficult linguistic choices to face, which can be
illustrated by the constrasting problems of oaths and dialects. The
use of oaths is ubiquitous in Aristophanes' plays. The main reason
for this is undoubtedly that they were a general feature of Attic
speech at all levels. Many of them, such as the commonest of all ('by
Zeus'), functioned as little more than expletives or exclamations.
Others lend varying degrees of intensification or emotional colour to

---

[59] It needs to be stressed that the success of a pun is not a matter of transparent
principle but of subtle contextual interplay between the aural and the semantic. We
are badly placed to judge whether *any* pun in Aristophanes would have struck his
contemporaries as witty or feeble (commentators often make dogmatic judgements
in this area).

their utterances. And some have further significance—for example, as markers of female speech[60] or as the basis of local comic effect. In the latter category belong, for instance, Poseidon's oath by himself at *Birds* 1614, Strepsiades' oath by Zeus in the very act of doubting the god's existence at *Clouds* 1234, the Commissioner's oath by Poseidon at *Lysistrata* 403 when responding to the old men's complaint about their watery suffering, or Dionysos' partly stifled cries to Apollo and Poseidon, which he tries to pretend are quotations from poetry, at *Frogs* 659 and 664. To translate each and every oath literally would probably lead to an excessively arch effect in English. To omit or tone down most of them, on the other hand, would be to lose both a distinctive feature of Athenian speech patterns and a source of much verbal pointing of comic dialogue. I have tried, therefore, to keep a fair proportion of oaths, especially those which are salient in one way or another.

In the case of dialects, however, I have diverged from the practice of most earlier translators by declining to employ a systematic differentiation of speech patterns in the case of characters who are depicted in the Greek as speaking dialects other than Attic (principally, the Megarian and Boiotian in *Acharnians*, Lampito in *Lysistrata*). This is for the simple but fundamental reason that no appropriate equivalent, making sense in both linguistic and cultural terms, is readily available. Athenians must have heard other Greek dialects spoken on many occasions, in the streets of their own city as well as elsewhere; the dialects as such were not intrinsically amusing (though their Aristophanic versions may contain some comic details[61]). In particular, giving the three characters in question a 'funny accent' is not the point. Many translators in the past have made Lampito speak Scots, but this is, and always was, unsuitable in a version which can be read as well in Scotland (where I happen to teach!) as anywhere else. Other translators have opted for a dialectal element which can be perceived, from the point of view of the implicit readership or audience, as markedly rustic or backward; in America, this usually means a hill-billy variety of speech. But such a strategy is certainly inapt for Lampito, and

---

[60] See the notes on *Lysistrata* 112, *Assembly-Women* 155.

[61] See, for instance, Lampito's perhaps excessive and mannered use of the Spartan oath (esp. *Lysistrata* 81–90). The visitors in *Acharnians* too have speech features which are markedly comic, but these can be conveyed in translation independently of an overall dialectal colouring.

probably for the two characters in *Acharnians* too, since we have no reason to suppose that Athenians perceived the relevant dialects in this light. I have, therefore, eschewed the use of a consistent dialectal presentation of these characters, while allowing individually comic speech peculiarities to come through in the translation.

STAGE DIRECTIONS

The Theatre of Dionysos in Athens, on the south-east slope of the Akropolis, was the location for both the City Dionysia and, almost certainly, the Lenaia too (cf. 'Aristophanes' Career', above). The details of its fifth-century form are contentious, since the archaeological remains are of much later date and literary evidence is scanty. We can be sure, however, that in the time of Aristophanes the main components of the theatre, apart from seating for the audience,[62] were a substantial, probably wooden stage building (*skênê*), and, in front of it, a large performance area, possibly rectilinear and elongated (trapezoidal) rather than circular in shape (as it was later to be), known as the orchestra (*orchêstra*, lit. 'dancing-floor') and used by both actors and chorus. The dimensions of the orchestra were perhaps of the order of some twenty metres in diameter and eight in depth, and to either side of it was an entrance/exit (*eisodos*) for the performers:[63] in my stage directions I refer to these as side entrances. The stage building had a main central door, a usable roof (cf. e.g. *Wasps* 136 ff., *Birds* 267 ff., *Lysistrata* 829 ff.), windows (cf. *Wasps* 156 ff., 317 ff., *Assembly-Women* 884 ff.), and, when required (*Acharnians, Clouds, Assembly-Women*), a second door. It is possible that there was a low wooden stage in front of the stage building and connected to the orchestra by two or three steps, but there can be no doubt that, if so, it did nothing to impede the physical interaction between characters and chorus which is often called for in Old Comedy, for example in the confrontational parodoi of plays such as *Knights* (247 ff.) and *Birds* (352 ff.). Also available, though employed by Aristophanes purely for the purposes of para-tragedy, were both the *mêchanê* ('machine'), a sort of crane which

---

[62] Probably a combination of wooden benches for most (cf. *Women at the Thesmophoria* 395) with some stone seats for dignitaries at the front.

[63] The term *parodos* (as for the chorus's entry: see 'Formality and Performance'), though common in modern books, is post-classical usage; *eisodos* (Aristophanes' own term at *Clouds* 326, *Birds* 296) is to be preferred.

suspended characters in simulated flight (see *Peace* 174, *Birds* 1199 ff., *Women at the Thesmophoria* 1009-14), and the *ekkuklêma* or wheeled platform, which represented interior scenes (*Acharnians* 407-79, *Women at the Thesmophoria* 101-265).

Most comedies were performed by three main actors, taking more than one role each when necessary and occasionally supplemented by a fourth and even fifth actor for smaller parts; mute parts were additional. All roles were played by males, and this probably held even for naked female figures such as the pipe girl in *Wasps* (1326 ff.) or Reconciliation in *Lysistrata* (1114 ff.): in such cases, the body stockings which seem to have been a standard part of comic actors' costumes would simply be designed to represent bare flesh and the appropriate anatomical externals.[64] Masks, typically exaggerated and often grotesquely so, were standardly worn, as was padding of the actor's belly and rump, with, for males, the conventional appendage of a phallus (which could be more or less prominent, cf. *Clouds* 537-9). These three accoutrements of the comic performer must have created a pervasive and inescapable sense of vulgar absurdity for Athenian audiences, ensuring that the action of a play was always suspended in a kind of generic world of its own. The chorus, as mentioned in previous sections, consisted of twenty-four singers/dancers, including a chorus-leader who spoke and declaimed certain sections solo, especially when in dialogue with individual actors.[65] Many of the choral dance sections took symmetrical strophic form, involving the musically and rhythmically matching pairing of strophe and antistrophe, as indicated in the margins of my translation. Musical accompaniment was provided by a piper, whose instrument was a pair of *auloi* or reed pipes (akin to oboes): comedy sometimes draws the piper temporarily into the dramatic sphere, as with the sounds of Prokne at *Birds* 209 ff., the same piper later in the play (859-61), or the old hag's address to the player at *Assembly-Women* 890-92.[66]

[64] Body stockings are regularly depicted in fourth-century vase-paintings of comic actors from Magna Graecia: see e.g. the illustrations in R. Green and E. Handley, *Images of the Greek Theatre* (London, 1995), ch. 5.

[65] We cannot always be confident whether particular choral utterances were collective or the leader's alone, but I have tried to follow a reasonably consistent practice of attribution in this respect.

[66] Additional musicians may, of course, be part of a play: see e.g. the Theban pipers at *Acharnians* 862; a Spartan 'bagpiper' has often been posited at *Lysistrata* 1242, but the reference is probably to the ordinary piper.

When the plays of Aristophanes were written down, they contained, like virtually all ancient dramatic texts, no stage directions. We are, therefore, left to make our own inferences about the kind of staging which the plays could or would have been given, guiding ourselves, wherever possible, by other sources of information about the Athenian theatre. So the reader of this, as of any other, translation of Aristophanes (or of Greek tragedy) should keep in mind that all stage directions are a matter of interpretation not independent fact, even though a fair number of them can be established uncontroversially, and more still can be persuasively justified, from the text. Readers should themselves cultivate the habit of picturing the realization of the script in an open-air theatrical space, and by a cast of grotesquely attired players, of the kind I have already described.

ARISTOPHANES AND POSTERITY

The works of Aristophanes have often aroused the curiosity of later writers, readers, and audiences of comedy, but they have rarely influenced them to an appreciable extent. The fundamental explanation of this state of affairs lies in two kinds of difficulty—difficulty of understanding, and ethical difficulty. The former arises from linguistic challenges (colloquial idioms, stylistic parodies, an immense range of imagery), historical references (to people, places, objects, and institutions), and imaginative exoticism. Ethical difficulty stems principally from scurrility of personal satire, irreverence in the treatment of religious matters, and a degree of obscenity, visual as well as verbal, not paralleled elsewhere in ancient literature: all three of these elements have regularly troubled those readers committed to the long predominant, indeed orthodox, view of comedy as a morally decent and edifying genre (see below). Yet these two sets of features, when seen from a different angle, can also be regarded as a large part of what makes Aristophanes' plays special and therefore worth having. The story of 'Aristophanes and Posterity', of which this section can provide only a partial sketch, is therefore one of rather delicately balanced considerations, in which factors of attraction and repulsion have often operated side by side.

Old Comedy was so closely tied to the society and culture of fifth-century Athens that it could never have had a fully sustained afterlife even in the ancient world. Unlike the New Comedy of Menander and other playwrights in the late fourth and early third centuries, which was transported to Rome about a century later by Plautus, Terence, and others, and was subsequently to be a fertile ground for the development of theatrical comedy in the Renaissance and beyond, Old Comedy's interest and importance do not lend themselves to ready imitation or emulation. Until recently it was thought likely that no Aristophanic play ever received a performance after the poet's own lifetime. Serious doubt has recently been cast on that claim, since vase-painting has given us probable evidence for the transference of Old comedies to the theatres of fourth-century Magna Graecia (South Italy and Sicily). The most compelling single item of such evidence is a south-Italian depiction of a moment from *Women at the Thesmophoria*, where the Kinsman threatens the women's 'baby', in reality a wineskin, with a sword, in a parody of Euripides' lost play *Telephos*.[67] In this particular instance it is germane that we are dealing with a comedy built around the (fictionalized) tragedian Euripides, whose works themselves received productions in the Greek theatres of South Italy and Sicily. It remains hard to imagine how, without considerable adaptation at any rate, some of Aristophanes' other comedies could have been transplanted to cities where their detailed references to matters Athenian would not have been fully intelligible. There remains no good reason to suppose that Old Comedy's performance life was much extended in this way.

For the rest of Graeco-Roman antiquity the works of Aristophanes were to be known only as texts, and then mostly to very small numbers of highly educated readers. The survival of eleven plays (out of more than forty) to the age of printing was, as with many other works of ancient literature, the result of a long and complex process, part cultural and part accidental. *Clouds*, for example, was preserved largely because of the lasting fascination of Sokrates, its central character; and a similar factor may have operated in the cases of *Women at the Thesmophoria* and *Frogs*, in both of which Euripides, the most popular tragedian throughout antiquity, is so prominent.[68] It was for very different reasons, however, that *Wealth*

---

[67] The vase is shown in O. Taplin, *Comic Angels* (Oxford, 1993), pl. 11.4, and in A. H. Sommerstein *et al.*, (eds.), *Tragedy Comedy and the Polis* (Bari, 1993), pl. 4.

[68] But the case of *Women at the Thesmophoria* also illustrates the importance of chance: the play survived the Middle Ages in only a single manuscript; if that one copy had been destroyed at any point between around 1000 and 1500, the play would now be on our list of lost works.

not only survived but became established as the most commonly
read of Aristophanes' works in antiquity and the Byzantine period.
Wealth was valued as the least taxing, both historically and linguistically, of the poet's plays, but also for the apparently clear-cut
morality of its plot; the second factor became increasingly operative
during the medieval centuries when pagan literature was subjected
to judgement, though hardly ever it seems to censorship, in the
light of Christian values. Clearly, though, such criteria were not
applied consistently. Otherwise, works such as *Knights*, with its
dense texture of contemporary political allegory, or *Wasps*, with its
detailed references to and travesty of the Athenian judicial system,
would not have been preserved and copied. In instances like these
it is tempting to suppose, though impossible to show, that survival
partly depended upon the interest of certain readers, especially
scholars, in precisely this rich element of historical allusiveness. Be
that as it may, it was *Wealth*, *Clouds*, and *Frogs* which became
standard 'set texts' in the schools of Byzantium; equally, and surely
not accidentally, the three 'women plays'—*Lysistrata*, *Women at the
Thesmophoria*, and *Assembly-Women*—were the least studied of the
eleven during the Byzantine centuries.

Among ancient readers of Aristophanes were probably the
Roman authors of poems in the genre of *satura*, 'satire'. By the time
of Horace, whose own *Satires* were composed in the 30s BC, the idea
had acquired some currency that Old Athenian Comedy was a pre-
cursor of, or partial model for, Roman satire. Horace refers to this
idea at the beginning of *Satires* 1.4, where he claims that the creator of the genre, Lucilius, was heavily indebted to the Old Comedy
of Kratinos, Eupolis, Aristophanes.[69] The connection, according to
Horace, takes the form of a shared concern for the public chastise-
ment of vice and crime. Horace's claim, which exemplifies a view of
Aristophanic satire which has had a long history (see 'Satire and
Seriousness', above), can probably best be interpreted as a mock-
formal arrogation of Greek pedigree for his literary genre. But the
view itself became a kind of academic orthodoxy, represented, for
example, in the statement by Quintilian, rhetorician and educa-
tionalist of the first century AD, that Old Comedy had been 'pre-eminent in the persecution of vice' (10.1.65).

The fullest reaction which we have from any one ancient reader

---

[69] Horace, *Satires* 1.4.1–6; cf. 1.10.16–17; Persius, *Satires* 1.123–4.

of Aristophanes is that of Plutarch in the later first and early second century AD, and it is a hostile reaction. Plutarch complains of Aristophanes' vulgarity, linguistic artificiality, confusions of tone, failures of consistent characterization, and acrid malice; in all respects he compares him unfavourably with Menander.[70] Plutarch's points suggest nothing so much as a chasm of taste between his own rather dry, academic leanings and the earthy scurrilities which had evidently answered to an Athenian need in the Dionysiac festivities of the classical period. It is an interesting index of the special status of Old Comedy in its culture that even so well informed an antiquarian as Plutarch is essentially nonplussed about its original significance.[71] Somewhat more creative observation of the genre's qualities can be traced in the Greek writer of comic dialogues, Lucian (second century AD), whose own combination of fantasy and satire owes something to Aristophanic precedent. Lucian's writing is, however, much blander, less sharply contemporary, and more reliant on generalized, stereotypical images of human vice; as a result, he was to exercise greater influence than Aristophanes himself on the classicism of the Renaissance.

While Lucian's works were quite widely translated into several European languages in the sixteenth century, the plays of Aristophanes were very rarely tackled in this context. The contrast with the Roman poets of New Comedy is even starker. The works of Plautus and Terence dominated both the theory and the practice of comedy in the Renaissance. They supplied scenarios, characters, and themes which could be so much more easily staged, imitated, and adapted than the peculiarities of the Aristophanic imagination, whose grotesque contortions were so much harder to reconcile with the prevailing notion of comedy as a 'mirror of life'. This situation was to hold good throughout the various phases of neoclassical drama, right up to the eighteenth century. For the whole of this period Aristophanes was a 'name' to be brandished in various contexts, the prime example of this, as mentioned earlier (see 'Satire and Seriousness'), being the repeated indictment of *Clouds* by puritans and moralists concerned about uncontrolled or malicious laughter. But the reading of Aristophanes, in any language, was the preserve of a few. In the sixteenth century Erasmus' wide

---

[70] Plutarch, *Moralia* 853-4.

[71] This did not stop Plutarch from citing Aristophanes, in his *Lives* and elsewhere, as though his plays were a straightforwardly reliable source of historical information.

knowledge of the author emerges from the frequency with which he cites him in his *Adages* and elsewhere. In England, we know that Ben Jonson possessed two editions of Aristophanes and read at least some of the plays in the original; Jonson's own works, both his plays and his notebook *Timber*, contain references to Aristophanes and Old Comedy. Jonson was undoubtedly interested in the ancient playwright, and occasionally indebted to him: perhaps the best instance is the mock trial of the dogs, an idea taken from *Wasps*, in Act V of *The Staple of News*. Yet even Jonson was none the less typical in knowing Lucian better than he knew Aristophanes, and modern claims about Aristophanic influence on his work have sometimes been exaggerated.

Later creative writers to have exhibited an active fascination with Aristophanes include Racine, whose only comedy, *Les Plaideurs* (1668), adapts its basic scenario and several motifs from *Wasps*, blending these with the style of *commedia dell'arte* characters to produce a result (as Racine acknowledged in the Preface) rather remote from the dominant Terentian model of comedy at the time; and Goethe, who read a good deal of Aristophanes at more than one point in his life and staged a loose imitation of *Birds*, as the basis for a satire on German literary culture, at Weimar in 1780. Productions of Aristophanes had, up to this date, been even more of a rarity than translations. In England, to which I shall largely confine my attention,[72] we know for certain of only two before the nineteenth century, both of them in sixteenth-century Cambridge. The first, at St John's College in 1536, was almost inevitably of *Wealth*, which was likewise later to be the first play to be translated into English (by Thomas Randolph, adopted son of Ben Jonson).[73] The second, *Peace*, produced at the newly founded Trinity College in 1546, seems at first sight an odd choice, until we note the involvement in it of John Dee, later notorious as an astrologer at the courts of Elizabeth and James I. The one recorded fact about the production is that Trygaios' ascent to heaven on his dung-beetle was effected illusionistically, a fact which points, I think, to Dee's famil-

---

[72] A much fuller discussion of the English material will be included in my book, currently in preparation, on *Aristophanic Satire*.

[73] Randolph's version may itself have been acted in Cambridge at some point before 1628: for this possibility, within the general context of performances of classical plays in this period, see B. R. Smith, *Ancient Scripts and Modern Experience on the English Stage 1500–1700* (Princeton, 1988), 168–77.

iarity with continental techniques of stage machinery and an interest in recreating the ancient use of the 'machine' or crane, *mêchanê*, which is mentioned in *Peace* itself (174: see 'Stage Directions', above). It is conceivable that the whole production was built around Dee's aspiration to merge modern theatrical technology with antiquarian experimentation.

Not long after the late Renaissance productions, the chances of staging any Aristophanic comedy in England must have diminished steadily, first under the pressure of puritanical attitudes to the theatre,[74] and later on account of the eighteenth century's predominant favouring of benign, humane laughter over more ribald, indecent varieties of humour. The eighteenth century was not a propitious time for the appreciation of Old Comedy. It is rather revealing that the title of 'the English Aristophanes' or 'the modern Aristophanes' was sometimes given to a dramatist of farces, Samuel Foote, who had very probably never read a word of his supposed model. Even practising satirists such as Swift and Pope ostensibly repudiated comparison with Aristophanes.[75] It was hard anywhere in Europe, in fact, to provide a publicly respectable justification of Aristophanic humour at this date, given the still strong sway of neoclassical canons of taste and decorum.

Increasing interest in Aristophanes starts to develop only in the later eighteenth century, and builds up during the nineteenth, with the growth of a more historically informed attempt to understand Old Comedy, alongside other ancient forms of literature, in its original cultural spirit and context. There was certainly no instant or total change of attitudes in this period, for in England, at least, the Victorian age saw a continuing concern over the potential moral dangers of too close a familiarity with the playwright: it is not surprising, for example, that the scholar who remarked that *Lysistrata* 'turns upon a proposal so gross, that we shall not insult our readers with it' subsequently published perhaps the most heavily bowdlerized translations of Aristophanes ever produced.[76] Yet

[74] One of the largest of puritan tracts on the stage, William Prynn's *Histriomastix*, refers to Aristophanes as 'that scurrilous, carping comedian . . . [who] personally traduced and abused virtuous Socrates' (1633 edn., p. 120).

[75] See the ironic couplet in Swift's 'A Letter to the Rev. Dr. Sheridan', and Pope's 'Epistle to Henry Cromwell', 102–4.

[76] The scholar was Thomas Mitchell: the quotation is from an anonymously signed review in *Quarterly Review*, 9 (1813), 139–61, at 142. Even Mitchell had a sense of new priorities: on the preceding page he had warned against coming to the

around this same time there are signs of a potential change of climate. In 1820, for example, Shelley wrote a savage satire, entitled *Oedipus Tyrannus, or Swellfoot the Tyrant,* on the contemporary royal *cause célèbre* of George IV's attempted divorce of Queen Caroline. Shelley, living in Italy at the time, was partly inspired by Aristophanic precedents: the work's animal chorus (of pigs) and its scurrilous and grossly fantastic political allegory, as well as a number of smaller details (such as compound Greek names: Wellington is Laoktonos, 'People-Slayer'), are undoubtedly reminiscent of Aristophanes, whom we know that Shelley had recently been reading.[77] Shelley's experimental work, which owed much to the radical traditions of English visual satire, is hardly part of a trend; nor was it successful (only seven copies were sold before a threat of prosecution led to its withdrawal). But it is none the less a harbinger of new possibilities opened up by Romanticism's more 'liberated' attitudes to ancient Greece.

In the course of the nineteenth century there was an increasing recognition in some quarters that Old Comedy, like so much else from antiquity, could not be instinctively appreciated from a standpoint of modern taste. By 1871 John Addington Symonds was able to write: 'The time has come at which any writer on Greek literature, if not content to pass Aristophanes by in silence, must view him as he is.' Symonds warned that ordinary canons of comedy were of no use in interpreting the author; he described the plays as 'Dionysiac daydreams', utterly alien to the expectations bred by Christian ideas, both ethical and religious.[78] Whatever reservations one might have about details of Symonds's essay, its direction of thought is clear. It represents an appeal for a fresh, informed, and unmoralistic appraisal of Aristophanes and his genre. The work of such an appraisal had, in fact, been under way for some time. We can find a major contribution to it in George Grote's great *History of Greece,* which started to appear in 1846, where amazement is expressed at the traditional tendency to treat the inventive materials of Old Comedy as though they could be made the basis of either

---

plays 'with English feelings and English ideas'; but he just could not practise what he preached.

[77] See F. L. Jones (ed.), *The Letters of Percy Bysshe Shelley,* ii (London, 1964), 468.

[78] Symonds's essay originally appeared in the *Westminster Review,* 39 (1871), 291–322, and was reprinted in *Studies of the Greek Poets,* 1st ser., vol. 2 (London, 1873), ch. 18.

historically or morally secure inferences. Like Symonds, though in rather more scholarly fashion, Grote perceived a cultural distance which could be bridged only by a careful combination of imagination and information; and in this fundamental respect he was concerned to create a framework of interpretation which holds good to this day. Certain aspects of Aristophanes' work remained inescapably problematic, of course, for most nineteenth-century readers. In particular the obscenity of Old Comedy continued to be bowdlerized[79] or tamed, in both translations and productions (which, as with Greek tragedy, became increasingly common from the 1880s onwards). Aubrey Beardsley's priapic illustrations to *Lysistrata*, produced in 1896, are an exception that proves the rule: they were printed in a small limited edition 'for private distribution', and confiscations of copies by the police, on grounds of obscenity, are recorded in England as late as 1966. At the same time the late Victorian period fostered the curious idea, which still has currency, that the light operettas of Gilbert and Sullivan were close in spirit to Aristophanic comedy. Although Gilbert was undoubtedly influenced by a few Aristophanic motifs, and more especially by the rhythmical translations of the author which had become standard in the nineteenth century,[80] the gulf between the two forms of drama, and between their cultural contexts, makes any attempt to assimilate them a historically very questionable enterprise. To turn the earthy, profane brio of Aristophanes into the arch tweeness of Gilbert is to emasculate the former's energy.

Despite the risk of excessive self-satisfaction, it is reasonable to claim that the twentieth century has seen a steady improvement in our understanding of Aristophanes. Scholarship has made enormous progress in the interpretation of Athenian culture as a whole in the classical period, and resulting benefit has accrued to our grasp of the city's politics, social life, festival culture, and theatrical resources, among much else besides. While older controversies over Aristophanes' point of view as an observer and satirist of his world have continued in their oscillations, criticism of the plays has learnt

---

[79] For a contrast between English and Continental practices in this respect, see K. J. Dover, 'Expurgation of Greek Literature', in his *The Greeks and their Legacy* (Oxford, 1978), 270–86.

[80] Gilbertian verbal mannerisms were in turn influential on the widely known translations by B. B. Rogers, published between 1902 and 1915.

to take their theatricality and their Dionysiac background into account, at every level, much more successfully than was the case in earlier periods. Rehabilitation has been implicit in these developments; George Bernard Shaw's repeated inclusion of Aristophanes in a 'great tradition' of comedy, and of theatre *tout court*, is a salient illustration of the new level of esteem. An escape from (in historical terms) the unduly moralistic concerns of neoclassicism has, of course, been facilitated by wider patterns of change in ethical and social attitudes. Where he previously appeared dangerously licentious (though his power to shock has certainly not yet been lost), Aristophanes has come to appear enjoyably bawdy and scurrilous to democratic audiences which flatter themselves that they are peculiarly well attuned to his outspokenness and licentiousness. There is, however, a subtle risk of misunderstanding lurking here. Classical Athens was not a 'liberated' society in sexual, social, and ethical terms: to grasp the special nature of Old Comedy, we need a historically careful approach to the plays, not a reliance on peculiarly modern instincts or assumptions. There may be a price to pay in other respects too. Twentieth-century translators have eschewed the somewhat mannered verse which had been the norm with their predecessors; but the predominant use of either prose or free verse has arguably tended to erase a sense of Aristophanes' distinctive combination of formality with freedom, virtuosity with vulgarity (see 'Translating Aristophanes', above). Here as elsewhere, one might be wise to conclude that there is something too multifarious about the playwright and his genre to be wholly or comfortably encompassed by later cultural responses.

The first commercial (as opposed to university and school) stagings of Aristophanic plays go back to the first decade of the twentieth century, when at least two productions of *Lysistrata* were put on in London. They were, naturally, still far from faithful to the sexual details of the original, and it was not until the 1990s that productions appeared, such as the one directed by Peter Hall in London in 1993 (with its attempt to recapture the spirit of the original phallic and padded costumes), of which this was no longer true. It is arguable that appreciation of Aristophanic humour, in principle at least, has benefited from the pluralism of modern styles of entertainment: to some extent a modern audience is disposed to find in his work elements of, say, stand-up comedy, farce, pantomime, cabaret, topical satire, variety or vaudeville shows, and even theatre of the Absurd,[81] all synthesized into a rich theatrical kaleido-scope. Similarly, it is possible to find recent works which, whether coincidentally or not, have a broadly Aristophanic ethos. Tom Stoppard's *Jumpers* (1972) is a case in point, with its central philosophical character, its quasi-animal chorus, its verbal wit, and its pervasive mixture of fantasy and reality. Direct influence, on the other hand, has been no more common in the twentieth century than in the past. T. S. Eliot's *Sweeney Agonistes*, drafted in 1924 and subtitled 'Fragments of an Aristophanic Melodrama', is a peculiar hybrid of music-hall routines and ritualistic overtones derived from theories of comedy's origins produced by the 'Cambridge School' of anthropologists: echoes of the comedies are few, and the so-called agon, with its rather morbid blurring of life and death, is remote from the Aristophanic form whose name it borrows (see 'Formality and Performance', above). Tony Harrison's *The Common Chorus* (first published in 1988), a version of *Lysistrata* set in the women's anti-nuclear peace camp at Greenham Common, contains obscenities which remarkably outdo even the original. The piece is extensively related to its Greek model, but the view of both war and sexuality which it projects is grimmer and more disturbing than anything to be found in Aristophanes' play.

I have tried in this final section of my Introduction, albeit in a highly selective manner, to convey some sense of the fluctuating responses to Aristophanes' work between antiquity and the present. For the post-Renaissance period I have concentrated largely on English examples, partly for obvious reasons of convenience and partly because in certain respects these represent a more complicated, often contradictory, set of attitudes than were sometimes found on the Continent.[82] But one overarching point, which I stress in conclusion, could have been made just as well by reference to other European countries. Aristophanes has never been central to

[81] There are, at any rate, passages in Samuel Beckett which remind one subtly of Aristophanes: compare, for example, the combination of suggested suicide, sexual humour, and exaggerated politeness in *Waiting for Godot* (*Samuel Beckett: the Complete Dramatic Works* (London, 1986), 18–19) with the prologue to *Knights*, where similar routines all occur. A short comparison of *Waiting for Godot* and *Birds* is offered by Segal, 'Aristophanes and Beckett', in A. Bierl and P. von Möllendorff (eds.), *Orchestra: Drama, Mythos, Bühne* (Stuttgart, 1994), 235–8.

[82] Outside Greece itself, at any rate, where Aristophanic revivals have sometimes carried a special political charge: see Gonda van Steen, 'Aristophanes on the Modern Greek Stage', *Dialogos*, 2 (1995), 71–90.

literary or artistic forms of (neo)classicism, yet his peripheral status in this respect has always been counterpoised by an underlying recognition of his importance as the sole survivor of an extraordinary phenomenon of classical Athens. It is not hard to see here a two-sided moral: Old Comedy has proved to be largely inimitable, and therefore an elusive model for classicizing writers and artists, for precisely the same reasons which tied it so closely to its original time and place. But, since understanding the past must embrace the experience of what is unlike as well as what is like ourselves, the plays of Aristophanes will always remain fascinating and rewarding material for anyone who wishes to come seriously to terms with the history of theatre, the possibilities of comedy, and the relationship between both these things and the culture of democracy.

NOTE ON THE TRANSLATION

Since there is as yet no wholly satisfactory edition of the Greek text of all Aristophanes' plays, my translations of individual works are based (though not rigidly) on separate editions, in most cases those of the Oxford series of commentaries on the plays. For the present volume these are: N. Dunbar (ed.), *Aristophanes Birds* (Oxford, 1995), J. Henderson (ed.), *Aristophanes Lysistrata* (Oxford, 1987), R. G. Ussher (ed.), *Aristophanes Ecclesiazusae* (Oxford, 1973) [= *Assembly-Women*], and, for *Wealth*, V. Coulon (ed.), *Aristophane*, v (Paris, 1963). Readers familiar with later dramatic texts may be surprised to learn that among the respects in which legitimate editorial disagreements over the text of Aristophanes can still occur is the attribution of lines to speakers in certain passages. Comparison with other translations of *Birds*, in particular, is likely to reveal significant variations in the utterances attributed to Peisetairos and Euelpides in the first part of the play; this is an area where my indebtedness to Dunbar's recent edition makes a material difference. Some of the more important of my divergences from the editions cited above will be indicated in the Explanatory Notes (see e.g. note 3 to my Introduction to *Assembly-Women*).

In accordance with the principles explained in the section of the Introduction entitled 'Translating Aristophanes', my translation follows the form of the Greek text closely. However, because the marginal numbers in the translation refer to the standard numeration of the Greek text, and since this numeration is sometimes (mostly in lyric passages) anomalous, readers should be warned that the sequence occasionally does not match exactly the printed lines of the translation itself. For consistency of reference, line numbers in the General Introduction, the Introductions to individual plays, and the Index of Names refer to the strict Greek numeration. However, line numbers as given in the lemmata to Explanatory Notes have, where necessary, been slightly adjusted for the convenience of the user of the translation.

SELECT BIBLIOGRAPHY

These suggestions for further reading are restricted to items written in, or translated into, English. Preference has generally been given to more recent and more accessible publications, through which, for those interested, older and more specialized secondary literature can be traced. I have tried, none the less, to give guidance to a reasonably wide range of publications, suitably flagged so that readers can follow up as much or as little as suits their interests. References to works which contain untranslated Greek have been minimized but not altogether excluded. Full publication details of books are given only at the first citation.

GENERAL WORKS

The most dependable introductions to Aristophanes and his genre are

Dover, K. J., *Aristophanic Comedy* (Berkeley and Los Angeles, 1972).
Handley, E. W., 'Comedy', in P. E. Easterling and B. M. W. Knox (eds.), *The Cambridge History of Classical Literature*, i. *Greek Literature* (Cambridge, 1985), 355-425.
MacDowell, D. M., *Aristophanes and Athens* (Oxford, 1995).

A lively book aimed specifically at sixth-formers and students is

Cartledge, P., *Aristophanes and his Theatre of the Absurd* (London, 1990).

Two effusive books which try to illuminate Old Comedy by modern comparisons, but are often free-wheeling and not to be trusted on details, are

McLeish, K., *The Theatre of Aristophanes* (London, 1980).
Reckford, K., *Aristophanes' Old-and-New Comedy* (Chapel Hill, NC, 1987).

A book full of ideas but often arbitrary in its interpretations is

Whitman, C. H., *Aristophanes and the Comic Hero* (Cambridge, Mass., 1964).

Various aspects of Aristophanes' literary technique are lucidly discussed in

Harriott, R., *Aristophanes Poet and Dramatist* (London, 1986).

An advanced discussion of all the plays, whose angle of approach (often stimulating, sometimes strained) is indicated by its title, is

Bowie, A. M., *Aristophanes: Myth, Ritual and Comedy* (Cambridge, 1993).

There is a recent collection of essays, several of which are cited separately below, in

Segal, E. (ed.), *Oxford Readings in Aristophanes* (Oxford, 1996).

ASPECTS OF ARISTOPHANIC COMEDY

On Old Comedy's use of traditional elements of 'sub-literary' entertainment, see

> Murphy, C. T., 'Popular Comedy in Aristophanes', *American Journal of Philology*, 93 (1972), 169–89.

The following deal with basic features of Aristophanic humour:

> Dobrov, G., 'The Dawn of Farce: Aristophanes', in J. Redmond (ed.), *Farce* (Themes in Drama 10, Cambridge, 1988), 15–31.
>
> Kaimio, M., 'Comic Violence in Aristophanes', *Arctos*, 24 (1990), 47–72.
>
> MacDowell, D. M., 'Clowning and Slapstick in Aristophanes', in Redmond (ed.), *Farce*, 1–13.

A sensitive discussion of the discontinuities of Aristophanic characterization in terms of 'imagist' logic (an alternative to what I have called the 'improvisatory' quality of many protagonists) can be found in

> Silk, M., 'The People of Aristophanes', in C. B. R. Pelling (ed.), *Characterization and Individuality in Greek Literature* (Oxford, 1990), 150–73; repr. without Greek, in Segal (ed.), *Oxford Readings*, 229–251.

Aristophanes' own (parabatic) statements about his dramatic activity are discussed, not always with a sufficient sense of their fictionalizing force, in

> Bremer, J. M., 'Aristophanes on his own Poetry', in J. M. Bremer and E. W. Handley (eds.), *Aristophane* (Vandœuvres-Geneva, 1993) 125–65.

The rhetoric of Aristophanic self-presentation, as found (chiefly) in the parabasis, is also discussed by

> Goldhill, S., *The Poet's Voice* (Cambridge, 1991), 188–205.
>
> Hubbard, T., *The Mask of Comedy: Aristophanes and the Intertextual Parabasis* (Ithaca, NY, 1991).
>
> Murray, R. J., 'Aristophanic Protest', *Hermes*, 115 (1987), 146–54.

Some brief but subtle remarks on deceptiveness, both in Aristophanes' presentation of himself and in his characters, are made by

> Heath, M., 'Some Deceptions in Aristophanes', *Papers of the Leeds International Latin Seminar*, 6 (1990), 229–40.

A detailed but often misguided use of Aristophanes as sociological evidence is made by

> Ehrenberg, V., *The People of Aristophanes* (2nd edn., Oxford, 1951).

For those interested in details of Aristophanic language, it is hard to avoid works which require knowledge of Greek. Two important articles are

Dover, K. J., 'The Style of Aristophanes', in his *Greek and the Greeks*
(Oxford, 1987), 224-36.
—— 'Language and Character in Aristophanes', ibid. 237-48.

Aristophanic obscenity receives a full analysis (but marred by errors),
whose introductory chapters are partly accessible to the Greekless, in

Henderson, J., *The Maculate Muse: Obscene Language in Attic Comedy* (New
Haven, 1975; repr. with addenda: New York, 1991).

On the development of 'Middle Comedy', during Aristophanes' later years
and beyond, see:

Arnott, W. G., 'From Aristophanes to Menander', *Greece and Rome*, 19
(1972), 65-80.

ARISTOPHANES' CAREER

Different views of the problems of Aristophanes' early career are taken by

Halliwell, S., 'Aristophanes' Apprenticeship', *Classical Quarterly*, 30
(1980), 33-45; repr. with Greek translated, in Segal (ed.), *Oxford
Readings*, 98-116.
MacDowell, D. M., 'Aristophanes and Kallistratos', *Classical Quarterly*, 32
(1982), 21-6.
Slater, N. W., 'Aristophanes' Apprenticeship Again', *Greek, Roman and
Byzantine Studies*, 30 (1989), 67-82.

A broader (but partly technical) argument for collaboration between comic
poets is put by

Halliwell, S., 'Authorial Collaboration in the Athenian Comic Theatre',
Greek, Roman and Byzantine Studies, 30 (1989), 515-28.

Aristophanes' relationship to his greatest comic predecessor (Kratinos) and
contemporary (Eupolis) is selectively examined in

Heath, M., 'Aristophanes and his Rivals', *Greece and Rome*, 37 (1990),
143-58.

FESTIVALS AND FESTIVITY

The outstanding work on festivals, actors, and so on, but containing
untranslated Greek and rather technical for the general reader, is

Pickard-Cambridge, A. W., *Dramatic Festivals of Athens*, 2nd edn., rev. J.
Gould and D. M. Lewis (Oxford, 1968; repr. with addenda, 1988).

Much of the same ground is more accessibly covered by an excellent source
book in translation:

Csapo, E., and Slater, W. J., *The Context of Ancient Drama* (Ann Arbor, Mich., 1995).

For comedy's festive status, and effective exemption from legal and other norms of decency, see

Halliwell, S., 'Comic Satire and Freedom of Speech in Classical Athens', *Journal of Hellenic Studies*, 111 (1991), 48-70.

The general place of dramatic festivals in the culture of Athens is explored by

Osborne, R., 'Competitive Festivals and the Polis: A Context for Dramatic Festivals at Athens', in A. H. Sommerstein *et al.* (eds.), *Tragedy Comedy and the Polis* (Bari, 1993), 21-38.

That the City Dionysia, the oldest dramatic festival, was of democratic (not Peisistratid) origin, and represented a celebration of civic freedoms, is argued by

Connor, W. R., 'City Dionysia and Athenian Democracy', *Classica et Medievalia*, 40 (1989), 7-32.

The relationship between tragedy and comedy is interestingly explored by

Taplin, O., 'Fifth-Century Tragedy and Comedy: A *Synkrisis*', *Journal of Hellenic Studies*, 106 (1986), 163-74, repr. with Greek translated in Segal (ed.) *Oxford Readings*, 9-28.

For the application to Aristophanes of the idea of 'carnivalesque' laughter, as developed by the Russian theorist M. Bakhtin, see (but with extreme caution about his simplified view of comic poets as 'conservatives')

Edwards, A. T., 'Historicizing the Popular Grotesque: Bakhtin's *Rabelais* and Attic Old Comedy', in R. Scodel (ed.), *Theater and Society in the Classical World* (Ann Arbor, Mich., 1993), 89-117.

FORMALITY AND PERFORMANCE

The three modes of delivery are technically analysed in

Pickard-Cambridge, *Dramatic Festivals*, 156-67.

Formal structures are discussed, with schematic analyses of the plays, by

Pickard-Cambridge, A. W., *Dithyramb Tragedy and Comedy*, 2nd edn. rev. T. B. L. Webster (Oxford, 1962), 194-229.

On the choral 'entrance', *parodos*, as manifesting Aristophanes' creative adaptation of formal conventions, see

Zimmermann, B., 'The *Parodoi* of the Aristophanic Comedies', *Studi Italiani di Filologia Classica*, 2 (1984), 13-24; repr. with Greek translated in Segal (ed.), *Oxford Readings*, 182-93.

The parabasis (see also under 'Aspects of Aristophanic Comedy', above) is the subject of two books, the first relatively technical, the second concerned with Aristophanes' creation of an autobiographical persona:

Sifakis, G., *Parabasis and Animal Choruses* (London, 1971).
Hubbard, *The Mask of Comedy*.

Demonstration that other poets of Old Comedy often made similar boasts to those of Aristophanes is provided by

Sommerstein, A. H., 'Old Comedians on Old Comedy', in B. Zimmermann (ed.), *Antike Dramentheorien und ihre Rezeption* (Stuttgart, 1992), 14–33.

On the genre's formal conventions, see also e.g.

Dover, *Aristophanic Comedy*, 49–53, 66–8.
Harriot, *Aristophanes Poet and Dramatist*, esp. chs. 2–3.

The evidence of the comic fragments for formal structures in other poets was analysed by

Whittaker, M., 'The Comic Fragments in their Relation to the Structure of Old Attic Comedy', *Classical Quarterly*, 29 (1935), 181–91.

A new analysis of Aristophanic plots in terms of narrative patterns and functional elements akin to those of folk tale is attempted by

Sifakis, G. M., 'The Structure of Aristophanic Comedy', *Journal of Hellenic Studies* 112 (1992), 123–42.

SATIRE

This is the most contentious area of Aristophanic criticism. A recent, balanced survey of opinions is supplied by

Carey, C., 'Comic Ridicule and Democracy', in R. Osborne and S. Hornblower (eds.), *Ritual, Finance, Politics: Athenian Democratic Accounts Presented to David Lewis* (Oxford, 1994), 69–83.

A much-cited older work, spirited but actually rather muddled, is

Gomme, A. W., 'Aristophanes and Politics', *Classical Review*, 52 (1938), 97–109; repr. in his *More Essays in Greek History and Literature* (London, 1962), 70–91.

An influential but extremely dogmatic modern reading of Aristophanes as a committed critic of radical democracy is

Croix, G. E. M. de Ste, *The Origins of the Peloponnesian War* (London, 1972), appendix XXIX, 355–71; repr., in abridged form with Greek translated, in Segal (ed.), *Oxford Readings*, 42–64.

The views of scholars cautious (in various ways) about the possibility of reading the poet's allegiances out of his plays can be found in

Chapman, G. A. H., 'Aristophanes and History', *Acta Classica*, 21 (1978), 59-69.

Halliwell, S., 'Aristophanic Satire', *Yearbook of English Studies*, 14 (1984), 6-20; repr. in C. Rawson (ed.), *English Satire and the Satiric Tradition* (Oxford, 1984), 6-20.

Heath, M., *Political Comedy in Aristophanes* (Göttingen, 1987).

Redfield, J., 'Drama and Community: Aristophanes and Some of his Rivals', in J. J. Winkler and F. I. Zeitlin (eds.), *Nothing to Do with Dionysos?* (Princeton, 1990), 214-335.

A conception of comedy as embodying the power of the democracy to humble individuals, and remind élite leaders of the sovereignty of the people, is elaborated by

Henderson, J., 'The *Dêmos* and the Comic Competition', in Winkler and Zeitlin (eds.), *Nothing to Do with Dionysos?*, 271-313; repr. with abridgements, in Segal (ed.), *Oxford Readings*, 65-97.

—— 'Comic Hero Versus Political Élite', in Sommerstein *et al.* (eds.), *Tragedy Comedy and the Polis*, 307-19.

For crucial differences between the festive traditions of comic satire and the power of aggressive laughter in Greek society, see

Halliwell, S., 'The Uses of Laughter in Greek Culture', *Classical Quarterly* 41 (1991), 279-96.

On the combination of honours and mockery in the traditions of Dionysiac festivals (but without reflections on the pertinence of this to comedy), see

Cole, S. G., 'Procession and Celebration at the Dionysia', in Scodel (ed.), *Theater and Society*, 25-38.

Arguments against the idea of Old Comedy as either a reliable reflector of, or a potent influence upon, the currents of Athenian publicity are put by

Halliwell, S., 'Comedy and Publicity in the Society of the Polis', in Sommerstein *et al.* (eds.), *Tragedy Comedy and the Polis*, 321-40.

For a negative case on the question of influence, see also

Stow, H. L., 'Aristophanes' Influence on Public Opinion', *Classical Journal*, 38 (1942), 83-92.

Old Comedy's satirical and obscene connections with the older, semi-dramatic genre of Iambos are discussed by

Rosen, R. M., *Old Comedy and the Iambographic Tradition* (Atlanta, 1988).

TRANSLATING ARISTOPHANES

For further discussion of the problems and the limits of their possible resolutions, see

Dover, *Aristophanic Comedy*, 230–7.

Halliwell, S., 'Aristophanes', in O. Classe (ed.), *Encyclopedia of Literary Translation* (London, 1998).

Sommerstein, A. H., 'On Translating Aristophanes: Ends and Means', *Greece and Rome*, 20 (1973), 140–54.

A challenging treatment of Aristophanic lyrics which suggests that their supposedly elevated elements are merely conventional, while their strength lies in the use of a 'low', popular idiom, is offered by

Silk, M., 'Aristophanes as a Lyric Poet', in J. Henderson (ed.), *Aristophanes: Essays in Interpretation* (*Yale Classical Studies*, 26, Cambridge, 1980), 99–151.

STAGE DIRECTIONS

On the Theatre of Dionysos, see e.g.

Csapo and Slater, *The Context of Ancient Drama*, 79–81.

The most comprehensive discussion of staging, but unreliable at many points, is

Dearden, C. W., *The Stage of Aristophanes* (London, 1976).

Some distinctively comic features of theatricality are analysed by

Lowe, N. J., 'Greek Stagecraft and Aristophanes', in Redmond (ed.), *Farce*, 33–52.

There is a detailed but irritatingly cluttered and disjointed treatment of theatrical aspects of all the surviving plays in

Russo, C., *Aristophanes an Author for the Stage*, Eng. trans. (London, 1994).

Specific points are, of course, treated by the editions of individual plays cited below, and my own interpretations have often been guided by these. Among other useful works on theatrical matters are

Dover, K. J., 'The Skene in Aristophanes', *Proceedings of the Cambridge Philological Society*, 12 (1966), 2–17; repr. in *Greek and the Greeks*, 249–66.

—— 'Portrait-Masks in Aristophanes', *Greek and the Greeks*, 266–78.

Handley, E. W., 'Aristophanes and his Theatre', in Bremer and Handley (eds.), *Aristophane*, 97–123.

Stone, L. M., *Costume in Aristophanic Poetry* (Salem, 1984).

A well-illustrated book for the general reader is

Green, R., and Handley, E., *Images of the Greek Theatre* (London, 1995), esp. chs. 4–5.

ARISTOPHANES AND POSTERITY

An interesting range of observations on the ancient evidence for knowledge of Aristophanes can be found in

Dover, *Aristophanic Comedy*, 221–9.

Sommerstein, A. H., 'Aristophanes in Antiquity', in D. Barrett and A. H. Sommerstein (trans.), *Aristophanes: the Knights etc.* (Harmondsworth, 1978), 9–20.

Evidence for fourth-century restaging of Aristophanes and other Old Comedy in Magna Graecia is presented and illustrated in

Taplin, O., *Comic Angels* (Oxford, 1993).

—— 'Do the "Phlyax" Vases have Bearings on Athenian Comedy and the Polis?', in Sommerstein *et al.* (eds.), *Tragedy Comedy and the Polis*, 527–44.

On Lucian's work, including some of its Aristophanic features, see

Branham, R. B., *Unruly Eloquence: Lucian and the Comedy of Traditions* (Cambridge, Mass., 1989).

Robinson, C., *Lucian and his Influence in Europe* (London, 1979).

There is a short sketch of Aristophanes' influence, unfortunately marred by sentimentality, silliness, and error, in

Lord, L. E., *Aristophanes: His Plays and his Influence* (London, n.d. [c.1925]).

The following items deal with particular aspects of Aristophanes' reception and influence:

Atkins, S., 'Goethe, Aristophanes, and the Classical Walpurgisnacht', *Comparative Literature*, 6 (1954), 64–78.

Gross, N., 'Racine's Debt to Aristophanes', *Comparative Literature*, 17 (1965), 209–24.

O'Sullivan, N., 'Aristophanes and Wagner', *Antike und Abendland*, 36 (1990), 67–81.

Segal, E., 'Aristophanes and Beckett', in A. Bierl and P. von Möllendorff (eds.), *Orchestra: Drama, Mythos, Bühne* (Stuttgart, 1994), 235–8.

Gonda van Steen, 'Aristophanes on the Modern Greek Stage', *Dialogos*, 2 (1995), 71–90.

BIRDS

My translation is based, with only occasional divergences, on the recent edition by

Dunbar, N., *Aristophanes Birds* (Oxford, 1995).

Dunbar's massive commentary is far and away the most important resource for the understanding of the play by those with Greek. See also the matching text and translation, with commentary, by

Sommerstein, A. H., *Aristophanes Birds* (Warminster, 1987).

In addition to the books cited in General Works above, there are notable discussions of the play in

Dobrov, G. (ed.), *Aristophanes' Birds and Nephelokokkugia* (Syracuse, NY, 1990).

Gelzer, T., 'Some Aspects of Aristophanes' Dramatic Art in the *Birds*', *Bulletin of the Institute of Classical Studies*, 23 (1976), 1–14; repr. with Greek translated in Segal (ed.), *Oxford Readings*, 194–215.

Konstan, D., 'Aristophanes' *Birds* and the City in the Air', *Arethusa*, 23 (1990), 183–207; rev. version in D. Konstan, *Greek Comedy and Ideology* (New York, 1995), 29–44.

LYSISTRATA

My translation is largely based on the Greek text edited by

Henderson, J., *Aristophanes Lysistrata* (Oxford, 1987).

See also the matching text and translation, with commentary, by

Sommerstein, A. H., *Aristophanes Lysistrata* (Warminster, 1990).

Henderson's and Sommerstein's Introductions include discussion of the difficult political chronology of early 411 in Athens. A view which detects hints of foreboding in the play is developed by

Westlake, H. D., 'The *Lysistrata* and the War', *Phoenix*, 34 (1980), 38–54.

In addition to the works cited in General Works above, questions of theme and structure are handled by

Henderson, J., '*Lysistrate*: The Play and its Themes', in Henderson (ed.), *Aristophanes: Essays*, 153–218.

Hulton, A. O., 'The Women on the Acropolis: A Note on the Structure of the *Lysistrata*', *Greece and Rome*, 19 (1972), 32–6.

Konstan, D., 'Aristophanes' *Lysistrata*: Women and the Body Politic', in Sommerstein *et al.* (eds.), *Tragedy Comedy and the Polis*, 431–44; rev. version in Konstan, *Greek Comedy*, 45–60.

Vaio, J., 'The Manipulation of Theme and Action in Aristophanes' *Lysistrata*', *Greek, Roman and Byzantine Studies*, 14 (1973), 369–80.

The play is discussed, both as a kind of metatheatre (male actors playing women) and as an implicit reaffirmation of masculine values, in

Taaffe, L. K., *Aristophanes and Women* (London, 1993), ch. 2.

That Lysistrata herself is not an entirely 'high-minded' character is argued by

> Wilson, N. G., 'Two Observations on Aristophanes' *Lysistrata*', *Greek, Roman and Byzantine Studies*, 23 (1982), 157–63, at 157–61.

A focus on the relationship between city (*polis*) and household (*oikos*) is adopted, perhaps rather too earnestly, by

> Foley, H. P., 'The "Female Intruder" Reconsidered: Women in Aristophanes' *Lysistrata* and *Ecclesiazusae*', *Classical Philology*, 77 (1982), 1–21.

ASSEMBLY-WOMEN

My translation is based, with occasional divergences, on the text and commentary of

> Ussher, R. G., *Aristophanes Ecclesiazusae* (Oxford, 1973).

See also

> Ussher, R. G., 'The Staging of the *Ecclesiazusae*', *Hermes*, 97 (1969), 22–37; repr. in H.-J. Newiger (ed.), *Aristophanes und die alte Komödie* (Darmstadt, 1975), 383–404.

A monograph which reads the play in terms of contrasting values (public/private, male/female) harmonized by persuasion is

> Rothwell, K. S., *Politics and Persuasion in Aristophanes' Ecclesiazusae* (Leiden, 1990).

Social and economic issues are discussed in

> David, E., *Aristophanes and Athenian Society of the Early Fourth Century B.C.* (Leiden, 1984).
> Said, S., 'The Assemblywomen: Women, Economy, and Politics', Eng. trans. in Segal (ed.), *Oxford Readings*, 282–313.

Also relevant (see under *Lysistrata*) are

> Foley, ' "Female Intruder" Reconsidered', 14–21.
> Taaffe, *Aristophanes and Women*, ch. 4.

WEALTH

The text on which my translation is based, with occasional divergences, is that of

> Coulon, V., *Aristophane*, vol. v (3rd impression, Paris, 1963).

Social and economic issues are discussed in

David, E., *Aristophanes and Athenian Society*.

In addition to relevant chapters of books listed in General Works, the following are among the more interesting discussions of the play:

Flashar, H., 'The Originality of Aristophanes' Last Plays', Eng. trans. in Segal (ed.), *Oxford Readings*, 314–28.

Konstan, D., and Dillon, M., 'The Ideology of Aristophanes' *Wealth*', *American Journal of Philology*, 102 (1981), 371–94; rev. version in Konstan, *Greek Comedy*, 75–90.

Olson, S. D., 'Economics and Ideology in Aristophanes' *Wealth*', *Harvard Studies in Classical Philology*, 93 (1990), 223–42.

Sommerstein, A. H., 'Aristophanes and the Demon Poverty', *Classical Quarterly*, 34 (1984), 314–33; repr. with Greek translated, in Segal (ed.), *Oxford Readings*, 252–81.

Willetts, R. F., *Blind Wealth and Aristophanes* (Inaugural lecture: Birmingham, 1970).

CHRONOLOGY

This chronology contains the dates of (a) Aristophanes' surviving plays, (b) certain prominent events mentioned in the plays themselves, and (c) a selection of other important occurrences. The chronology of Aristophanes' lost plays will be separately discussed in an appendix to volume iii of the translation.

c.525 Birth of Aischylos, tragic playwright.

514 Murder of Hipparchos, brother of the Athenian tyrant Hippias, by Harmodios and Aristogeiton.

510 With Spartan help, the Athenians expel the tyrant Hippias.

508 Kleomenes, Spartan king, occupies Athenian Akropolis but is forced to withdraw.
    Kleisthenes' democratic reforms of Athenian politics, including creation of demes.

c.496 Birth of Sophokles, tragic playwright.

490 First Persian invasion of Greece, under Dareios. Battle of Marathon.

486 Comic drama introduced into the official programme of the City Dionysia festival (spring).

480 Second Persian invasion of Greece, under Xerxes. Battles of Artemision, Thermopylai, and Salamis.

c.480 Birth of Euripides, tragic playwright.

478 Founding of Delian League of Greek states against Persia, under Athenian leadership; subsequently turns into Athenian empire.

469 Birth of Sokrates, Athenian philosopher.

462 Further democratic reform at Athens, promoted by Ephialtes and Perikles.

456 Death of Aischylos.

c.455 Birth of Thucydides, Athenian historian.
    Athenian system of democratic law courts strengthened; payment introduced, on Perikles' proposal, for jurors.

c.450 Birth of Aristophanes.

447 Building of Parthenon started, financed by Athenian imperial revenues; completed in late 430s. Cult statue of Athena Polias designed by Phidias, sculptor.

446–5	Thirty-year peace treaty concluded between Athens and Sparta.
c.440	Comic drama introduced into the official programme of the Lenaia festival (mid-winter).
c.432	Megarian decree passed by Athenians, on Perikles' proposal, prohibiting Megarian trade/business with Athens and her allies.
431	Thirty-year peace collapses: friction between Athenian and Spartan spheres of influence erupts into major conflict (Peloponnesian War, spanning 431–404).
	First of annual series of Spartan invasions of Attika, to damage crops and property.
430–29	Major outbreak of plague at Athens. Death of Perikles. Ascendancy of Kleon as democratic leader begins: he proposes increase in rate of jury pay.
427	Aristophanes' first play, *Daitaleis* (*Banqueters*), produced. Gorgias, Sicilian rhetorician, visits Athens.
426	Aristophanes' *Babylonians* (Dionysia) leads to official complaint by Kleon.
425	Aristophanes' *Acharnians* (Lenaia), 1st prize; produced by Kallistratos.
	Athenian capture of Spartans on island of Sphakteria, after special military intervention by Kleon.
424	Aristophanes' *Knights* (Lenaia), 1st prize.
423	Aristophanes' *Clouds*, first version (Dionysia), unsuccessful.
422	Aristophanes' *Wasps* (Lenaia), probably 2nd place; produced by Philonides.
	Death of Kleon in Battle of Amphipolis.
421	Aristophanes' *Peace* (Dionysia), 2nd place.
	'Peace of Nikias' concluded between Athens and Sparta.
419–17	Gradual breakdown of peace, and renewal of outright war, between Athens and Sparta.
415	Athens sends major expedition to Sicily; scandalous mutilation of city's herms takes place on eve of fleet's departure. Alkibiades, suspected of involvement, flees into exile.
414	Aristophanes' *Birds* (Dionysia), 2nd place; produced by Kallistratos.
413	Sparta establishes fort at Dekeleia in northern Attika. Sicilian expedition ends in catastrophic defeat.

412	Defection of Miletos and other cities from Athenian empire.
411	Aristophanes' *Lysistrata* (Lenaia, probably), result unknown; produced by Kallistratos.
	Oligarchic *coup* at Athens, led by Peisandros and others; suspension of democratic government.
	Aristophanes' *Women at the Thesmophoria* (Dionysia, probably), result unknown.
410	Democracy restored at Athens.
407–6	Return of Alkibiades to Athens, later followed by his second exile.
406	Athenian victory in naval battle at Arginusai, but followed by trial and execution of several generals.
	Deaths of Euripides and Sophokles.
405	Aristophanes' *Frogs* (Lenaia), 1st prize; produced by Kallistratos.
	Athenian defeat in battle of Aigospotamoi; effective destruction of the city's military capacities.
404	Final surrender of Athens to Sparta; Spartans destroy city's Long Walls and impose rule of Thirty Tyrants.
403	Expulsion of the Thirty from Athens; restoration of democracy.
c.400	Agyrrhios proposes introduction of pay for attendance at Athenian Assembly.
399	Sokrates executed on charges of impiety and corrupting the young.
396–5	Athens and Thebes form anti-Spartan league, later joined by Korinth and Argos.
395	Athens begins rebuilding its Long Walls.
394	Battle of Knidos: Spartan fleet destroyed by Persian fleet under Athenian leadership.
c.393	Aristophanes' *Assembly-Women* (festival and result unknown).
388	Aristophanes' *Wealth* (festival unknown), possibly 1st prize.
c.387	Plato opens philosophical school, the Academy.
c.385	Death of Aristophanes.

Birds

INTRODUCTION

Birds, produced for Aristophanes by Kallistratos at the City Dionysia in 414, is by some way the longest surviving Aristophanic comedy. It is conceived and constructed around as extravagant (as well as literal) a flight of fancy as occurs in any of his works. It begins, somewhat *à la* Samuel Beckett, with a scene of two old, shabby, disenchanted Athenians stumbling around the countryside outside their city, attempting to interpret the directions they are supposedly receiving from a pair of birds; and it ends with one of these same characters celebrating a marriage which marks his displacement of Zeus as the supreme ruler of the universe. In between that bizarre beginning and that cosmically triumphant conclusion, we pass through an increasingly exorbitant adventure which moves from earth to sky, and which sees the creation of a bird-city (the eponymous Cloudcuckooland) whose existence impinges upon—indeed, places a decisive barrier between—the human world below and the Olympian gods above. The shape of the plot thus follows a typical Aristophanic pattern. The first half embraces the achievement of a fantastic piece of comic 'heroism', as Peisetairos employs his creative (and sophistic) imagination to encourage the birds to recover the power which he claims they once held over the world, and persuades them that the way to do so is to build a new city state in the sky. The second half then pursues the consequences of this scheme in a sequence of visits by 'outsiders' (an unusually long sequence, hence *Birds*' exceptional size), mixing together would-be intruders from earth with divine visitors from Olympos (Iris the spy, Prometheus the defector, and finally the three diplomat-gods of an official embassy).

The simple yet memorably exotic scenario of *Birds* draws on sources which include the material of dreams, animal fable, and myth. It combines all of these with generic traditions which include the use of animal choruses[1] and the egotism of the comic protagonist. The motifs of flying, bird-like humans, and birds which take on

---

[1] A bird-chorus had been used as early as Magnes, the leading comic playwright of the 470s–460s: see the allusion at *Knights* 522. Vase-paintings of dancers in bird costumes also reflect this comic tradition: see e.g. R. Green and E. Handley, *Images of the Greek Theatre* (London, 1995), pl. 3.

human characteristics, occur in the art and storytelling of many cultures. When a character in Plato cites the possession of wings and the ability to fly as an example of the delusions which we experience in dreams (*Theaitetos* 158b), he picks on an archetypal and perhaps universal human fantasy. In reassuring his two guests, at *Birds* 654-5, that there is a magic root which, when eaten, will cause them to sprout real wings, the Hoopoe is drawing on a motif which would almost certainly have been familiar to Aristophanes' audience from the realms of folklore. Certainly the Athenians, like all Greeks, were familiar with a wealth of animal fables, especially those which went under the name of Aesop, in which birds could speak, think, and act intelligently; *Birds* refers twice to Aesop (471, 651), and may allude to such fables at several other points. In the realms of Greek myth, two stories of winged humans stand out. One is the tale of Daidalos' prodigious technology, which allowed him to make artificial wings for himself and his ill-fated son, Ikaros. Daidalos is nowhere alluded to in *Birds*, but a second myth with a tragic element, that of Tereus' metamorphosis into a bird, was evidently a crucial part of the inspiration for the play.

In the appalling story of Tereus, who raped and maimed his sister-in-law, Philomela, before being tricked by her and his wife, Prokne, into eating his own son, Itys, the metamorphosis from human to bird (a hoopoe for Tereus, nightingale for Prokne, and swallow for Philomela) is an image which half-blurs, half-freezes the horrors of the earlier events. This block of myth had been treated by a number of tragedians in Athens, including Sophokles, before the date of *Birds*. There can be no more remarkable illustration of the forms of transmutation which Aristophanes' imagination relishes than the way in which a myth whose tragic version embraced rape, mutilation, murder, and incest was used to generate some of the material of an airily ludicrous fantasy. Old Comedy can, it seems, invert and convert for its own purposes even the bleakest of subjects. The appeal of Tereus to Aristophanes was in part the possibility of discovering (or inventing) absurdity even within the materials of tragedy, and in part his comically promising status as a twin-natured creature who could help to mediate the transition from human to bird which he had lived through himself. Tereus is, then, in a sense the key figure in the genesis of the plot of *Birds*.

In very broad terms, *Birds* weaves together three main types of story pattern familiar from myth and folklore. The first leads us from human to animal: this is the metamorphosis theme for which Tereus is the crucial precedent, and which the two main humans in the play carry out after the parabasis (801 ff.), in a way which simultaneously foregrounds the basic pretence of comic costuming. The second reverses the direction of imaginative change, leading us from animal to human: this, for which the paradigm is already provided by Aesopic animal fables, and which sustains the well-established comic tradition of animal choruses, is the humanization of the birds themselves. In *Birds*, humanization is taken to the ultimate point of *urbanization*, and therefore politicization, as the birds are organized into the central institution of Greek society, the polis or city state. Thirdly and finally, Peisetairos' idea of building a bird-city in order to challenge the Olympian gods is, at a barely submerged level of significance, a comic counterpart to myths of conflict within the divine world, especially the Titanomachy, or war between the Titans (pre-Olympian gods led by Kronos) and the Olympians (led by Kronos' son, Zeus), and the Gigantomachy, in which the Olympians in turn faced and overcame a challenge from the Giants. Both these myths were extremely familiar from Greek literature and art; *Birds* refers three times to the Gigantomachy (553, 823–5, 1249–52). In the later parts of the comedy, an Athenian audience could not have failed to have a sense that Peisetairos, by wresting Zeus' power and sceptre from him, was succeeding where the Giants had failed, and was displacing Zeus in the way in which he himself had once displaced his own father.[2]

In so far as *Birds* is both the fulfilment of a blatantly escapist impulse, and the realization of an ultimate egotism, its comic dynamics can to a considerable degree be left to speak for themselves. But a large dimension of the richness and humour of the play lies in the ways in which those undeniable features become complicated and qualified by twists and turns that increasingly assume an air of paradox. At the start of the play, the old figures of Peisetairos and Euelpides are simply looking for an escape from Athens, with its supposedly vexing climate of taxes, debts, and, above all, litigiousness. To the modern reader or audience, the rural setting might initially suggest the search for a specifically anti-urban utopia or Shangri La. But that would be a mistake. The old

[2] Nan Dunbar, in her edition of *Birds* (7–9), points out that Aristophanes effectively confuses the motifs of Titanomachy and Gigantomachy, since it was in the former that Prometheus had lent crucial help *to* Zeus.

men are carrying, among other things, a basket, pots, and myrtle wreaths, which would make an Athenian audience think not only that they are on the move, but also that they hope eventually to make a sacrifice for a new-found homeland (a sacrifice that will in fact turn out to be for a newly *founded* homeland: 848 ff.). The 'land that's free from trouble' for which they are searching (44) is, as is made clear (48, 121 ff.), a new city. They venture into the countryside only to make enquiries of Tereus, whose existence as a bird, superimposed on his previous experience as a man, makes him a potential informant about the whereabouts of promising places to settle.

The old men seem at first little better than self-indulgent fantasizers: people who dream of a world which would be like 'a place to curl up in, like a big soft blanket' (122), where all the usual problems of social life would be inverted to their specific and irresistible advantage (128 ff.). But this prospect is overtaken and modified by a sudden inspiration from Peisetairos, who is prompted by Tereus' own metamorphosis to wonder about the possibility of living with the birds themselves. Now, after all, the idea of escaping altogether from human civilization does come into view. Yet it is almost at once given an ironic slant (foreshadowing much of the comedy's later development) by Peisetairos' 'grand design' (162), which involves the creation of a new city that, far from lying outside the realms of trouble and strife which the Athenian characters wanted to leave behind, sounds like a recipe for trouble on a massive scale. *Power* (163) lies at the heart of Peisetairos' scheme, a power for the birds that will involve them not only in 'colonizing' (183) and controlling the whole sky, but also thereby in blockading the territory and intercepting the trade of their rivals, the gods. This is power politics and international relations on the largest scale imaginable, and it makes the social problems which irked Peisetairos and Euelpides in Athens look very petty indeed.

This shift from the crude escapism of the opening to the hugely ambitious 'grand design' of a bird-city that will challenge the gods themselves is also a process whereby the character Peisetairos is transformed from a down-at-heel, disgruntled old man into an exponent of comically remarkable acumen and vision, first in the role of military general (356 ff.), commanding his imaginary forces against the resistance from the birds, and then in that of oratorical advocate and persuader. This is a striking comic instance of the combination of words and action which was a traditional Greek formula for the outstanding leader or hero (cf. e.g. Homer, *Iliad* 9.443). It is also a salient example of the 'improvisatory' qualities which I have identified in my general Introduction as a hallmark of the characterization of Aristophanic protagonists. So Peisetairos' transformation naturally has something in common with, say, the creativity of Dikaiopolis in *Acharnians* or Trygaios in *Peace*. But there is a substantial difference too. The pivotal motivations of both Dikaiopolis and Trygaios—their dissatisfaction with war, their longing for peace—are a datum from the beginnings of their plays; and their subsequent arguments are at any rate congruent with those motives. But it would be impossible, from the nature of Peisetairos' original disillusionment with Athens, to anticipate anything like the arguments which he goes on to produce (or invent) for the original power of birds in the universe, and the possibility of retrieving that power by challenging Zeus himself.

In Peisetairos' case, the transformation of character or behaviour takes on a particularly rhetorical and intellectual colouring. It is only the dynamo of Peisetairos' *ideas* which brings the concept of Cloudcuckooland into being. To an extent which is not really matched by any other Aristophanic protagonist, and which fulfils the meaning of his name ('persuader of companion(s)'), Peisetairos evolves into a figure who forges his destiny, and the destiny of those around him, by the force of persuasion. At an early stage the Hoopoe tells the other birds that a human has arrived whose mind 'is full of new ideas' (256), and he will later describe him, even before the agon bears out the description in abundance, as both 'amazingly wise' and

> a wily old fox—
> Sophist and quibbler and spiv, so smooth and so subtle!
>
> (428–31).

This last passage contains terms which suit a rhetorical adept, not least one who is a product, or for that matter a purveyor, of sophistic techniques.[3] Although the implications of the description are patently double-edged, the extraordinary success to which persuasion carries Peisetairos surely removes him from the plane on which

---

[3] The closest parallel, significantly, is at *Clouds* 444–51, where the Chorus is envisaging the benefits of a rhetorical training in the Thinking Institute.

real anxieties about sophistic rhetoric might operate. It is, in any case, consistent with this description that the arguments which Peisetairos uses in the agon involve a sharpness of debating style, an array of cosmogonical, historical, and religious lore, and a sense of how power can be wrested from the gods back to the birds, all of which give him something of the character of a rhetorical politician or ambassador. This prepares the way for the situation after the parabasis, where the notional divinity of the birds in general will be entirely subordinated to the egotistical authority of Peisetairos himself—an authority which even allows him to have rebellious birds, political 'dissidents', put to death and cooked for his own dinner (1583–5). It is a related aspect of the protagonist's transformation that, by the stage at which Iris flies into Cloudcuckooland, Peisetairos has established, and expects to be effective, an apparatus of officialdom (guards, immigration officials, etc.), which seems a highly ironic creation for someone who originally left Athens to escape the workings of its legal and bureaucratic system.

There is a sense in which Peisetairos can plausibly be regarded as an apotheosis of one view of the collective Athenian 'character'. In Thucydides' account of the Congress at Sparta in 432, during the diplomatic prelude to the Peloponnesian War, the Corinthian delegates describe the Athenians as people who are 'perpetually innovative and acute at having ideas and then putting them into practice'.[4] Peisetairos, once his grand design occurs to him, embodies such features in a supremely confident and high-flying style. The first half of the play shows him deploying a combination of soaring imagination and rhetorical talent, while the post-parabatic scenes survey the aggrandizement which grows from his plans. Moreover, as has already been mentioned and as has frequently been stressed by earlier critics, the city which Peisetairos founds bears an ironic resemblance in certain respects to the colonizing and imperialistic practices of Athens itself.[5] For these and other reasons, some interpreters have wanted to read *Birds* as an allegory on Athenian 'international' ambitions, particularly in view of the fact that the play was produced during the great expedition to Sicily which had left Athens in the summer of 415 and was to be disastrously crushed

---

[4] Thucydides 1.70.2; cf. 1.102.3.

[5] The earliest moment at which this point becomes salient is 186, where Peisetairos invokes the Athenian siege of Melos as a model for the birds to follow; a reference to 'tribute' a few lines later (191) underlines the point.

in the early autumn of 413. In so far as this expedition had the possible aim of bringing the whole of Sicily under Athenian control, it certainly provided a topical example of the city's political aspirations which Aristophanes could, if he had wished, have exploited in constructing his comedy.

But any totalizing allegorical interpretation of *Birds* must fail, and for one reason above all. While it is feasible to see in Peisetairos an enterprise and inventiveness which might have a special resonance for an Athenian audience, it would be absurd for Aristophanes to allegorize the city's own policies by a figure who starts the play with the overriding intention of *escaping* from Athens. Of course this starting point leaves scope for later ironies in the protagonist's behaviour, but it also rules out the possibility of reading Athens itself in Peisetairos *tout court*. This latter observation can be reinforced by a reminder of the two successive scenes in which the protagonist brusquely expels, first, the Inspector, a figure explicitly representative of Athenian imperial officialdom (1021 ff.), and then the Decree-Seller, whose wares forcefully bring imperial legislation to mind (1035 ff.). Besides, given Aristophanes' treatment of allegorical elements in other comedies, especially *Knights*, *Wasps*, and *Peace*, it is telling that *Birds* does not contain a single direct cue for an allegorical interpretation in the sustained sense. Overtones and allusiveness are one thing, allegory another altogether: the latter cannot be constructed out of the purely tacit and hypothetical. Peisetairos can legitimately be perceived as more typically 'Athenian' in his energies and ideas than he ever realizes, but he does not make us much the wiser about the nature of the city he wants to leave behind.[6]

In fact, *Birds* does not make us any the wiser about *anything* other than the dreamlike capacity of the comic hero to carry his desires through to ultimate fulfilment. The second half of the play is a celebration of pure egotism. This brings us back to the comedy's paradoxical nature. Peisetairos' success was prepared by an act of persuasion at whose heart lay the idea of bird-deities and their recovery of a long-lost power. But after the parabasis, where the chorus demonstrates that it has learnt something from the

---

[6] It might be worth adding that there is nothing remotely Athenian (Athens was the most cosmopolitan city in the Greek world) about vetting new arrivals and violently rejecting most of them: Peisetairos' behaviour in this respect owes everything to the traditions of comic egotism.

protagonist's manipulation of mythical motifs, very little more is heard, and nothing at all is *seen*, of this earlier fantasy. If the birds as a whole are benefiting from the worship of human beings, this seems of slight weight when compared to the accumulation of authority and kudos in the hands of Peisetairos, their sole and dictatorial ruler, *turannos* (1708), a highly charged term for Athenian ears.[7] His power makes it a delicious absurdity that he should be preparing (in typical comic fashion: cf. *Acharnians*, *Peace*, *Wealth*) to *sacrifice*. To whom? The conundrum is not, of course, resolved but only compounded by the observation that Peisetairos is himself nominally a bird-deity. In any case, the first part of this idea is comically skin-deep. Peisetairos is scarcely treated as a bird by any of his visitors, human or divine;[8] indeed he is referred to as a man by Prometheus (1545), Herakles (1575), and Poseidon (1581), and he explicitly acknowledges his anthropic status in the first of these passages. Peisetairos may have wings, but that does not stop him doing what only people can do: cooking birds, for example (1579 ff.). Is he the only cannibal in Aristophanes?

The theme of bird-deities remains a necessary part of the background, a premiss of the ongoing action, in the second half of the play, and comes briefly to the fore in the second parabasis (1058 ff.). But, in addition to being absorbed into the increasingly self-centred glorification of Peisetairos, it is also subordinated to two other sources of comic material: the attempts of various human beings to gain 'wings' of their own or access to the new city; and the mythological burlesque of the scenes involving Iris, Poseidon, and the three-god embassy. The 'intruder-scenes' with humans form, as usual, a loosely bound concatenation, each of them exploiting in its own way some of the associations of a new city and/or the aerial setting. Two of the human arrivals, the Inspector and the Decree-Seller, are legalistic 'bureaucrats' who see an opportunity for official intervention in the creation or running of the city. We might have expected the Informer to be a comparably meddlesome

---

[7] Since *Birds* contains a reference, albeit humorous, to Athenian fears about the return of tyranny (1074-5), we might say that Peisetairos' achievement legitimizes, or at any rate celebrates, in the world of wish-fulfilment (the id?) what has to be condemned and suppressed in the reality of the social world.

[8] There are a number of passages where second-person plurals, denoting the bird community, are addressed to Peisetairos (e.g. 1515, 1592); and Peisetairos himself refers to 'us birds' at 1600. But the overwhelming impression is of an egotistically manipulated fiction.

nuisance, like the ones in *Acharnians* (818 ff.) and *Wealth* (850 ff.). But he turns out not to be plying his trade on Peisetairos, only to want a pair of wings that would enable him to fly all the more efficiently around the Athenian empire in pursuit of victims. Then there are the airy(-fairy), mantic types, the Poet, the Soothsayer, and Kinesias, who use their lofty inspiration to celebrate or endorse the appearance of Cloudcuckooland, and hope thereby for some rewarding patronage. This leaves two figures who are more *sui generis*. Meton is the boffin, the mathematician-cum-scientific 'town-planner', whose references to radial roads and the like do reflect real ideas held by contemporary intellectuals but are none the less punctured by the underlying implication (important for much of the comic ethos of *Birds*) that he wants to make something inflatedly portentous, not to mention some lucre, out of the situation. Finally, there is the Father-Beater, the rebellious adolescent who is ready-made for the role of fighting-cock, which humorously symbolizes a spell in the army to work off his aggression. It hardly repays careful thought to ask why, of all these, the nameless Poet (but not Kinesias) and the Father-Beater should be the two who succeed in extracting something from Peisetairos. The protagonist's limited sympathy for them is little more than another manifestation of his arbitrary power.

When it comes to the divine visitors, two of whom Peisetairos greets, once he recognizes them, as though old friends (1504, 1586), Aristophanes' imagination is influenced, as we saw earlier, by the thinly submerged pattern of myths which tell of challenges to the power of a supreme god and his supporters. This is the story pattern which leads to the climactic appearance of Peisetairos as the new Zeus, fitted out with that god's accoutrements (sceptre and thunderbolt). But over this narrative of triumph and succession within the world of gods Aristophanes superimposes scenes whose comic rationale exhibits a kind of mythological burlesque, the reduction of divine figures to the level of idiosyncratic and humanly defective characters.[9] This style of humour, represented elsewhere in the surviving plays by the Dionysos and Herakles of *Frogs* and the Hermes of both *Peace* and *Wealth*, appeals to cultural familiarity with the established images and personae of the gods, but only

---

[9] Full-blown mythological burlesque involves the comic transformation of a mythical narrative: many other Old Comedies, including some of the lost plays of Aristophanes, belonged to this category.

in order to subvert them by collapsing their religious and mythological grandeur into the mundanely less-than-perfect. In the case
of Iris, this is done not only by a good deal of paratragic language,
but also through a sharp juxtaposition of the goddess's own shrill,
prima-donna-like squeamishness with the protagonist's lustful
aggressiveness. In the second of these respects the scene is likely to
have reminded the Athenian audience of the specific kind of mythological burlesque associated with satyr plays. We have several Attic
vase-paintings depicting satyric assaults on Iris, and Peisetairos'
coarse threat of rape at 1253–6 is of a piece with their ithyphallic
violence.[10]

Rather different in ethos is the presentation of Prometheus as a
kind of neurotic, even paranoiac personality: driven to befriend
'men', as he paradoxically puts it (1545), and betray Zeus once
more, yet obsessed with fear of persecution by the latter (1494 ff.).
The mythological prototype is unmistakable, yet utterly remote: the
fretful coward who needs to skulk beneath a parasol could hardly
be further from the defiant hero of *Prometheus Bound*; such is comedy's paradigmatic drop from the sublime to the ridiculous. What is
more, his parasol is a rich piece of absurdity in itself: while serving
the practical purpose of concealment, its association with female use
in religious processions (of which Prometheus is aware, 1550–1)
gives an effeminate tinge to his behaviour, and this is perhaps complicated further by the occasional status of parasols as quasi-Asiatic
status symbols in Athens.[11] Finally, the divine embassy is a piquant
combination of sharply divergent personae: Poseidon's proud
seniority and stuffy conservatism (he is worried even about the
Triballian's poor form in dress, 1567–9); Herakles' readiness to slip
from the aggression of a hero used to killing with his own hands
(1574–8) to the impulses of the traditional stage gourmand who
cannot resist the demands of his belly;[12] and the Triballian's presence as a token barbarian god, unable to make even the simplest
remark in Greek, and there to be exploited by the others.

[10] The best known of the relevant vases, a cup by the Brygos painter in the British
Museum (E65), is illustrated in e.g. Green and Handley, *Images*, pl. 9.

[11] Athenian use of parasols is discussed in scholarly detail by M. C. Miller, 'The
Parasol: An Oriental Status-Symbol in late Archaic and Classical Athens', *Journal of
Hellenic Studies*, 112 (1992), 91–105.

[12] Aristophanes is (mock-)contemptuous at *Wasps* 60, *Peace* 741, of the well-
worn use of Herakles as a comic glutton.

In addition to the details of its burlesque mode, the embassy scene as a whole fits perfectly into the comedy's final crescendo, because it shows the triumph of the comic fundamental of self-gratification, here typified by Herakles' voracious appetite, over the cautious, rational balance of considerations which Poseidon attempts to argue for. In its characteristically condensed way, this encourages a sense that the entire cosmos might be manipulated for the hedonistic satisfaction of embodied desires, especially for food and sex. And yet this celebration of physical pleasure and power is itself, of course, only an idea, a piece of wishful imagination. It is, as Peisetairos pointed out to one of his visitors, (only) *words* which give human 'wings' (1446). *Birds* is, we might conclude, the extreme, the paradigmatic case of the Aristophanic comic imagination as the realm of an 'airy nothing': it acts out a gigantic, compound metaphor for the mind's capacity to take flight from reality into fantasy, yet does so in order to realize urges which remain, in the final analysis, all too human, all too (back) down to earth.

BIRDS

Speaking Characters

EUELPIDES: an elderly Athenian
PEISETAIROS: his companion; the same age
SERVANT: bird-slave of the HOOPOE
HOOPOE: the metamorphosed Tereus
CHORUS: of twenty-four different species of bird
LEADER: of the CHORUS
PRIEST
POET
ORACLE-MONGER
METON: scientist and town-planner
INSPECTOR: Athenian imperial official
DECREE-SELLER: vendor of copies of state documents
MESSENGER^A: a bird
MESSENGER^B: another bird
IRIS: messenger of the gods
HERALD: a bird, envoy from Cloudcuckooland to earth
FATHER-BEATER: a disillusioned young man
KINESIAS: Athenian poet
INFORMER: a young Athenian who lives by malicious prosecutions
PROMETHEUS: traitor to Zeus
POSEIDON: leader of the divine embassy
HERAKLES: colleague of POSEIDON's on the divine embassy
TRIBALLIAN: a Thracian god, representative of barbarian deities
MESSENGER^C: a bird

Silent Characters

FLAMINGO
MEDE: an exotic bird
Second HOOPOE
GOBBLER: an obese bird
PROKNE: wife of the HOOPOE
RAVEN: a bird-piper? (see note on 861)
PRINCESS: a beautiful girl, symbolic incarnation of Zeus' power
Various BIRD-SLAVES

[*The scene building represents, in the first instance, part of a wild, rocky area of countryside. Two elderly Athenians enter:* EUELPIDES *has a jackdaw on his wrist,* PEISETAIROS *a crow. Between them they also carry a jumble of belongings, including a basket, various pots and pans, cooking skewers, myrtle wreaths, and bedding.*]

EUELPIDES [*to jackdaw*]. D'you mean straight on, towards that
    tree just there?
PEISETAIROS [*to crow*]. To hell with you! [*to* EUELPIDES] It's
    cawing *back*, that way!
EUELPIDES. For crying out loud! Just why are we roaming like
    this?
    We'll kill ourselves by shuttling back and forth.
PEISETAIROS. What a wretched fool I was to trust this crow!
    I dread to think how far I've walked—in circles.
EUELPIDES. What a miserable fool I was to trust this jackdaw!
    I've broken all my toenails, stumbling round.
PEISETAIROS. I haven't the faintest notion where we are.
    D'you think you'd find your way back home from here?   10
EUELPIDES. Not even Exekestides could do!
PEISETAIROS. Damnation!
EUELPIDES [*sarcastically*]. *That's* a route for you, old
    mate!
PEISETAIROS. The man who sold these birds has swindled us—
    That market-trader, mad Philokrates!
    He said this pair would show us the way to Tereus.   15-16
    This jackdaw—right old son of Tharreleides!—
    Cost us an obol; that crow of yours cost three.*
    But the only thing they know is how to bite!
    [*To jackdaw*] What's making you gawp this time? D'you   20
    mean continue
    Across those rocks? There's certainly no path here.
EUELPIDES. And there isn't a trace of track on *this* side, either.
PEISETAIROS. This crow of mine's now trying to show the route.
    It caws away, but keeps on changing its mind.
EUELPIDES. Well what's it trying to say?
PEISETAIROS.   I'd swear it's saying
    It won't stop gnawing until it's chewed my fingers!

[EUELPIDES *turns to the audience, while* PEISETAIROS *remains preoccupied
with his crow.*]

EUELPIDES. Now *what* a dreadful business! Here we are,
    All keen and ready to go and join the crows,*
    But quite unable to find the path to take!
    Our problem, all you people listening to this,   30
    Is not old Sakas's sickness. Quite the reverse.*
    He wants to force his way to citizenship,
    While *we*, although our ancestry's quite clear—
    We're citizens all right—have now decided
    [*Flapping*] To fly away from Athens on both our—feet.
    It's not because we loathe the city itself.
    We'd like to see it flourish and keep its greatness,
    And give a share to all in—paying taxes.
    Cicadas whine each year a month or two
    While sitting in the trees. But Athenians   40
    Sit in the *courts* and whine throughout their lives!*
    Now that's the reason why we're on the road,
    And why we've brought this basket, pot, and wreaths*
    To roam in search of a land that's free from trouble:
    That's where we'd like to settle ourselves for good.
    Our quest's to find where Tereus lives, the hoopoe.
    We want to ask him whether, while flying around,
    He's ever seen a city that meets our needs.
PEISETAIROS. Hey you!
EUELPIDES.   What now?
PEISETAIROS.   This crow of mine's still restless:
    It's pointing up in the air.   50
EUELPIDES.   This jackdaw too
    Keeps gawping up—perhaps it's giving a signal.
    There must be nests of birds somewhere nearby.
    We'll soon find out: let's start to make a noise.
PEISETAIROS. I'll tell you what: just give that rock a kick.
EUELPIDES [*facetiously*]. No, bang it with your head—the sound's
    more hollow.
PEISETAIROS. Just take a stone and knock it.
EUELPIDES.   All right, I will.
    [*Banging.*] Yoo-hoo!*
PEISETAIROS.   What's that? D'you think you're
    calling a slave?

You should call the hoopoe's name, not shout a slave.

EUELPIDES. Yoo-*hoop*! [*He waits.*] I suppose you want it twice. 60
    Yoo-*hoop*!

[*The door opens to reveal a preposterously large-beaked creature.*]

SERVANT.   What have we here? Who's shouting my master?

[EUELPIDES *and* PEISETAIROS *fall down in fright; their birds fly away.*]

EUELPIDES. Apollo preserve us! His beak's a gaping cavern!

SERVANT. Here's trouble for us: not one but *two* bird-catchers!

PEISETAIROS. I must say, that's a shocking way to greet us.

SERVANT [*fiercely*]. You're doomed!

PEISETAIROS [*improvising*].   Don't think we're *humans*.

SERVANT.   What
    are you, then?

PEISETAIROS [*nervously*]. Well *I'm* a yellow-belly—a Libyan bird.

SERVANT. What nonsense!

PEISETAIROS.   Look at the droppings between my legs!

SERVANT. And what's this other bird? Come on, speak out.

EUELPIDES. A—shitterling, the kind that comes from Phasis.*

PEISETAIROS. What kind of beast are *you*, in heaven's name?

SERVANT. A servile bird. 70

EUELPIDES.   You mean you came off worst
    In a cock-fight?*

SERVANT.   No. I changed to match my master.
    When he became a hoopoe, he begged me too
    To turn into a bird, as his attendant.

PEISETAIROS. So birds require attendants too, like us?

SERVANT. Well this one does, because he'd once been human.
    Sometimes he craves for Phaleron anchovies;*
    So then I get a dish and run to fetch them.
    Suppose he fancies soup but needs a ladle,
    I run for one.

PEISETAIROS [*ornithologically*].
               This bird's a real roadrunner.
    Well let me tell you what we want, roadrunner: 80
    Please call your master out.

SERVANT.   He's gone to sleep,
    After eating lunch of myrtle berries and gnats.

PEISETAIROS. Then wake him up.

SERVANT.   He's bound to be annoyed:

But just as a favour for you, I'll wake him up.   [*Goes in.*]

PEISETAIROS [*after him*]. And damn your eyes! You frightened
   me to death!

EUELPIDES. O blast it all! My jackdaw's gone and flown,
   From fright.

PEISETAIROS.   Oh what a spineless beast you are!
   You were so afraid you let your jackdaw go?

EUELPIDES. Well didn't you too fall down and lose your crow?

PEISETAIROS. No, certainly not.   90

EUELPIDES.   Well where's it gone?

PEISETAIROS [*shrugging*].   It's flown.

EUELPIDES [*sarcastically*]. So you didn't let go. O what a brave
   fellow you are!

HOOPOE [*within*]. Open up the boscage; let me go outside.

[*The door opens, and the* HOOPOE, *with long bill and large crest but rather
   vestigial plumage, emerges.*]

EUELPIDES. O Herakles! What kind of creature is this?
   [*Grandly*] What plumage have we here? What triple crest?*

HOOPOE. Who's looking for me?

PEISETAIROS.   It seems that all twelve gods*
   Have tried to finish you off!

HOOPOE.   Don't laugh at me
   Because of this plumage you see. I used, my guests,
   To be a man.

EUELPIDES.   We're not mocking *you*.

HOOPOE.   Well what?

EUELPIDES [*stifling laughter*]. It's just that beak we find quite
   ludicrous.

HOOPOE [*indignantly*]. Well this is the sort of outrage Sophokles   100
   Inflicts on me in those tragic plays of his.*

PEISETAIROS. You're Tereus, ah! But are you bird or—peacock?*

TEREUS. Of course I'm a bird!

EUELPIDES.   In that case, where are your
   feathers?

TEREUS. They've fallen off.

EUELPIDES.   Is there something wrong with you?

TEREUS. No, all birds moult their feathers in the winter,
   But later on we grow fresh ones again.
   Now, tell me who you are.

PEISETAIROS. What, *us?* [*proudly*] Two mortals.

HOOPOE. And where are you from?

PEISETAIROS. The land of lovely triremes.*

HOOPOE. Don't tell me your *jurymen?**

EUELPIDES. No, quite the reverse:
We're *anti*-jurors. 110

HOOPOE. Athens grows that sort too?

EUELPIDES. You'll find a few, if you look for them in the fields.

HOOPOE [*formally*]. What venture motivates your journey
here?*

PEISETAIROS. We want to talk to *you.*

HOOPOE. But what about?

PEISETAIROS. You used to be a man—just like us two.
And owed the city money—just like us two.
And liked not paying your debts—just like us two.
But then you changed your nature for a bird's,
And flew across the land and over the sea.
Your mind contains the thoughts of man and bird.
That's why we've come as suppliants to your door, 120
To ask if you know a city that's warm and woolly—
A place to curl up in, like a big soft blanket.

HOOPOE. You want a greater city than rugged Athens?

PEISETAIROS. Not greater—just more comfortable for *us.*

HOOPOE. You obviously want to live as an aristocrat.

PEISETAIROS. What, *me?* Not at all. I hate Aristokrates.*

HOOPOE. Then what's the sort of city you'd like to live in?

PEISETAIROS. One where life's greatest problems would be like
this.
[*Vividly.*] At the crack of dawn a friend knocks on my door,
And says: 'In the name of Zeus, lord of Olympos, 130
You must come round to my house, as soon as you're
washed.
Bring your children too. I'm having a wedding-feast.
You simply can't refuse—but if you do,
Don't bother visiting me when I'm in deep trouble.'

HOOPOE. I see you've set your heart on a pitiful life!
And *you?*

EUELPIDES. I fancy similar things.

HOOPOE. Explain.

EUELPIDES. A place where in the street I'd be rebuked

By some good-looking boy's indignant father:
'Well, what a splendid way to treat my son!
You saw him as he left the gymnasium,   140
But didn't kiss, or speak, or try to touch him.
A family friend, and you didn't squeeze his balls!'*
HOOPOE. Poor wretch, what a sorrowful life you hanker for!
[*Ponders*] There *is* a happy city that's just like that.
It's by the Red Sea*—
EUELPIDES.   No thanks! That's out of the question.
We mustn't be near the sea: an Athenian galley*
Might pop up at any time, to serve a summons.
There must be a city you know somewhere in Greece.
HOOPOE. Why don't you go and live in Lepreon?
EUELPIDES. Never seen the place, of course; but its leprous name 150
Sounds terribly mangy—like Melanthios.*
HOOPOE. There's also where the Opountians live, in Lokris;
You should go and live there.
EUELPIDES.   What, become Opountios?
I wouldn't do *that* in return for a talent of gold!*
[*Thinking*] But what's life like round here, among the birds?
You know it so well.
HOOPOE [*nonchalantly*].   Not uncongenial, really.
To start with, no one needs a purse up here.
EUELPIDES. Well that's a major source of fraud removed.
HOOPOE. We feed ourselves in gardens: sesame seeds,
And myrtle-berries, poppies, and leaves of mint.   160
EUELPIDES. It sounds as though you lead a bridegroom's life!*
PEISETAIROS [*excited*]. I can see a grand design for the race of
    birds.
There's potential for power here, if you take my advice.
HOOPOE. And what's the advice you've got?
PEISETAIROS.   Well, in the first
    place,
Stop flying everywhere with your beaks agape;
It's really undignified. Down there on earth
If flighty types are seen and someone asks,
'What kind of person's this?', Teleas will answer:
'This man's a *bird*—unstable, always in flight,
Untraceable, always moving from place to place.'   170
HOOPOE. That's true enough; your criticism's fair.

So what should we do?

PEISETAIROS.   Inhabit a single city!

HOOPOE. But how could birds inhabit a city at all?

PEISETAIROS [*grandly*]. 'You need to ask, O speaker of foolish
    words?'*

    Look down.

HOOPOE.   All right, I'm looking.

PEISETAIROS.   And now look up.

HOOPOE. All right.

PEISETAIROS.   Now turn your neck around.

HOOPOE [*straining*].   My god,
    It'll do me a lot of good if I crick my neck!

PEISETAIROS. I suppose you saw?

HOOPOE.   Yes, clouds and deep blue sky.

PEISETAIROS. Well, isn't this all a natural *sphere* for birds?

HOOPOE. A sphere? In just what sense?   180

PEISETAIROS.   Their private space.

    Because the sky revolves, and everything
    Traverses it, it's called the celestial sphere.
    If *you* could colonize and fence it off,
    You'd turn this sphere into a global city.
    You'll lord it over men—they'll be your locusts!
    And you'll starve the gods, just like the siege of Melos.*

HOOPOE. But how?

PEISETAIROS.   By cutting them off from earth below.
    You know how Athens must always ask Boiotia
    For permission to cross its land to get to Delphi.
    Now, when the humans sacrifice to gods,   190
    If the gods don't pay the tribute you demand
    This aerial city of yours won't give free passage
    To the smoke of sacrifice from earth below.

HOOPOE. I swear by every snare that catches birds,
    I've never heard a more creative scheme!
    I'd love to help you found this great new city,
    Provided all the other birds agree.

PEISETAIROS. Then who'll explain the plan to them?

HOOPOE.   Why, *you*!
    [*Reassuringly*] They used, of course, to be barbarians once:
    But I've taught them Greek since settling here with them.   200

PEISETAIROS. Well why not summon them now?

HOOPOE.   It's easily done.
   I'll just step back inside this thicket here
   And start by waking up my nightingale.*
   With her I'll call the rest: to hear us both
   Will make them all come rushing along at speed.
PEISETAIROS. My dearest bird, don't stand around!
   I beg you, go inside this thicket at once
   And wake from sleep the nightingale, your wife.

      [*The* HOOPOE *steps inside the door and starts to chant.*]

HOOPOE. Come, nest-mate of mine, wake up from your sleep!
   Issue forth all the strains of the sacred chants   210
   In which you lament, with a mouth that's inspired,
   For the child of us both, oh piteous Itys!*
   Let your voice thrill the air with its liquid notes,
   Through your vibrant throat! For your song is so pure
   As it echoes around, through the rich-leaved trees,
   Till it reaches the throne of lord Zeus up above,
   Where Phoibos as well, golden-tressed god of song,
   Hears your grief and responds on his ivory lyre,
   As he summons the gods to take part in the dance.
   Then is heard from above an immortal choir,   220
           All in unison clear,
   As the gods cry in grief for your plight.

[*The pipe is heard playing a melody imitative of the nightingale's cry.*]

EUELPIDES [*ecstatic*]. O Zeus in heaven! The birdy's lovely
   voice!
   It filled the wood with a sound as sweet as honey!
PEISETAIROS. Eh you there!
EUELPIDES.   What's the matter?
PEISETAIROS.   Keep quiet!
EUELPIDES.   But why?
PEISETAIROS. The Hoopoe's on the point of singing again.

HOOPOE.   Hoopoopoo! Poopoopoo!
      Ee-oo! Ee-oo! Come everyone!
      Come all my feathered friends!
   All you who live on well-sown farmers' fields,   230
      You myriad flocks of barley-eaters,
      Seed-peckers of countless kinds,

Fly quickly here, emit your mellow cries!
And all you birds that crowd in furrows
To twitter round the crumbling clods
　　With such elated sounds,
　Twee-twee, twee-twee! Twee-twee, twee-twee!

And all you birds of garden habitats
　　Where ivy branches sprout,
You mountain species, feeders on olives and berries,　　　240
　Take wing at once in answer to my call!
　　Trrrr, trrrr! Trrrr, trrrr!

And you who on the rolling hills
Gulp down shrill gnats, and you who live
In the dew-soaked plains and Marathon's lovely meadows,
　With you of mottled-wings, O francolin, francolin!
　And birds which over the sea's great swell　　　250
　　Soar out among the halcyons,
　Come here to learn the latest news!
　Yes, every class of long-necked bird
　　Must congregate around me.
　　An old and wily man's arrived;
　　His mind is full of new ideas
　　And new the deeds he plans to do.
Come, all you birds, to hold discussion,
　Quickly, quickly, quickly, quickly!
　　Tsee-tsee, tsee-tsee!　　　260
　　Kee-wick! Kee-wick!
　Tsee-tsee, tsee-tsee, tisisisi!

PEISETAIROS [*puzzled*]. Can you see any birds?
EUELPIDES.　　　　　　　　　　Not a single beak
　or feather.
And yet I'm standing gawping at the sky.
PEISETAIROS. It looks as though the Hoopoe cried in vain,
　When filling the wood with his waterfall of sound.
HOOPOE [*still inside*]. Toro-tinx, toro-tinx!

[PARODOS: 268–433]

[*A* FLAMINGO, *soon followed by other birds, appears on the roof of the scene building; the characters begin to declaim in recitative rhythms.*]

PEISETAIROS. This way, my friend! Look over there! I've seen a
    bird at last.

EUELPIDES. A bird, for sure, but just what kind? A peacock?
    Surely not.

PEISETAIROS. Look, here's the Hoopoe coming back. He'll know.
    [*to* HOOPOE] What bird is that?   270

HOOPOE. No common-or-garden bird at all, familiar to you
    humans.

  It lives where marshy ground is found.

PEISETAIROS.   Crikes! Such a lovely
    pink!

HOOPOE. Indeed it is! And flaming wings are why they're called
    flamingos.

EUELPIDES [*to* PEISETAIROS].

  Hey you there, psst!

PEISETAIROS.   Well, what's it now?

EUELPIDES.   Look, here's a second
    bird.

PEISETAIROS. How right you are! And once again it looks 'of
    colour rare'.*

  What *could* it be? A songster strange, from mountains of the
    wild?

HOOPOE. Its name is actually the Mede.

EUELPIDES.   The *Mede?* Well blow me
    down!

  How could a Mede have flown so far, without a camel's help?*

PEISETAIROS. Now here's another bird again, perched on that
    crest up there.

EUELPIDES. I can't believe my eyes! It seems you're not the only
    hoopoe,   280

  For he's one too.

HOOPOE.   He's Philokles' son, and had a hoopoe-
    mother.

  And I'm his grandad. Think of how your families pass on
    names:

  From Hipponikos to Kallias, then back to Hipponikos.*

PEISETAIROS. I suppose this bird is Kallias! He's losing all his
    feathers.

HOOPOE. Yes, noble breeding means he's torn to pieces—by
    informers.

[*Suggestively*] And *female* birds are also fond of plucking off
 his plumage.

EUELPIDES. Good heavens above! Here's yet one more, a bird of
 coloured hue.

Now what's the name of this one here?

HOOPOE.   This one is called a
 gobbler.

PEISETAIROS. If that's a gobbler, I suspect that means
 Kleonymos!

HOOPOE. That can't be right. Kleonymos would have dropped
 his crest by now.   290

PEISETAIROS. Well never mind. But tell us why these birds are
 highly crested.*

Perhaps they plan to race in arms?

HOOPOE.   They're like the Karian
 tribes:

You see, my friend, they live on crests because it makes
 them safer.

[*Enter, from both sides, the members of the* CHORUS, *costumed as twenty-
four different birds.*]

PEISETAIROS. Poseidon save us! Look at this! A nasty throng of
 birds!

EUELPIDES. Apollo help! They're like a cloud: I'm really quite
 alarmed.

Their wings are flurrying everywhere. They're blocking up
 the entrance.*

PEISETAIROS. Look, there's a partridge.

EUELPIDES.   Zeus above! And that's a
 francolin there.

PEISETAIROS. This one's a widgeon.

EUELPIDES.   That one there must be a
 green kingfisher.

But what's the bird behind it now?

HOOPOE.   What, that one? That's
 a snipper.

EUELPIDES. A snipper? *Is* there such a bird?   300

HOOPOE.   Yes, Sporgilos the
 barber!*

Look, that's an owl.

PEISETAIROS.   That can't be true! Who's brought an owl to
     Athens?*

HOOPOE [*pointing*]. A jay, a turtle-dove, a lark. A warbler,
     wheatear, pigeon.
   A vulture, falcon, ring-dove too. A cuckoo, redshank, shrike.
   A moorhen, kestrel, grebe, and finch. Then lammergeyer,
     woodpecker.

PEISETAIROS [*shrieking*].
                         I've never seen so many birds!
                         So many blackbirds everywhere!
   What chirping sounds, what twittering cries, they make
     while running round.
   [*To* EUELPIDES] Perhaps they mean to threaten *us*: their beaks
     are gaping wide!
   It's you and me they're staring at.

EUELPIDES.   I must confess, you're right.

[*As the* CHORUS *continues to flutter around, its* LEADER *exclaims in excited,
                    stammering bursts at first.*]

LEADER.   Whe-whe, whe-whe, whe-whe, whe-whe,   310
               Where lives the bird that called me?

HOOPOE. I'm here, just where I always was. I won't desert my
     friends.

LEADER.   Wha-wha, wha-wha, wha-wha, wha-wha,
               What message for your friends?

HOOPOE. It's something free of risk for all; it's fair and sweet
     and useful.
   Two human males have just arrived, a pair of subtle
     thinkers.

LEADER.   Where, where? I don't believe it!

HOOPOE. I'm telling you, two ageing men have come to pay a
     visit.   320
   They've brought a quite prodigious plan, a tree of many
     branches.

LEADER [*no longer singing*]. You've made a blunder quite
     immense, the worst since I was hatched.
   What *can* you mean?

HOOPOE.   Don't feel alarmed.

LEADER.   What action have you
     taken?

HOOPOE. I've welcomed here a pair of men: they're lovers of
　　our life style.*
LEADER. You mean you've done this dreadful deed?
HOOPOE. 　　　　　　　　　　　　　　　I've done it,
　　and with pleasure.
LEADER. And are they both among us now?
HOOPOE. 　　　　　　　　　　　　If *I* am, so are they.

[*The birds move into a new dance sequence, expressive of fluttery
　　　　　　　　　　anxiety.*]

CHORUS. 　　　Sound the alarm! Sound the alarm! 　　　　*Strophe*
　　　　　　Our world's betrayed, we've been defiled!
　　　　　　A former friend, a fellow-creature,
　　　　　　Who shared these plains, our habitat, 　　　　330
　　　　　　Has now transgressed our ancient laws,
　　　　　　Transgressed the oaths of birds,
　　　　　　And lured me here into a trap.
　　　　　　He's placed me in the hands of men,
　　　　　　The race of foul, defiling men,
　　　　　　Who've been the enemies of birds
　　　　　　Throughout their whole existence.

LEADER [*to* HOOPOE]. We'll leave it to a later date to settle our
　　score with *you.*
　　But now's the time for these old men to face their
　　punishment:
　　They'll both be torn to bits by us.
PEISETAIROS. 　　　　　　　　　　It's clear we're doomed
　　already.
EUELPIDES. It's *you* who should be blamed for this: it's you who
　　caused this mess.
　　Why *did* you bring me here from Athens? 　　　　340
PEISETAIROS [*casually*]. 　　　　　　　Oh, just for company.
EUELPIDES. To plunge me into tears and trouble!
PEISETAIROS. 　　　　　　　　　　What balderdash
　　you're talking!
　　You won't be able to weep at all—with both your eyes
　　pecked out.*

CHORUS [*dancing aggressively round the men*].

Shriek battle-cries! Shriek battle-cries!   *Antistrophe*
Advance, attack, begin the war,
The bloody war! Vibrate your wings
And whirl them round on every side.
This pair of men must howl with pain:
My beak must tear their flesh.
No mountain top, with forest dense,
No cloud that floats across the sky,
No depths of ocean's grey expanse,   350
Will give a hiding-place to them
Or save them from my vengeance.

[*The* CHORUS *approaches, following its* LEADER's *quasi-military instructions.*]

LEADER. No holding back, go straight for them! Pluck out their
    hair and bite!
  Now where's the taxiarch?* Bring up your forces on the
    right.
EUELPIDES [*panicking*]. I told you so! I can't escape.
PEISETAIROS.   Don't start to
    run away!
EUELPIDES. What, stay to let them tear my limbs?
PEISETAIROS.   But what's the
    point of fleeing?
EUELPIDES. It's true, there's no escape route here.
PEISETAIROS.   Just follow my
    instructions.
  We need to stand and make a fight; [*pointing*] these pots
    will soon prove useful.
EUELPIDES. What use are pots?
PEISETAIROS.   Athena's craft! No *owls* will dare
    attack us.*
EUELPIDES. But what about these *vultures*, then?
PEISETAIROS.   Quick, grab a
    skewer here,
  Then hold it firm in front of you.   360
EUELPIDES.   But what about my eyes?
PEISETAIROS. Just take a saucer or a dish, and hold it up like
    this.   [PEISETAIROS *puts a dish on his head as helmet.*]
EUELPIDES. A stroke of outright genius! Such great strategic flair!

Your machinations quite surpass old Nikias's tactics.

LEADER. Ee-ee! Advance! Direct your beaks! No holding back
 from combat.

Now pluck and stab and mutilate! And strike the front pots
 first.

HOOPOE. I'd like to know the reason why, you vile and brutish
 things,

You're trying to rip these men apart, who've done you all
 no harm.

I'll have you know they're relatives, yes kinsmen of my
 wife.*

LEADER. What makes you think that they deserve more mercy
 than would wolves?

We know no greater enemies: to take revenge is right.   370

HOOPOE. Perhaps by *nature* they're your foes, but in their minds
 they're friends:

They've come to make proposals which could benefit you
 all.

LEADER. But how could anything they say bring benefit to us?
 Our enmity with humankind is generations old.

[*Preparations for the attack continue, but it becomes steadily clear that
 the birds are frightened by the men's skewers.*]

HOOPOE. It's often from their enemies that wise men learn good
 lessons.

For instance, caution keeps you safe, but *friends* won't
 teach you that.

It's enemies who make us see the value of this point.

Or then again, it's enemies not friends who teach Greek cities

The need to build the highest walls, and get themselves
 good navies.

And that's a lesson which helps preserve their children,
 homes, belongings.   380

LEADER [*to* CHORUS]. It's always prudent, in our view, to listen
 before acting.

The wise can even benefit from what their foes may say.

PEISETAIROS [*like a commander*]. It seems they're less aggressive
 now. Pull back the ranks with caution.

HOOPOE [*to* LEADER]. You owe some gratitude to *me*, for giving
 good advice.

LEADER. You know full well we've never crossed your will in
    any venture.

EUELPIDES. They're coming round to peaceful terms.

PEISETAIROS.   So let's put
    down our pots,
        And place these dishes on the ground.
        But hold your spear—I mean your skewer:
        We need to keep an armed patrol
        Inside our camp, along the lines   390
        Formed by our pots, and watch from here
        The enemy: we mustn't flee.

EUELPIDES. But if we really lose our lives,
    What burial-ground will then be ours?

PEISETAIROS [*pointing to the pots*].
        The Kerameikos cemetery!*
        To guarantee a public grave,
        We'll tell the generals how we fought,
        Engaging with the enemy,
        And died at Birdsnest Creek.*

[*The* CHORUS *now starts to back off slowly but surely. The following
exchange between the* LEADER *and the* HOOPOE *is sung.*]

LEADER.
    Fall back into rank! Now return to your base!   400
    Just drop your aggression—back down on the ground,
    Let it lie with your anger, like soldiers' arms.*
    Let's enquire of these men who they are, where they're from,
    What objective has brought them to come to us here.
        Yoo-hoo, hoopoe! I'm calling you.

HOOPOE.
    And what's the reason for your call?

LEADER.
    Who *are* these men, and where's their home?

HOOPOE.
    They're guests of mine, from clever Greece.

LEADER. And what adventure brings them here   410
    To the land of birds?

HOOPOE.   They're passionate
    About your style of life up here.
    They want to share your world with you.

LEADER. To share our world? Incredible!
　　[*Pointing to* PEISETAIROS]
　　　　What arguments does *he* advance?
HOOPOE. Things hard for you to comprehend!
LEADER. Does he discern some profit in staying here?
　　Does he believe that living here with me
　　He'll vanquish foes and benefit his friends?　　　　420
HOOPOE. He speaks of happiness surpassing words.
　　But none the less you'll find yourself convinced
　　When he describes a plan to change your life.
LEADER. 　　*Is* he just out of his mind?
HOOPOE. 　　No: he's amazingly wise!
LEADER. 　　Does he have brain power, then?
HOOPOE. 　　Yes, he's a wily old fox—
　　Sophist and quibbler and spiv, so smooth and so
　　　　subtle!*　　　　　　　　　　　　　　430
LEADER. 　　Tell him to speak, to speak at once!
　　For what you've told me of his words
　　Has set my wings aflutter.

HOOPOE [*speaking to* BIRD-SLAVES]. Now, you and you, pick up
　　this armour here.
　　Take it and hang it up where it belongs
　　Inside the kitchen, where equipment's stored.
　　[*To* PEISETAIROS] And *you* must tell the birds the reason why
　　I've called them here. Explain.
PEISETAIROS. 　　　　　　　Not on your life!
　　Unless they first agree some terms with me,
　　Like those the woman was offered by the monkey,　　　440
　　You know, the cutler:* namely, not to bite,
　　Nor grab my balls, nor poke inside my—
LEADER. 　　　　　　　　　　　　What?
　　You don't mean—
PEISETAIROS. 　　　　No, not *that*—I mean my eyes!
LEADER. I agree these terms.
PEISETAIROS. 　　　　　　Then swear an oath to prove it.
LEADER. I will—[*towards audience*] if all the judges vote for *us*,*
　　And all the audience too.
PEISETAIROS. 　　　　　　　Of course they will!
LEADER. If I break my oath, may we win—by just one vote!

PEISETAIROS [*like a herald*]. Attention, all! The campaign's been
    suspended:
  Take up your weapons, hoplites; go back home;
  But watch for announcements on the noticeboards.*   450

[AGON: 451–637]

CHORUS.   Treacherous always, in all respects,   *Strophe*
       Is human nature. Still, let's hear your case.
      Perhaps you'll draw attention to an asset,
         Or some great power of mine,
      Neglected by me through a lack of insight.
          Make public your vision!
         For any good you render me
      Will be a public gain for all the birds.

LEADER. Now what's this large idea you've brought, of which
    you would convince us?   460
  Speak loud and clear: you need not fear that *we* shall
    break the truce.
PEISETAIROS. I'm bursting with excitement now. My speech is
    ripe and ready.
  Before you wouldn't listen. [*like a banqueter*] Slave, a
    wreath! My guests, recline!
  Bring water quickly for our hands!
EUELPIDES.   Is dinner on its way,
    then?*
PEISETAIROS. Of course not. But I'd like to make a large and
    beefy speech.
  Its force will overawe their minds. [*to* CHORUS] My grief for
    you is deep:
  In former times you lived as kings.
LEADER.   We lived as *kings*—of
    what?
PEISETAIROS. You lived as kings of *everything*—of me, of him,
    of Zeus!
  Your origins are older far than Kronos and the Titans,*
  And even Earth.   470
LEADER.   Than Earth?
PEISETAIROS.   I swear.

LEADER. I hadn't heard *that*
before!

PEISETAIROS. You're not inquisitive enough—you haven't
thumbed your Aesop.

Now Aesop said the lark was born the first of all the
birds.*

There *was* no earth, so when she lost her father from
disease,

His body lay exposed for days; she could not find a grave.

Until at last, in sheer despair, she lay him in her head.

EUELPIDES. Well what a lark! I suppose that means he's buried
in a headland!*

PEISETAIROS. So if the birds were older than the earth and than
the gods,

Primeval status ought to mean that kingship's theirs by
right.

EUELPIDES. I quite agree. You'd better start to grow a beak
yourself;

Zeus won't return his sceptre to woodpeckers in a hurry!   480

PEISETAIROS. Now, long ago the human world was ruled by
birds not gods,

And birds were kings of everyone. I've many proofs of this.

For instance, I shall demonstrate the cock was once a
monarch:

He ruled the Persians long before Dareios or Megabazos;

It's from that famous reign he gained the name of 'Persian
bird'.*

That's why he still struts round the place just like the
Persian king;

No other bird's allowed to wear his headdress all erect.*

His former power was so immense that even to this day

It lingers on and shows itself in how his dawn-time song

Makes everyone jump up for work—yes, bronzesmiths,
potters, tanners,   490

Oh, cobblers, bathmen, merchants-of-grain, and lathe-and-
joinery-craftsmen.*

They all set off before it's light.

EUELPIDES. Now *I* can tell a story!

I lost a cloak of Phrygian wool because of a blasted cock.

I'd been invited into town, for a baby's naming-day;*

I'd had some drinks, and fell asleep; then *he* crowed out at
  evening!
I thought it must be dawn by now, so I set off to the
  country.
I'd hardly got outside the walls, when a mugger clubbed
  my back:
I fell and wanted to shout for help, but the blighter swiped
  my cloak!

PEISETAIROS. Well anyway, in early times the kite was king of
  Greece.

LEADER. Of Greece? 500

PEISETAIROS.   That's right. And while he reigned, he first
  required all humans
To do obeisance to the kites.*

EUELPIDES.   I did so once myself!
I'd seen a kite and grovelled down, my head back, mouth
  all open:
I swallowed a coin,* and had no money to buy myself
  some grain!

PEISETAIROS. Now, Egypt and Phoenicia had a cuckoo for their
  king.
And every time he called 'cuckoo!', Phoenicians would
  rush out
To harvest all the wheat and barley growing in their
  fields.

EUELPIDES. So *that*'s the point of what they say, 'Cuckoo!
  Skinned pricks to work!'*

PEISETAIROS. Because the birds held such control, it meant that
  when a human—
Say Agamemnon or Menelaos—became a king in Greece,
A bird would sit atop his sceptre, to take a share of bribes. 510

EUELPIDES. I'd never heard of that before. No wonder I was
  puzzled
Each time I went to tragedies and Priam held a bird:*
The bird kept watch to see what bribes—Lysikrates
  would take.

PEISETAIROS. But most remarkable of all is how king Zeus
  himself
Stands with an eagle on his head.* His children too have
  birds:

Athena has an owl; Apollo, more servant-like, a goshawk.*

LEADER. How right you are, but tell us why they carry round
   these birds.

PEISETAIROS. It's so that when, in sacrifice, the god receives the
   innards,

The birds themselves can eat them all, before Zeus has a
   chance.

In former times all humans swore their oaths by birds not
   gods.   520

Lampon still does: he swears 'By Goose'—whenever he's
   trying to swindle.*

Thus, long ago all men believed you birds were great and
   sacred,

      Yet now they think you're just their slaves,
      And treating you like lunatics
      They just throw stones—in temples too!
      Now everyone's for catching birds:
      They set the snares, the wires, the springes,
      The traps, the nets, the decoy cages,
      Then take you off for market sale,
      Where customers can squeeze your flesh.   530
      And once they've bought, they're not content
      To roast and serve you up to eat:
      They coat your skin in grated cheese,
      With silphium,* oil, and vinegar;
      They then prepare a further dressing,
      A greasy one at that,
      And pour it hot all over you,
      As though on knacker's beef!

CHORUS.   Hard to our ears are your words, O human! *Antistrophe*
        I weep to hear the shame upon our fathers.   540
        Inheriting these honours from their forebears,
           They lost them in my youth.
      But now some god, some great propitious fortune,
           Brings you as saviour.
         My nestlings and myself I shall
       Entrust to you, to care for all our lives.

LEADER. Advise us what we need to do: our life is not worth
   living,

Unless we find a way to gain our former kingship back.

PEISETAIROS. Well first of all I recommend you birds should
    found a city.   550

You then should build a circuit wall around the upper air,

Just like the one round Babylon, with giant, sun-baked
    bricks.*

LEADER. In the name of all the Giants themselves, that sounds
    an awesome city!*

PEISETAIROS. Then once your settlement is built, ask Zeus to
    give back power.

And if at first he just declines, and won't concede your
    claim,

Declare a holy war on him, and ban the gods from
    travelling*

Across your city's territory with members all erect,

The way they used to visit earth to sleep with married
    women—

Alkmene, Alope, Semele.* If they persist, then fasten

A seal upon their outsize cocks, to stop them fucking
    women.   560

I urge a second herald-bird be sent to visit humans,

To tell them, 'Birds are now in power, so sacrifice to *them*,

And only afterwards to the gods.' Then match up birds
    with gods,

And make each pair appropriate, to fit each other's
    features:*

At Aphrodite's sacrifice, give coots, those lovebirds, barley;

And when Poseidon gets a sheep, the duck must have
    some wheat;

If Herakles gets sacrifice, the gull should get stuffed loaves;

And if it's a ram for Zeus the king, the wren will now be
    'king',

And *he* must have his victim first: an uncastrated—gnat!

EUELPIDES. A sacrificial gnat, how nice! Let Zeus rage down
    with thunder!   570

LEADER. But how will humans ever think we're really gods
    not jackdaws,

When all we do is fly around?

PEISETAIROS.   What nonsense! Look at
    Hermes:

He too's a god but flies with wings; and so do many others.
There's Nike, with her golden plumes, and then again
    there's Eros.
And Iris too: for Homer said she's 'like a quivering dove'.*
And doesn't Zeus's thunder bring 'a wingéd lightning-
    bolt'?*

LEADER. But just suppose they're ignorant, and think we birds
    are worthless,
While those are gods up on Olympos?

PEISETAIROS.   A cloud of rooks and
    sparrows
Will gather and attack their fields, and guzzle all their
    seeds.
And *then* we'll see, when famine strikes, if Demeter finds
    them grain!   580

EUELPIDES. I'm sure she won't, you wait and see! She's bound
    to make excuses.

PEISETAIROS. I've got another test for them. Just send the
    ravens down
To peck the eyes out from their sheep, and from their
    pairs of oxen,
Then let Apollo heal them all. They'll have to *pay* him,
    though!*

EUELPIDES. Don't do it yet! Please give me time to sell my dear
    old oxen.

PEISETAIROS. But once they treat you as their gods—Kronos,
    Zeus, Earth, Poseidon—
They'll gain so many benefits.

LEADER.   Just give me one example.

PEISETAIROS. For one thing, locusts won't devour the blossoms
    on their vines:
They'll be annihilated by a troop of owls and kestrels.
In just the same way, ants and gall-flies won't devour
    their figs: 590
They'll all be picked off, one by one, by a flock of hungry
    thrushes.

LEADER. But how will birds make humans *rich*? For that's
    their ruling passion.

PEISETAIROS. When they consult their oracles, the birds will
    lend advice:

They'll tell them where to dig their mines, and where to
    trade for profit.
No merchant will be drowned at sea.

LEADER.   Explain why that
    won't happen.

PEISETAIROS. When someone asks about a trip, a bird will give
    the answer.
'Don't set sail now; a storm's due soon.' 'Sail *now*; you'll
    make good profits.'

EUELPIDES. I'm off to buy a cargo ship; I won't stay here with
    you.

PEISETAIROS. The birds will show them where to find old buried
    hoards of silver.
It's only birds who know these things; that's why we're
    fond of saying   600
'There's no one knows where *my* gold lies—except a
    dicky-bird.'

EUELPIDES. My boat's for sale! I'll buy a spade, to dig up crocks
    of treasure.

LEADER. But how will birds give humans *health?* It's in the gift
    of gods.

PEISETAIROS. Well once prosperity is theirs, they'll feel they've
    got well-being.
For no one's really healthy when he's suffering deprivation.

LEADER. And how will long life be assured? That too comes
    from Olympos.
Or will they die in infancy?

PEISETAIROS.   They won't. The birds will give
    them
An extra thirty years of life.

LEADER.   But how?

PEISETAIROS.   From their reserves.
Remember that 'five human ages lives the cawing crow'.*

EUELPIDES. No doubt at all, these birds will make far better
    kings than Zeus.   610

PEISETAIROS.   Of course they will!
                   And *we* won't need to build for them
                   Great temples made from marble,
                   With doors of gilded timbers too.
                   Instead, in woods and shrubbery

They'll make their homes. The grandest birds
Will have an olive tree to serve
As sanctuary. No more to Delphi,
No more to Ammon will we go
To sacrifice. We'll stand instead 620
Among wild olive and strawberry trees,
And offering barley grains and wheat
We'll pray to them with outstretched hands
For all our wants. And lo and behold
     We'll get them too,
In return for seeds of grain!

LEADER [*to* PEISETAIROS]. I thought you once my greatest foe:
    you're now my dearest friend!
I'm certain I could never wish to lose this mind of yours.
CHORUS [*singing*].
    Pride swells in me, pride in your words.
    I issue warning, I swear on oath: 630
    Make me a pledge of lasting concord;
    Be righteous, guileless, pious (*against* the gods!),
    And if we plan in harmony, those gods won't hold
    My sceptre in their hands much longer now!

LEADER. For all the tasks that need brute strength, we birds
    are standing ready.
But where shrewd thinking's still required, it's *you* who's
    got to act.
HOOPOE. It's certainly time we roused ourselves for action:
We shouldn't procrastinate like Nikias.
So let's proceed at once. But first of all, 640
I'd like you both to come inside my nest—
It's made of cosy straws and bits of twig—
And let us know your names.
PEISETAIROS.   That's easily done.
My name is Peisetairos. He's my friend,
Euelpides, from deme Krioa.*
HOOPOE.   Welcome!
PEISETAIROS. Well, thank you very much.
HOOPOE.   Now come inside.
PEISETAIROS. That's very kind. Lead on.
HOOPOE.   Then follow me.

[*The* HOOPOE *starts to go in, but* PEISETAIROS *suddenly pulls him back by the wings.*]

PEISETAIROS. Oh, just a moment! Row the ship back here.
　My friend and I still have one little problem.
　How can we live with you? We've got no wings!   650
HOOPOE. Quite simple!
PEISETAIROS.　　　　　　Wait a moment, doesn't Aesop
　Tell somewhere how the fox once came unstuck
　Because of a pact of friendship with an eagle?*
HOOPOE. You needn't be concerned. We know a root:
　Just chewing on that will make you sprout some wings.
PEISETAIROS. In that case let's go in. [*to two* BIRD-SLAVES, *using
　　human names*] Right, Xanthias
　And Manodoros,* bring in all our bedding.
　　　　　　　　　　[*The remaining belongings are taken in.*]
LEADER [*to the* HOOPOE].
　You there, yes you, I'm calling you.
HOOPOE.   What for?
LEADER.   Take *them* inside,
　And feed them well. But please send out the sweet-tongued
　　nightingale,
　The bird who sings just like a Muse. We'd like to play with
　　her.   660
PEISETAIROS. O do oblige! It's such a good idea.
　Fetch out the little birdie from the sedge.
EUELPIDES. Yes, fetch her out at once. O please agree!
　We too would love to see the nightingale.
HOOPOE. Well if that's what you want, I shall. [*calling in*]
　　Prokne!
　Come out and show yourself before our guests.

[*The door opens and the piper, costumed in brown, red, and white as
　　　　　　PROKNE, a female nightingale, emerges.*]

PEISETAIROS. O holy Zeus, what a gorgeous little birdie!
　Her skin's so soft and fair.
EUELPIDES.   I'll tell you what:
　I'd love to get myself between her thighs!
PEISETAIROS. She's wearing so much gold—just like a girl.   670
EUELPIDES. I think I'd rather like to kiss those lips.
PEISETAIROS. Deluded fool! Her beak's just like two skewers.*

EUELPIDES [*approaching* PROKNE]. Well first you must remove the
    outside layer,
  Just like an egg—and then you kiss like this.
HOOPOE [*urgently*]. Let's go inside!
PEISETAIROS [*pulling* EUELPIDES *away*].
                    Lead on: let's celebrate.   [*All in.*]

[PARABASIS: 676–800]

CHORUS.   Lovely female, tawny female,
            Loveliest of all the birds!
            Partner in the songs I sing,
            Companion constant, nightingale,
       You've come, you've come, you've shown yourself,   680
            You bring us your melodious sounds.
            With calls of spring you weave
            A pleasing tune upon your pipes
            And introduce our formal chant.

LEADER [*addressing the audience with mock-hieratic gravity*].
  Hark, you whose lives are dark and dank, who fall like
    leaves in autumn,
  You puny beings, formed from clay, you shadowy, feeble
    peoples,
  You wingless creatures-of-a-day, pathetic dreamlike
    humans,
  Pay close attention to our words, for we are true
    immortals,
  Who live in air and never age, whose thoughts will never
    wither.
  From us you'll hear a true account of elevated matters: 690
  The origins of birds and gods and rivers and all creation.
  Then once you've heard the truth from us, tell Prodikos
    to hang!*
  At the start of time there was Chaos and Night, black
    Erebos, Tartaros deep.
  But Earth and Air and Heaven were not. In Erebos'
    boundless bosom
  Black-wingéd Night produced an egg, an egg from wind
    created,*

And from that egg, as time revolved, there grew the lovely
    Eros,
Whose back gleams bright with wings of gold, whose flight
    is swift as winds.
Next, Eros lay in Chaos' wings, in Tartaros' secret depths,
And hatched this race of birds you see, and brought us to
    the light.
The universe contained no gods, till Eros mingled all.   700
But once the elements intermixed, then Heaven and Ocean
    formed
And Earth herself, with all the race of blessed, deathless gods.
This means that *we* are older far, because we're Eros'
    offspring;
That's why we fly, and why we keep the company of lovers.
Now pretty boys quite often swear they'll never yield to
    lovers,
But through our might it comes about: they're screwed
    between their thighs
For quails and purple coots and geese and cocks, their
    lovers' gifts.*
The finest things in human life all come from us, the birds.
To start with, we announce the start of winter, spring,
    and autumn.
Migrating off to Libyan shores, the crane cries, 'Sow your
    seed!',   710
And to the merchant, 'Winter comes: hang up your rudder
    and sleep!'
He tells Orestes, 'Weave a cloak!'—to keep him warm while
    mugging.*
Then later on the kite appears, to signal change of season:
It's time to sell your heavy cloak and buy some summer
    clothes.
To you we're Ammon, Delphi too, Dodona, Phoibos Apollo.
In everything you undertake, you seek bird-omens first,
When trading, buying property, or contemplating marriage.
You call a 'bird' whatever gives you hints for augury.•
A *word* can be a 'bird' for you; you call a sneeze a 'bird';   720
Chance tokens, voices, slaves, and asses: you treat them all
    as 'birds'.
It's surely plain that we're as good a prophet as Apollo!

So if you treat us as your gods,
We'll sing our oracles to you
Through all the seasons of the year,
In winter, summer, cold and heat.
We'll never fly and sulk on high,
The way that Zeus hides in the clouds.
We'll always give to each of you,
And to your families evermore,   730
Great wealth-and-health, long lives of peace,
With youth and laughter, dancing, feasts—
In short, *birds' milk* for you to drink.*
You'll wallow in such luxury,
You may be quite exhausted!

[CHORUS, *to* PROKNE.]

    Muse of the boscage—   *Strophe*
      Twee-twee, twee-twee—
Singer of filigree song, with whom
In valleys and on mountain peaks—   740
Twee-twee-twee, twee-twee-twee—
Perched on frondiferous ash tree—
Twee-twee-twee, twee-twee-twee—
My vibrant throat emits the sound
Of sacred strains of song to Pan,
And solemn dances for the Mountain-mother.*
Tri-tri-tri, tri-tri-tri, tri-tri-triii!
Our calls were borrowed by Phrynichos,
Extracting nectar like a bee
From our ambrosial melodies   750
To make his lovely music.*
Twee-twee-twee, twee-twee-twee!

LEADER. *Any* time that one of you, spectators, wants to join our
    world,
Living out a life of pleasure, let him come and visit us.
All the things that human beings count as shameful and deter,
We consider splendid and encourage birds to practise them.
If, on earth, the law decrees it's wrong for fathers to be struck,
In the sky we think it's good for someone to accost his dad,
Strike him first, and then declare: 'Hold up your spur! You want
    a fight?'*

If, down here, a slave escapes, then when he's caught gets
      branded,   760
In the sky he'd win some fame, admired for coloured
      markings.
If, down here, someone should be as Phrygian as, say,
      Spintharos,
We'd just change his race to *Pigeon*—member of Philemon's
      clan.*
If you're born a Karian slave—say, just like Exekestides—
Come to us and grow some plumage, then you'll be
      respectable.
If the son of Peisias should wish to let the exiles back,
Let him turn into a partridge, then he'll be his daddy's boy:
Here there's nothing shameful in the use of partridge-
      artifice!*

CHORUS.   Swans once made music—   *Antistrophe*
                 Twee-twee, twee-twee—   770
            Mixing calls with sound of wings,
            Invoking with acclaim Apollo—
            Twee-twee-twee, twee-twee-twee—
            Assembled on Hebros's river-bank*—
            Twee-twee-twee, twee-twee-twee—
            Sending cries through the floating clouds.
            Herds of mottled beasts then cowered,
            Windless calm held all the sea.
            Tri-tri-tri, tri-tri-tri, tri-tri-trink!
            Olympos resounded with the noise,   780
            A sense of awe transfixed its lords.
            The Graces and the Muses too
            Cried back in answering song.
            Twee-twee-twee, twee-twee-twee!

LEADER. *What* could be more wonderful, more lovely than a
      pair of wings?
   Say, for instance, some spectator here possessed the power
      of flight:
   When he felt quite hungry, and was bored with tragic
      choruses,
   Nothing could impede him from just winging off to eat at
      home,

Then returning, nice and full, to come and watch the
    comedies.*
Just suppose some Patrokleides in the audience needs to
    shit:*   790
Rather than allowing all to ooze its way into his cloak,
Winged escape would soon be his: he'd fly off, crap, and
    fly straight back.
Likewise, think of someone who's a practising adulterer;
Say he sees the woman's husband sitting in the Council
    seats:*
With his wings he'd have no problem flying up and off
    from here,
Fucking her and then returning to resume his seat again.
Don't these thoughts convince you that a pair of wings is
    bliss itself?
After all, Dieitrephes, whose only 'wings' are wickerwork,
None the less was chosen phylarch, even hipparch. Goes to
    show
Lowly backgrounds lead to power: now he *struts*, a 'red
    horse-cock'!*   800

[*As the* CHORUS *steps back, the door opens:* PEISETAIROS *and* EUELPIDES
*emerge, adjusting the less than convincing bird feathers with which they
have been equipped.*]

PEISETAIROS. Well, that will do. [*looking at* EUELPIDES] My god,
    I really think
I've never seen so ludicrous a sight!
EUELPIDES. What's making you laugh?
PEISETAIROS.   The plumage on your
    arms!
You know just what an impression those feathers make?
You look like a painted goose, and a cheap one too!
EUELPIDES. And *you* resemble a blackbird whose scalp's been
    cropped!
PEISETAIROS [*urbanely*]. I suppose our jokes are somewhat
    Aischylean:
    [*Mock-grandly*] 'Shot not by others but by my very own
    feathers'!*
LEADER. Right. What's to be done?
PEISETAIROS.   We've got to find a name,

A big impressive name, for this city of ours;   810
  Then sacrifice to the gods.
LEADER.   I quite agree.
EUELPIDES. Now let me see, what name shall we give the city?
  The Lakedaimonians use a grand old name:
  Shall we call it Sparta?
PEISETAIROS.   You must be barking mad!
  You think I'd want to call my city Sparta?
  That's a name that makes me spit!
EUELPIDES.   I feel the same.
PEISETAIROS. Well, what name *shall* we give it?
LEADER.   Perhaps a name
  That suggests the clouds and atmosphere up here—
  A light and airy name.
PEISETAIROS.   'Cloudcuckooland'?
LEADER. Hurrah!
  What a wonderful, grandiose name you've hit upon!   820
EUELPIDES. I suppose Cloudcuckooland must be the place
  Where the wealth Theogenes boasts about is hidden,
  And Aischines' money too!*
PEISETAIROS.   No, better still,
  It's the plain of Phlegra, where the gods surpassed
  Their foes, the Giants, in braggadocio!*
LEADER. What a lustrous city we've got! Which god will be
  Its patron, and receive the sacred robe?
EUELPIDES. Why not just keep Athena Polias?*
PEISETAIROS. But how could you ever expect a well-run city,
  If you have a female god who carries armour,   830
  While a woman's work is left to Kleisthenes?
LEADER. Which god, then, *will* control our battlements?
PEISETAIROS. A bird, of course—the Persian bird, in fact:*
  It's the one which has the fiercest reputation
  As the war-god's chick.*
EUELPIDES.   O chick, our lord and master!
  I'm sure he's the perfect god to live on rocks.
PEISETAIROS [*to* EUELPIDES, *officiously*]. I'd like you now to go
  across the sky
  And help the birds who are building the city walls.
  Strip off to bring the rubble and mix the mortar,
  And carry a hod, and then—fall off the ladder!   840

Post sentries there, and keep the braziers lit.
Run round to ring the bell, and sleep on site.*
Remember to send a herald up to the gods,
And another down to humans on the earth:
They should both report back here.

EUELPIDES.   And *you* stay put
And stew yourself 'back here'!

PEISETAIROS.   Please hurry along!
Without your presence the job will never get done.

[*Exit* EUELPIDES.]

It's time we made our new gods sacrifice;
I'll go to fetch the priest to lead procession.
[*Calling, as he goes in*] Slaves, fetch the ritual basket and
    holy water.   850

CHORUS.   I lend applause, I share your wish,   *Strophe*
                I quite approve of your desire
            That grand processional hymns be sung to gods,
            And a little sheep be sacrificed to them,
                To win a favourable response.
            Let a resonant chant ascend, ascend, ascend!
                Let Chairis pipe our song with us!*

[*As the piper continues to play,* PEISETAIROS *re-enters, together with a
            garlanded* PRIEST, *who carries a goat.*]

PEISETAIROS [*to the piper*]. Stop blowing that thing! Good god,
        what's going on here?
    I've certainly seen some strange things in my time,   860
    But never a raven wearing a piper's cheek-band!*
    Prepare the victim, priest, for our new gods.

PRIEST. I shall, but where's the slave who's got the basket?

[*A* BIRD-SLAVE *comes forward.*]

    [*Intoning*]
                Make prayer to Hestia, goddess of bird-hearth,*
                To Kite, the hearth-protector,
                To all bird-deities of Olympos,
                Both male and female—

PEISETAIROS [*speaking throughout*]. O Sounion's holy hawk, hail,
        ancient lord!*

PRIEST.   To the swan of Pytho and Delos,*
                To Leto, quail-mother,   870

           To Artemis, goldfinch—

PEISETAIROS. 'Artemis goldfinch': there's a new cult-title!

PRIEST.   To Sabazios, Phrygian-pigeon,
           To ostrich-mother great
           Of gods and men.

PEISETAIROS [*mockingly*]. Queen Kybele, ostrich-mother of
    Kleokritos!*

PRIEST.   May health and well-being be bestowed
           Upon Cloudcuckooland's inhabitants,
           For themselves and for the Chians—

PEISETAIROS. I like the way the Chians are always added!*   880

PRIEST.   And upon bird-heroes and sons of heroes,
           Purple coot and woodpecker,
           Pelican and spotted eagle,
           Pin-tailed sandgrouse, peacock,
           Reed-warbler and teal,
           Harrier and heron,
           Tern and blackcap,
           Titmouse and—

PEISETAIROS. Enough, to hell with you! Don't call any more.
    You must be crazy, inviting all these vultures   890
    When we've got so little meat for sacrifice.
    A single kite could snatch this clean away!
    Get out of here, and take your garlands with you!   [*Exit* PRIEST.]
    I'll sacrifice this victim on my own.   [*Starts to wash his hands.*]

CHORUS.   Just as before, it now appears,   *Antistrophe*
           A second song must be performed,
        A sacred hymn to accompany ritual washing.
        Now gods must be invoked—but only one,
           If you want the meat to be enough.
        The sacrificial beast that's lying there   900
           Is little more than jaw and horns!

PEISETAIROS [*ceremonially*]. Let us pray and sacrifice to feathered
    gods.

        [*Enter a* POET, *long-haired and scruffily dressed.*]

POET [*singing*].   Cloudcuckooland,
           Land of happiness, be acclaimed,
           In odes inspired by you,
                My Muse.

PEISETAIROS. What on earth has shown up here? Well, what's
   your name?
POET [*still singing*].
            A sender-forth of song in honey-tongued words,
            The Muses' zealous servant
            (To borrow Homer's phrase).*   910
PEISETAIROS. You mean you're just a slave, yet wear long hair?
POET [*speaking*].
            I'm not a slave, but all we chorus-trainers
      [*Singing*] Are the Muses' holy servants
            (To borrow Homer's phrase).
PEISETAIROS [*inspecting him*]. No wonder, then, your clothes are
      hole-y too!
   What's made you, poet, come mucking around up here?
POET. I've written some lyrics about Cloudcuckooland—
   Yes, several lovely dithyrambs, for instance;
   Some maiden-songs; some works *à la* Simonides.*
PEISETAIROS [*suspiciously*]. How *long* ago were all these works
      composed?   920
POET. Your city has been a theme of mine for ages.
PEISETAIROS. It's only a few days old! It's like a baby:
   I was just about to hold its naming-day.*
POET [*singing again*].
            Swift is the Muses' report,
            As swift as horse-hooves' coruscation.
      [*Begging*]
            Come, father, founder of Aitna,*
            Whose name is linked with hallowed rites,
            Donate to me whatever you are willing
            To grant with beneficent nod of your head.   930
PEISETAIROS. I can see this nuisance is going to cause us trouble,
   Unless we give him something to shake him off.
   [*To* BIRD-SLAVE] You there, you're wearing a jerkin over your
      tunic:
   Take it off and let this masterly poet have it.
   [*To* POET] Here, take the jerkin; you look quite frozen to me.
POET [*singing*].   With no reluctance my dear Muse
                  Accepts this gift.
               Now ponder in thy mind
                  Pindaric utterance.*

PEISETAIROS. This person doesn't intend to leave us alone!   940
POET [*singing loftily*].
     'Among the nomadic Scythians he wanders,
     The man who possesseth no loom-woven garment.
        Ignoble is the fate—'
      Of jerkin without tunic.
     'Comprehend my words to you.'*
PEISETAIROS. I comprehend all right! You want a tunic.
  [*To* BIRD-SLAVE] Strip off your tunic: this poet needs our
    help.
  [*To* POET] Take this and leave us alone.
POET.   I'm on my way.
                              [*Moving off*]
  And when I've gone, I'll sing about your city:
  [*Singing*]
     Acclaim, O gold-throned Muse, the trembling, frozen
       city!   950
     I visited its snow-clad, many-tracked plains.
           Hurrah for the joy!   [*Exits.*]
PEISETAIROS [*calling after*]. You've already found a way to escape
    the cold
  By getting your hands on that little tunic we gave you!
  Well, that was trouble I simply hadn't expected—
  That news of our city should reach his ears so soon.
  [*To* BIRD-SLAVE] You, take the water around the altar again.

[*As the* BIRD-SLAVE *begins to sprinkle the holy water,* PEISETAIROS *resumes the sacrificial ritual, just as an* ORACLE-MONGER, *carrying oracle-scrolls, enters.*]

PEISETAIROS. Let ritual silence reign!
ORACLE-MONGER.   Don't kill the goat!
PEISETAIROS. Who's this?   960
ORACLE-MONGER.   An oracle-monger.
PEISETAIROS.   Go to hell!
ORACLE-MONGER. I beg you, please don't treat religion rudely.
  I've got an oracle here that comes from Bakis:*
  It's all about Cloudcuckooland.
PEISETAIROS.   How comes it
  You didn't offer this oracle in the past,
  Before I founded this city?

ORACLE-MONGER [*evasively*].
Religious scruples.

PEISETAIROS. We'll soon find out: let's hear your verses then.

[*The* ORACLE-MONGER *unrolls a scroll and begins to chant.*]

ORACLE-MONGER. '*Should* the time ever arrive, when wolves and
grey-hooded crow-birds
Set up a homeland together, mid-way between Korinth and
Sikyon—'*

PEISETAIROS. Now *what*, I wonder, has Korinth to do with me?

ORACLE-MONGER [*blustering*]. That's Bakis's riddling way of
saying 'the air'.   970
[*Continuing*] 'Sacrifice first a white ram, and offer it up to
Pandora,*
Then, when a prophet appears, and starts to interpret my
verses,
Grant to him gifts for himself—both a pristine cloak and
new sandals.'

PEISETAIROS. Does it really mention sandals?

ORACLE-MONGER [*offering the scroll*].   Take the scroll!
'Give to him also a bowl, and fill up his hands with the
innards.'

PEISETAIROS. Does it really mention innards?

ORACLE-MONGER.   Take the scroll!
'*If*, sacred youth, you obey, and carry out all my
instructions,
High in the clouds you will live as an eagle. But if you
ignore me,
Neither a dove will you be, nor a woodpecker, nor yet a
blue thrush.'

PEISETAIROS. Is *all* that really mentioned?   980

ORACLE-MONGER.   Take the scroll!

PEISETAIROS. This oracle's wholly different from the one
I copied down from the lips of Apollo himself:
[*Chanting like the* ORACLE-MONGER] '*Should* the time ever
arrive, when a *charlatan* comes uninvited,
Meddling in other men's rites, and seeking a share of the
innards,
Pay him at once with some blows, and aim them with
care at his ribcage—'

ORACLE-MONGER. I don't believe you're serious.
PEISETAIROS.   Take the scroll!
  '*Nothing* should make you hold back, not even wild claims
      about eagles;
  Not if it's Lampon himself, nor even the great Diopeithes.'*
ORACLE-MONGER. Is *all* that really mentioned?
PEISETAIROS.   Take the scroll!
  [*Attacking him*] Clear out of here! To hell with you!   990
ORACLE-MONGER [*fleeing*].   Help, help!
PEISETAIROS. Skedaddle, and peddle your oracles somewhere else!

[*As the* ORACLE-MONGER *runs off on one side,* METON, *carrying compasses
  and other apparatus, enters confidently by the opposite side entrance.*]

METON [*pompously*]. I've come to visit—
PEISETAIROS.   Oh, surely not further
      trouble!
  [*Quasi-tragically*] What aim, what shape of purpose brings
      you here?
  What motive, nay what boot, explains your journey?*
METON. I want to practise geometry on the air
  And help you portion it into fields.
PEISETAIROS.   My god!
  And who exactly are you?
METON.   Meton, of course,
  Whose fame pervades all Greece and all—Kolonos.*
PEISETAIROS. And what are these things you've got?
METON.   They're
      aerial rulers.
  I'll try to explain. [*gesturing*] The entirety of the air   1000
  Is rather like a baking-lid in shape.*
  [*Demonstrating*] So if I place on top this rounded ruler,
  And use these compasses—you see?
PEISETAIROS.   I'm baffled!
METON. I'll measure with my level ruler here,
  And make the circle square. Then, at the centre
  Your Agora will stand, and to its hub
  Will lead straight roads—just like a star
  Whose centre forms a circle but whose rays
  Shine in straight lines.
PEISETAIROS.   I think he's really Thales!*

[*Confidentially*] Meton, 1010

METON. Yes, what?

PEISETAIROS. You know I'm fond of you:
Take my advice and slip away quietly now.

METON. Is something wrong?

PEISETAIROS. It's like what happens at Sparta:
They're driving foreigners out. There's trouble around,
With violence breaking out.

METON. Not a revolution?

PEISETAIROS. No, certainly not.

METON. Then what?

PEISETAIROS [*menacingly*]. There's popular feeling
It's time to use our fists on all *impostors*!

METON. I'd better get out.

PEISETAIROS. You should! I can't be sure
You've still got time: the trouble's close at hand!   [*Strikes him.*]

METON [*running*]. My life's at risk!

PEISETAIROS. Well didn't I give you
warning?
Just scarper—go and measure yourself elsewhere! 1020

[*As* METON *runs off on one side, an* INSPECTOR, *carrying voting-urns and
sumptuously dressed, enters on the other.*]

INSPECTOR. Now where are the consuls?*

PEISETAIROS. Who's this fancy playboy?

INSPECTOR. I've come as Inspector, appointed at Athens by lot
To Cloudcuckooland.

PEISETAIROS. You've come as Inspector, you say?
Who sent you here?

INSPECTOR. Some paltry document
In Teleas' name.

PEISETAIROS. Well would you like some payment
To go back quietly home?

INSPECTOR. I certainly would!
I wanted to stay at home for Assembly business:
[*Self-importantly*] I've been an agent in dealings with
Pharnakes.*

PEISETAIROS [*hitting him*]. Well *there*'s your pay—so take it and
on your way!

INSPECTOR. And what was that? 1030

PEISETAIROS.   An Assembly for Pharnakes!
INSPECTOR [*fleeing*]. Ho, witnesses! An Inspector's being
    attacked!
PEISETAIROS [*throwing the urns*]. Buzz off! And don't forget your
    pair of urns!*   [*Exit* INSPECTOR.]
    It beggars belief! They even send Inspectors
    Before the city's had time to sacrifice.

    [*Enter a* DECREE-SELLER,* *carrying a stack of documents.*]

DECREE-SELLER [*reading, in prose*]. 'Should a citizen of
    Cloudcuckooland commit an offence against a citizen
    of Athens,—'
PEISETAIROS. And what's this latest curse—another scroll?
DECREE-SELLER. I've got the freshest laws and new decrees:
    I've brought them all for sale.
PEISETAIROS.   What sort of thing?
DECREE-SELLER [*reading*]. 'The people of Cloudcuckooland shall   1040
    adhere to the aforementioned weights, measures, and
    decrees, as stipulated for the people of Olophyxos.'*
PEISETAIROS [*hitting him*]. I'll Olo-fix you right and proper now!
DECREE-SELLER. Hey, what's the matter?
PEISETAIROS [*chasing him*].   Pack up your laws and
    run!
    I've got some *different* laws which will make you smart.
DECREE-SELLER [*coming back, as if reading again*]. 'I summon
    Peisetairos to appear next month on a charge of assault.'*
PEISETAIROS [*chasing again*]. What, back for more? You haven't
    vanished yet?
INSPECTOR [*reappearing, and reading*]. 'If anyone expels Athenian
    officials, and refuses to receive them according to the
    terms of the inscribed decree,—'   1050
PEISETAIROS. I don't believe my eyes! Not *you* again!
INSPECTOR. I'll bring a charge—the fine's ten thousand
    drachmas.*
PEISETAIROS. And *I'll* smash up this pair of voting-urns!
    [*Chases him off.*]
DECREE-SELLER [*returning*]. I remember how you used to crap
    on pillars.*
PEISETAIROS. You stinking rat! [*to* SLAVES] Quick, grab him!
    [PEISETAIROS *calls after.*] Come back here!   [DECREE-SELLER *escapes.*]

Let's get away at once, before more trouble:
We can sacrifice the goat inside the house.   [*All inside.*]

[SECOND PARABASIS: 1058-1117]

CHORUS. To me, all-seeing deity,   *Strophe*
         All-puissant god, the human race
         Will sacrifice with pious prayers.   1060
         My eyes survey the whole of earth,
         I keep its copious fruits quite safe
         By killing teeming broods of beasts
         Who feed on all that grows in soil,
     Crushing the produce of plants in omnivorous jaws,
     And sitting on branches devouring the fruit of the trees.
         I also kill the ones which blight
         All fragrant gardens with their stains.
     All manner of insects which creep and which bite
         Are caught in the sweep of my wings   1070
         And fall to destruction in bloodshed.

LEADER. Now's the time, this very day, official edicts fill the
           air:
         [*Solemnly*] 'Let it be known that if you kill Diagoras the
           Melian,
         You can claim reward—one talent. Likewise for a tyrant's
           head
         (Even if he's dead already), claim a talent as reward.'*
         We too, therefore, want to make a proclamation to you
           all:
         [*As before*] Let it be known that if you kill Philokrates the
           sparrow-man,
         You can claim reward—one talent. Take him captive,
           you'll get four!
         What's the reason? He's the man who sells dead siskins
           on a string,
         Puffs up thrushes, furthermore, to put them cruelly on
           display,   1080
         Hangs up blackbirds too, with feathers crammed through
           nasal cavities,

Captures doves, what's more, and keeps them prisoners in
    his ruthless style,
Forcing them to act as decoys while they're fastened in a
    net.*
Here's what we desire to say, then: *any* man who's
    breeding birds,*
Caging them inside his house, we urge him now to set
    them free.
Should this order go ignored, you'll find yourselves seized
    by the birds:
We, in turn, will fasten *you*, and make you serve as decoys
    too!

CHORUS.   Happy the race of feathered birds!   *Antistrophe*
        In wintertime they have no need
        To wrap themselves in woollen cloaks.   1090
        In summer's stifling heat, in turn,
        The sun's effulgence burns us not:
        In blossoming meadows' leafy bosoms
        I make my nest and make my home,
      Just when cicadas, melodious creatures, are singing,
      Drunk with delight in the sun and the heat of midday.
        In winter I retire to caves,
        To frolic with the mountain nymphs.
      In springtime we feed on the berries of myrtles
        (Their flowers all virginal white)   1100
        And fruits of the Graces' own garden.

LEADER. Now's the time for us to tell the judges who award
    the prize
All the lovely things we'll bring them, if they vote that
    we're the best.*
Greater gifts by far they'll have than even Paris once
    received.*
First of all the thing that every judge desires with all his
    heart.
Owls of silver, mined at Laurion, won't run out at any
    time.*
Hoards of them will fill your houses; in your purses you
    will find

Nests have been laid down and from them baby coins will
   be produced.
Furthermore we'll make your homes as spacious as your
   temples are;
All your houses we'll rebuild—we'll give them all new
   wings, in fact!   1110
Should you hold a minor post and then desire to filch
   some cash,
We'll provide a keen-eyed hawk to add to your
   rapaciousness.
Lastly, when you're out to dine, we'll lend you gullets to
   store more food.
Should you *fail* to vote for us, you'd better buy some caps
   of bronze
Like the ones that statues have.* For if you leave
   yourselves exposed,
Retribution will be ours: we'll wait until your clothes
   are clean,
Then we birds will guarantee we'll drop our crap all over
   you!

       [PEISETAIROS *enters from the scene building.*]

PEISETAIROS [*to* CHORUS]. That's taken care, my birds, of the
   sacrifice.
But it's strange we've had no messenger from the wall
To bring us up-to-date with progress there.   1120
[*Pointing*] Oh, here's one running—a right Olympic
   sprinter!

     [*On rushes* MESSENGER^, *in a highly flustered state.*]

MESSENGER^. Whe-whe, whe-whe, whe-whe, whe-whe,
   whe-whe, whe-whe,
Whe-where's our leader, Peisetairos?
PEISETAIROS.   Here!
MESSENGER^. Your wall's been built—it's finished!
PEISETAIROS.   That's
   splendid news!
MESSENGER^. It's the finest, most magnificent piece of work!
The top's so wide that even a pair of braggarts,
Theogenes and Proxenides, could drive
A pair of chariots past one another up there,

With horses as big as the Wooden Horse!*
PEISETAIROS.   Astounding!
MESSENGER^A. And as for height—I measured it out myself—   1130
    It's a hundred paces!
PEISETAIROS.   Poseidon, what proportions!
    So who were the builders who made it so immense?
MESSENGER^A. Just birds, that's all. Not a single Egyptian navvy
    To carry the bricks; no mason or carpenters, either.
    The birds did it all themselves. I watched in awe!
    From Libya came some thirty thousand cranes;
    They'd swallowed all the stones for the wall's
        foundations.*
    The stones were faced by corncrakes, using their beaks.
    Ten thousand storks were making all the bricks.
    The water they needed was carried across the sky   1140
    By curlews and other birds that live by rivers.
PEISETAIROS. But who was bringing the mortar?
MESSENGER^A.   Oh that, the
        herons—
    In hods.
PEISETAIROS.   But how did they get the mortar *in*?
MESSENGER^A. Now *that* was a problem solved ingeniously:
    The geese just used their feet as if they were shovels,
    And pressed the mortar into the hods for them.
PEISETAIROS [*loftily*]. What deed, then, lies beyond the grasp
        of—feet!*
MESSENGER^A. There's more to come! The ducks put aprons on
    And laid the bricks. Meanwhile the swallows flew up
    With trowels behind them, trailing like their tails,*   1150
    And carrying lots of mortar in their mouths.
PEISETAIROS. There'll never again be jobs for building-workers!
    Let's see, what else? What about the timberwork,
    Who built those parts of the wall?
MESSENGER^A.   The carpenters—
    And skilful too—were woodpeckers.* Yes, they used
    Their beaks to saw the gates. The noise they made,
    All hacking away at once, was like a shipyard!
    So now the wall's been fully equipped with gates;
    The gates are bolted, the wall's all under watch;
    The sentries go on their rounds and ring the bell;*   1160

There are guard-posts everywhere, and beacon-stations
On all the towers. [*turning away*] But now I need to wash;
I must be running. I'll let you do the rest.
                    [*Exits*; PEISETAIROS *is left looking rather dazed.*]
LEADER. Is something wrong? You're surely not surprised
The wall's been built in quite so short a time?
PEISETAIROS. I certainly am! How else could one react?
It truly seems a work of first-rate—fiction!
[*Pointing*] But here's a guard from the wall: he's
     bringing a message
And running towards us wearing a frenzied look.

     [*Enter* MESSENGER[B], *another bird, squawking in panic.*]

MESSENGER[B]. Alarm! Alarm! Alarm!   1170
PEISETAIROS. What on earth is wrong?
MESSENGER[B].   There's terrible trouble afoot!
Some god who comes from Zeus's palace above
Flew through the gates, invading our tract of air,
Unnoticed by jackdaw guards on daytime duty.
PEISETAIROS [*portentously*]. Outrageous deed! Audacious
     malefaction!*
But *which* of the gods?
MESSENGER[B].   We don't yet know—except
It was one with wings.
PEISETAIROS.   Then send the frontier guards
To track him down at once!
MESSENGER[B].   We've already sent
A mass of mounted archers—hawks, in fact.
And every bird with crooked talons is going,   1180
The kestrels, buzzards, vultures, as well as eagles.
There's a rush of whirring wings on every side.
The search is so intense, the air's vibrating.
He can't be far away; he must be here
Or hereabouts.
PEISETAIROS [*shouting*].
               Then fetch some slings at once,
And bows as well! Let everyone lend help!
Use arrows and stones! I want a sling myself.

[*Various birds appear with bows and slings*; PEISETAIROS *starts to look
               around for signs of the intruder.*]

CHORUS.   *Strophe*

> We're on the brink of war, war beyond all words,
> Between the gods and me. Now everyone must guard   1190
> The cloud-filled air, offspring of Erebos,
> In case some god should fly unseen past here.

LEADER [*solemnly*]. Keep watch now, one and all, on every
> side!
> A deity is in these lofty regions:
> The whirring sound of wings has reached my ear.*

[IRIS *appears, swinging across the stage on the crane. She is dressed in a
billowing dress, and wears a rainbow headdress.* PEISETAIROS *attempts, far
from successfully, to catch her legs, before she comes to rest on the roof
of the stage building.*]

PEISETAIROS. Hey! Hey! You, there! Stop flying around at once!
> Stay still! Right there! Don't think of running away!   1200
> Who *are* you? Where are you from? And answer sharp!
IRIS. I've come from the gods above, the gods of Olympos.
PEISETAIROS. Well what's your name? And are you ship—or
> helmet?*
IRIS. I'm Iris the swift.
PEISETAIROS.   Is that an official galley?*
IRIS. What on earth d'you mean?
PEISETAIROS [*calling*].   Quick, send a buzzard up
> there
> And put her under arrest.
IRIS [*indignant*].   Me under arrest!
> Just what's the meaning of this?
PEISETAIROS.   You're in real trouble!
IRIS. I find this quite extraordinary.
PEISETAIROS.   What gate
> Did you use to enter the city, you lousy bitch?
IRIS. I haven't the faintest idea what gate I used.   1210
PEISETAIROS [*to* CHORUS]. Did you hear her answer? What sheer
> evasiveness!
> [*To* IRIS] Did you see the jackdaw officials? Well, answer
> the question!
> Did you get your documents stamped by the storks?
IRIS.   How
> dare you!

PEISETAIROS. You mean you didn't?

IRIS. You're mad!

PEISETAIROS. No bird-official
Was there to block your entry and check you over?

IRIS [*outraged*]. I'll have you know my entry's *never* been
blocked!

PEISETAIROS. So you have the gall to fly in secrecy
Right through the air of a city that isn't yours?

IRIS. What *other* route d'you think the gods should take?

PEISETAIROS [*mimicking her*]. 'I haven't the faintest idea.' But
not this one!   1220
Right now you're trespassing. You ought to know
We've every right to seize all Irises
And kill you off. That's clearly what you deserve!

IRIS. But I'm immortal!

PEISETAIROS. We'll put a stop to that!
We've got big problems ahead, it seems to me,
If we aim to rule the world, yet all you gods
Continue to misbehave and won't accept
It's now your turn to follow higher orders.
So tell me, *where* are you steering those wings of yours?

IRIS. My father's sent me down with a message for men,   1230
To tell them to sacrifice to Olympian gods:
[*Solemnly*] To slaughter sheep at hearths where oxen burn,
And fill the streets with fumes.*

PEISETAIROS. What gods are these?

IRIS. What gods? Why *us*, the gods in the sky!

PEISETAIROS. You think you're gods?

IRIS. What other gods exist?

PEISETAIROS. The birds have now become new gods for men:
It's *they* who need the sacrifice, not Zeus.

IRIS [*gravely*]. Avoid such folly! Don't stir the gods to wrath!*
Beware lest Justice take the mattock of Zeus
To tear your family up by all its roots,   1240
And lest your body, and the confines of your palace,
Be turned to smouldering cinders by lightning bolts!

PEISETAIROS. Now listen here, that's quite enough flapdoodle!
Just pack it in! D'you think I'm just some slave
Who'll be alarmed by all this bogey talk?
I'll have you know, if Zeus annoys me further

[*Stiltedly*] 'Amphion's halls, and all his palace walls,
I'll turn to cinders with eagles that breathe out fire.'*
I'll also send porphyrion-birds against him,
All dressed in leopard-skin to look more fierce.   1250
Six hundred or more, there'll be; yet long ago
Just one Porphyrion caused Zeus lots of trouble.*
And as for *you*, if you irritate me further
I'll lift those little servant's legs of yours
And screw you well and proper!* You'll be surprised:
I can get it up three times, despite my age.

IRIS. What scandalous words! You ought to be dismembered!

PEISETAIROS [*clapping, as to a bird*]. Now shoo away! Get out of
    here! Brrr! Brrr!

IRIS. My father will put a stop to this violence of yours!
                          [*Exits, lifted aloft by the crane.*]

PEISETAIROS. Oh what a life! Just fly off somewhere else,   1260
    And find a younger man to turn to cinders!

CHORUS.   *Antistrophe*

    Now we've barred the way, to Zeus and all the gods.
    They can't come here again, they can't traverse my city.
    No smoke of oxen, victims of sacrifice,
    Will rise to gods from men across our space.

PEISETAIROS. There's something wrong if the herald we sent to
    earth
    Doesn't come back here to make report to me.   1270

[*Enter, from a side entrance, an excited bird* HERALD, *carrying a golden
                          garland.*]

HERALD [*extravagantly*]. O Peisetairos! Blessed! O wisest of men!
    Illustrious! Most wise! Most brilliant too!
    O three-times-blessed! [*faltering*] What's next?

PEISETAIROS.   Well what's
    your *message*?

HERALD. I've brought this golden garland to crown your head:
    All humankind desires to honour your wisdom.

PEISETAIROS. Well I'll accept. But what's behind this honour?

HERALD [*formally*]. O you who founded this famous aerial city,
    You do not know what honour you win from men,
    Nor how many lovers this land of yours now has!*

Some time ago, before you built this city,   1280
The human race had a craze for Spartan ways—
Long hair, starvation, no washing (like Sokrates),
And carrying round those curious message-sticks.*
But now that's changed: they've all become bird-crazy,
And love to emulate all bird behaviour.
I saw them all jump out of bed together
And *fly* at once, like us, to find some food.
Next thing, they all descended upon the bookstalls,
And there they nibbled around among decrees.*
This bird-craze then became so widely spread   1290
That many men acquired the *names* of birds!*
'Partridge' they called a certain tavern-keeper
Who had a limp. Menippos' name was 'Swallow'.
Opountios was dubbed 'the one-eyed Raven',
Philokles was 'Lark', Theogenes 'the Goose-fox',
Lykourgos 'Ibis', Chairephon 'the Bat',
And Syrakosios 'Jay'. To Meidias
They gave the name of 'Quail', because he looked
Just like a quail whose head had been concussed.
Their love of birds made everyone sing poems   1300
In which they found a way to mention swallows,
Or wigeons, geese, or sometimes even pigeons,
Or wings of any kind, or even feathers!
So that's the news from earth. I warn you, though:
You'll find an endless stream of humans coming
To ask for wings—and sets of crooked talons.
You'll need supplies of wings for the immigrants!
PEISETAIROS. By god, we mustn't stand here any longer.
    [*To a* BIRD-SLAVE] Rush off and find a pile of wicker baskets,
    And get them all filled up with wings at once: 1310
    Let Manes bring the wings outside to me;*
    I'll stay and greet our visitors as they come.

[*During the following exchange of song between the* CHORUS *and*
    PEISETAIROS, *a* BIRD-SLAVE *carries baskets of wings in and out.*]

CHORUS.   It won't be long till someone calls   *Strophe*
                 Our city a richly peopled place.
PEISETAIROS.   Let's hope good fortune's ours!
CHORUS.   Love for my city now fills the world.

PEISETAIROS [*to* BIRD-SLAVE].
                    Bring out the stuff much faster!
CHORUS.   Here there is all that one could wish
                    To make a splendid life:
                    Wisdom, love, immortal Graces,   1320
                    With the clear and placid face
                    Of Peacefulness, sweet deity.

PEISETAIROS [*to* BIRD-SLAVE].
                    You're doing the job so sluggishly.
                    Show lively there and move along!

CHORUS.   Bring further baskets full of wings!   *Antistrophe*
[*To* PEISETAIROS] And you should lend encouragement—
PEISETAIROS [*striking* BIRD-SLAVE]. With hefty blows like this!
CHORUS.   He's quite as slow as a stubborn ass!
PEISETAIROS.   Manes is an idle wretch!
CHORUS.   You ought to group these pairs of wings   1330
                    In order over here:
                    Wings of songbirds, birds of omen,
                    Seabirds too. Inspect each person,
                    And fit them with the wings they need.

PEISETAIROS. I swear by the kestrels, I can't restrain myself
    When I see how idle and slow you manage to be.

        [*Enter a young* FATHER-BEATER, *singing in elevated style.*]

FATHER-BEATER.   'O for the wings of a soaring eagle!
                    I'd fly aloft above the barren sea,
                    Across the grey waves' swell.'*

PEISETAIROS. The messenger's warning's proving all too true!   1340
    Here's someone coming along now, singing of eagles.
FATHER-BEATER. What thrills! What joy!
    [*To* PEISETAIROS] There's nothing in the world as sweet as
        flight!
    I'm simply crazy on birds: I want to fly
    And live with you and share your way of life.
PEISETAIROS. Which way of life? The birds have many ways.
FATHER-BEATER. I love them all—especially the way they think
    It's fine for birds to strangle and bite their fathers.*
PEISETAIROS. Oh yes, we think it's really rather tough
    For any young bird to set about its father.   1350

FATHER-BEATER. That's why I want to come and live up here:
  I want to strangle my father—and then inherit.
PEISETAIROS. We birds, though, have another law as well;
  The storks have an ancient copy, inscribed on boards:*
  [*Reciting*] 'When the time is reached at which the
      father-stork
  Has fed his storklets, and sees them fully fledged,
  The young must then take care of their fathers in turn.'
FATHER-BEATER. A fat lot of use, after all, to come up here,
  If I've actually got to *feed* my father as well!
PEISETAIROS. No need. Because you came with good intentions,   1360
  I'll fit you out with the wings of an orphan-bird.
  [*Gravely*] What's more, young man, I'll give you sage
      advice—
  The things I learnt myself when once a boy.*
  You *mustn't* strike your father. [PEISETAIROS *takes a shield,
      spear, and helmet from a basket, treating them as a bird
      outfit.*]   Take this wing,
  And take this cock's spur in your other hand.*
  Then telling yourself that's a cock's crest on your head,
  Go off and serve as a soldier, to earn your keep.
  Just leave your father alone. Since you're aggressive,
  Fly Thracewards; go and find some fights up there.
FATHER-BEATER. I really think you've given me good advice;   1370
  I'll do as you say.
PEISETAIROS.   You'll show good sense if you do.

[*Exit the* FATHER-BEATER, *costumed as a hoplite, while, from the other side,
the dithyrambic poet* KINESIAS, *of markedly gawky appearance, enters.*]

KINESIAS [*singing.*]
    'I fly aloft to Olympos on pinions light.'*
    I fly now here, now there, along the paths of song—
PEISETAIROS. It looks as though we'll need a ton of wings!
KINESIAS.
    With fearless heart and body, a new course charting.
PEISETAIROS [*recognizing*]. Old spindle-legs Kinesias! Well,
    greetings!
  What brings you spinning your crooked feet round here?
KINESIAS [*still singing*].

A bird I long to be, a nightingale of limpid voice.   1380-1
PEISETAIROS. Just stop the lyrics and tell me what you mean.
KINESIAS [*speaking*]. I'd like some wings from you, with which
    I'd float
In flight above, to use the clouds to make
New air-swept, snow-clad dithyrambic preludes.*
PEISETAIROS. You think you'd find good preludes in the *clouds*?
KINESIAS. But that's the source of all this kind of art.
    In dithyrambs the very finest things
    Are airy, murky, streaked by gloomy light,
    And full of high-flown sounds. Just listen to this—   1390
PEISETAIROS. I'd rather not!
KINESIAS.   You must, you simply must.
    You'll hear me course my way through all the air.
    [*Singing again*]
          To the phantom forms of wingéd,
            Aether-skimming,
          Slender-necked creatures of flight—
PEISETAIROS. Give over!
KINESIAS.   Surging over the sea
          May I fly on breaths of wind—
PEISETAIROS. By god, I'll put a stop to these breaths of yours!
        [PEISETAIROS *starts to thrash* KINESIAS *with assorted wings.*]
KINESIAS.   First roaming a southern path,
          Then bearing my body northwards,
          Cutting the aether's ocean in endless furrows.   1400
               [KINESIAS *is forced to stop singing.*]
    [*Sarcastically*] I suppose you think that's clever work,
    old man!
PEISETAIROS. What, don't you like becoming an air-swept poet?
KINESIAS. What a way to treat the famous dithyramb trainer!
    My services are in demand in Athens.
PEISETAIROS. Then why not stay with us and train a chorus
    Of flying birds for Leotrophides
    And his squawking tribe.*
KINESIAS.   I see you're poking fun.
    I want you to know I won't give up my plans
    Until I get some wings to roam the sky.

[*He exits, as a young* INFORMER, *dressed in a ragged and patchy cloak,*
      enters from the opposite side entrance.]

INFORMER [*singing*].

    'Who are these poor and dappled-winged birds,   1410
    O long-feathered, dappled swallow?'*

PEISETAIROS. A right old piece of bother has reared its head!

  Here's someone else approaching, humming a song.

INFORMER [*still singing*].

    Long-feathered, dappled one, again I say.

PEISETAIROS. I think his song's addressed to that cloak of his!

  With such poor clothes, he needs the swallows of summer!

INFORMER [*speaking*]. Who's giving out wings to all the new
    arrivals?

PEISETAIROS. That's me. But first I have to know your needs.

INFORMER. It's wings, real wings I need. Don't ask again.   1420

PEISETAIROS. D'you want to fly in search of a warmer cloak?

INFORMER. I travel round the islands as accuser,

  Informer too—

PEISETAIROS [*ironically*].

    Oh what a fine profession!*

INFORMER. And sniffer-out-of-mischief. I want some wings

  With which to swoop and issue summonses.

PEISETAIROS. Will wings improve these summonses of yours?

INFORMER. No, I'll avoid the muggers on the roads,

  And fly back home in company of cranes,

  But full of prosecutions not of stones!*

PEISETAIROS. Is this the way you work, at your young age,   1430

  By prosecuting foreigners for gain?

INFORMER. Why not? [*evasively*] I don't know how to use a
    spade.

PEISETAIROS. There are lots of other decent jobs to do:

  A fit young man should choose an honest life,

  Instead of making money from the courts.

INFORMER. I don't need preaching, thanks—just give me wings.

PEISETAIROS. I'm giving you wings by speaking now.

INFORMER.   But how

  Can words give wings?

PEISETAIROS.   Well words set everyone

  Aflutter.

INFORMER.

    What, everyone?

PEISETAIROS.   You've surely heard

How fathers sit around in barbers' shops*   1440
Discussing their adolescent sons like this:
'My lad's been listening to Dieitrephes;
And now he's all aflutter to ride a horse!'
Another claims his son loves tragedy:
It sets him all aflutter and blows his mind!

INFORMER. It's words that give them *wings?*

PEISETAIROS.   It really is.
For words can make the mind soar high above
And lift us up. And that's how I would like
To give you wings by urging you to do
A decent job.   1450

INFORMER.   But that's not what I want!

PEISETAIROS. Then what's to be done?

INFORMER.   I've got my family pride:
We've been informing since my grandad's time.
Please give me swift, light wings, just like a hawk's.
Then when I've issued summonses abroad,
I'll get back here to bring the charge to court
Before I fly away again.

PEISETAIROS.   I see.
You mean you'll have the time to win the case
Before the foreigner even comes.

INFORMER.   Dead right!

PEISETAIROS. And while he's sailing *here*, you'll fly back *there*
To confiscate his property.   1460

INFORMER.   You've got it!
I'll imitate a spinning-top.

PEISETAIROS.   I see,
A spinning-top. [*produces a whip*] Well, here I've got some
    wings,
A lovely pair that come from old Korkyra.*   [*Lashes him.*]

INFORMER. Ouch, help! You've got a whip!

PEISETAIROS.   No, no, they're
    wings,
With which I'll make you whirl a spinning-top!

INFORMER. Ouch, help!

PEISETAIROS.   Just flap yourself away from here!
Go on now, scarper! Scram, you filthy devil!
I'll show you how to twist the law, all right!   [*Exit* INFORMER.]

[*To* BIRD-SLAVES] Let's gather up these wings and go indoors.

[*All exit into the stage building.*]

CHORUS.   *Many* strange and wondrous sights   *Strophe*   1470
                     Underneath our gaze have passed,
                     From our vantage in the sky.
                     Take a quite exotic tree
                     Found in far, secluded parts:
                     What's its name? *Kleonymos*!
                     Bulky it may be, but useless;
                     Signs of danger make it shrink.
                     Every spring it sprouts its foliage,
                     Causing nasty lawsuit rashes.
                     Every winter down it sheds   1480
                     Leaves that have the shape of—shields!*

                     Take another strange location,   *Antistrophe*
                     Far away in darkest regions,
                     Where no lamp is ever seen.
                     This is where the local people
                     Eat and fraternize with heroes
                     All the time—except at night.
                     When the daylight's disappeared,
                     Meeting heroes isn't safe.
                     If, at night, you met a hero—   1490
                     Someone, say, who's called Orestes—
                     Beaten up and stripped you'd be, and
                     Paralysed right down one side!*

[*Enter, from a side entrance,* PROMETHEUS, *skulking very nervously with
     his cloak over his head, and carrying a parasol.**]

PROMETHEUS. I really must make sure Zeus doesn't spot me.
    Where's Peisetairos?

            [PEISETAIROS *happens to come out from the door.*]

PEISETAIROS.   Crikey! What's this lark?
    Who's hiding there?
PROMETHEUS [*gesturing edgily*].
                        Please check behind me here:
    Are any gods to be seen?
PEISETAIROS.   Not a single one!

Who *are* you?
PROMETHEUS.   Tell me, what's the time of day?
PEISETAIROS. The time? It's early in the afternoon.
　　Who *are* you?   1500
PROMETHEUS [*coyly*].
　　　　　　　'Oxen-loosing hour', or later?*
PEISETAIROS. I've had enough!
PROMETHEUS.   It's crucial: what's Zeus doing?
　　Is he clearing the sky or drawing clouds together?
PEISETAIROS [*turning away*]. O stew yourself!
PROMETHEUS.   All right, I'll let you see.
　　　　　　　　　　　　　　　　　　　　　[*Peers out.*]
PEISETAIROS. My *dear* Prometheus!
PROMETHEUS.   Shh! Shh! Lower your voice!
PEISETAIROS. But what's the matter?
PROMETHEUS.   Keep quiet, don't mention
　　my name.
　　You'll have me ruined, if Zeus should spot me here.
　　If you want to know the news from up above,
　　Please keep this parasol held above my head,
　　To stop the gods from noticing me down here.
PEISETAIROS [*taking the parasol*]. Aha!   1510
　　It's that Promethean brain of yours again!
　　Stand underneath, and speak with confidence.
PROMETHEUS. Well listen, then.
PEISETAIROS.   You've got my full attention.
PROMETHEUS [*portentously*].
　　He's done for—*doomed*—is Zeus.
PEISETAIROS.   Since when?
PROMETHEUS. It happened when you built your aerial city.
　　All sacrifice from men has finished now;
　　No smoke of animal thighs has risen up
　　Since the very day you colonized the sky.
　　Burnt offerings? None. We're *fasting*—like the women
　　At the Thesmophoria. Now the barbarian gods   1520
　　Have become so hungry they're screeching out at us:
　　They say they'll bring an army *down* on Zeus*
　　Unless he gets their markets opened up,
　　To make their entrail imports safe again.
PEISETAIROS. You mean that other gods, barbarian gods,

Live *over* you?
PROMETHEUS.   Of course barbarians do—
    Ancestral gods of Exekestides!
PEISETAIROS. And what's the name of all these foreign gods?
PROMETHEUS. Their name? They're called Triballians.*
PEISETAIROS [*cornily*].   Ah, I see.
    That's why we think the gods send *tribul*ations.   1530
PROMETHEUS. Exactly right. But let me warn you now:
    You'll find that envoys come to seek a peace,
    From Zeus himself and from the Triballians too.
    But you *mustn't* make a treaty unless Zeus gives
    His sceptre back again to all the birds,
    And gives you Princess, too, to be your wife.
PEISETAIROS. Who's *Princess?*
PROMETHEUS.   She's a gorgeous nubile girl
    Who oversees the thunderbolt of Zeus,
    And all the gifts he gives: intelligence—
    Good government—moderation—shipyards too—   1540
    Verbal abuse—state treasurers—even three obols!*
PEISETAIROS. She oversees them all for him?
PROMETHEUS.   She does.
    So if he gives you *her*, you'll have the lot.
    That's why I came down here, to tip you off:
    I've always been a friend of men's, of course.
PEISETAIROS. That's right: it's thanks to you we cook our food!
PROMETHEUS. I loathe all other gods—you must have heard.
PEISETAIROS. By *Zeus*, that's true! You always hated gods.
    You're quite a Timon!
PROMETHEUS.   Well, I must be off.
    I'll take the parasol: that way, if Zeus sees me,   1550
    He'll think I'm in a basket-carrier's train.*
PEISETAIROS. If that's your role, you'd better take this stool!*

[PEISETAIROS *gives* PROMETHEUS *a stool, with which he leaves, while*
    PEISETAIROS *himself goes back into the stage building.*]

CHORUS.   Near the land of Shadow-footers*   *Strophe*
               There's a lake where, all unwashed,
               Sokrates can conjure *souls!*
               Once, Peisandros came along,
               Yearning to reclaim the soul which

Left him in the midst of life.
Creature strange he brought to slaughter,
Hybrid camel-lamb, whose gullet   1560
In Odysseus' style he severed.
Then there rose up from below,
Thirsting for the camel's blood,
Chairephon—you know, 'the bat'!*

[*Enter a trio of divine ambassadors:* POSEIDON, *the senior member and a
haughty aristocratic figure; the* TRIBALLIAN, *who is struggling with a
Greek cloak that is unfamiliar to him; and* HERAKLES, *bearing his usual
club and lionskin but possessed of a gourmand's belly.*]

POSEIDON [*pompously*]. The buildings which we see before us
    here
  Are Cloudcuckooland: that's where we've come as envoys.
  [*To* TRIBALLIAN] What *are* you up to there? Your cloak's all
    skew.
  Adjust it, so it's properly draped like mine.
  What a vagabond! A right old Laispodias!*
  Democracy! Just where will it all end up,   1570
  When people like this get appointed by the gods?
  [*Trying to help him*] Stop squirming around! To hell!
    You're much the most
  Barbarian god I've ever set eyes upon.
  Right, Herakles, what next?
HERAKLES.   I've told you once:
  I'd like to get my hands around his throat,
  Whoever he is—blockading the gods like this.
POSEIDON. I must remind you, friend, we've been elected
  To negotiate a *truce.*
HERAKLES.   Then strangle him twice!

[*The stage door opens and* PEISETAIROS *emerges, together with* BIRD-SLAVES
*carrying cooking utensils, to prepare a meal. The gods start to approach
him.*]

PEISETAIROS. Cheese-grater, please. Some silphium as well.*
  Pass me the cheese, and stir the charcoal there.   1580
POSEIDON [*diplomatically*]. The three of us, all gods, would like
    to offer
  Our friendly greetings.
PEISETAIROS.   I'm grating the silphium.

HERAKLES [*approaching with fascination*].
  What kind of meat is this?
PEISETAIROS.   It's certain birds,
  Condemned for rising in revolt against
  The democratic birds.*
HERAKLES [*interested*].   You're grating on
  The silphium first?
PEISETAIROS [*looking up*].
                      Oh *Herakles*, hello!
  What brings you here?
HERAKLES.   The gods have sent us three
  As envoys, to negotiate a peace.
PEISETAIROS [*to* BIRD-SLAVES]. The olive oil's run out: the bottle's
      empty.
HERAKLES [*sympathetic*]. Yes, bird-meat ought to glisten in
      plenty of oil.   1590
POSEIDON. We recognize we're suffering from the war,
  And *you* would gain from being good friends with gods:
  We'd always fill your ponds with fresh rainwater;
  Your lives would just consist of halcyon days.
  We've got the power to negotiate these things.
PEISETAIROS. It wasn't *us* who ever took the step
  Of starting war with you. So if you're now
  Prepared to stick to justice, we'll be willing
  To make a peace. What 'justice' means is this:
  That Zeus must give the sceptre back to us,   1600
  The birds. And if we come to full agreement
  Upon those terms, you're welcome then to dinner.
HERAKLES [*avidly*]. The terms seem fine to *me*. I vote for them.
POSEIDON. You *what*, you dolt! Your brain's as soft as your
      belly!
  Will you give away your father's very kingship?
PEISETAIROS. What's wrong? You gods will surely grow in
      strength
  If down below the power is held by birds.
  At present mortals skulk beneath the clouds
  Whenever they want to swear false oaths by you.
  But if you have the birds to be your allies,   1610
  Whenever a person swears by raven and Zeus,*
  The raven will notice what the perjurer does

And fly back down to knock out one of his eyes!
POSEIDON. Well, by *Poseidon*, that sounds a good idea!
HERAKLES. I quite agree.
PEISETAIROS [*to* TRIBALLIAN].

              And you?
TRIBALLIAN.   Ya, Beisitairi.
HERAKLES. You see, he's all in favour.
PEISETAIROS.   Then listen now
  To further benefits we'll soon bring to you.
  If anyone vows an offering to a god,
  And then equivocates by trying to say
  'The gods are patient',* and stingily withholds,   1620
  We'll make him pay the price.
POSEIDON.   But tell us how.
PEISETAIROS. We'll wait until he's counting out his money
  Or sitting soaking in a nice warm bath,
  Then a kite will swoop and, while he's quite distracted,
  Snatch up two sheep in payment to the god.
HERAKLES. I vote, a second time, for giving back
  The sceptre to them.
POSEIDON.   Then ask the Triballian too.
HERAKLES [*aside, raising his club*]. Triballian, would you like to
  feel some pain?
TRIBALLIAN [*alarmed*]. No bashy stick!
HERAKLES [*suavely*].   He quite agrees with me.
POSEIDON. Well if you're both agreed, I'll play along.   1630
  [*To* PEISETAIROS, *stiffly*] We've decided, fellow, to give the
  sceptre back.
PEISETAIROS. But just a moment: I mentioned *two* conditions.
  I don't object if Zeus holds on to Hera,
  But he's got to let me have that Princess girl
  To be my wife.
POSEIDON [*outraged*].

            You've no desire for peace!
  [*Turning*] Let's go back home.
PEISETAIROS.   I couldn't care two hoots!
  [*To* BIRD-SLAVE] Remember, chef, to make the sauce taste
  sweet.
HERAKLES [*alarmed*]. My dear old chap, Poseidon, don't rush off!
  You can't believe one *woman*'s worth a war?

POSEIDON. Then what should we do? 1640

HERAKLES. Why, come to terms, of
course.

POSEIDON. You dunce! He's been deceiving you throughout.
You're harming yourself, what's more. If Zeus should die
When he's handed over dominance to these birds,
It's *you* who'll be impoverished: you're the one
Who gets whatever Zeus leaves behind at death.

PEISETAIROS. How dreadful! What outrageous sophistry!
[*To* HERAKLES] Come over here: I'd like a private word.
Your uncle's cheating you, you silly ass:
The law decrees you can't inherit at all
Because you're not legitimate, just a bastard. 1650

HERAKLES. A bastard? What d'you mean?

PEISETAIROS. You really are!
You had a foreign mother.* How d'you think
Athena would have been a sole heiress,
If Zeus had had legitimate sons as well?*

HERAKLES. But can't my father leave his property
As a bastard-legacy?

PEISETAIROS. No, he's not allowed.
Poseidon here, who's trying to rouse you up,
Will grasp your father's property right away,
Because he's Zeus's lawful brother himself.
I'll quote the very words of Solon's law:* 1660
[*Like a lawyer*] 'No bastard shall have the right of
inheritance where legitimate children exist; but in the
absence of legitimate children, property will go to those
who are closest in kinship.'

HERAKLES. So *I* would have no right to property
Of my father's?

PEISETAIROS. None at all. Just tell me this:
Did your father ever induct you into the phratry?*

HERAKLES. He missed me out. I've often wondered why. 1670

PEISETAIROS. Then why stand open-mouthed and look so fierce?
Come, if you'll side with us, I'll give you power,
And keep you well supplied with birds' milk too.*

HERAKLES. Your claim on the girl seems fair enough to me.
I've thought so all along: I'll hand her over.

PEISETAIROS. And what's your view, Poseidon.

POSEIDON.   I vote against.

PEISETAIROS. The Triballian has the casting vote. Well then?

TRIBALLIAN. Di luvvli tawli girli Princi-cinsi.

  Di birdi handi ova.

HERAKLES [*emphatically*].

                              He votes in favour.

POSEIDON. He doesn't vote to hand her over at all!   1680

  He's simply twittering on just like the swallows.*

PEISETAIROS. That means he wants her handing *to* the
  swallows!

POSEIDON [*to* HERAKLES *and* TRIBALLIAN]. In that case, you two
  settle the whole agreement.

  And since it's what you want, I'll say no more.

HERAKLES [*to* PEISETAIROS]. Your terms are all acceptable to us.

  So come with us yourself, back up to heaven,

  To fetch the girl and everything else as well.

PEISETAIROS. How nice these birds were chopped up just in time

  For my *wedding*!

HERAKLES [*nonchalantly*].

                        If you like, I'll stay behind

  To roast the meat, while you go on ahead.   1690

POSEIDON. What, *you* to roast the meat? You greedy glutton!

  You'll come with us.

HERAKLES [*disappointed*].

                        I would have liked the job.

PEISETAIROS [*shouting in*]. Could someone bring my wedding
  garment out.

[*A* BIRD-SLAVE *appears with the cloak, and all exit by a side entrance,* en
                        route *to Olympos.*]

CHORUS.   In the country of informers,   *Antistrophe**
                By the water-clock* you'll find them—
                Nasty beasts who live by tongue-work.*
                All they sow and all they reap,
                All that falls into their hands,
                Comes to them by use of tongue.
                Aliens they are—yes, men like   1700
                Gorgias, Philippos too!*
                Now because of all these tonguesters,
                Like Philippos and his crowd,

> Everywhere in Attic ritual
> Victims' *tongues* are specially prized!*

[MESSENGER^c *rushes on and addresses the* CHORUS *in grandiose profusion.*]

MESSENGER^c. Hail, you whose great achievements beggar
      speech!
  Hail, three-times-happy, feathered race of birds!
  Come welcome your triumphant ruler home.
  He now draws near, resplendent more by far
  Than any meteor's streaming path of gold   1710
  Or even than the sun's own brilliant beam,
  Such is the radiance flashing out from him!
  He brings a bride whose beauty words can't tell;
  He wields a thunderbolt, Zeus' wingéd weapon.
  An indescribable fragrance fills the vault
  Of heaven. The breezes waft into the air
  Light wreaths of incense fumes from where he moves.
  Here comes the man himself! Now let resound
  The sacred chant the Muse's mouth inspires!

[*Enter* PEISETAIROS *and* PRINCESS *in a wedding-chariot, the former still wearing his wings but also bearing a thunderbolt and other symbols of Zeus himself.*]

CHORUS. Move back, make room, make space for him!   1720
        Fly round the jubilant man with jubilant cheer.
        Behold his bride: how fresh and lovely!
        This marriage means felicity for our city.
            What great prosperity awaits
                The race of birds
        Because of this man! With wedding-songs
        And bridal-songs, come welcome them home,
            The groom and Princess!   1730

        With Hera on Olympos   *Strophe*
        The king of gods himself,
        The lord of towering throne,
        Was joined in wedded bliss
      By Fates who sang this wedding-cry:*
        Hail Hymen, Hymen of marriage!
        Hail Hymen, Hymen of marriage!

Love's rich bestower, Eros, *Antistrophe*
With gold wings on his back,
Controlled the chariot's reins:
He sat as groomsman there 1740
For Zeus and Hera, happy bride.
Hail Hymen, Hymen of marriage!
Hail Hymen, Hymen of marriage!

PEISETAIROS.
I love your cries, I love your songs!
I'm thrilled to hear your words!
CHORUS. Come lift the voice,
Acclaim his earth-oppressing thunder,
And Zeus's fiery lightning flash
With dread white thunderbolt.

O great and golden lightning glare,
O Zeus's eternal, fire-bearing sword,
O thunder-claps, whose boom rolls round the earth 1750
While storm-clouds burst and break!
With you this man now shakes the earth,
Because of you he rules the universe
With Princess, Zeus's helpmate, by his side.
Hail Hymen, Hymen of marriage!

[PEISETAIROS *and* PRINCESS *descend from the chariot.*]

PEISETAIROS. Come, all you feathered flocks of birds, attend our
wedding feast,
And follow in procession to the wedding-bed of Zeus.
[*To* PRINCESS] Stretch out your hand, my happy bride, and
hold my bristling feathers: 1760
Then dance with me and I shall make you weightless in
my arms.

[*Groom and bride perform a celebratory dance before exiting into the
stage building, followed by the repeated cries of the cheering* CHORUS, *who
exit after them.*]

CHORUS. Three cheers! Hurrah! Congratulations!
We salute you, brilliant victor, highest of gods!

Lysistrata

INTRODUCTION

The comic heart of *Lysistrata*, and the secret of its lasting appeal, lies in its combination, interweaving, and ultimately its confusion of a pair of archetypal human interests: sex and war. The play's brio stems from the evocation of a great and oversimplified dichotomy of the kind which Aristophanes had already exploited to some extent in *Acharnians* (425) and *Peace* (421). This dichotomy aligns sex, and indeed comedy itself, with the life-giving, procreative, and celebratory associations of peace, and sets this cluster of ideas against the negative, disruptive, and destructive effects of war. If we wanted a suggestive slogan to sum up this imaginatively enlarged and (in both senses of the word) theatrically polarized contrast, it might be: war is tragic, peace is comic.

It is arguable, as I shall later suggest in more detail, that the perspective on war which *Lysistrata* offered its first audience in 411, probably at the Lenaia festival (early February that year), had little explicit contact with the military or political realities of the time. In early 411 Athens was making strenuous efforts to rebuild her military strength after the devastating defeat, involving massive losses of both men and ships, suffered by the great expedition sent to Sicily in 415–413. The results of that defeat, in September 413, were intensified by the presence, from spring 413, of a permanent Spartan garrison at Dekeleia, affecting land access to Attika from the north and engaging in periodic plundering (see *Lysistrata* 1146, with Thucydides 7.19, 27). Another pressing factor was that by 412 several of Athens' allies, including Miletos (cf. *Lysistrata* 108), had attempted to secede from the empire. In addition, the Spartans were now building up their own fleet, with the help of Persian funds, to match the Athenian navy in size at least. Yet mass reaction at Athens to the Sicilian débâcle, or to these other developments, showed little interest in making peace. On the contrary, the city voted to make use of a special financial reserve of a thousand talents which had been deposited on the Akropolis in 431.[1] Money was there, in other words, to rebuild the fleet, and the political will

---

[1] Aristophanes' plot does incorporate one realistic reflection of the economics of this situation: the women's occupation of the Akropolis is designed to prevent further spending of the city's financial reserves (cf. esp. 488).

was there to fight on doggedly. It was probably the democracy's determination to renew the war effort with economic abandon which most prompted a group of disenchanted Athenians to respond to approaches from the exiled Alkibiades in the winter of 412–411, and to make plans for constitutional restrictions on the democratic system. We cannot be sure what stage these plans, which led to an oligarchic *coup* in the spring of 411, had reached by the date of *Lysistrata*'s performance. Rumours at least are likely to have been in circulation, since the would-be reformers had made an initial statement to the army in Samos in December 412 (Thucydides 8.48.2–3). But the play itself, which would have been in advanced preparation by that date, contains nothing which can safely be regarded as hinting at contemporary tensions or forebodings.[2] Its scenario does indeed presuppose an entrenched commitment to war on the part of Athenian (and other Greek) males; but the solution which it produces to the continuing conflict with Sparta emerges from a decidedly unexpected and 'alternative' source of initiative.

Lysistrata connects the war/peace dichotomy with the age-old functional opposition of the sexes whereby the men go out to fight while the women stay at home and wait to see if their husbands and sons will return alive. It is the women's dissatisfaction with this state of affairs which Lysistrata concentrates into her double scheme of a 'sex-strike' and an occupation of the Akropolis. But while this creates a scenario which involves a kind of 'battle of the sexes', the women's aim is purely and simply to bring the war to an end and thereby to restore a world of peace in which marital harmony and erotic fulfilment (which they interestingly regard as interlocking) can prevail. Unlike their counterparts in the later *Assembly-Women* (393), the women of *Lysistrata* do not seek a permanent change in the balance of power between the sexes. They want a return to normality in their married and family lives.

---

[2] Most telling is the fact that Peisandros (see Index of Names), leader of the *coup* in 411, is the subject at *Lysistrata* 490 of a gibe normal in comedy for demagogic politicians. The allusion at 1048 is too vague to tell us anything. Nor could Aristophanes' women be regarded in more general terms as an analogue to possible political revolutionaries: apart from anything else, the oligarchs in 411 did not *at first* think of making peace (Thucydides 8.48.1, 63.4). See the Select Bibliography for further reading on the play's chronological context, with my notes on 490, 578, 1048.

Critics have often tried to discover in the play the expression of serious insights into relations between the sexes in Athens, especially *vis-à-vis* the experience of war. *Lysistrata*, as we shall see, does contain some thought-provoking passages on its twin themes of sex and war, but the way in which it runs these themes together is also the reason why its treatment of them leaves us, as I shall contend, with nothing more solid than an alluring fantasy. As in both of Aristophanes' previous 'war plays', *Acharnians* and *Peace*, the root of the fantasy is the notion that conflict with Sparta could be ended by a solution which completely bypasses the reality of military campaigns and the complexities of political negotiations between states. In all three cases, moreover, the solution has a strongly personal and even 'domestic' cast to it: Dikaiopolis' private peace, restricted to his own family, in *Acharnians*; Trygaios' personal journey up to Olympos in *Peace*; and Lysistrata's plan of compelling Athenian, Spartan, and other troops to make peace by denying them sexual gratification from their wives.

The broad sweep of *Lysistrata*'s action, whereby the women use both a seizure of funds on the Akropolis and a suspension of marital sex to compel their husbands to accept peace, is complicated by the various inconsistencies which appear, on closer inspection, in the details of the plot. Most obvious of these is the fact that the women initially complain how military service takes their husbands away from home (99-107), so that the city is allegedly empty of males (107); yet the idea of a sex-strike implies—as the later Kinesias scene exemplifies, and other references (e.g. 17, 555-64) confirm—the presence of men after all.[3] At its acutest, the potential contradiction which lurks here amounts to the notion that it is precisely the women's lack of sex (107-110) which motivates their sex-strike! A further oddity is that the opening scene of the play seems to posit a situation in which the younger wives will participate in the sex-strike in their homes (149-66, 217 ff.), while the older women, who are no longer sexually active, occupy the Akropolis (177-9). Yet in the upshot, Lysistrata and the others all go inside the Akropolis, and there is only one later passage which alludes to the motif of a domestic refusal of sex (551-4). As the scenes after the parabasis demonstrate (706 ff.), and in keeping with the idea that the women themselves find sexual abstinence

---

[3] The male chorus and the Commissioner are a different matter, of course: they represent men who are both over fighting-age and past their sexual prime.

near-impossible, Lysistrata's plan eventually depends on segregating the wives from their husbands.[4]

These anomalies are typical enough of the spirit of inconsequence which runs through and colours the zaniness of Aristophanic comedy in general; but they are not all on quite the same level. Lysistrata's exclamation about the paucity of men at 107 can readily be taken in context as a piece of psychological exaggeration, of the sort which parallels, and perhaps reflects, the anxieties about diminished Athenian manpower which we know were in the air around this time.[5] In any case, periods of military campaign were usually limited by the seasonal nature of Greek warfare, and different men would be out of the city at different times. None of this lessens the fundamental motivation appealed to by Lysistrata, a desire on the part of the wives to end the frequent and sometimes prolonged absences caused by war. The anomaly involved in the shift from domestic sex-strike to mass occupation of the Akropolis, however, is a matter of dramatic telescoping or condensation.[6] It allows Aristophanes to maintain a more concentrated focus of scene, without denying himself the 'striptease' comedy of a confrontation between an individual wife and her husband (845 ff.). Above all, it makes it easier for the play to make the eventual transition from the men's despairing discomfiture to the peace council which Lysistrata convenes on the Akropolis (1103 ff.).

The difficulties just considered hardly impinge on an audience's or reader's enjoyment of *Lysistrata*, since they do not deflect from the combined impetus of the women's physical and sexual strategies. Much more important and dramatically pertinent is a tension which takes us close to the work's comic kernel—namely, the sharp divergence of character between the heroine herself, Lysistrata the 'disperser of armies',[7] and the other Athenian wives. This diver-

---

[4] For what it is worth, 999–1001 imply that the Spartan side of the sex-strike was carried out according to Lysistrata's original suggestion; but this is, of course, a marginal detail.

[5] Such anxieties are characterized by Lysistrata in reporting the snatches of male conversation (themselves involving paradoxical hyperbole) at 524; they are independently attested by Thucydides for the aftermath of the Sicilian expedition (8.1.2, cf. 2.44.3). Cf. also the implication of *Women at the Thesmophoria* 1169.

[6] It might also be regarded as a typically Aristophanic piece of 'improvisatory' behaviour at 245–6: on this trait of comic protagonists, see the general Introduction, 'The Dynamics of Fantasy'.

[7] Lysistrata was a real name, but Aristophanes exploits it, as he does with e.g. Lamachos ('Great Fighter') in *Acharnians*, for its comic potential. On the speculation

gence is prominently displayed in the first scene, and later in the attempted escapes after the parabasis (706 ff.), though it is temporarily resolved in the Myrrhine-Kinesias scene when we see that at least one wife who originally jibbed at Lysistrata's scheme (130) has now developed the strength to carry it through with precisely the right style of paradoxically provocative self-control. But Myrrhine's successful arousal-cum-deception of her husband does nothing to erase the overall impression of Lysistrata's superiority to the ordinary women. And this impression arises from the heroine's ability to rise above what is projected as the norm for Athenian wives, and to embody a more elevated conception of the power of women.

The norm which Lysistrata transcends is a mixture of social reality and comic stereotyping.[8] When Lysistrata opens the play with exasperation at the women's failure or lateness to appear, Kalonike reminds her that domestic duties make it 'hard for women to leave the house' (16). It is Kalonike who here draws attention to the actualities—in this case, the norms of respectability—which obtain in the audience's own world, and Lysistrata who presupposes something exceptional. As the scene progresses, Lysistrata comes more and more to embody a commitment, a seriousness,[9] and a kind of vision which escapes the other women, with the slight exception of the Spartan Lampito (142-4). Two themes, above all, mark this development. One of these is Lysistrata's ability to see beyond the women's underlying obsession with sexual gratification. Kalonike's

that Lysistrata was in some way modelled on a contemporary priestess of Athena Polias, called Lysimache (cf. 554), see J. Henderson, *Aristophanes Lysistrata* (Oxford, 1987), pp. xxxviii-xli: I would go further than Henderson in playing down this point; at the most it should be regarded as an 'optional' association or overtone which might have occurred to a few spectators.

[8] The general presentation of women in *Lysistrata* is an amalgam of three main elements: aspects of social reality (e.g. the status of wives as domestic stewards, 495, 894 ff.; their domestic role as clothes-makers, 519, 567 ff.; the expectation of female modesty, 473-4), comic stereotypes (scheming mischief, 11-12, 1014-15; secret eating/drinking, n. 12 below; ecstatic sensuality, 1-3, 387 ff.; high sex drives, 124 ff., 715 ff.), and the quasi-mythical resonance of both the refusal of sex and the assault on the Akropolis (cf. especially the reference to Amazons at 678).

[9] Although references to facial expression in Greek drama cannot always be translated into the features of the characters' masks, it is possible that the mention of Lysistrata's frowning, dark looks at 7-8 and 707 reflects the use of a semi-tragic mask for the heroine (cf. *Wealth* 423-4 for a somewhat different instance). Lysistrata is reminiscent of tragic women at a number of points: e.g. near the beginning of her great speech, with the Euripidean quotation at 1124 (see note *ad loc.*).

first and, as it turns out, dramatically ironic guess about Lysistrata's purpose in calling the women together is that it must be for sexual excitement of some kind (23-4). Lysistrata quickly quashes her, but the suggestion that sex matters more than anything else to the wives reappears with a vengeance once the proposal of a sex-strike is mooted (125 ff.), and it is this which leads the heroine to an indecent exclamation about female libido (137). As with the later scene where she restrains the women whose sex drive makes them try to escape from the Akropolis (esp. 708-9), Lysistrata's mentality is defined precisely by contrast to what she herself acknowledges to be the characteristic attitudes of her sex. In the heroine, the comic stereotype of women is simultaneously corroborated and transcended.

Yet Lysistrata's greater self-control should not be allowed to obscure the ambiguities of her comic status. In explaining the frustrations which have generated her idea of a sex-strike, she dwells, with a brio that qualifies and complicates the solemnity she shows elsewhere, on the shortage not only of males eligible for adultery, but also of Milesian leather dildoes (107-10). It would be pedantically beside the point to suppose that Lysistrata merely simulates feelings which she knows will appeal to the other women. Although we are given no personal details about her husband or family (the same is true of all the women, except Myrrhine), Lysistrata is herself a wife like the others.[10] We are invited to think of her not as lacking the strong sex drive which the others all too readily reveal, but as a woman who *knows* the workings of sexual arousal (cf. the calculated imagery of 149-54)[11] yet is able to exploit these for a grander purpose. Something similar could be said, though this motif is much less important for the play as a whole, about the related comic stereotype of Athenian wives as secret, heavy drinkers:[12]

[10] This is sometimes wrongly denied: the point is not only implied by her repeated use of first-person plurals in such passages as 120-4, 149-54, 495, 1184, but made explicit at 513-20.

[11] In the eventual negotiations for peace, Lysistrata continues to exploit her understanding of sex in the phallic references at 1119-21, another passage which refutes the claim sometimes made that Aristophanes gives her no scurrilous utterances.

[12] The stereotype of bibulous wives appears at e.g. 114, 395, 465-6; see my note on 64. The comic idea of women as excessive consumers of food and drink partly (and wryly) reflects their responsibility for the economy of the household in their typical role as *oikonomos* or 'household-steward' (e.g. Lysias 1.7, Xenophon, *Oikonomikos* 7-10, with *Lysistrata* 493-5, *Assembly-Women* 211-12).

Lysistrata herself suggests an oath which betrays the female love of strong alcohol (195–7), and is keen to take the first drink from the wine-cup once the oath is sworn (238).

If Lysistrata's exceptional earnestness and discipline in the realm of sexuality turn out to be less than pure, so, in a rather different way, does the second main quality which differentiates her from the other Athenian wives, her political awareness and acumen. This is glimpsed at an early stage in her reference to a pan-Hellenic cause for the women to pursue (29 ff.). Pan-Hellenism remains a vital strand throughout the execution of the scheme,[13] and I shall shortly return to it. But it is worth stressing at once what is often overlooked, namely that this element in the plot is entwined by comic logic with the very notion of a sex-strike to end the war. A sex-strike by Athenian women alone might have compelled their husbands to seek peace with Sparta, but that would have left the dramatic problem of how, and on what terms, to bring about Spartan compliance. As it is, the play's pan-Hellenism is, in part at least, an expression and consequence of the universal sexual susceptibility of Greek males. None the less, Lysistrata's own perception of the need for women to 'save' or 'rescue' the whole of Greece from war (30, etc.) reinforces her presentation as a politically motivated character. In the opening scene this motivation is glimpsed but not explained: the explanation comes first in the agon with the Commissioner, and later still in the speech which she delivers to the two sets of ambassadors. Each of these passages calls for close attention in turn, not least because around them hinges the issue of whether Aristophanes' play can be read as containing a politically intelligible message beneath the fantastic daring of the women's sex-strike.

The agon (476–613) pits Lysistrata against an official representative of the contemporary democracy, the testy and misogynistic Commissioner. Following on from her quasi-military victory over his archers, the contest is extremely one-sided: as in *Birds*, the protagonist dominates the argument throughout, and this gives a strong stamp to Lysistrata's political vehemence and sharpness. An important general observation about this part of the play deserves to be emphasized. Because the comic agon is intrinsically a representation (as well as a travesty) of adversarial rhetoric, designed to

[13] In addition to the involvement of Lampito and her allied companions, see esp. 342–3, 525, 1128–34.

appeal to an audience reared in the Athenian culture of public
speech and debate,[14] Aristophanes uses the form in *Lysistrata* to
foreground the heroine's mastery of verbal persuasion and argumentative forcefulness. But it is an almost inevitable consequence of
this that the motif of the sex-strike, which relies on the women's
collective eroticism not on the quasi-political intelligence of their
leader, is here relegated to the background. The agon contains a
single, free-floating reference to it, at 551-4; no attempt is made to
integrate this point into the case for a diplomatic solution which
Lysistrata goes on to expound at 565 ff. In this respect the agon
structurally mirrors and reproduces the anomalies of the plot as a
whole by juxtaposing but failing to harmonize the sexual and political components in the women's strategy for ending the war.

Lysistrata's arguments in the agon can be summarized very easily. The root of the war, she claims, is money; conflict has been fostered by corrupt politicians who profit from its perpetuation.
Athenian women have suffered the democracy's misguided policies
with increasing vexation, but their husbands would never allow
them to express their own political views. Now they have had
enough, and intend to lift the military blight from the city's life by
reforming its politics on the principles of domestic wool-working:
they will separate out the 'strands' of the war by diplomacy; get rid
of the filthy elements in the city; and integrate all well-disposed
groups, binding them together into a ball of wool from which to
weave 'a nice warm cloak for all the city's people' (586). And
Lysistrata finishes by momentarily emphasizing, despite the
Commissioner's objections, why women are entitled to shape the
city's future: it is they, after all, who bear male offspring to fight for
the city, while they themselves suffer from war in various ways,
either losing their sons (and husbands) in the fighting,[15] or in some
cases growing old without husbands at all because of the shortage
of males.

From the point of view of Athenian men, Lysistrata's case is a
tour de force of bravado, ingenuity—and wishful thinking. That it
contains a number of potentially thought-provoking aspects and
aperçus should not be disputed. Although 507-20 caricatures a

---

[14] See the general Introduction, 'Formality and Performance'.
[15] This is the point Lysistrata is about to make, when interrupted, at 590; it is
not made anywhere else in the play (though 651 harks back to 589-90), but it
recurs as a general, less highly charged idea at *Assembly-Women* 233-4.

paradigmatic separation of male and female roles, culminating in the echo of *Iliad* 6.492 and similar Homeric passages, the context evokes a world of partially submerged female political consciousness which probably had some reality, however limited, among well-informed Athenian women.[16] More obviously, the account of women's sufferings from war at 589-97 refers to elements of social reality which all Athenian men could have recognized; and the Commissioner's failure to grasp this point, either before (587-8) or after (598) Lysistrata has made it, marks the blindness of his prejudices as clearly as anything in the entire debate. But suggestive though these details are, and however much they may help to load comic sympathy on the women's side, they are subordinate to the two major thrusts of Lysistrata's case: her analysis of why Athens has no need to be at war (488 ff.), and her proposals for bringing the war to an end and reuniting the city. Do *these* elements in the agon stand up to careful scrutiny, or are they, as the Commissioner alleges, 'woolly nonsense' (587)?

To ascribe the war to the corrupt machinations of politicians like Peisandros (490), as Lysistrata does, is certainly not compelling. It is the sort of cynicism which no doubt many Athenians could sympathize with in certain moods, and it was a standard piece of comedy's satirical repertoire.[17] Indeed, it now seems ironic that Lysistrata should pick out Peisandros as a typical demagogue at the very time when, as we know, he was preparing the way for potentially revolutionary restrictions to democracy in Athens.[18] But in any case the analysis of war as fundamentally due to the financial corruption of political leaders is (at face value) hopelessly reductive, and we can be sure that, in this blunt form, it is unlikely to have struck otherwise a general Athenian audience, many of whom had themselves been persuaded to vote for the continuation of war over a period of many years. Lysistrata's arguments do, as we have seen, indirectly acknowledge the democratic support for the war (507-20), but this only reduces the cogency of her basic analysis.

---

[16] An independent glimpse of wives' interest in political business is found at pseudo-Demosthenes 59 (*Against Neaira*), §§110-11: the speaker assumes that, when individual Athenians return home from the courts, they may face questions from wives and other female kin; and he imagines the possibility that some women will be angry about what they hear. Cf. also the implication of *Assembly-Women* 553.

[17] See e.g. the accusations against Kleon in the 420s, esp. *Knights* 801-9; Thucydides unworthily echoes this crude judgement at 5.16.1.

[18] For Peisandros, see the Index of Names.

It is particularly significant that when she alludes, at 513-14, to the reopening of hostilities with Sparta in the winter of 418, she does not so much as hint at the reasons for this decision, any more than she goes on to discuss the complex factors which had sustained Athenian war policy over the intervening seven years. This omission does not matter if we take her case as a kind of parody of political rhetoric, only if we look for a substratum of coherent meaning. Lysistrata's flamboyance resides in the gap between her confident air of persuasiveness and the synthetic nature of her programme.

The same is true of her recipe for ending the war, which, as already noted, sounds like an *ad hoc* argument whose thrust ignores the sex-strike strategy already activated by the women. Lysistrata's proposals are dominated by a magnificent piece of female imagery, which not only thoroughly 'domesticates' the war to the conditions of wool-working, but also by its cumulative energy outruns any practical correlation with internal or external politics at Athens. No Athenian could have failed to notice that Lysistrata says *nothing* that could be concretely applied to the situation which faced the city in 411. Lines 569-70 refer to the mechanism of diplomacy, but in a gloriously vacuous manner: diplomacy *tout court* is empty, and we hear nothing of the details of bargaining claims and counter-claims which such a solution to the war would have had to deal with (if, that is, diplomacy was an option at all at this date). When the Commissioner expresses disbelief on this point, Lysistrata does not address the immediate issue at all. Instead she shifts, with a discontinuity typical of Aristophanic dialogue, to the further idea that Athens should model *all* its politics on wool-working principles (572-3). In the imagery which she goes on to manipulate, there are difficulties in gauging the resonance of some of her language, especially at 576-8;[19] but we can be confident that, as so often in Aristophanes, there is a comic excess of sentiment over pragmatism in this entire context. 'Common goodwill' (579), and a 'cloak for all the city's people' (586), are stirringly democratic phrases, but they represent slogans divorced from reality when coming from the leader of a group of women which has overturned the city's functioning democracy. This is, however, not a failure of sense but an integral part of Lysistrata's fantastic persona: that she should argue

[19] See my note *ad loc.* for the (vague) possibility of an allusion to oligarchic manœuvrings in the early months of 411.

with such stylish and forceful aplomb, while saying nothing that could be translated into a feasible policy in the circumstances of 412–411, is an integral part of her status as comic heroine. In sum, the agon leaves us with a Lysistrata who dominates the blustering Commissioner by a combination of potently sentimental rhetoric and unfeminine force (531–8, 599–613); her triumph would have given an Athenian audience more entertainment, not least in its visual enactment of a gender-reversal for the Commissioner, than concentrated food for political thought.

One of the (comic) deficiencies I have noted in the agon—namely, the lack of practical suggestions for diplomatic negotiations with Sparta—seems at first sight to be made good by the later demonstration of Lysistrata's political prowess in her speech at 1112–88. But the first thing to be said about that subsequent speech is that it has been made possible by, and brings to final fruition, the women's sex-strike. The judgement of some critics that Lysistrata's address to the ambassadors carries a convincing message flies in the face of the ripely comic eroticism of the setting. The ambassadors are in a painfully priapic state (duly highlighted by Lysistrata, 1119–21), and are accordingly obsessed with the erogenous zones of the naked Reconciliation, the female symbolization both of peace and of Greek territory. The central absurdity of the scene blatantly lies in the piquant contrast between Lysistrata's adoption of an ostensibly lofty tone of pan-Hellenic sentiment, and the recurrent indecencies of the ambassadors on both sides. A reference to the war's destruction of 'Greek men and cities' by Lysistrata elicits an Athenian's riposte that it is his erection which is destroying *him* (1134–6): physical exigency—one of Old Comedy's favourite resources—obliterates the note of would-be gravity. Similarly, Lysistrata's claim that the Spartans had helped Athens to win freedom from tyranny, a century earlier, prompts nothing more than lascivious remarks about Reconciliation's anatomy (1157–8). The dramatic significance of the heroine's speech cannot be separated from its obscene ambience, both visual and verbal.[20]

Let us look a little closer at Lysistrata's case for ending the war. She starts from, and in a sense never goes beyond, an ideal of

---

[20] The claim of G. E. M. de Ste Croix, *The Origins of the Peloponnesian War* (London, 1972), 368–9, that Lysistrata's speech at 1114–77 is 'completely serious . . . and without a single jest', shows a basic failure to grasp the subtleties of register and context in a comic text.

pan-Hellenic solidarity of the kind whose roots lay in Greek dealings with Persia during the first thirty years of the fifth century.[21] Athenians and Spartans, as well as their allies, are Greeks of common race and religion, so the argument runs, and it is barbarians (Persians) who are their natural enemies; yet they kill one another relentlessly (1128-35). As with parts of the agon, there are sentiments here which could, in a different context, carry real resonance, but which are undermined by the ridiculous irony in which they are enveloped by both visual and verbal aspects of the comic setting. When, as already mentioned, the Athenian at once refers to his conspicuous phallus, the juxtaposition of emotional rhetoric and practical compulsion accentuates the point that military conflicts are not solved by sentiment alone. Moreover, the airiness of Lysistrata's rhetoric only increases when she proceeds to cite two supposed examples of previous co-operation between Athens and Sparta. The first (1138-44), which recalls how Kimon, a major Athenian politician and general in the 460s, had taken an army to assist the Spartans during the Helot revolt in 463/2, is pointedly distorted: Lysistrata claims that Kimon 'saved' Sparta, when in fact he was sent back home prematurely in a way which led, according to Thucydides (1.102), to a *deterioration* in Athenian-Spartan relations. In the second case, where Lysistrata refers to Spartan help in expelling the tyrant Hippias in 510, the irony is more oblique but just as fatal to the cogency of the heroine's case. We need not wonder whether Aristophanes' audience would have remembered that only two years later, in 508, the same Spartan king, Kleomenes, had returned to Athens to try and quash the nascent democracy: the chorus of old men has already reminisced about this event at 273-80. So much for Spartan assistance in allowing Athenians 'to wear the cloak of freedom' (1156)!

Lysistrata, then, has offered pan-Hellenic sentiment which carries an abstract appeal but whose practical relevance to the messy, embedded actualities of war in 411 is, to say the least, hazy; and she has supported it with historical precedents whose inappropriateness is comically ironic. After all this, the effect of which is reinforced by the libidinous inattention of the ambassadors, she brings her case to a point: 'Why not be reconciled? Well, what's to stop it?' (1161). The seemingly rhetorical questions receive a response

---

[21] See Herodotos 8.144 for a clear indication of the original link between pan-Hellenism and a Greek sense of a 'common enemy'.

which, while it redoubles the vulgar farce of the ambassadors' sexual desperation, also adds to the paradoxes of the scene. For what was *actually* stopping peace in 411 was a combination of deeply rooted attitudes with an elaborate web of territorial and related issues. When at last we get some allusion to the territorial dimension, in a few lines of highly condensed wit (1162–74), Aristophanes simultaneously hints at some of the real difficulties which would bedevil any attempt at peace negotiations, and yet allows these to be dissolved, for the sake of comic harmony, in the overt imagery of bodily desire. There are enough parts of Reconciliation's anatomy to satisfy the pleasures of both sides to the conflict: the intricacies of political geography can be wished away by the ultimately simple imperatives of sexual longing.

When I first raised the question of the play's pan-Hellenism, I pointed out that it is an entailment of the comic logic of a sex-strike to end the war. What *Lysistrata*'s final speech confirms, I suggest, is that pan-Hellenism is a necessary and convenient sentiment for the heroine's arbitration between Athens and Sparta, but is also entirely secondary to the sexual forces which drive her plan from start to finish. I have referred several times to the heroine's use of 'sentiment', and *Lysistrata* is, after all, a thoroughly sentimental play. It spins its comic fantasy out of the notion that, beneath the extensive political and social disjunctions of male and female in Athenian society, sexual need is something which brings them together and could even triumph over the dynamics of war. However disappointing some modern readers may find the conclusion, this is a play which contains little to disturb the feelings of Athenian males, since it presents an image of women as ultimately unsubversive in their instincts.[22] In this connection it is notable that, while *Lysistrata*'s plot effectively represents not only a political revolt but also a blow against the heart of each Athenian husband's power and status as head of his *oikos*, this latter aspect of the matter is almost entirely suppressed in the interests of concentration on the physically sexual consequences of the strike. *Lysistrata* caricatures both the stereotyped misogyny of men, embodied above all in the antics of the male chorus, and the women's supposed lack of self-control in the face of bodily appetites. But it transcends these weaknesses with an indulgent illusion of concord that emerges, in

---

[22] Cf. the female chorus's statement at 473–4, that underneath their toughness and aggression they really retain the 'modesty' of maidens.

the end, less from the heroine's disciplined calculations than from the cravings of both sexes. In Plato's *Symposium* Socrates describes Aristophanes at one point as someone whose whole activity as a comic playwright 'is concerned with Dionysus and Aphrodite' (177e). *Lysistrata*, we can conclude, is a perfect illustration of this claim: rather than being in any realistic or sustainable sense an anti-war play, it is an unfettered celebration, of the kind possible only in Dionysiac festivity, of the irresistible power of sexuality.

LYSISTRATA

Speaking Characters

LYSISTRATA: leader of the Athenian wives
KALONIKE: a young Athenian wife
MYRRHINE: likewise
LAMPITO: a Spartan wife
COMMISSIONER: member of the Commission of Ten
KINESIAS: Athenian citizen, husband of MYRRHINE
HERALD: Spartan messenger
SPARTAN: spokesman of the Spartan ENVOYS who come to sue for peace
ATHENIAN: leader of the Athenian ENVOYS

OLD MEN: half-chorus of 12
WOMEN: half-chorus of 12
CHORUS: incorporating the two half-choruses (from 1043 onwards)
LEADER^M: of OLD MEN's half-chorus
LEADER^W: of WOMEN's half-chorus
LEADER: of combined CHORUS
(There are also several small parts for individual unnamed women.)

Silent Characters

BOIOTIAN WOMAN
KORINTHIAN WOMAN
SLAVE-GIRL: LYSISTRATA'S
ARCHERS: slaves attending the COMMISSIONER
BABY: child of KINESIAS and MYRRHINE
RECONCILIATION: naked female personification of peace
ENVOYS: official representatives of both Athens and Sparta
SLAVES (various)

[*Early morning. The scene is an Athenian street, in the vicinity of the Akropolis; there is at least one door in the background.* LYSISTRATA, *accompanied by a* SLAVE-GIRL, *enters and paces up and down with growing impatience.*]

LYSISTRATA [*exasperated*]. Now, if they'd been invited to a *Bacchic* rite,
　　Or a grotto of Pan's, or Aphrodite's shrine,
　　You wouldn't be able to move for their tambourines!*
　　As it is, not a single woman has shown up yet.　[*A door opens.*]
　　Oh—my neighbour Kalonike's coming out.
　　Kalonike, greetings!
KALONIKE.　　　　　　　You too, Lysistrata.
　　What's agitating you? Don't frown, my dear.
　　Those arching eyebrows just don't suit your face.*
LYSISTRATA [*gravely*]. Kalonike, I feel a burning pain at heart—
　　A sense of bitter grievance for us women.　　　　　　　　　　IO
　　Among the men we've gained a reputation
　　For being fond of schemes—
KALONIKE.　　　　　　　　And so we are!*
LYSISTRATA. Yet when they're told to gather for this meeting,
　　To come and discuss a matter of such importance,
　　They stay in bed—no sign of them!
KALONIKE.　　　　　　　　　　　Look, darling,
　　They'll *come*. It's hard for women to leave the house.*
　　I dare say some are getting their husbands—up,
　　Or waking the slaves, or putting a baby to sleep,
　　Or maybe washing and feeding their little ones.
LYSISTRATA. There are *other* things that ought to matter far more. 20
KALONIKE. But what's the reason, dear Lysistrata,
　　Which makes you ask us women to meet together?
　　What kind of thing? What scale?
LYSISTRATA.　　　　　　　　　　It's big.
KALONIKE [*suggestively*].　　　　　　　And beefy?
LYSISTRATA. It's beefy, all right.
KALONIKE.　　　　　　　It sounds worth coming for!
LYSISTRATA. It's not like *that*, or else they'd all be here.
　　It's something I myself have pondered hard
　　And tossed around through many sleepless nights.
KALONIKE. And is this thing you've 'tossed'—well, *delicate*?
LYSISTRATA. So delicate that Greece's whole salvation
　　Depends entirely on the female sex.　　　　　　　　　　　　30

KALONIKE. The female sex? Well, what a slender hope!
LYSISTRATA. It's up to *us* to run the city's affairs.
If we don't, there won't be any Spartans left—
KALONIKE. No Spartans left? How simply wonderful!
LYSISTRATA. And every single Boiotian will be wiped out—
KALONIKE. No, please just spare a few—of their *eels*, that is.*
LYSISTRATA. And as for Athens, my tongue can't bring itself
To say the worst. You grasp my implication.
But if the women attend the meeting here—
Boiotian and Spartan women as well as ours— 40
We'll launch a common effort to rescue Greece.
KALONIKE [*sententiously*]. 'What clever, illustrious deed could
women achieve?'*
[*Normal voice*] We spend our idle lives at home, dolled up
And draped in chiffon dresses, or prettified
In slinky gowns and ritzy evening shoes.
LYSISTRATA. It's *just* these things that could save the situation:
Little chiffon numbers, perfumes, ritzy shoes,
And all that rouge and see-through lingerie.
KALONIKE. But what could they do?
LYSISTRATA.   They might prevent the men
From threatening one another with their spears— 50
KALONIKE. For *that* I'll have my chiffon dress re-dyed!
LYSISTRATA. Or waving shields—
KALONIKE.   Straight on with that slinky
gown!
LYSISTRATA. Or swords.
KALONIKE.   I'll fetch some ritzy evening shoes!
LYSISTRATA. Well, shouldn't the rest of the women be here by
now?
KALONIKE. They should have simply *flocked* here long ago.
LYSISTRATA. But, dear, you'll see the women from Attika
Do everything too late; it's always the same.
Not a single woman has come from the coastal region,
And no one's here from Salamis yet.
KALONIKE.   I bet
That *they* were up at dawn for an early ride!* 60
LYSISTRATA. And as for those I felt quite confident
Would be here first—the women from Acharnai—*
They haven't come.

KALONIKE.   I know Theogenes' wife
  Was bracing herself with a drink before she left.*
  Oh look! Here *are* some women approaching now.

[*Women start to appear from both side entrances, among them* MYRRHINE.]

LYSISTRATA. And here's another group over here.
KALONIKE.   Good heavens,
  What deme are they from?
LYSISTRATA.   Anagyrous.
KALONIKE [*sniffing*].   Yes, I see:
  No wonder, then, they're raising such a stink.*
MYRRHINE. I hope we're not too late, Lysistrata?
  Well, what? No answer?   70
LYSISTRATA.   You've let me down, Myrrhine,
  Turning up so late for such important business.
MYRRHINE. I'm sorry, I had to find my bra in the dark.
  But now we're here, explain, if it's really urgent.
LYSISTRATA. Not yet: we ought to wait a little longer
  Until the Boiotian and Spartan wives have time
  To get here too.
MYRRHINE.   Quite right: I'm sure we should.
  But here, in fact, comes Lampito right now.

[*Enter, from a side entrance,* LAMPITO, *a muscular beauty, with two other
young wives, all three wearing short, revealing dresses. The new arrivals
    immediately become the object of close physical attention.*]

LYSISTRATA. Warm greetings, Lampito, dear Spartan friend.
  Sweetheart, you're looking simply ravishing.*
  What gorgeous skin—and, oh, those *muscles* of yours.   80
  You could throttle a bull!
LAMPITO.   By the Twins,* I swear I could.
  My exercise includes rump-stretching kicks.
KALONIKE. I've *never* seen a finer pair of breasts.
LAMPITO. Stop feeling my flesh: I'm not for sacrifice!
LYSISTRATA. And what about this other girl—who's she?
LAMPITO. A Boiotian—and a fine one, by the Twins.
  She's come for the meeting too.
MYRRHINE [*examining her*].   A true Boiotian!
  Her belly's as flat as any Boiotian plain.
KALONIKE [*peering*]. And look at her little bush, how cutely
    trimmed!*

LYSISTRATA. This other girl?   90

LAMPITO.   A choice piece, by the Twins.
  Korinthian, what's more.

KALONIKE.   A real 'choice piece'!*
  That's all too clear in front as well as behind.

LAMPITO. Now, who's the one who's summoned this gathering
  Of all us women?

LYSISTRATA.   It's me.

LAMPITO.   I'd like to hear
  What it is you want.

KALONIKE.   Yes, tell us now, dear friend.
  Explain this grand idea that's on your mind.

LYSISTRATA. I'll tell you, then. But first I'll ask a question.
  It's something small I need to know.

KALONIKE.   Feel free.

LYSISTRATA. Don't you ever miss the fathers of your children
  When they're off on active service? I certainly know   100
  You've all got husbands away from home like this.

KALONIKE. You're right, my dear. My husband's been in Thrace
  The last five months: he's guarding—Eukrates.*

MYRRHINE. And *mine*'s been gone for seven whole months, at
    Pylos.

LAMPITO. While *mine*, even when he comes home, has hardly
    time
  To hang up his shield before he flies off again.

LYSISTRATA. Not a glimmer of males—not a single adulterer
    left!
  And since Miletos ditched our old alliance,
  I haven't set eyes on a single five-inch dildo
  Which might at least have given synthetic relief.*   110
  So, are you ready, if I devise a scheme,
  To help me end the war?

KALONIKE.   By the two goddesses!*
  I'd even be prepared to pawn this dress
  To raise the funds for celebratory drinks!

MYRRHINE [*frivolously*]. And I'd be willing to cut myself in half
  And serve myself as a sacrificial flat-fish!

LAMPITO. And *I* would climb up mount Taÿgetos
  To gaze upon a land of peace below.

LYSISTRATA. I'll tell you then; no need for secrecy.

I assure you, assembled women: to have a chance   120
Of ever compelling our husbands to live in peace,
We really must—
KALONIKE.   Do what?
LYSISTRATA.   Well, *will* you do it?
KALONIKE. We promise we will, if death itself's the price!
LYSISTRATA. We *must* give up the pleasure of—the prick.
                         [*Women shudder and start to leave.*]
What makes you turn away? Don't try to leave.
You there, why grimace and shake your heads like that?
[*Melodramatically*] 'What means this pale complexion, these
    tears that flow?'*
Well, will you or won't you do it? Please tell me that.
KALONIKE. I simply *couldn't*. The war must take its course.
MYRRHINE. I feel the same. The war must take its course.   130
LYSISTRATA. So that's your view, you 'flat-fish'! Just before
    You said you'd even cut yourself in half.
KALONIKE. Ask *anything*, anything else. I'd be prepared
    To walk through fire. But not give up the prick!
    There's nothing like it, dear Lysistrata.
LYSISTRATA. Well, what about *you*?
MYRRHINE.   I too would walk through fire.
LYSISTRATA. The female sex! Sheer lustfulness, that's us!
    No wonder they write such tragedies about us!
    Our lives are simply full of sex and intrigue.*
    [*Pleadingly*] But you, dear Spartan friend—if only you   140
    Would stick with me, we'd save the situation.
    Please lend support.
LAMPITO.   It's difficult, by the Twins,
    For wives to sleep alone without a dick.
    And yet we must: we need peace back so badly.
LYSISTRATA. O dearest friend, you're the only genuine *woman*!
KALONIKE. Suppose we really did abstain from *it*,
    Though god forbid! What difference would it make
    To getting peace?
LYSISTRATA.   A difference like no other.
    If we were to sit at home, our faces powdered,
    And wore short silken shifts to give a glimpse   150
    Of nicely trimmed small triangles of hair,*
    So our husbands started to swell and wanted to shag,

But *we* held back and refused to let them do it—
I tell you now: they'd make peace in a flash.
LAMPITO. It's true, when Menelaos caught a glimpse
Of Helen's breasts, it made him drop his sword.*
KALONIKE. But what if our men reject us then, my dear?
LYSISTRATA. To borrow Pherekrates' phrase: try self-abuse!*
KALONIKE. A useless substitute! It's just not real.
And what if they turn quite rough, and drag us upstairs?   160
LYSISTRATA. Then grab the bedroom door and cling for life.
KALONIKE. But what if they beat us up?
LYSISTRATA.   Keep on resisting.
They can't derive much pleasure from *forcing* us.*
We've got to make them suffer in every way.
They'll soon give in: no husband can enjoy
A life of constant friction with his wife.
KALONIKE. Well, if you two agree, we'll go along.
LAMPITO. But how will *we* persuade our Spartan husbands
To keep the peace without duplicitous guile?*
And who could hope to persuade the Athenian rabble   170
To keep its mind fixed on negotiations?*
LYSISTRATA. Don't worry, we'll soon convince our people here.
LAMPITO. Not while their triremes still having rigging intact,
And your goddess's vault contains such limitless funds!*
LYSISTRATA. I've made provisions to cover this very point:
We're going to seize the Akropolis today.
This task has been assigned to older women:
While we talk here, they're going to use the pretext
Of a sacrifice to occupy the hill.
LAMPITO. A perfect ploy—you've thought of everything.   180
LYSISTRATA. In that case, Lampito, let's swear an oath
. At once, to make our pact unbreakable.
LAMPITO. Reveal the oath you want us all to swear.
LYSISTRATA. Right, where's my Scythian slave?
                    [*The* SLAVE-GIRL, *carrying a shield etc., steps forward.*]
                                        Hey you, look

    sharp!
Come here and place the shield there, facing down.
Can someone pass the meat?
KALONIKE [*interrupting*].   Lysistrata,
What oath is this you're going to make us swear?

LYSISTRATA. The sort, I've heard, occurs in Aischylos—
  A blood-oath over a shield.*
KALONIKE.   Lysistrata!
  Don't use a shield to swear an oath for *peace*!   190
LYSISTRATA. What oath, then, would you like?
KALONIKE.   Perhaps we ought
  To find a pure white horse for sacrifice?*
LYSISTRATA. A pure white horse!
KALONIKE.   Well think of something better.
LYSISTRATA. All right, I will; just listen to this suggestion.
  Let's place a large black *drinking*-cup down here,
  And sacrifice a jar of Thasian wine,
  Then swear we won't pour in a drop of water.*
LAMPITO. A quite magnificent oath! I'm lost for words.
LYSISTRATA. Let someone fetch a cup, and a jar of wine.
            [*The* SLAVE-GIRL *fetches a huge wine-jar and drinking-cup.*]
MYRRHINE. My dears, what specimens! What ceramic art!   200
KALONIKE [*fondling the cup*]. Could anyone fail to handle this
      with pleasure?
LYSISTRATA. Just place it here, and help me hold the beast.
      [*She picks up the jar and speaks with the solemnity of a priest.*]
  Divine Persuasion*—cup of female friendship—
  Be kind to women, receive our sacrifice.
                              [*Some wine is poured from the jar.*]
KALONIKE. The blood's a lovely colour; it flows so well.
LAMPITO. And what a fine bouquet, in Kastor's name!
MYRRHINE. Allow me, ladies, to be the first to swear.
LYSISTRATA. By Aphrodite, no! Please wait your turn.
  Now all must touch the cup. Come, Lampito.
  Let one of you, for the group, repeat my words,   210
  Then all will solemnly ratify this oath.
  [*Gravely*] 'No male, be he adulterer or spouse,'
KALONIKE. 'No male, be he adulterer or spouse,'
LYSISTRATA. 'Shall come near me with prick erect.' [KALONIKE *hesitates.*]
      Repeat!
KALONIKE. 'Shall come near me with—prick erect.' Oh dear!
  My knees are feeling weak, Lysistrata.
LYSISTRATA [*persisting*]. 'At home I'll stay as chaste as any virgin,'
KALONIKE. 'At home I'll stay as chaste as any virgin,'
LYSISTRATA. 'Draped in a chiffon dress, my face made up,'

KALONIKE. 'Draped in a chiffon dress, my face made up,'   220
LYSISTRATA. 'To make my husband hot with lust for me.'
KALONIKE. 'To make my husband hot with lust for me.'
LYSISTRATA. 'And never shall I do my husband's will.'
KALONIKE. 'And never shall I do my husband's will.'
LYSISTRATA. 'But if he uses force and tries to rape me,'
KALONIKE. 'But if he uses force and tries to rape me,'
LYSISTRATA. 'I'll still resist and never writhe with pleasure.'
KALONIKE. 'I'll still resist and never writhe with pleasure.'
LYSISTRATA. 'I'll never lift my sexy legs up high.'
KALONIKE. 'I'll never lift my sexy legs up high.'   230
LYSISTRATA. 'I'll never kneel in the lioness position.'*
KALONIKE. 'I'll never kneel in the lioness position.'
LYSISTRATA. 'If I keep this oath, may wine be mine to drink.'
KALONIKE. 'If I keep this oath, may wine be mine to drink.'
LYSISTRATA. 'But if I transgress, may the cup be filled with water.'
KALONIKE. 'But if I transgress, may the cup be filled with water.'
LYSISTRATA. Do all you others swear this oath?
ALL.   We do.
LYSISTRATA [*starting to drink*].
   Now, let me sanctify this cup.
KALONIKE [*anxiously*].   Fair shares,
   My dear! Let's all be best of friends.
                        [*As they drink, an off-stage cry is heard.*]
LAMPITO. I heard a shout.   240
LYSISTRATA.   Well, didn't I tell you so?
   It means Athena's hill, the Akropolis,
   Is in the women's hands. Come, Lampito,
   You go and settle business back in Sparta,
   But leave these girls as hostages with us.

[*Exit* LAMPITO *by a side entrance: the stage building now assumes the
          identity of the Propylaia, gateway to the Akropolis.*]

   The rest of us must join the women inside
   And help them bolt and bar the Akropolis gates.*
KALONIKE. You mean you think the men will send a force
   To deal with us at once?
LYSISTRATA.   I couldn't care less!
   Suppose they threaten to storm the place with fire:
   We're never going to open these gates to them   250

Unless they come to terms with our demands.

KALONIKE. We'll never give in! We'd lose our reputation
For being nasty and fighting tooth and nail!

[*All the women enter the Akropolis. Soon afterwards, the* OLD MEN's *half-chorus, struggling to carry logs and a brazier up the hillside, appears from a side entrance.*]

[PARODOS: 254–386]

LEADER^M. Keep up, old chap, with steady steps; ignore your
    aching shoulder
That carries such a heavy load of fresh-cut olive-wood
    logs.

OLD MEN.   *Strophe*
        Long life brings many surprises, shiver me timbers!
        Who would have thought, my friends, we'd ever hear
            That *women*, whom we reared   260
            As blatant mischiefs in our homes,
            Should seize Athena's statue,
            And occupy our sacred hill,
            And fasten up these massive gates
            With bolts and bars?

LEADER^M. Come on, my ancient comrade, let's push on up to
    the summit.
We've got to pile these logs around the site that's occupied
By all the women who've carried out this bold, audacious
    deed.
Let's get to work to build it up and then ignite the bonfire:
We'll burn them all at one fell swoop; not least, the wife of
    Lykon.*   270

OLD MEN.   I swear that while I live their plot will fail. *Antistrophe*
            Why, even when Kleomenes seized this hill,
                He did not leave unscathed.*   275
                For all his Spartan puff and prowess,
                I made him drop his weapons.
                He wore a little, patchy cloak;
                He starved, he stank, he hadn't shaved
                For six full years.*

LEADER^M. That's how I showed my fierceness once, in laying
    siege to *him*.
  We kept a vigil by the gates, in rank on rank of troops.
  What trouble could I find it, then, to end the brazen scheme
  Of women whom the gods detest—as Euripides does too!*
  If I fail, then may my monument at Marathon collapse.*

OLD MEN.   Well, all that's left for me to do   *Strophe*
          Is climb this steep part here
      Up to the top: that's where I've got to aim.
       How ever will we haul this stuff
           Without an ass?   290
  My shoulder's crushed beneath this pair of logs.
        And yet we must proceed
        And keep the fire well fanned,
  In case we lose the flame before we're there.   [*They blow.*]
    Pfff! Pfff! Oh, what disgusting smoke!

        How terrible, lord Herakles!   *Antistrophe*
        The flame leapt out at me:
    It's like a mad bitch biting at my eyes.
   This fire must come from Lemnos way,*
         I'm sure of that.   300
  That must be why it has the teeth to bite.
       But onwards, nevertheless!
       Athena needs support.
  Whenever could we help her more than now? [*They blow.*]
    Pfff! Pfff! Oh, what disgusting smoke!

LEADER^M. This fire has woken up, I swear; it's really come
    alive.
  So let's halt here and lay our logs along this bit of ground.
                    [*They deposit the logs.*]
  Now dip your vine-wood torches in the brazier, till they
    burn.
  Then when they're lit, we'll make a ram to batter down
    the door.
  And if the women still refuse and won't unlock the bolts,   310
  We'll burn the doors and force them out by blinding them
    with smoke.

Let's drop our burdens on the ground. Yuck, what
    disgusting smoke!
Can we expect a helping hand from the generals now in
    Samos?*
Thank god that's off my back; that wood had almost
    crushed my backbone.
It's up to you, my brazier, now to fuel the coals inside.
I want my torch to be the first to set light to the bonfire.
Athena Nike, goddess proud, help us defeat these women
And place a monument to show we crushed their
    shameless deed.

[*As the men continue to prepare their attack, the* WOMEN's *half-chorus,
carrying water-jars, hurries on from the opposite side entrance.*]

LEADER^w. Look up, my women, the atmosphere is full of soot
    and smoke.
There's fire somewhere, it's obvious: we must be quick
    to find it.   320

WOMEN.	Look everywhere, before the flames *Strophe*

Look everywhere, before the flames   *Strophe*
Engulf our dear companions.
The flames are fanned
By gusting winds
And senile windbags!
My fear is that I've come belatedly.
Just moments ago, in dawn's half-light,
Down by the spring, among noisy crowds
Of women and slave-girls jostling one another for room,   330
I snatched my jug, and rushed up here,
To use this water
To save my friends from burning.

I heard that some deranged old men   *Antistrophe*
Have come with tons of timber.
They're arsonists
And threaten 'to cook
These filthy bitches'.   340
Athena, please don't let the women burn!
They'll stop the war, the crazy war,
And rescue Greece, as well as Athens.
Gold-crested,* patron goddess, that's why they've seized

your shrine.   344-6
O ally, hail! Tritogeneia!*
Help us fetch water
To quell the old men's fire.

[*The two half-choruses now face up to one another: they move and act with a stylized 'pantomime' aggression which reflects their leaders' words.*]

LEADER^W. Just wait a moment! What *have* we here? Some right old nasty codgers.   350

God-fearing men, the decent sort, would never behave like this.

LEADER^M. Well here's a real surprise for us; we didn't see it coming.

A hornet's nest of women here is bringing reinforcements.

LEADER^W. What makes you look so stinking scared? Our numbers aren't so large.

Mind you, you've so far only seen a fraction of our forces.

LEADER^M. Can we, my friends, allow these women to jabber in this fashion?

It's time we took these logs of ours and gave them all a thrashing.

LEADER^W. Well let's respond by putting down our pitchers on the ground.

If one of them should raise a hand, we mustn't be encumbered.

LEADER^M. They should, like Boupalos, have had their jaws both broken for them.*   360

That way, they wouldn't have the voice to be so impudent.

LEADER^W. Well here's my jaw! Just throw a punch! I'll stand and let you try.

But if you do, you'll find this bitch will grab your *testicles*.

LEADER^M. Unless you shut your mouth, I'll knock your stuffing out, old hag.

LEADER^W. You better hadn't even try to lay a finger on me.

LEADER^M. Suppose I beat you with my fists? What will you do about it?

LEADER^W. I'll sink my teeth into your ribs and rip your innards out!

LEADER^M. We always knew Euripides possessed poetic insight:

There is no creature on the earth as shameless as a
woman.*

LEADER^W. Let's lift our pitchers up again: it's time to use this
water.   370

LEADER^M. What made you, god-forsaken crone, come here with
so much water?

LEADER^W. And what made *you* bring fire along, you
tombstone—your cremation?

LEADER^M. I've come to build a funeral pyre, and burn your
friends inside.

LEADER^W. And *I've* come here to quench the flames by dousing
them with water.

LEADER^M. You think you'll quench the fire I've brought?

LEADER^W.   You'll
see in just a moment.

LEADER^M. I've half a mind to take this torch and grill you right
away.

LEADER^W. Perhaps you've brought some soap along; you'll need
it for this bath.

LEADER^M. A *bath* from you, you putrid hag?

LEADER^W [*sarcastically*].   A nuptial bath,
what's more.

LEADER^M. Did you hear her outright impudence?

LEADER^W.   I'm not a slave,
you know.

LEADER^M. I'll stop this noisy rant of yours.   380

LEADER^W.   You're not a juror
now!*

LEADER^M [*brandishing torch*]. It's time to set her hair on fire.*

LEADER^W [*tipping water*].   Now
do your job, my water!

LEADER^M [*pathetically*]. You're soaking me!

LEADER^W.   Was the temperature
right?

LEADER^M.   The temperature! You've got to stop.

LEADER^W.   I'm watering you to help you grow.

LEADER^M.   But I'm shivering like a wilting plant.

LEADER^W. Well, as you've brought your fire with you, I'm sure
you'll soon get warm.

[*As the half-choruses separate, an aged* COMMISSIONER* *enters, accompanied by two* SLAVES *and four* ARCHERS. *He appears more concerned with airing his views than with taking control of the situation.*]

COMMISSIONER. So the women's dissipation has flared again?
　　The usual tambourines and Sabazios stuff,
　　And all this roof-top nonsense with Adonis!*
　　[*Rambling*] I heard it once while sitting in the Assembly.　　390
　　Demostratos—ill-fated fool!—was urging
　　We send a fleet to Sicily.* Nearby,
　　His *wife* was dancing, shrieking 'O Adonis!'
　　He then proposed we fetch troops from Zakynthos,*
　　While his drunken wife was shouting on the roof
　　'Bewail Adonis!' *He*, though, persevered—
　　The god-forsaken, impious lunatic!
　　So there you have it: women's wantonness!
LEADER^M. Just wait till you hear the crime of *this* lot here.
　　On top of all their other outrageous deeds,　　400
　　They've soaked us to the skin; so now our cloaks
　　Are dripping as though we've gone and pissed ourselves.
COMMISSIONER. In Poseidon's watery name, it serves us right!
　　When we abet our own wives' turpitude
　　And give them lessons in depravity,
　　Such are the schemes they're bound to breed and hatch.
　　Just think of how we talk in craftsmen's shops:
　　[*Lubriciously*] 'You made a necklace, goldsmith, recently,
　　But while my wife was dancing in the evening,
　　The pin came out of the hole it's meant to fit.　　410
　　Now, *I'm* about to leave for Salamis,
　　So if you've time, bring round your tools one evening
　　And re-insert the pin: my wife will like it.'
　　Another husband, talking to a cobbler
　　Who's young and has a virile prick, says this:
　　'My wife is having trouble with her foot:
　　The strap is squeezing round the fleshy cleft.
　　The skin's so soft; so come at noon one day
　　And stretch it for her: make more width inside.'
　　Now what a pretty pass affairs have reached:　　420
　　Here's me, a city Commissioner—I've come
　　To see that timber's bought to make new oars,*

And I find myself locked out by *women*, no less!
There's no use standing round. Just bring the crowbars.
I'll put a stop to this criminal act of theirs.
[*To his* SLAVES] Stop gawping, will you, wretch! You too,
    you dolt!
You look as though you're waiting for a drink.
Get moving with those bars beneath the gates,
And start to prise them open. I'll do the same
With a lever here.   430

    [*The gates suddenly open and* LYSISTRATA *comes out.*]

LYSISTRATA.   No need to force the gates.
    I'm coming out voluntarily. Why use crowbars?
    It's not such tools you need but careful thought.
COMMISSIONER. How dare you, filthy bitch! Arrest her, archers!
    Seize her and tie her hands behind her back.

         [*One* ARCHER *starts to approach her.*]
LYSISTRATA. By Artemis!* If he lays a finger on me,
    This public slave will get it in the eye.   [*The* ARCHER *hesitates.*]
COMMISSIONER. You're afraid of *her*? Just grab her round the
    waist.
    [*To another* ARCHER] *You* help him too: I want her tied at
    once.

[*As the second* ARCHER *moves forward nervously, an* OLD WOMAN, *carrying a basket of wool etc., steps out from the gates behind* LYSISTRATA.]

OLD WOMAN^A. By Pandrosos!* Just lay a finger on her,
    And I'll trample you until the shit falls out.

         [*The* ARCHER *backs off.*] 440
COMMISSIONER. 'The shit'—what shocking language! [*To the third
    ARCHER*] Hey you, come here.
    Tie up this woman first, to stop her prattle.
OLD WOMAN^B [*appearing*]. By Phosphoros!* Just lay a finger on
    her,
    And you'll soon acquire a shiny blue-black eye.

         [*This* ARCHER *too backs away.*]
COMMISSIONER. What, another one! [*To the fourth* ARCHER] Quick,
    archer, here! Grab *her*.
    I'll stop them coming out here to face me down.
OLD WOMAN^C [*emerging*]. By Artemis goddess of bulls! Just take
    one step!

I'll tear your hair and make you scream to hell.

> [*The final* ARCHER *retreats.*]

COMMISSIONER [*looking round*]. What wretched fate! I've now
used all my archers.

We can't accept defeat at the hands of women: 450
[*To the* ARCHERS] Get into line, you Scythians; be prepared
To charge head-on.

LYSISTRATA.   And when you do, you'll find
That we too have our troops: four companies
Of warlike women, all waiting armed inside.

COMMISSIONER [*raging*]. Twist back their arms, you Scythians:
truss them up.

[*The* ARCHERS *approach tentatively.* LYSISTRATA *calls to those inside.*]

LYSISTRATA. Come, allied women, rush to our defence!
You market-trading-vegetable-vending swarms,
You tavern-keeping-bread-and-garlic wives,*
Get hold of them and give them all a bruising.
Call them the filthiest names, show no restraint! 460
> [*Various women appear and repulse the half-hearted attack of the*
> ARCHERS.]

[*Like a commander*] The battle's won. Pull back: no booty-
taking.

COMMISSIONER. My archery division's been destroyed!

LYSISTRATA. Well what did you expect? Did you believe
That we'd obey like slaves? Or don't you know
That women too have spunk?

COMMISSIONER.   And plenty too,
Provided alcohol is close at hand!

LEADER^M [*stepping forward*]. Commissioner of our city, you've
expended many words.

Why lock yourself in argument with *animals* like these?
Aren't you aware of what a bath they doused us in just now,
While we were wearing all our clothes—and had no soap,
what's more? 470

LEADER^W. Well now you've learnt your lesson, mate: you
shouldn't harry neighbours.

But if you do, you must expect to get a pair of shiners.

[*Demurely*] I didn't want to start a fight; my aim is like a
maiden's,

To trouble no one here at all, and keep my modest manner,
Provided no one stirs me up and rouses me to anger.

[AGON: 476-613.]

OLD MEN.   O Zeus, how shall we deal   *Strophe*
                             With monsters like these?
                       Intolerable it is. Commissioner, *you*
                             Must help investigate:
                       What motive could have brought them   480
                       To occupy this rocky mound? And why
                             Should they have seized our great,
                             Our sacrosanct Akropolis?

LEADER^M. Come question them, and don't be duped; be sure to
     test each answer.
   What shame there'd be if this affair were left unscrutinized.
COMMISSIONER. Indeed there would. And here's the first enquiry
     I shall make.
     [*To* LYSISTRATA] What reason made you shut and bolt the
     Akropolis' gates like this?
LYSISTRATA. We aimed to seize the treasury, and block your
     funds for warfare.
COMMISSIONER. You think it's money that makes us fight?
LYSISTRATA.   And
     causes *all* our turmoil.
   That's why Peisandros and the rest who set their sights on
     power   490
   Created turmoil everywhere—to cover up their thieving.
   They'll never get their hands again upon the city's silver.
COMMISSIONER. What makes you sure?
LYSISTRATA.   You need to ask? Well
     we'll be treasurers now.
COMMISSIONER. You *women* look after the city's funds?
LYSISTRATA.   What
     makes you think that's strange?
   Don't we, your wives, already hold the purse strings in
     your houses?*

COMMISSIONER. It's not the same.

LYSISTRATA.   Why not?

COMMISSIONER.   Because the city pays
  for *warfare*.

LYSISTRATA. There isn't any need for war.

COMMISSIONER.   How else could we
  survive?

LYSISTRATA. We women will keep you safe and sound.

COMMISSIONER.   You women?

LYSISTRATA.   Yes, we.

COMMISSIONER.   Outrageous!

LYSISTRATA. We *will*, no matter what you want.

COMMISSIONER.   How shocking!

LYSISTRATA.   Now you're angry.
  There's really no alternative.   500

COMMISSIONER.   Such rank contempt for justice!

LYSISTRATA. You *must* be saved, old thing.

COMMISSIONER.   Against my will?

LYSISTRATA.   Yes,
  all the more so!

COMMISSIONER. What gives you women the right to take control
  of war and peace?

LYSISTRATA. I'll tell you, then.

COMMISSIONER.   And make it sharp, or else you'll pay.

LYSISTRATA.   Then
  listen.
  And please stop waving round your arms.

COMMISSIONER.   I can't: it isn't
  easy
  To keep my anger bottled up.

OLD WOMAN^ [*chipping in*].   Well, *you're* the one who'll pay,
  then.

COMMISSIONER. I hope you croak to death, old crone. [*to* LYSISTRATA]
  But *you*, explain.

LYSISTRATA.   I shall do.
  For quite some time we've seen your faults, yet suffered
    them in silence.
  We tolerated everything decided by our husbands.
  You wouldn't let us grumble, yet your actions didn't please
    us.

We learnt precisely what you did, and often in our houses   510
We heard reports of bad mistakes in very serious business.
Then, inwardly distressed, we'd wear a smile as we asked
    nicely:
'What vote went through today? Perhaps to change the
    peace inscription?'*
But all my husband ever said was 'What's it all to you,
    then?
Now hold your tongue.' And so I did.

OLD WOMAN^.   Well, *I* would never
    have done so!

COMMISSIONER [*to latter*].
    You would have earned a thrashing, then.

LYSISTRATA.   And that's
    why *I* kept quiet.
But later on we'd learn about an even worse decision.
And then we'd ask: 'How can you, husband, all be quite
    so crazy?'
He'd scowl at me and tell me I should stick to spinning
    yarn
If I didn't want a battered head. 'Just leave the war to
    menfolk.'*   520

COMMISSIONER. *Precisely* what he should have said.

LYSISTRATA.   But how,
    benighted fool,
Was it ever right we weren't allowed to give you good
    advice?
Then, when we heard you in the streets complaining, broad
    as daylight:
'There isn't a man left in the land', 'You're right, it's quite
    deserted',
That's when we women came to think we ought to stand
    together
And share our strength to save all Greece. We *couldn't* hold
    off longer.
So, if you men are now prepared to take some good
    suggestions,
And hold your tongues as we did then, we'll try to rescue
    you.

COMMISSIONER. You 'rescue' us! What shocking talk! Insufferable!

LYSISTRATA.   Keep quiet!

COMMISSIONER. Keep quiet for *you*, you loathsome thing—a
    woman with a veil*   530
  Wrapped round her head? I'd rather die.

LYSISTRATA [*removing her veil*].   Well if my veil's the
    problem,
            Then take it: have it for yourself
            And wrap it round your own head.
                      [*She attaches it to him.*]
            And *then* keep quiet!

OLD WOMAN^A. And take this basket, while you're at it!
                  [*She thrusts it into his arms.*]

LYSISTRATA.   Then hitch your tunic, chew some beans,
            And work your wool.*
         Just leave the war to *women*!

LEADER^W. Come, women, put your jugs aside, and rouse
    yourselves for action.
  It's now our turn to give our friends the help which they
    deserve.   540

WOMEN.   I never could grow tired   *Antistrophe*
                Of dancing like this.
      My knees could never ache with weariness.
            I'll go to any lengths
           To help my fellow women.
       For they've got verve and courage,
          Wisdom and patriotism,
         With virtue and intelligence.

LEADER^W. O bravest woman of us all, both grannies and
    young mothers,
  Proceed with passion, don't relent: you have the wind
    behind you.   550

LYSISTRATA. Now if delicious Eros, with the Kyprian, Aphrodite,
  Will make our breasts and thighs appear seductively
    attractive,
  And then subject our husbands to exquisite priapisms,
  I'm sure the Greeks will hail us all, 'Lysimache, war-
    breaker!'*

COMMISSIONER. But what's your plan?

LYSISTRATA.   We'll make a start by
    banning from the market
    All lunatics in military dress.
OLD WOMAN.   We shall, by Aphrodite!
LYSISTRATA. At present, in the Agora, among the traders' stalls
    These people wander round in arms, like frenzied
        Korybantics.
COMMISSIONER. Of course they're armed, our soldiers brave.
LYSISTRATA.   But
    what a silly sight
    To see a man with Gorgon-shield just buying fish for
        supper.*   560
OLD WOMAN. The other day I saw a long-haired cavalry
        commander,
    Yes, buying porridge on his horse: he put it in his helmet!
    Nearby, a Thracian mercenary, with weapons just like
        Tereus,
    Had petrified a poor old woman, and then gulped down
        her figs.
COMMISSIONER. Well how could *women* like yourselves resolve
        such tangled matters
    In all the various parts of Greece?
LYSISTRATA.   Dead easy!
COMMISSIONER.   Oh? Then show
    me.

[LYSISTRATA *takes some wool and a spindle from the basket: she gives a*
                    demonstration as she speaks.]

LYSISTRATA. We'll deal with them precisely like a tangled skein
        of wool.
    We use our spindles in this way, to separate the strands.
    And that's how we'll resolve this war, if only we're allowed,
    By using embassies to separate the warring factions.   570
COMMISSIONER. You think that all your skeins of wool, and
        implements like spindles,
    Can show you how to stop a war? What fools!
LYSISTRATA.   If you were
    sane,
    You'd model *all* your politics on our wool-working methods.
COMMISSIONER. Explain your point, and let me see.

LYSISTRATA [*proceeding to demonstrate from the basket*].

To start with, treat the city
As women do a filthy fleece, by washing off the grease,
Then stretching it and picking out the nasty, prickly bits.
Next, find the ones who club together and press themselves all tight
In quest for power:* then comb them out, and pluck off all their heads.
Now fill your basket with communal fabric of goodwill,
With room for everyone, including well-disposed outsiders,   580
And even debtors to the state; there's space to mix them in.
Then don't forget the colonies sent out abroad by Athens:*
You ought to recognize that each is like a flock of wool.
Then take together all these strands, from all these different sources,
And draw them, bind them into one great mighty ball of wool,
From which to weave a nice warm cloak for all the city's people.

COMMISSIONER. How shocking that these women spin out all this woolly nonsense!
They've played so small a part in war.

LYSISTRATA.   'So small', repulsive blockhead!
We pay a *double* price for war. For first we bear our children,
And send them out as fighting troops, but—   590

COMMISSIONER.   Silence! Don't stir trouble.

LYSISTRATA. Then, when we should be finding joy and pleasure in our marriage,
We sleep alone, because of war. And it's not just wives who suffer.
Think of the maidens growing old, unmarried. How it grieves me!

COMMISSIONER. And don't men too grow old?

LYSISTRATA.   Of course, but things are rather different.
Even a grey-haired man can find a youthful bride to marry.

A *woman*'s chance is very brief, and if she doesn't seize it
No man will ever marry her: she sits and waits for omens.*
COMMISSIONER.   Well while a man can get it up—
LYSISTRATA [*aggressively*].
                    Look, isn't it time you just dropped dead?
                    There are burial plots, and coffins for sale;   600
                    I'll bake your funeral cake myself.
      [*Setting about him*]
                    And *there*'s a wreath to boot!
OLD WOMAN^A.
                    And take some ribbons for your corpse!
OLD WOMAN^B.
                    And there's another wreath for you!*
LYSISTRATA.   You've everything. Get in the boat:
                    Old Charon's calling you aboard,
                    He's waiting just for *you*.

[*The* COMMISSIONER *manages to extricate himself, and starts to leave.*]

COMMISSIONER. It's shocking I should be abused like this.
    I swear I'll go directly, in this garb,
    And show my fellow magistrates my plight.   [*Exits.*]   610
LYSISTRATA [*calling after*]. You won't complain we failed to wash
      the corpse?
    In two days' time we'll come at crack of dawn
    And have our offerings ready for your grave.

[LYSISTRATA *and the* OLD WOMEN *go back inside the Akropolis, leaving the
                two half-choruses to face one another.*]

[PARABASIS: 614-705]

LEADER^M. Now's no time for idle dozing; every free man must
      look sharp.
    Let's remove our cloaks, my fellows: down to business
      straight away.

                              [*The* OLD MEN *remove their cloaks to dance.*]

OLD MEN.   I swear I'm on the scent   *Strophe*
                      Of bigger and more dangerous plots.
                Indeed, I get a whiff of Hippias's tyranny!*
                      My fear is that some Spartan males   620
                      Have rendezvoused with Kleisthenes:

They're now inciting god-forsaken women
To use their stealth and seize our revenues—
    The source of all my jury-pay!*   625

LEADER^M. I'm shocked, completely shocked. To think that *they*,
    the female sex,
  Should lecture all us citizens and prate about bronze shields,
  While seeking ways to make a truce between us and the
    Spartans—
  The Spartans, who deserve our trust no more than hungry
    wolves!*
  They've woven snares against the city; it's tyranny they're
    after.   630
  But *I* won't let them tyrannize, I'm always on my guard.
  Yes, I shall 'wear my sword' for ever 'beneath a myrtle
    branch',*
  And stand in arms by Aristogeiton in the market place.
        [*Raising their right arms, they move towards the women.*]
  I'll stand like this, in tight-knit rank, all poised to aim a
    blow
  Against the jaw of this decrepit, god-forsaken hag.

LEADER^W. *If* you do, you'll find your own face soon gets
    smashed into a pulp.
Now's the time, my aged friends, to place our cloaks down
    on the ground.
      [*The* WOMEN *remove their cloaks, matching the* OLD MEN'*s earlier*
                              action.]

WOMEN.   O citizens of Athens,   *Antistrophe*
           We have some useful things to say.
  Why should we not? I too was reared in splendour by the
                  city.   640
          At seven, I served Athena's cult,
          At ten, I ground the goddess's corn,
      And shed my dress to be a bear at Brauron;
    As basket-carrier too I served when young,
      Adorned in dried-fig necklace.*

LEADER^W. Now, who'll dispute my right to give the city good advice?
  It's true that I'm a woman, but suspend your prejudice
  And wait to see if I propose improvements to our plight.   650

Yes, I too make a contribution: *I* produce the men!
But as for you sad geriatrics, what do *you* provide?
For all the funds our grandpas earned by fighting Persian
     Wars*
You've squandered now, although you pay no taxes of your
     own.
Yet you're the ones who want the war, and make us risk
     extinction.
          [*Raising their boots, they approach the men, echoing 634–5.*]
I hope your grumbling's going to cease. But if you cause
     me trouble,
You'll find my leather boot will land a kick right on your
     jaw.

OLD MEN.   Isn't their behaviour scandalous?   *Strophe*
     My suspicion tells me that there's more than meets the
                                        eye.   660
Now's the time for every man with testicles to stand and fight.
[*Shedding their tunics*]
          Let's remove more clothes: a man should *smell*
          Well and truly virile—not stay all wrapped up.
               Rouse yourselves, white-footed soldiers,
                    We who in our prime
                    Went to Leipsydrion.*
               Now, yes now let's find our youth again,   670
          Sprout wings of strength, and slough off our old age.

LEADER^M. If anyone allows this lot to get a slight advantage,
     We'll never see a limit to their scheming artifice.
     Perhaps they'll use our funds to build a navy of their own,
     Then try to smash our ships to bits, like Artemisia did.*
     Or if they turn to cavalry, who'd give the knights a
          chance?
     For legs astride is *the* position every woman loves;
     They grip so hard and never slip. Recall the Amazons:*
     They rode on horseback into war, as Mikon's painting shows.
          [*They move threateningly, once more, towards the women.*]
     But what we need for all these women is sets of wooden
          stocks: 680
     We'd grab them by the neck like this, and lock them in for
          good!

WOMEN.   If you rouse me up to fever pitch,   *Antistrophe*
                Then you'll find my anger turns into a blazing sow.
    First of all I'll tear your hair, until you start to scream for help!
        [*Imitating*]
                Women, we should also shed more clothes,
                    Till we 'smell' of women with a rage to *bite*.   690
                        Now let anyone attack me!
                        If he does, he's finished:
                        He's had his final supper.
                Now my anger's boiling: watch your tongues,
                Or I'll play Aesop's beetle to your eagle's eggs.*

LEADER^W. Your threats don't make me flinch at all, while
        Lampito's alive,
    As well as that dear girl from Thebes, the fine Ismenia.*
    You'll find you've lost the power you had, your votes
        won't count a jot,
    Especially since you're hated by your neighbours all
        around.
    The other day I planned a feast to honour Hekate;   700
    I wanted to invite along a friend from down the road,
    A fine and sweet young thing she is—a Boiotian eel, in
        fact!*
    'She can't be sent,' the answer came, 'your state-decrees
        forbid it.'
        [*They move towards the men, mirroring the aggression of 680–1.*]
    Well, what will stop these mad decrees? There's one sure
        remedy:
    To take you by the leg, then throw you down and break
        your neck.

[*The parabasis complete, the half-choruses move aside. Some days have
now passed since the occupation.* LYSISTRATA *emerges anxiously from the
Akropolis. The following exchange burlesques the ethos of tragedy—until*
                                715.]

LEADER^W. O mistress of this deed, this mighty scheme,
    What brings you out of doors with such dark looks?
LYSISTRATA. The acts, the female thoughts of wicked women
    Oppress my spirit—and make me pace out here.
WOMEN [*wailing*]. Say more! Say more!   710
LYSISTRATA [*similarly*]. It's true, it's true.

LEADER^W. Reveal the horror! Disclose it to your friends.

LYSISTRATA. To speak is shameful; silence too is hard.

LEADER^W. Do not conceal the woe that now is ours.

LYSISTRATA [*plainly*]. Well, in a word—we're dying to be
    fucked!

WOMEN. Alas, O Zeus!

LYSISTRATA. Why call on Zeus? What difference can he make?
  I've lost the power to keep the women up here,
  Cut off from their husbands like this. They're slipping away.
  I caught the first one trying to open a hole   720
  Just down the slope, right next to Pan's old grotto.
  Another I caught wriggling down a pulley, no less.*
  What a way to desert! A third was ready to fly
  Astride a *dicky* bird, to find some Johnny;
  I caught her by the hair and pulled her back.
  There's no excuse beyond them, to make a chance
  To go back home. [*The door opens and* WOMAN^A *emerges furtively.*]
    Look, here's another one now!
  Hey you, why such a hurry?

WOMAN^A.   I must get home.
  I've left my woollen fabrics from Miletos;
  They're being ravaged by the moths.   730

LYSISTRATA.   The moths!
  Get back inside!

WOMAN^A.   I promise I'll come straight back,
  As soon as I've spread my things out on the bed.

LYSISTRATA. You'll spread out nothing! You certainly can't go
    home.

WOMAN^A. But surely my fabrics will be destroyed.

LYSISTRATA.   Hard luck!
                    [*A second woman appears.*]

WOMAN^B. Oh dear, oh dear! My poor old stalks of flax,
  They're waiting to be stripped.

LYSISTRATA.   Another one!
  [*Suggestively*] She wants to go and finger stalks of flax.
  Get back inside!

WOMAN^B.   But *please*, in Hekate's name!
  I'll be straight back when I've peeled the outside off.

LYSISTRATA. You'll peel off nothing! For if you make a start,   740
  Every other woman will want to do the same.

[*A third woman rushes out, clutching her belly.*]

WOMAN^C. O mistress Eileithya, stop the birth
   Until I get myself to sacred ground!

LYSISTRATA. What's all this guff?

WOMAN^C.   I'm almost giving birth!

LYSISTRATA. But I didn't see you pregnant *yesterday*.

WOMAN^C. I am today! Please send me home at once.
   I need a midwife, quickly.

LYSISTRATA [*examining her*].   What d'you mean?
   There's something hard in here.

WOMAN^C.   A baby boy.

LYSISTRATA [*tapping*]. By Aphrodite, it sounds as though you've got
   A bronze and hollow belly. I'll soon find out.   750

                                        [*Opens the dress.*]

   Oh how absurd! To use Athena's helmet*
   To claim you're pregnant!

WOMAN^C.   Listen—I *swear* I am!

LYSISTRATA. So why take *this*?

WOMAN^C.   In case of emergency.
   Suppose I had to give birth on the hill,
   [*Demonstrating*] I'd squat on this—the way that pigeons do.

LYSISTRATA. What cock and bull! A patent pack of lies.

                                        [*Removes the helmet.*]

   You'll stay with us for your helmet's family party.*

WOMAN^C. I just can't get a wink of sleep up here,
   Ever since I caught a glimpse of the guardian snake.*

WOMAN^B. And *I* can't sleep as well; it's all those owls.*   760
   They spend the whole night hooting endlessly.

LYSISTRATA. I beg you, please give up this silly twaddle.
   No doubt you miss your husbands. Don't you think
   That they miss *us*? I'm certain they must find
   Their nights unbearable. Stand firm, my friends:
   An oracle predicts that victory's ours,
   Provided we don't feud. [*producing a scroll*] Look, here it is.

WOMAN^C. Oh, tell us what it says.

LYSISTRATA.   Keep quiet, then.
   [*In solemn tones*] 'Should swallows huddle together, and stay
      in a single enclosure,   770
   Fleeing away from the hoopoes,* abstaining from genital
      contact,

Then will their sufferings cease, and the higher be turned
    into lower,
All by high-thundering Zeus—'
WOMAN^c [*interrupting*].   We women will now lie on
    top, then?
LYSISTRATA. '*Should* the time ever arrive when swallows will
    quarrel and flutter,
Flying away from the holiest shrine, then all will discover
No other bird in the sky loves debauchery more than this
    creature.'
WOMAN^c. I've never heard an oracle quite so clear!
LYSISTRATA. So let's not tire or give it up just yet.
Come back inside. It really would be shameful
For us, my dears, to let the oracle down.   780

[*All back inside. The two half-choruses take up their positions for an
exchange of songs.*]

OLD MEN.   Time to tell a little fable   *Strophe*
          Which I heard while still a child.
There lived a young man once, his name Melanion,*   785
      Who fled from marriage off into the wild,
          To live on mountain slopes.
          Now there he hunted hares
           By means of woven nets,   790
          And kept some sort of dog,
But never came back home, such was his hate.
So that's how much disgust he felt for *women*.
We share his feelings too—and his good sense!

[*The* OLD MEN *start to approach the* WOMEN; *the* LEADERS *speak, while the
other dancers perform matching actions.*]

LEADER^M. [*with mock affection*].
          May I have a kiss, old hag?
LEADER^W.   First, stop eating onions!
LEADER^M.   May I lift your legs*—and kick you?
LEADER^W.   What a bushy pubic region!*   800
LEADER^M.   Yes, Myronides was like this,
          With a black and bristling rump
          Which he showed to all his foes.
          And Phormio was just the same.*

WOMEN. I too want to tell a fable *Antistrophe*
Quite unlike Melanion's.
There lived a homeless drifter: Timon was his name.
He hid his face inside a thorny thicket, 810
His life was grim as death.
So Timon now, this fellow,
Went off and fed on hate,
And lived on mountain slopes.*
He called down curses on all evil men.
And that's how much he shared our hate for males;
To *women*, though, he stayed the best of friends. 820

[*The women approach the men, copying their action at 797 ff.*]

LEADER^W. Shall I thump you on the jaw?
LEADER^M [*ironically*].
Please don't. I'm quite afraid.
LEADER^W. What about a hefty kick?
LEADER^M. If you do, I'll see your pussy.
LEADER^W. What you'd see would not be hairy.
Old I may be, but you'd find
All is neatly trimmed and tidy:
I know how to use a lamp.*

[*A scream of alarm is heard.* LYSISTRATA, *soon followed by* MYRRHINE *and other women, appears on the roof of the stage-building, which represents the battlements of the Akropolis.*]

LYSISTRATA. Help! Help! Come over here at once, my women.
WOMAN. Is something wrong? What's all the shouting for? 830
LYSISTRATA. A man, a man! I can see him coming near.
[*Coyly*] He's stricken by Aphrodite's sacred needs!
O goddess, queen of Kypros, Kythera, Paphos,
Please keep us safe—but keep it up as well!
WOMAN. Where *is* this man you mean?
LYSISTRATA [*pointing*]. By Chloe's shrine.*
WOMAN. Oh yes, I see. Whoever could he be?
LYSISTRATA. Look, all of you. Does anyone know him?
MYRRHINE. Eeek!
I certainly do. It's Kinesias, my husband.
LYSISTRATA. It's *your* job, then, to roast him on a spit.
Seduce him—but withhold the love you offer. 840
And *dangle* everything—but keep our oath!

MYRRHINE. Of course. I'll get to work.

LYSISTRATA.   And I'll stay here
   To lend you help in working your seduction,
   And help you make him *sizzle*. The rest should leave.

[*Other women off, and* MYRRHINE *stands back. Enter* KINESIAS, *with erect phallus beneath his cloak and accompanied by a* SLAVE *carrying a* BABY.]

KINESIAS. I just can't take much more of this distension!
   The strain's as bad as torture on the wheel!*

LYSISTRATA [*aggressively*]. Who's there, inside the sentry line?

KINESIAS.   It's

   me.

LYSISTRATA. A man?

KINESIAS.   Of course a man.

LYSISTRATA.   Then clear right off!

KINESIAS. And who are *you* to eject me?

LYSISTRATA.   I'm the look-out.

KINESIAS. I beg you, by the gods, call out Myrrhine.   850

LYSISTRATA. Call out Myrrhine for *you*! But what's your name?

KINESIAS. Kinesias, from Paionidai*—her husband.

LYSISTRATA [*softening*]. O greetings, dear. Your name's familiar
      here:
   We've heard a lot about your reputation.
   Your wife forever has you on her *lips*.
   So when she takes an apple or an egg,*
   She says, 'For my Kinesias!'

KINESIAS.   Ye gods!

LYSISTRATA. She does, by Aphrodite! When we start
   Discussing our husbands' lives, then straight away
   Your wife claims you're a *man* without compare.   860

KINESIAS. Then call her out.

LYSISTRATA.   Well, are you willing to pay?

KINESIAS. I certainly am, if it's what you really want.
   [*Pointing to phallus*] Look what I've got: I'll happily make it
      yours.

LYSISTRATA. I'll go inside and call her out.

KINESIAS.   Be quick!
                                   [LYSISTRATA *goes inside.*]
   [*Sentimentally*] My life has been without a trace of joy
   Ever since my wife departed from the house.

I feel oppressed each time I come back home.
The whole place seems deserted. Even food
Gives me no pleasure at all. It's this erection!

[MYRRHINE *appears above, speaking back to* LYSISTRATA.]

MYRRHINE. I love, I love him so. But he doesn't want 870
  To be loved by me. So please don't call me out.
KINESIAS. My sweetie-pie Myrrhine, what are you doing?
  Please come down here.
MYRRHINE.   Down there? You must be joking.
KINESIAS. Not even when it's me who asks, Myrrhine?
MYRRHINE. You don't have any need to call me out.
KINESIAS. No *need*! I'm in excruciating pain!
MYRRHINE [*retreating*]. Goodbye.
KINESIAS [*desperately*].   No, please don't go. You can't
    ignore
Our *baby*. [*He touches the* BABY.] Call your mummy, little one.
BABY. Ma-ma, ma-ma, ma-ma.
KINESIAS [*to* MYRRHINE]. What's wrong? You don't feel sorry for
    your baby, 880
Who's not been washed or breastfed five whole days?
MYRRHINE. Of course I do. But its *father* couldn't care less.
KINESIAS. Don't wrangle, just come down for the baby's sake.
MYRRHINE. What it is to be a mother! I'd better go down.
                        [*She goes inside.*]
KINESIAS [*excited*]. I'm sure my wife looks younger than before;
  Her eyes have somehow got a softer look.
  And all this temper and this haughtiness,
  It only makes me want her all the more.

[MYRRHINE *appears from the Akropolis gates and goes to the* BABY.]

MYRRHINE. My little darling! What a wicked father you've got!
  Just let me kiss you, mummy's little darling. 890
                        [*She takes the* BABY.]
KINESIAS [*approaching*]. You're cruel! What's made you do these
    things and follow
These other women? You're just oppressing me
And feeling pain yourself.
MYRRHINE.   Just keep your hands off!
KINESIAS. And as for all our property in the house,
  You're letting it go to ruin.

MYRRHINE.   What's that to me?

KINESIAS. You mean you're not concerned if valuable wool
  Is damaged by the poultry?

MYRRHINE.   I'm certainly not.

KINESIAS [*coyly*]. You haven't practised Aphrodite's rites
  For such a long time. You really must come home.

MYRRHINE. No, never—unless you men will stop the war   900
  And make a peace.

KINESIAS.   Well, once it's been decided,
  Of course we will.

MYRRHINE [*sarcastically*].
                     Well, 'once it's been decided'
  I'll come back home. For now, I've sworn I won't.

KINESIAS [*desperately*]. It's been so long, please lie down here
  with me.*

MYRRHINE. I can't—and yet I won't deny I love you.

KINESIAS. You do? Then, lie down straight away, my Myrrhi!

MYRRHINE. How ludicrous! Right here in front of the baby?

KINESIAS. Of course not. [*He gives the* BABY *to the slave.*] Manes,*
    take the baby home.   [SLAVE *exits.*]
  So there: the baby's well and truly dealt with.
  You'll surely lie down now?   910

MYRRHINE.   But where, my dear,
  Could we *do* it?

KINESIAS [*looking around*]. Where? Inside Pan's grotto is fine.

MYRRHINE. But I'd be impure; I couldn't go back inside.

KINESIAS. Why not, if you washed in the spring, Klepsydra, first?

MYRRHINE. I've sworn an oath. You want me to perjure myself?

KINESIAS. May the punishment fall on *me*: forget your oath.

MYRRHINE. All right—but let me fetch a small bed.

KINESIAS.   No!
  The ground will do.

MYRRHINE.   You may be desperate,
  But it's out of the question to lie down on the ground.
                                        [*She goes inside.*]

KINESIAS. My wife still loves me: that's entirely clear.
                     [MYRRHINE *returns with a light bedframe.*]

MYRRHINE. Right, lie straight down; I'm taking my clothes off now.
                          [KINESIAS *gets onto the bed.*]   920
  But no—I'll tell you what: we need a mattress.

KINESIAS. A mattress! I certainly don't.

MYRRHINE. Of course you do:

The straps are hard.

KINESIAS [*trying to hold her back*].

But let me kiss you first.

MYRRHINE. Well there you are.

KINESIAS. Mmmmmmm! Now come back soon.

[MYRRHINE *goes inside again, and returns with a mattress.*]

MYRRHINE. Right, there's the mattress. Lie on it, while I strip.

But no—I'll tell you what: you need a pillow.

KINESIAS. I've everything I need!

MYRRHINE. Well *I* need more. [*In again.*]

KINESIAS. My prick's like Herakles—hungry but cheated of food!

MYRRHINE [*returning with pillows*]. Come on, lift up. That's

everything I want.

KINESIAS. It's more than enough! Please lie down now, my

treasure. 930

MYRRHINE. I'll just undo my bra—but don't forget,

You won't deceive me, will you, over peace.

KINESIAS. If I do, then damn my eyes!

MYRRHINE [*suddenly*]. You need a blanket.

KINESIAS. It's not a blanket I need—it's just a fuck!

MYRRHINE. Of course, you'll get your chance. I won't be long.

KINESIAS. This woman will finish me off, with all her bedding!

MYRRHINE [*returning with blanket*]. Just lift yourself.

KINESIAS [*pointing to phallus*]. Is *this* not

high enough?

MYRRHINE. Would you like some perfume?

KINESIAS. No, for god's sake, no!

MYRRHINE. You've got to have some, whether you want or not. [*In.*]

KINESIAS. I hope to heaven her perfume all gets spilt! 940

MYRRHINE [*returning with perfume*]. Now give me your hand and

rub that on yourself.

KINESIAS [*smelling*]. This perfume isn't suitable at all:

Its fragrance doesn't *penetrate* enough.

MYRRHINE. Oh dear, I've gone and brought the Rhodian scent.*

KINESIAS. No, look—it's fine. Forget it, please.

MYRRHINE. You're silly. [*In again.*]

KINESIAS. Damnation on the man who first made perfume!

MYRRHINE [*returning*]. Here, take another bottle.

KINESIAS.   I don't need two.

    Stop being heartless. Lie down, just forget
    The rest.

MYRRHINE.   I'll do exactly what you want.   [*Stepping backwards.*]
    I'm taking off my shoes. Remember, darling,   950
    Be sure you vote for peace.   [*She slips back into the Akropolis.*]

KINESIAS.   Of course I will.

        [*Looks round and realizes that* MYRRHINE *has gone.*]

    My wife's sadistic! Such a fierce tormentor!
    To stretch my skin so far, then disappear!

  [*Chanting like a lamenting hero*]

        What's left for me? What chance of a fuck?
        The loveliest woman has made me her dupe.
        How will I nurse this thing of mine?

  [*To the audience*]

        Where's Foxy the pimp?*
        Procure a wet-nurse for me!

LEADER^M [*with mock-tragic sympathy*].

        You're in a dreadful plight, poor wretch.
        Your life's been crushed by harsh deceit.   960
        I'm moved to pity you.
        What innards could withstand such woe?
        What kind of mind? What testicles?
        What groin, what haunch
        Could stand this strain
        Without an early-morning fuck?

KINESIAS.   O Zeus, what spasms of fresh pain!

LEADER^M.   All your afflictions are due alone
        To a loathsome, hateful female.

KINESIAS.   No—dear, delicious wife!   970

LEADER^M.   Delicious? *Vile*, she's vile.

KINESIAS.   You're right, she's vile. O Zeus, O Zeus,
        I pray that you may sweep her up
        With a mighty blast of hurricane
        And swing her, fling her through the air
        Before releasing her once more,
        And letting her fall to earth again
        Where, lo and behold, she'd find herself
        Astride my swollen cock!

[*As* KINESIAS *turns, enter a Spartan* HERALD,* *an erect phallus bulging beneath his cloak.*]

HERALD. Can you tell me where to find the Athenian Elders,*   980
Or the Council committee? I've got some news for them.
KINESIAS. And what are *you*? A man—or priapic god?*
HERALD. A herald, young man, from Sparta, by the Twins!
I've come to ask for peace negotiations.
KINESIAS [*pointing to the* HERALD's *phallus*]. I suppose that's why
you've brought a spear along!
HERALD [*embarrassed*]. I swear I've no such thing.
KINESIAS.   Why turn
away?
Then what's this bulge beneath your cloak? Perhaps
The journey's swollen your groin?
HERALD.   I swear, by Kastor,
This man's deranged!
KINESIAS.   You've got a hard on, liar!
HERALD. I swear I haven't. Stop babbling utter nonsense!   990
KINESIAS [*lifting the* HERALD's *cloak*].
And what's this here?
HERALD.   A Spartan message-stick.*
KINESIAS [*gesturing*]. Well if that's so, I've got one here myself!
You can speak the truth to one who understands.
Now, what's the situation back in Sparta?
HERALD. The whole of Sparta's up in—well, just *up*.
Our allies too. They've all got hards. It's dire.
KINESIAS. But what's the cause of all your tribulation?
A curse from Pan?
HERALD.   No, Lampito led the way,
And all the other Spartan women joined her.
They reached agreement when to hatch their plot,   1000
Then banned their husbands from their entrances.
KINESIAS. Can you cope?
HERALD.   Of course we can't. We walk bent over,
As though we're screening lamps, to keep them lit.
      [*He mimics the walk of a lamp-carrier, with his arms round his
                                                            phallus.*]
Our wives won't let us touch their bushy plants*
Until we all, by common accord, decide
To make a peace that binds the whole of Greece.

KINESIAS. This whole affair's one huge conspiracy
  By all our wives. At last, I understand!
  Look, hurry home and tell your countrymen
  To send ambassadors back with open mandate.   1010
  I'll ask the Council here to do the same:
  They can't refuse—I'll let them see my prick!
HERALD. I'll rush back home. An excellent suggestion.
                                   [*Both exit by opposite side entrances.*]

[*The two half-choruses once again confront one another, but this time the*
WOMEN'*s approach is different. As before, the dancers follow their*
                          LEADERS' *example.*]

LEADER^M. *Nowhere* will you find a beast that's quite as fierce as
    womankind.
  Fire itself is not so harsh. No leopardess is quite so bold.
LEADER^W. Now you understand my nature, will you still make
    war on me?
  Even though you've got the chance, you brute, to have
    me as a friend?
LEADER^M. Rest assured I'll never cease to execrate the female sex.
LEADER^W. *Should* you change your mind, the offer stands. But
    anyhow,
  Surely now you need some clothes on. What a funny sight
    you are!   1020
  Let me come and wrap you in the tunic which you shed
    before.*
                          [*She wraps his tunic round his shoulders.*]
LEADER^M. *That,* I must confess, was not an altogether hostile act.
  When I threw it off, my own hostility was goading me.
LEADER^W. Now you're looking somewhat manly; now you're
    not so ludicrous.
  If you weren't so petulant, I might consider helping you
  Take this insect from your eye: it's clearly causing irritation.
LEADER^M [*softening*]. Ah! so that's what made me angry. Here's
    a ring to help remove it.
  Scrape it out, and when you've got it, let me see just what
    it was.
  All along it's been so vexing, interfering with my sight.
LEADER^W. Count on me to show you kindness, all despite your
    peevishness.   1030

[*She touches his face, as though removing something from his eye.*]
Zeus above! I've never seen so large a gnat in someone's
    eye.
Take a look: you'll rarely find an insect species so immense.
LEADER^M [*sentimentally*]. Thanks for being so kind! That gnat
    was digging a well inside my eye:
Now it's out, my eyes are watering—tears are running
    down my cheeks.
LEADER^W. Never mind, I'll wipe them for you—even though
    you *are* a brute.
Here's a kiss too.
LEADER^M.   No, don't kiss me!
LEADER^W.   Yes I will, whatever
    you say.
LEADER^M. Oh confound you! How can I resist a woman's
    artfulness?
Now the truth of that old saying starts to dawn upon my
    brain:
'Life with women's too appalling; life without them's just
    the same.'
Time has come to make a truce, upon the understanding
    that   1040
Neither party does the other any harm in word or deed.
Let us join our ranks together, then embark upon a song.

[*The two half-choruses now, and for the rest of the play, amalgamate
themselves into a single* CHORUS *of twenty-four.*]

CHORUS.   First a message for our audience: *Strophe A*
               We do not propose to slander
                 Any Athenian citizen.
Everything we say and do will fill your minds with happy
                     thoughts,   1046-7
Since the city's present troubles hardly need to be increased.*
       Let the word be spread by every man and woman: 1050
            When a person's short of money,
      We have lots at home—yes, bags of it.
        If, one day, the war is over,*
        Those who sign for loans with me
          Never, ever need repay—
       Since they'll never see the cash!

We're about to wine and dine   *Strophe B*
Some Karystian visitors—
Actually, they're VIPs.   1060
Soup will start the menu off, and then we'll eat a sucking-pig:
Ready-roasted this is waiting, tender cuts of pork for all.
See you round at mine today, but don't be late:
Have a bath before you come;
Bring your children; feel no need to knock;
Just imagine that you're walking
Into your own property—
Since you'll find in any case   1070
Bolts are fastened on the door!

[*Enter, from a side entrance, long-haired Spartan* ENVOYS, *with erect phalluses beneath their cloaks.*]

LEADER. Here come some Spartan envoys now: their hairy faces
    prove it.*
And what a bulge around their thighs! It seems they're
    wearing tents.

Official greetings to you, men of Sparta,
Do tell us what has brought you here today.
SPARTAN. What need is there for lengthy explanation?
You see precisely what has brought us here.
LEADER. Phew! Yes, a tense condition you're suffering from!
I see that matters now are worse *inflamed*.
SPARTAN. Incredibly! The facts speak for themselves.   1080
We badly need an offer of terms for peace.

[*Enter Athenian* ENVOYS, *bent over by the same affliction and accompanied by* SLAVES.]

LEADER. Look over here. Some natives are approaching:
They're bending forwards just as wrestlers do,
To make their cloaks hang loosely from their groins.
[*Mock-medically*] I diagnose a case of grave tumescence!
ATHENIAN. We need to find Lysistrata at once.
[*Revealing his phallus*] The plight we're in is plain for all
    to see.
LEADER [*pointing*]. *This* sickness is a perfect match for *that*.
[*Diagnostically*] D'you find distension most acute at dawn?
ATHENIAN. Not half! We've been reduced to desperation!   1090

Unless a resolution's quickly found,
We'll be compelled to fuck old Kleisthenes.
LEADER. I'd recommend you promptly close your cloaks:
In case those herm-defacers notice you.*
ATHENIAN. My god! That's good advice.
SPARTAN.   Yes, by the Twins!
I quite agree. Let's fasten up our garb.
ATHENIAN [*regaining dignity*]. We're glad you've come; we've
been through misery here.
SPARTAN. We too, dear friend, have been in real distress.
To think of people seeing us all aroused!
ATHENIAN. Right, let's begin negotiations proper.   1100
What brings you here?
SPARTAN.   We've come to seek a truce,
As envoys.
ATHENIAN.   Good to hear! We want the same.
We ought to call Lysistrata at once.
There's no one else who knows the way to peace.
SPARTAN [*desperately*]. Be quick, or else I'll need to take a *man*!
ATHENIAN. But look, no need for us to call her out.
She must have heard; she's coming out here herself.

[*Enter* LYSISTRATA *from the Akropolis gates.*]

LEADER [*declaiming*]. Hail, boldest of the female sex. It's time
for you to be
Both fierce and gentle, fine and coarse, quite haughty yet
benign.
The foremost men in all of Greece are captured by your
spell: 1110
They're here, and have agreed that you should mediate
between them.
LYSISTRATA. The task will not be hard, provided that
Their passions are inflamed but lack deceit.
I'll soon find out. Call Reconciliation!*
[*Enter the naked* RECONCILIATION *from the Akropolis.*]
To start with, bring the Spartans here to me.
And don't adopt a rough or surly manner—
Not like our husbands' former boorishness—
But lead them in a feminine, friendly way.
If they refuse their hands, just grab their knobs.

[RECONCILIATION *ushers the Spartans to* LYSISTRATA's *side.*]
Now bring the Athenians over here as well:　　　　　　　1120
Take hold of any part they offer you.

[RECONCILIATION *does the same with the Athenians.*]
Envoys from Sparta, stand right by me here,
And you Athenians there. Now hear my speech.

[LYSISTRATA *begins solemnly, though the* ENVOYS *concentrate on* RECONCIL-
IATION's *anatomy.*]

'A woman I am, but not without sharp wits.'*
My own intelligence is quite robust,
And hearing words of wisdom from my father
Has added greatly to my education.
So now I wish to take both parties here
And reprimand you justly—you who share
A common ritual, just like men of kin,　　　　　　　　1130
At Olympia, Thermopylai, and Delphi*
(The list could be extended, if required),
Yet while barbarian armies lie nearby,*
You send Greek men and cities to destruction.

[*Formally.*] 'That is my first contention now complete.'*
ATHENIAN. Well, *my* destruction stems from this erection!
LYSISTRATA. Now, Spartans, I'll address myself to you.
Don't you remember how your countryman,
Perikleidas, came here once as suppliant?
At the altar, pale-faced in a scarlet cloak,　　　　　　1140
He begged for troops. For at that time Messene
Was in revolt, and Poseidon's earthquake shook.
Kimon went off, and with four thousand hoplites
He saved the whole of Sparta's territory.*
Yet in return for this Athenian help,
You ravage the very land which rescued you.*
ATHENIAN. That shows they're in the wrong, Lysistrata.
SPARTAN. We're in the wrong. [*Examining* RECONCILIATION] But
　　　what a magnificent arse!
LYSISTRATA [*turning*]. You think I've no reproof for *you*, Athenians?
Don't you remember how in turn the Spartans　　　　　1150
Came armed with spears, when you were dressed like slaves,
And slaughtered many Thessalian combatants
And many other friends of Hippias?*
It was they alone who forced the tyrants out,

And liberated you: they gave the people
The chance to wear once more the cloak of freedom.*
SPARTAN [*as before*]. I've never seen a more voluptuous woman.
ATHENIAN. Nor I, in all my life, a finer cunt.
LYSISTRATA. Why, then, when precedents like these exist,
　　D'you go to war and keep up all your hatred?　　　　1160
　　Why not be reconciled? Well, what's to stop it?

[*Both* SPARTAN *and* ATHENIAN *treat* RECONCILIATION's *anatomy as a map of Greece*.]

SPARTAN. Well, *we* want peace—provided we get back
　　This round, enclosed part.
LYSISTRATA.　　　　　　　Which?
SPARTAN.　　　　　　　　　　　The rear—of Pylos.
　　We've long requested it, and tried to probe.
ATHENIAN. Poseidon hear my oath, that's *not* for you!
LYSISTRATA. Please let them have it.
ATHENIAN.　　　　　　　　But where will *we* thrust
　　then?
LYSISTRATA. Demand another part in return for this.
ATHENIAN [*pointing between the legs*]. Let's see, then: we
　　demand that you return
　　This scrubby part—Echinous—and the orifice
　　Of the Malian gulf, as well as Megara's legs.*　　　1170
SPARTAN. No, by the Twins! Not *both* legs, my good friend.
LYSISTRATA. O let them! Don't start squabbling over legs.
ATHENIAN. I want to get this land and sow my seed.
SPARTAN. And I to spread manure out, by the Twins!
LYSISTRATA. You'll get your chance, once fully reconciled.
　　Now if you're sure, then formally decide
　　And go to get agreement from your allies.
ATHENIAN. Consult our allies! But look at our erections!
　　Both sets of allies surely won't dissent:
　　They'll want to fuck.　　　　　　　　　　　1180
SPARTAN.　　　　　I'm certain, by the Twins,
　　That goes for *ours*.
ATHENIAN.　　　　And for the Karystians too!
LYSISTRATA. Well said! In that case, purify yourselves,
　　In order that we wives may entertain you
　　With all the contents of our festive baskets.*

Inside you'll swear an oath to show good faith.
And then each one of you can take his wife
And go back home.

ATHENIAN.   Well, let's waste no more time.

SPARTAN. Lead on, Lysistrata!

ATHENIAN.   Without delay!

[LYSISTRATA *leads the* ENVOYS *into the Akropolis; their* SLAVES *sit down outside the gates. The* CHORUS *gathers for a dance which matches* 1043–71 *in form.*]

CHORUS   Woven blankets, finest mantles,   *Antistrophe A*
                   First-rate cloaks, gold jewellery—   1190
                   I'm prepared to lend the lot.
Never would I hesitate to lend you clothes for all your sons,
Or for when your daughter serves as basket-carrier to the state.*
              Everyone is welcome, I invite you all:
              Come and borrow from my house.
          Nothing need be locked away from you.
              All that's there is yours to take.   1200
                   Only, be prepared to find
                   (If my eyes aren't going blind)
                   That there's nothing left at all!*

                   Anyone who's short of food   *Antistrophe B*
              For his slaves and little children,
              Ought to get supplies from me.
Finest barley-grain is stored inside my house. The bread it makes
Swells to loaves of handsome size, all baked for you in quantity.
          All who live in penury should come to see me;   1210
              Bring your sacks and bags with you,
              They'll be filled up by a slave of mine.
                   On the other hand, be warned
                   Not to come too near my door:
                   If you do, you'll find yourself
                   Bitten by my vicious dog!

[*Enter, from the Akropolis,* ATHENIANS, *inebriated from their peace-celebrations and carrying torches.*]

ATHENIAN^A [*to door-keeper*]. Just open the door! You shouldn't
    be in the way.

[*To* SLAVES] Get up, you lot! Don't tell me I need to singe
Your hair with my torch? [*to audience*] A *vulgar* old routine:
I couldn't stoop to that.* Oh, if we must,
We'll bring ourselves to gratify your tastes.   1220
        [*He starts to threaten the* SLAVES *with his torch.*]
ATHENIAN^B [*entering*]. And we'll join in, though sharing your
    distaste.
[*To* SLAVES] Clear off! Or else you'll find your hair on fire!
ATHENIAN^A. Clear off! We want the delegates from Sparta
    To leave the celebration undisturbed.
ATHENIAN^B. My eyes have never seen a finer banquet.
    The Spartans were such sparkling company,
    While *we* are at our best when drinking wine.
ATHENIAN^A. Quite right. It doesn't suit us being sober.
    If I can get the Athenians to agree,
    All envoys will negotiate when drunk.*   1230
    At present, when we make a trip to Sparta,
    We're sober—so we're bent on causing trouble.
    We take no notice of their actual words,
    But keep detecting what they leave unsaid,
    And can't agree on what has taken place.
    Today, though, all was perfect harmony.
    If someone got the drinking-songs mixed up,
    We just applauded, swore that nothing was wrong.
    But, look, these slaves are coming back again.
    Clear out of here, before you get a whipping!   1240
ATHENIAN^B. Yes, just in time—the Spartans are coming out.

        [*Enter Spartan delegation from the Akropolis.*]

SPARTAN [*to piper*]. Come, take your blowers up, my merry
    friend.*
    I'd like to dance a Spartan jig and sing
    A song for our Athenian hosts and us.
ATHENIAN^A. Yes, take your puff-pipes, do; you really must.
    I always love to watch you Spartans dancing.

      [*Space is cleared for the* SPARTAN *to sing and dance.*]

SPARTAN.
        Send down, o goddess Memory, to your singer young
             The Muse, your daughter,
        Who remembers glorious deeds of both our peoples.   1250

How, first, at Artemision, Athenians
　　　Assailed like gods
　The Persian ships and won the day.*
　Remember, too, how Leonidas
　　Led Spartans whose ferocity
Was like wild boars with sharpened tusks:*
　Like boars their faces foamed with rage,
　　And foam ran down their limbs;
　The Persian hordes were numberless   1260
　　　As are the grains of sand.
O goddess of the wild and of the hunt,
　　Come down, O virgin Artemis,
　　Attend the peace we make
　And help preserve it evermore.
May friendship's bounty always overflow
　Upon our pact! And may we cease
　　To act like wily foxes!*   1270
　　Come down, come down,
　　　O virgin huntress!

[*During the music, the wives have emerged from the Akropolis, to be
reunited with their husbands.*]

ATHENIAN. Well, now our other business is complete,
　You Spartans can escort these women home.*
　Let every man and wife stand reunited,
　Then let us, for the sake of happiness,
　Perform a dance in honour of the gods
　And vow we'll never err again in future.

[*Husbands and wives move into pairs for the dance, as the* ATHENIAN
starts to sing.]

　Draw up the dance! Draw in the Graces.
　　　Invoke, first, Artemis!   1280
　　Invoke her brother-twin,
　Who leads the dance and brings us joy!
　　Invoke mount Nysa's god,*
　　Who revels with his maenads,
　　　His eyes aflame with light!
Invoke, too, Zeus, illuminated by his fiery bolt!
Invoke his queen and wife, fortune's bestower!
Invoke all other gods, whose memories

Will serve as witnesses for evermore
To the life of gentle-minded peace
Restored for us by the Kyprian goddess.   1290

Alalai! Cry for joy!
Lift up your legs to dance,
To dance for victory!
Shout out in ecstasy!

[*To* SPARTAN] Now sound your own new strain, to match
that song.

SPARTAN [*singing and dancing*].
Leaving the lovely summit of Taÿgetos,
Come Muse, O Spartan Muse, help us to call
In fitting fashion on Apollo, god of Amyklai,*
And on Athena, goddess of Bronze-House shrine,*
And on the noble Tyndaridai   1300
Who play beside Eurotas' banks.*
Come tread in time,
Tread lightly to the dance's step.
Let our singing honour Sparta,
Where the love of dance is nurtured
With the beat of stamping feet,
And where the girls, like colts,
Upon Eurotas' banks
Leap in rhythm, kicking up the dust   1310
Into the breeze,
And let their hair stream out
Like Bacchants swirling with their wands.*
At their head moves Leda's daughter,*
Sacred, charming leader of the dance.

LEADER. Come, bind your hair up neatly for a further dance.
Prepare
To move with feet like deer, and clap your hands to keep
in time.
Let's raise a song in honour of the warlike, Bronze-House
goddess.   1320-1
[*Exit all, dancing.*]

Assembly-Women

INTRODUCTION

Assembly-Women (*Ecclesiazousai*) was probably staged at one of the dramatic festivals of 393, or perhaps 392, and therefore belongs to the last few years of Aristophanes' career. A gap of some twelve years separates it from the next earliest of the surviving plays, *Frogs* of 405. Athens's eventual defeat in the Peloponnesian War, in 404, had been an event of such gravity as to form a kind of watershed in the city's history. It brought to an end a long period, stretching back as far as the Persian Wars of 490 and 480, during which Athens had risen to a position of both political and cultural pre-eminence in the Greek world. While defeat by Sparta did not prevent an eventual and gradual resurgence of Athenian buoyancy, even (to a degree) imperialism, it dented the city's power and confidence in ways which had lasting repercussions.[1] It may not be entirely fanciful to detect hints of a somewhat jaded Athenian mood in certain passages of *Assembly-Women*, such as Chremes' report that the Assembly voted for a female government on the grounds that it was the only thing 'still left untried' (456-7). It is, of course, now impossible for us to trace, and perhaps anyway unnecessary to posit, anything like a close connection between Athens's (relative) decline after the Peloponnesian War and the changing trends in comic drama which can be glimpsed in Aristophanes' last two extant plays, *Assembly-Women* and *Wealth*. The evolution of comedy must have been affected by many factors, some of them internal to its own theatrical traditions. But, whatever the reasons for change, these two late Aristophanic works do allow us to observe something of the developments in Attic comedy which ancient critics subsequently came to denote by the distinction between Old and Middle Comedy.

From our own distant perspective, to regard *Assembly-Women* as 'transitional' is inevitably a simplification of comedy's complex and partially unrecoverable theatrical history; but it is none the less a useful starting-point from which to interpret the work's dramatic character. Such a judgement involves a recognition that the play

---

[1] The change was reflected, both symbolically and psychologically, in the ceremonies of the Great Dionysia, where the traditional parading of allied tribute and of war orphans both ceased some time after 404 (see Isocrates, *On the Peace* 82).

contains much that continues the style and ethos of Aristophanes'
fifth-century comedies, yet diverges from them in ways which not
only are salient in themselves but also anticipate the type of entertainment that eventually became standard in the New Comedy of
Menander and other poets in the later fourth and third centuries.
Among the features reminiscent of earlier Aristophanic ways are
the larger-than-life dynamism of the protagonist, Praxagora; the
central fantasy of 'women on top' or women in power (gynaecocracy); the cross-dressing 'travesty' played out both by the women's
disguises in the first scene and by the embarrassed appearance of
Blepyros in his wife's dress; and the farcical tug-of-war between the
old Hags and the Girl for the sexual attentions of the Youth. But
alongside these features there are others which seem to represent a
new direction for the genre. Most obvious as signs of change are the
formal or structural differences from earlier norms. In particular,
the general contribution of the chorus to the play is greatly reduced,
partly by the scaling down of the parodos (here, paradoxically, an
exit not entrance, 285–311)[2] and the reduction of the agon to a
half-agon (571–709), but above all by the total disappearance of its
former parabasis and the lack of any integrated choral songs (as
opposed to interlude entertainments[3]) in the second half of the play.
Nor are these points of merely technical interest: they are symptoms
of a marked turn away from the theatrically mixed exuberance of
Old Comedy towards a more concentrated and narrowly focused
style of social drama.

As regards *Assembly-Women*'s affinities with earlier Aristophanic
plays, it is superficially tempting to see the link with *Lysistrata* as
especially important. Certainly it is hard to avoid the supposition
that the playwright had his earlier play actively in mind when com-
posing the later. In both cases we witness a female political conspiracy organized by a central and dominant woman who proves
capable not just of assuming 'masculine' qualities of intelligence
and determination, but even of outflanking the city's officials, leaders, and democratic structures. Praxagora—she who is 'active in
the Agora (i.e. in public life)'—duplicates some of the special attributes of Lysistrata, 'disperser of armies': in both comedies the hero-

---

[2] 478–503 mark a kind of second (and stricter) parodos.
[3] My translation diverges from Ussher's edition in accepting the manuscript evidence for choral interludes (the words and music for which may not have been supplied by the poet) after 729 and 876; see my note on the first of these passages.

ine is motivated by a desire to 'save' or 'rescue' the city, or even the whole of Greece;[4] and both are characterized by sharp differentiation from the mass of ordinary Athenian women. This heightening of the protagonist's stature is initially established by broadly similar opening scenes. In each case the women meet secretly, around or just before dawn, to hear the plans of their leader. Their apparent inability to live up to the standards asked of them, whether in terms of sexual discipline (*Lysistrata*) or quasi-male deportment and political behaviour (*Assembly-Women*), is a source of temporary despair for the heroine; but the latter's forcefulness and exhortation lead eventually to the female solidarity required for the reversal of power between the sexes which is subsequently and decisively enacted. Part of the significance, in both plays, of this contrast between the protagonist and the rest is that it sets up a comic paradox, and a kind of dialectic, between two ideas of women's nature. Collectively, it appears, women exhibit weaknesses and failings which make their political and social inferiority to men easy (from a male point of view) to understand. At the same time, they are led by individuals whose acumen, boldness, and powers of argument are too much for the male characters with whom they deal. Comedy exploits existing stereotypes of gender, but simultaneously insinuates that such ideas might not be the whole story.

While *Assembly-Women* involves a sort of creative engagement with, and reworking of, some of the comic materials earlier used in *Lysistrata*, there are also a number of rather telling differences between the two. The plot of *Lysistrata* was woven from a pair of motifs, a sex-strike and an occupation of the Akropolis, which owed something, in spirit at least, to mythical prototypes of female daring such as that of the Amazons. Yet the motivation of the women of that play is nothing other than a restoration of domestic, social, and political 'normality' through the making of peace. In *Assembly-Women*, on the other hand, we watch the establishment of a revolutionary gynaecocracy, the acquisition of power by women. And that gender-inversion on the political level is the launch pad for two further and comically utopian revolutions: first, *economic* communism, which involves abolition of private property, the creation of public dining halls (converted from the law courts, no longer needed once all live in harmony), and the satisfaction of everyone's material

---

[4] See *Lysistrata* 30, 342, 498–501, 525–9, *Assembly-Women* 107–8, 202.

needs; secondly, *sexual* communism, which removes the most fundamental social unit, the oikos or family (to be replaced by a new
sense of general kinship), and allows for widespread promiscuity.
Assembly-Women thus fulfils the characteristically comic impulses of
hedonism in an exceptionally populist and 'democratic' manner.[5]
That is one reason why Praxagora (and here a parallel with
Lysistrata reasserts itself), unlike several other Aristophanic protagonists, is not a glorious egotist but the leader of a scheme which
promises pleasure for all.

Although the components of Praxagora's scheme are more intricate and far-reaching than Lysistrata's, *Assembly-Women* is in one
sense a less original conception than the earlier play. This is because
its materials are to a considerable extent borrowed, with due adaptation and distortion, from contemporary intellectual ideas about
the relationship of male and female natures.[6] The most striking indication of this fact is the remarkable resemblance between parts of
Assembly-Women and Book 5 of Plato's *Republic*, in which arguments are advanced for the inclusion of female Guardians in the
government of the ideal state, as well as for the abolition of the family, with a consequent sexual communism, among the members of
this same ruling class.[7] There is much, both large and small, which
separates what is envisaged in the two works, especially the difference between a universal and a class-based system of communism.
But such divergences, as well as the vexed question of the date of
composition of the *Republic*, are less relevant for our purposes than
the basic point that Aristophanes can be seen to have made use of
speculations, arguments, and ideas which were explored by a number of Greek intellectuals in the later fifth and early fourth centuries.
In that sense, *Assembly-Women* is a comic adaptation of, though
scarcely a satire on, contemporary forms of radicalism and utopi-

[5] Praxagora specifically says that the principle of her sexual revolution will be
dēmotikē (631), i.e. favourable to the common people. Note also the notion that
women would never destroy democracy (452–3): in a somewhat paradoxical sense,
the play bears this out.

[6] Something similar may have been true of a comedy by Theopompos, *Female
Soldiers*, which may be some years earlier than *Assembly-Women*. Later in the fourth
century, two comic poets, Amphis and Alexis, wrote plays called *Rule by Women*
(*Gunaikokratia*).

[7] A summary of both connections and differences between Aristophanes' and
Plato's schemes, and further bibliography, can be found in my edition, *Plato: Republic*
5 (Warminster, 1993), 224–5; see ibid. 9–12 for other evidence on fifth- and fourth-
century ideas about both communist principles and female equality.

anism. Aristophanes could expect his audience, in particular, to have heard at least vaguely of reports of non-Greek societies in which sexual communism was supposedly practised, and he can therefore count on their appreciation of a plot which transplants this possibility with extravagant aplomb, alongside the utopian details of economic communism, to contemporary Athens itself.

The schemes which are implemented in *Assembly-Women* are explicitly designed for the benefit of all, even though the implicitly male point of view shared by playwright and audience leads at certain stages to a concentration on the enjoyment which men will derive from the new regime.[8] Yet the sole instigator and supreme controller of these schemes is an individual, Praxagora, who in that respect not only recalls the leadership qualities of Lysistrata but is more broadly reminiscent of the Aristophanic protagonists who conceive 'big ideas' and sweep aside all resistance to their accomplishment. Praxagora's distinction is highlighted, as we saw earlier, through contrast to the supposedly typical feminine foibles of the rest of the Athenian women who participate in her plot. It is also emphasized by the way in which she, first, outwits her puny husband, Blepyros, to his great embarrassment, and then comprehensively out-argues both him and Chremes in the half-agon (571 ff.). The power of rhetoric is always available to comic protagonists; it is vital to the self-confidence with which they manipulate the world for their own ends. The forceful use of rhetorical persuasion by women is, by the norms of Athenian culture, pointedly paradoxical, but perhaps not much more so than when we find it in the hands of (initially) decrepit old men like Dikaiopolis in *Acharnians* or Peisetairos in *Birds*. And persuasion is matched, in Praxagora's case, more formally than in Lysistrata's, by political-cum-military authority. She becomes known as the '(lady-)general', the generaless (246, 491, 500, 727, 835, 870).

But here we encounter an interesting point of tension in the comic design. For all her success and elevation, Praxagora does not appear on stage after line 724; she is absent, in other words, for

---

[8] It has often been noticed that women, though now in charge, will continue to be responsible for their traditional tasks of cooking (599–600) and clothes-making (654); in addition, 676 and 693 make it sound as though only the men will dine in the common messes. On the other hand, the sexual tug-of-war between Hags and Girl leaves us in no doubt that some women have much to gain from sexual communism!

approximately the last two-fifths of the play, and receives just a handful of brief mentions during that section (835, 1113, 1126, 1137). While no doubt is left about her continuing responsibility for the running of the city's new way of life, the dramatic focus shifts from her to a series of lesser characters; and in the finale it is the comparatively feeble Blepyros, not his wife Praxagora, who enjoys the limelight that is usually reserved for the protagonist. There is only one other surviving Aristophanic play in which the central character may not be on stage at, or very close to, the end, typically as the unambiguous centre of attention.[9] That other exception, perhaps not surprisingly, is *Lysistrata*. There, as in *Assembly-Women*, the heroine's absence at the end reflects the expansion of the dramatic celebration to embrace the mood of the entire city, or even, in *Lysistrata*, the whole of Greece. But in *Lysistrata* the protagonist is missing for only 130 lines,[10] and the play's coda brings to a joyous conclusion the peace negotiations which the heroine herself had commandingly conducted. In Praxagora's case, however, her much earlier 'fading' from the play seems to compromise the dramatic design in a more intrinsic way. It is as if Aristophanes' shaping of his comic conception becomes suspended somewhere between the protagonist-driven model typical of his fifth-century plays, and a more fluid scenario which opens out to explore the general consequences of the city's social and sexual communism. That would perhaps help to explain the rather hybrid nature of the ending, where the revelry usual in earlier plays makes a vestigial, slightly perfunctory appearance, but with Blepyros, not Praxagora, at its centre.

If there are thematic reasons for the reduction or curtailment of the main character's dominance in *Assembly-Women*, this feature of the play may none the less be indicative of a larger tendency in Middle Comedy, at least as represented by Aristophanes' last two plays, towards an interest in characters who are socially less idiosyncratic, more 'typical' and low-key in behaviour, than many of

---

[9] In *Knights* and *Women at the Thesmophoria* the protagonist shares attention with another character, Demos and Euripides respectively; something comparable occurs in *Frogs*, where it is not clear whether Dionysos reappears at 1500 ff. for Aischylos' triumphant departure from Hades.

[10] The manuscripts keep Lysistrata on for the whole finale, and speaking at 1271 ff. This is almost certainly incorrect: see J. Henderson, *Aristophanes Lysistrata* (Oxford, 1987), 214-15, who suggests (very speculatively) that Lysistrata may have appeared silently at the play's conclusion.

the figures of Old Comedy. That generalization is particularly apt for the ethos of several scenes which take place while Praxagora is off stage: first, the encounters between Blepyros and his Neighbour, and Blepyros and Chremes (311–477); later, the further scene with Chremes and the Neighbour (728–833). All three of these male characters are relatively bland and sluggish by the standards of earlier plays. The Neighbour's somewhat acrid cynicism is a mild feature compared to, say, the wilfulness of a Dikaiopolis or the imagination of a Peisetairos, and his selfishness seems merely grubby, unlike the energetic self-centredness of many earlier Aristophanic figures. Blepyros's initial embarrassment, when he is forced to come outside in his wife's dress (311 ff.), is a circumstance that only accentuates the dim-wittedness of which Praxagora has taken advantage. His ineffectual nature is foregrounded not only by his general inability to keep up with his younger wife, but also by the sexual taunts which he receives from her (522–6, 622): like the Neighbour (see 350), we are made to feel that it would not take much to cuckold such a character. Chremes, finally, is the most naïve and trusting of the three, and his willingness to obey the new law is set in counterpoint to the Neighbour's wily cautiousness about anything recently voted by the Assembly.

Unlike the mostly rural male figures of the earlier plays, all three of these characters are vaguely urban types, socially somewhat nondescript in background,[11] concerned in the first place about their personal or family affairs and in danger of being swept along by the currents of political change in the city. Their mentalities and the world they are used to inhabiting have a rough if caricatured plausibility about them, and they are certainly much closer to the realistic than the fantastic end of the Aristophanic spectrum. Their principal dramatic importance lies in the fact that they are used to create a comic tension between the revolutionary nature of Praxagora's economic communism and the ordinary social conditions on which she imposes it. The very mundaneness of these three men's characters offsets the extraordinary nature of the protagonist's reforms, and in a sense brings the utopianism of the latter back down to earth.

[11] There are hints that we are to think of them all as relatively poor, hence concerned about Assembly pay or jurors' pay: see 353, 382, 547–8, 562–3, 750. Chremes refers to selling grapes at 817, but status in Aristophanes cannot be read from isolated remarks, and there is nothing earlier in the play to stamp him as a 'countryman'.

Something similar can, with a significant qualification, be said about the longest scene which takes place without Praxagora, the sexual tug-of-war between the Hags and the Young Girl (877–1111). Here the implementation of a (supposedly) utopian revolution also comes up against the problems posed by the established inclinations of human nature. The idea that people could agree, in the interests of sharing out pleasure throughout the population, to a sexual communism which gives priority to the physically *undesirable* is a paradox which Aristophanes exposes to merciless and farcical treatment, suggesting, in the process, the comic potential for an 'infinite regress' in the appearance of increasingly ugly claimants on the new law. Unlike the scenes involving Blepyros, Chremes, and the Neighbour, there is no interplay here between the unheard-of and the socially humdrum, but rather the development of a 'cabaret' vignette which simultaneously burlesques the idealism of young love and the indecency of the brothel. It is no coincidence that Praxagora had earlier announced the abolition of slave-prostitutes, so as to increase the sexual opportunities of citizen women (718–24). Sexual communism turns the latter effectively into *free* prostitutes, whose competition for clients is regulated only by their degree of beauty or ugliness. And it was also Praxagora herself who had envisaged how the new set-up would operate, with women touting like whores for men on the streets and from their windows (693–701).[12]

The behaviour of the Hags, then, conjures up the ambience of a low brothel, but a brothel at which attendance is compulsory. The relationship between the Young Girl and her lover is set against this, but hardly as a model of pure eroticism. The girl herself almost seems to be soliciting for men too (885–7), even though she is waiting for one young man in particular; and her exchanges with the first Hag, including their saucy songs, involve sexually crude insults on both sides. At the same time, the girl apparently has to escape her mother's control in order to meet her young man (913), and the songs which she and her lover eventually sing are evocative less of a socially realistic meeting for respectable Athenian citizens than of a tryst between figures from traditional folk tales, ballads, or the

---

[12] Compare the images of would-be adulteresses, appearing alluringly at doors and windows, at *Peace* 979–85, *Women at the Thesmophoria* 797–9.

low-life sketches of sub-theatrical mimes.[13] We can safely go further and assert that a socially realistic assignation involving a respectable Athenian girl would have been virtually a contradiction in terms, given the usually tight chaperoning of adolescent females. Having posited a new and radical sexual freedom, Aristophanes' imagination finds it most comfortable to explore it from an angle whose comically polarized vision (predatory hags versus serenaded maiden) conveniently avoids the delicate sensitivities which would be touched by the abandonment of male control over the sexuality of wives and daughters.

Assembly-Women draws such comic energy as it has from a combination of two main ideas: the female usurpation of male roles and powers, and the reform of Athenian society along utopian-communist lines. But the success of Praxagora's plans seems to come about, as I have tried to suggest, *despite* rather than with the assistance of most of the play's other characters, and the upshot is a less than completely convincing new order. Moreover, the coherence of the heroine's own politics is undermined by multiple inconsistencies. In the 'rehearsal' for the Assembly meeting, Praxagora's speech contains a specific complaint about Athenian addiction to innovation, in the context of a claim that women can be relied on as natural 'conservatives' (214–28); yet unprecedentedly radical innovation is what she proceeds to introduce and to boast of.[14] Praxagora and the Chorus more than once grumble about contemporary reliance on Assembly pay (185–8, 206–8, 300–10), yet their own regime institutes a communism which goes much further than this in making 'free' economic provision for ordinary citizens. An existing politician like Euaion might be pictured, satirically, as taking his populism to the point of proposing special welfare, comprising clothes and beds, for the poor (408 ff.), but Praxagora makes this look trifling by her programme to guarantee the material needs of all. If Athens needs saving from contemporary democracy, Aristophanes invites his audience to contemplate a solution which

[13] Sexual impropriety was a favourite theme in the short sketches of vulgar characters and incidents which the Greeks called mime. The ethos of the young man's doorstep serenade at *Assembly-Women* 960 ff. can be glimpsed on comic vases such as that shown in R. Green and E. Handley, *Images of the Greek Theatre* (London, 1995), pl. 31 (with wreaths, torch, wine, and the girl at the window).

[14] 577–85 represents both Praxagora's boast about her own scheme, and, implicitly, the playwright's boast about his own comic inventiveness. Blepyros' response, 586–7, harks back to his wife's earlier criticisms of the city.

has the supremely populist merit of pleasuring everyone at no one's expense, and which stems from the only group of Athenians independent of existing political affiliations, women. A quintessential comic dream, we might well think—and comic in both its escape from, and its wry reminders of, the constraints of reality.

ASSEMBLY-WOMEN

Speaking Characters

PRAXAGORA: Athenian woman, wife of BLEPYROS, organizer of the women's plot

WOMAN^A
WOMAN^B } Athenian citizen-wives
WOMAN^C

BLEPYROS (*Blepúros*): elderly Athenian, husband of PRAXAGORA

NEIGHBOUR: of BLEPYROS'

CHREMES: elderly Athenian citizen

HERALD: female replacement for the city's male herald

GIRL: young unmarried Athenian

YOUTH: lover of the GIRL

HAG^A
HAG^B } three elderly Athenian women
HAG^C

SERVANT: female slave of PRAXAGORA'S

CHORUS: of Athenian wives, associates of PRAXAGORA'S

LEADER: of the CHORUS

Silent Characters

PARMENON: slave of CHREMES
SIKON: slave of CHREMES

[*The scene is an Athenian street shortly before dawn; the scene building contains at least two doors. From one of them enters a woman dressed in a man's cloak and shoes, carrying a lamp, walking-stick, and some garlands. After looking round impatiently, she starts to address the lamp in an exaggeratedly solemn, prayer-like manner.*]

PRAXAGORA. Bright eye of light that issues from my lamp,
　　Most beautiful design of clever minds!
　　Your birth, just like a god's, I celebrate,*
　　Since born upon a potter's turning wheel
　　Your nostrils shed a light fit for the sun.
　　[*Waving the lamp*] Send out the signs of fire that we agreed!
　　Yes, you alone are privy to our deeds,
　　When in our bedrooms all we women move
　　In Aphrodite's twists, and you stand near.
　　As bodies writhe and bend, your eye is there　　　　　　　10
　　To look on all; you never get removed.
　　You alone see what lies hidden between our thighs,
　　When shining there to singe our bushy hair.*
　　Or when for food or juice of grape we steal
　　Into the larder, you assist us well,
　　Yet never blab our secrets to the neighbours.*
　　So in return for this I'll let you share
　　The plans my friends decided at the Skira.

　　　　　　[*She looks around, and her tone now becomes much plainer.*]
　　Yet not a single woman's here on time.
　　It's getting close to dawn, and very soon　　　　　　　20
　　The Assembly starts: we need to find good seats
　　(To use a phrase Phyromachos made famous)*
　　And settle down without attracting notice.
　　What's held them up? Perhaps they can't get hold
　　Of the woollen beards they were told to bring along.
　　Or maybe creeping out in their husbands' cloaks
　　Proved difficult for them. Ah, now I see
　　A lamp approaching. I'd better stand back here,
　　In case a *man* is coming down the street!

　　　　[*Enter several more women dressed in men's clothes.*]

WOMANᴬ. We'd better get along: just now I heard　　　　　　30
　　The herald's voice crow out a second time.*
PRAXAGORA. I've been out of bed and waiting for you to come

Right through the night! Well, now's the time for me
To call my neighbour here with a tap on the door.

       [She scratches on one of the doors.]

Her husband mustn't be disturbed.

WOMAN^B *[emerging on tip-toe].*   I heard
Your fingers scratch as I fastened on my shoes.
I wasn't asleep, my dear, because my husband—
He comes, this man of mine, from Salamis—
Was *rowing* me all night on top of the bed.
I've only managed to get his cloak just now.   40

PRAXAGORA. Look, here come other women along the street:
They're friends of ours; I recognize their faces.

*[In what follows, various women arrive from both side entrances, either
alone or in small groups, all of them at least partially disguised as men.]*

WOMAN^A *[calling].* Well hurry up there! You know an oath was
 sworn
The last of us to arrive would pay a fine—
Nine litres of *wine*, and a bag of chickpeas too!

WOMAN^B. D'you see that woman there, old thingummy's wife?*
She's running in her husband's shoes.

WOMAN^A *[bitchily].*   But surely
With a husband like *him*, she can't be busy at night!

WOMAN^B. Can you see the publican's wife, that thirsty girl?
Is that a torch she's waving in her hand?   50

WOMAN^A. And *I* can see two other familiar faces,
And lots of other women approaching here:
It looks as though we're turning out in force.

WOMAN^C *[entering, to* PRAXAGORA*].* My dear, I had a simply
 dreadful time
Slipping out of the house. My husband coughed all night—
He'd had too many anchovies for supper.

PRAXAGORA. Right, all sit down. I'll start by asking you,
Now that I see that everyone's arrived:
Have you done what we decided at the Skira?

WOMAN^A *[showing off].* I certainly have! I've let my armpits grow 60
Far shaggier than a bush, as we agreed.
And whenever my husband went to the Agora,
I covered my body in oil and spent the day
Standing in the sun, to try to get a tan.*

WOMAN^B. Me too. I actually threw my razor out,
  To guarantee I'd grow *hirsute* all over
  And lose all trace of femininity!
PRAXAGORA. And have you got the beards which we agreed
  You'd all bring with you to the meeting here?
WOMAN^A [*producing one*]. Not half, by Hekate! Look at this
    beauty here.   70
WOMAN^B. And mine's a better beard than Epikrates'!*
PRAXAGORA. And the rest of you?
WOMAN^A.   They've got them: look they're
    nodding.
PRAXAGORA. I can see you've made the other preparations:
  You've all obtained your husbands' shoes and sticks
  As well as their cloaks, exactly as agreed.
WOMAN^A [*producing a huge stick*]. Yes, this is Lamios' stick I've
    brought along:
  I smuggled it out while *he* was fast asleep.
WOMAN^B. Are you sure it's Lamios' stick—not farting Lamia's?*
PRAXAGORA. With a stick that size, he only needs a jerkin
  Like that of Argos, hundred eyes and all,   80
  To make himself a terrifying cowherd!*
  But now we must proceed with preparations,
  Before the stars have vanished from the sky.
  The Assembly which we're ready to attend
  Will start its meeting once the dawn's arrived.
WOMAN^A. You're right; you must make sure we get the seats
  Below the platform, facing the Prytaneis.
WOMAN^B [*producing wool*]. I thought I'd bring these things along
    with me.
  I'll comb the wool while the meeting's filling up.
PRAXAGORA. 'Filling up', you silly thing!   90
WOMAN^A.   Of course; why not?
  I'd still be able to listen while combing wool.
  My children haven't a stitch of clothing to wear.
PRAXAGORA. You'd sit there combing wool? You're not supposed
  To give the men a glimpse of a woman's body!
  What a pretty mess we'll face if the meeting's full
  And one of us steps in with clothes hitched up,
  Revealing a large and hairy—Phormisios!*
  But if we're first to occupy our seats,

We won't be noticed wrapped up in our cloaks.
And once we've got our long beards fastened on,   100
No one will doubt our male identity.
Agyrrhios borrows his beard from Pronomos,*
So people forget he used to be a woman!
And now he dominates political life.
Well, *he*'s the reason why, this very day,
We've got to execute our daring deed,
In the hope that we can seize the city's affairs
And manage to change its fortunes for the better.
As things stand now, 'we've neither sails nor oars'.*
WOMAN^A [*mock-gravely*]. 'But how could female minds in
    congregation'*   110
Make public speakers?
PRAXAGORA.   Perfectly, you'll see!
  It's said the young men who get 'knocked' the most
  Grow up to make outstanding politicians.*
  Well, *we* possess this qualification too!
WOMAN^A. I'm not so sure. We badly lack experience.
PRAXAGORA. But that's precisely why we've gathered here,
  To rehearse our lines before the meeting starts.
  So get your beard attached without delay,
  And likewise anyone else who's practised speaking.
WOMAN^A. Aren't *all* we women experts with our tongues?   120
PRAXAGORA. Then fasten your beard, and turn into a man.
  I'll put these garlands aside, and fasten on
  My own beard too, in case I decide to speak.

                [*All the women start to attach false beards.*]
WOMAN^B. O look at us all, Praxagora darling, here!
  We really are a terribly funny sight.
PRAXAGORA. Why 'funny'?
WOMAN^B.   It's just as though you fastened beards
  On cuttle-fish that had a light brown grilling!*
PRAXAGORA [*playing the herald*]. Official purifier, carry the—cat.*
  Stand forward, people. Ariphrades, stop talking!*
  You, come to the front for a seat. Who wants to speak?   130
WOMAN^A. I do.
PRAXAGORA.   Then wear this garland for good luck.
WOMAN^A. All right.
PRAXAGORA.   Now speak.

WOMAN^A.   Before I've had a drink?
PRAXAGORA. A drink!
WOMAN^A.   That's why I put the garland on!*
PRAXAGORA. Away with you! You would have made this gaffe
  In the real Assembly.
WOMAN^A.   But surely they drink there too?
PRAXAGORA. Just listen to her!
WOMAN^A.   I swear they really do,
  And it's unmixed too!* Well, think of their *decisions*,
  The kind of things they bring themselves to do.
  Their craziness suggests inebriation!
  What's more, they're always pouring out libations—   140
  Why else, if not to help themselves to wine?
  And then they swap abuse just like real drunks,
  And the archers have to carry the worst ones out.*
PRAXAGORA. Well, *you* can sit back down! You're simply useless.
WOMAN^A. My god, I wish I'd never worn that beard!
  I feel so warm I'm going to die of thirst.
PRAXAGORA. Does another woman wish to speak.
WOMAN^B.   I do.
PRAXAGORA. Then put on a garland. We need to press ahead.
  Make sure you speak in a good deep masculine voice,
  While leaning stylishly upon your stick.   150
WOMAN^B [*like a male speaker*]. I would have preferred that one
    of the usual speakers
  Should put the case, while I stayed in my seat.
  As it is, I need to put my own proposal—
  That taverns mustn't fill their vats with water.
  That's my suggestion, by the two goddesses!*
PRAXAGORA. The two goddesses! Are you mad, you silly woman?
WOMAN^B. What's wrong? At least I didn't request a drink.
PRAXAGORA. That's true, but you swore an oath no *man* would
    use,
  Though the rest of your speech was quite a skilful piece.
WOMAN^B [*adjusting*]. By *Apollo*, so I did!   160
PRAXAGORA [*taking the garland*].   That's quite enough!
  I won't advance one step towards the Assembly,
  Unless we get our speeches polished up first.
WOMAN^B. Give me back the garland, then; I'll try again.
  I think I understand what's needed now.

[*In a man's voice*] I wish to state my view, assembled
   women—
PRAXAGORA. You address the men as 'women', you imbecile?
WOMAN^B [*pointing to audience*]. It's because of Epigonos there:*
   I glanced across
And thought that I was speaking just to women.
PRAXAGORA. I've had enough of you as well: sit down!
   You've left me with no choice. I'll take this garland   170
And speak myself. I call upon the gods
To send success and fortune to my plans.
[*Like a politician*] This land belongs to me as well as you,
My citizens. I'm vexed and grieved to see
The poor condition the city's affairs are in.
I notice how she always has as leaders
The rotten types. If one of them is decent
For one whole day, he's rotten then for ten!
If you switch to another, he'll only make things worse.
Now it's hard to give advice; you're easily piqued.   180
But you shy away from those who wish you well
And keep on turning to those who wish you ill.
There *was* a time when Assemblies hardly mattered,
And everyone was sure Agyrrhios
Was a rotten man. But now the Assembly counts;
Those who draw pay adore Agyrrhios;
While those who don't regard the rest as frauds
For living on their payment from the Assembly.*
WOMAN^A. You're absolutely right, by Aphrodite!
PRAXAGORA. An oath by *Aphrodite*, you silly thing?   190
   How fine that would have sounded in the Assembly!*
WOMAN^A. I wouldn't have said it there.
PRAXAGORA.   Then don't do now!
   [*Continuing*] And just remember how the people thought
The city would never survive without this league.*
But when it happened, they hated it so much
The one who proposed it disappeared for good.
Suppose we need to launch a fleet: the poor
Will vote for that, but not the rich or farmers.*
At one time Korinth and you feel mutual spite;
But soon you're back in one another's credit.*   200
'Argives are stupid'; 'Hieronymos is shrewd'.*

We caught a glimpse of peace, but Thrasyboulos
Is angry that his services aren't required.*
WOMAN^A. This man's astute!
PRAXAGORA.   Now *that's* the way to praise.
   [*Continuing her speech*] The blame for all these things is *yours*,
     the people's.
   You're happy to draw your pay from public funds,
   Yet each one thinks in terms of private gain
   While the common good just *reels*—like Aisimos.*
   Well, if you heed my words there's still some hope:
   I propose we hand the city's business over   210
   To *women*. After all, inside our homes
   They hold the purse strings tight and run our affairs.*
WOMAN^A [*applauding*]. Quite wonderful!
WOMAN^B.   Let's hear some more,
   good chap!
PRAXAGORA. Their traits are quite superior to ours,
   As I'll explain. For one thing, all of them
   Maintain traditional ways of dyeing wool;
   You'll never find them trying to *innovate*.
   Contrast that point with what the city does:
   If something old seems fine, it won't be kept
   But has to be replaced by novel schemes!*   220
   The women sit and cook—they always have.
   They carry things on their heads—they always have.
   They hold the Thesmophoria—always have.
   They bake their pastry cakes—they always have.
   They grind their husbands down—they always have.
   They keep adulterers hidden—they always have.
   They keep their secret rations—they always have.
   They like to drink pure wine—they always have.
   They really love being *fucked*—they always have.
   So let us, men of Athens, halt debate
   And hand the city over to the women.   230
   No need to ask what policies they'll have;
   Let's simply give them power, remembering this:
   As mothers of our sons they'll want to save
   The soldiers' lives, but also send them food
   To boost their rations when they're on campaign.
   A woman's good at finding new resources,

And once in power could never be deceived:
They're too familiar with deceit themselves!
I'll say no more. If my proposal's followed,
The future holds prosperity for all. 240

WOMAN^A [*in her normal voice*]. O darling Praxagora, what
    amazing speech!

Where on earth, my dear, did you learn rhetorical skills?

PRAXAGORA. In the war I lived with my husband on the Pnyx:*
    I used to listen to speakers and learn their words.

WOMAN^A. That explains how you made such a *terribly* clever
    speech.

We women will now elect you on the spot
To be our general* and carry out your plans.
[*Thinking*] But what if confounded Kephalos shouts abuse?*
What kind of response will you give him in the meeting?

PRAXAGORA. I'll tell him his mind's all muddled. 250

WOMAN^A.   But everyone
    Knows that already.

PRAXAGORA.   I'll say that he's *demented*!

WOMAN^A. They know that too.

PRAXAGORA.   Then I'll say his pottery
    Is dreadful stuff, and his politics are potty!

WOMAN^B. What if bleary Neokleides abuses you?

PRAXAGORA. I'll say to *him*: he should squint up a dog's
    backside!

WOMAN^B. And if the people start to shout and heckle?

PRAXAGORA. I'll love every minute—I'm used to being knocked!

WOMAN^A. But there's one more thing: supposing that the
    archers
    Try to drag you off, what then?

PRAXAGORA [*like a wrestler*].   I'll use my elbows,
    Like this: they'll never grab me round the waist! 260

LEADER. And if they lift you up, we'll shout 'lay off'!

WOMAN^A. I think we've planned for all contingencies.
The only thing we haven't discussed is how
We mustn't forget to vote by raising *hands*:
We're all so used to lifting up our legs!*

PRAXAGORA. That might prove problematic; we'd better vote
By keeping one arm free outside our cloaks.
[*To all*] Well, now we must be moving: hitch up your tunics,

And don't delay in putting on your shoes
Just like you've often seen your husbands do   270
When going off to the Assembly or to town.
Then, after taking care of all these things,
Tie on the beards you've brought. And when that's done,
And you've adjusted them to fit you well,
It's time to fasten up your husbands' cloaks
Which you smuggled from the house. Then take your sticks
And lean on them when walking down the road,
While singing an old-men's song, just like the ones
The country people sing.*

LEADER.   A good idea!
WOMAN^A. The rest of us should go ahead of them,   280
   To meet the country women who've gone straight there
   To the Pnyx.
PRAXAGORA.   Yes, hurry along! You know that those
   Who don't turn up at the Pnyx at the crack of dawn
   Must slink back home with nothing at all to show.*

[PRAXAGORA, WOMAN^A, WOMAN^B *make their way off by a side entrance. The
remaining women, now fully costumed in false beards and their husbands' clothes, take up formation as the* CHORUS.]

[PARODOS: 285-310]

LEADER. The time has come, my fellow men, for us to be
      proceeding.
   Yes, *men*'s the word, we must remember, despite our
      female nature.
   The danger that we face is great: suppose we were detected
   While in the act of secretly embarking on this venture!

[*They start to mimic, in movements and singing, a group of old
      countrymen on their way to the Assembly.*]

CHORUS.   Let's get to the Assembly, fellow men.   *Strophe* 290
             The Archon has made a threat:*
             Unless you're there at dawn,
             And can show the dust on your feet,
             With a breakfast of garlic inside you
             And a sour old look on your face,
             You *won't* get your three obols' pay.*

So come on now, old greybeards!
We really must rattle along.
Be sure keep pace with me.
You must be on your guard: 295
We can't afford wrong notes.
You must maintain the show.
And when we've got our tickets,*
Ensure we sit together,
To vote *en masse* for measures
Proposed by fellow women—
Oh dear, what *am* I saying?
I meant our fellow *men*!

Be sure to push aside these urban folk.   *Antistrophe*
Before, when the pay was low,
Just a single obol in fact,*   302
They'd sit there in the market,
By the garland-makers' stalls,
To gossip the whole day long.
But *now* they come crowding in here!
It was different in the old days.
Myronides was general,
A man of finest stock.
Then no one got a payment
For running the city's affairs.
No, people would come along
With a flask of wine and some bread,
Two onions and maybe three olives.
These days they come for the money:
Three *obols* is all they want.
They've turned this public service   310
Into a labourer's job!

[*As the song ends, the* CHORUS *exits by a side entrance. From a door in
the stage building emerges, sheepishly, a man wearing a woman's yellow
dress and shoes.*]

BLEPYROS. What's going on here? And where on earth's my wife?
No sign of her—and yet it's nearly dawn!
I've been lying awake for ages, needing a shit,
And trying to find my shoes and cloak in the dark.

I felt all over the bed without success,
While the dung-collector kept knocking at my door.*
That's why I grabbed this dress that belongs to my wife
As well as pulling on these boots of hers.
[*Looking round*] But where, oh where can I find a spot to
    shit? 320
Perhaps it doesn't matter during the night:
No one will see me shitting as early as this.
What a wretched fool I was to take a wife
At *my* great age. I deserve to be flogged as an ass!
My wife has surely left the house to do
Some mischief. Anyhow, time to ease myself.

[*He squats; another door opens, and a* NEIGHBOUR, *also dressed in women's
clothes, emerges with a lamp.*]

NEIGHBOUR. Who's over there? Blepyros from next door?
BLEPYROS. I'm afraid it's me all right.
NEIGHBOUR.   What's going on here?
You look all yellow; there must be something wrong.
[*Facetiously*] Don't say Kinesias has crapped on you? 330
BLEPYROS [*embarrassed*]. He certainly hasn't. I've had to come
    outside
Just wearing this yellow dress which belongs to my wife.
NEIGHBOUR. But where's your cloak?
BLEPYROS.   I haven't the faintest idea.
I looked but couldn't find it on the bed.
NEIGHBOUR. Then didn't you tell your wife to find it for you?
BLEPYROS. Some hope! She isn't inside the house at all.
She's managed to slip outside without my knowledge:
I'm afraid she must be up to some scheme or other.
NEIGHBOUR. Well I'll be blowed! Your experience matches mine
Precisely. *My* wife too has left the house 340
And taken with her the cloak that I was wearing.
I wouldn't mind, but she's taken my shoes as well!
At least, I couldn't locate them, search high and low.
BLEPYROS. By Dionysos! I had that problem too.
I couldn't find my shoes, but needed to shit,
So I had to shove my feet inside these boots.
Otherwise I would have soiled my nice clean blanket!
What's it all about? Don't tell me one of her friends

Has invited her to breakfast.

NEIGHBOUR.   That's what I think;

I can't believe she's doing anything *worse*.   350

[*Turning away*] That must be a rope you're excreting; I've
   got to go.

It's time to be off to attend the Assembly meeting—

That's *if* I can find my one and only cloak!

BLEPYROS. I'll do the same, once I've managed to ease myself.

At the moment there must be something causing a block.

NEIGHBOUR [*as he goes in*]. Surely not the blockade Thrasyboulos
   mentioned!*

BLEPYROS. By Dionysos! It's certainly clogging me up.

Well, what am I going to do? It isn't just

My present discomfort. But when I eat again,

I don't know how my shit will find an exit.   360

This door of mine's been well and truly bolted.

It's the work of some anonymous constipator!

[*To audience*] Could someone fetch a doctor? But which of
   them?

I need someone who's trained in anal matters.

What about Amynon? Wait: he might deny it.*

Let someone hurry and fetch Antisthenes.*

To judge by all the groans he makes, he knows

The meaning of an arse that needs to shit.

[*Melodramatically*] O goddess of childbirth, Eileithya! *Please*

Don't let me burst, don't keep me bolted up!   370

I don't want to be a comic chamber pot.*

[*Enter an elderly man along the street.*]

CHREMES. Eh you! What's up? You're surely not *shitting*?

BLEPYROS [*rising*].   What, *me*!

I'm certainly not: I can't. I'm just getting up.

CHREMES. Is that your wife's little dress I see you're wearing?

BLEPYROS. It's all I could lay my hands on in the dark.

But where have *you* just been?

CHREMES.   The Assembly meeting.

BLEPYROS. Is it over already?

CHREMES.   It finished right after dawn!

And Zeus above, you should have seen the mirth

At the number of people smeared by the crimson rope.*

BLEPYROS. Did you manage to get three obols?   380
CHREMES.   If only I had!
  I arrived too late, which makes me feel ashamed.
BLEPYROS. No need to feel that way—though you'll probably
    starve!
  But what was the problem?
CHREMES.   A massive crowd of people,
  Unprecedented hordes that filled the Pnyx.
  In fact, we started comparing them all to cobblers
  When we looked at them: it really beggared belief
  To see so many white faces in the Assembly.*
  That's why there were plenty of us who missed the pay.
BLEPYROS. So *if* I turned up now, I'd get no pay?
CHREMES. You wouldn't have got the pay if you'd even arrived   390
  At second cockcrow!
BLEPYROS [*like a tragic actor*].
                        O alack alas!
  'Antilochos, lament your fill for me
  And not for my—three obols. The loss is mine.'*
  [*Normally*] But what was happening there, to make this
    throng
  Turn up in such good time?
CHREMES.   The reason was
  The Prytaneis had put down on the agenda
  The city's preservation.* And straight away
  Bleary-eyed Neokleides sidled to the rostrum.
  You can just imagine the way the people shrieked
  'It's scandalous that *he* should dare to speak,   400
  When the subject is the city's preservation.
  He doesn't know how to preserve his own eyesight!'
  He looked around and shouted back to them:
  'Well, what else can I do?'
BLEPYROS [*like a heckler*].   'Just take some garlic,
  Mix it with fig juice, add the bitterest spurge,
  Then smear it on your eyelids in the evening!'*
  That's what I would have said if *I'd* been there.
CHREMES. Euaion, brilliant fellow, came up next,*
  Without a cloak—or so it seemed to *us*,
  But he himself insisted he had one on.   410
  His speech was full of populist arguments:

'You see that *I*'m in need of preservation;
I need some decent clothes. But none the less
I'll tell you how to save the whole of Athens.
If all the needy folk were given cloaks
By tailors every winter, then we'd find
That no one ever suffered from pleurisy.
And those who have no bed or blankets either,
Should wash and then go off to sleep the night
In the tanners' shops: any tanner who refuses,   420
In winter time, should pay a three-cloak fine.'

BLEPYROS. What excellent proposals! He would have found
   Unanimous support if he'd also said
   The grain-retailers ought to supply the poor
   With enough for everyone's dinner, or else be thrashed.
   In either case, Nausikydes would have paid!*

CHREMES. The next to speak was a young and handsome man.
   His face was white; he looked like Nikias.*
   He leapt to the rostrum to speak, and started to say
   We ought to hand the city over to *women*!   430
   Applause broke out at once, and cries of approval—
   From the horde of cobblers, that is;* the country folk
   Just rumbled dissent.

BLEPYROS.   And quite right too, by Zeus!

CHREMES. But they lacked the numbers. The speaker shouted on,
   With nothing but praise for women, but calling *you*
   Abusive names.

BLEPYROS.   Like what?

CHREMES.   He said, to start with,
   That you're a rogue—

BLEPYROS.   And *you*?

CHREMES.   Please let me finish.
   And also a thief.

BLEPYROS.   Just *me*?

CHREMES.   And furthermore
   An informer.*

BLEPYROS.   Just *me*?

CHREMES [*gesturing to the audience*].
           And all of them as well,
   Yes, every man jack.   440

BLEPYROS.   Who disagrees with *that*?

CHREMES. A woman's head, he said, is packed with sense
   And ideas for making money. He said they never
   Divulged their secrets from the Thesmophoria,
   While you and I keep leaking Council business.
BLEPYROS. I swear by Hermes, that's absolutely true!
CHREMES. He said our women lend each other things—
   Like clothes and precious jewels and drinking-cups—
   Informally, no witnesses involved,*
   Yet always give them back and never steal,
   While most of *us* just can't be trusted at all.   450
BLEPYROS. We even cheat in front of witnesses!
CHREMES. There are many other things he praised in women:
   They never inform, bring prosecutions, or try
   To destroy democracy. And much besides.
BLEPYROS. Well what was decided?
CHREMES.   To give the women power.
   The Assembly thought that this was the *only* thing
   Still left untried!
BLEPYROS [*amazed*]. It's been agreed?
CHREMES.   Indeed.
BLEPYROS. You mean that everything we males controlled
   Is now entrusted to women?
CHREMES.   Precisely so.
BLEPYROS. So it won't be me, but my wife, who goes to court?   460
CHREMES. And it won't be you, but your wife, who keeps the
   family.
BLEPYROS. So I won't have to get out of bed with a groan at
   dawn?
CHREMES. No, all these things are now the task of women,
   And *you* can stay in bed and fart at ease.
BLEPYROS. But I've got one fear for men as old as us:
   Suppose that when they hold the reins of power,
   The women resort to force to—
CHREMES.   Make us what?
BLEPYROS. To give them sex.
CHREMES.   And if we just can't manage?
BLEPYROS. They won't allow us breakfast.
CHREMES.   Then better comply,
   To guarantee we get both sex and breakfast!   470
BLEPYROS. *Compulsory* sex is a horrible thing!*

CHREMES [*grimly*].   But surely
   If it serves the city, each man must do his duty.
BLEPYROS. It goes to show there's truth in that old saying:
   No matter what foolish plans we make in Athens,
   It all turns out eventually for the best.*
CHREMES. I pray to Athena and all the gods it does!
   I must be off. Keep well!
BLEPYROS.   You too, Chremes.

[BLEPYROS *goes into his house and* CHREMES *off down the street. From the
   opposite direction the* CHORUS *returns from the Assembly.*]

CHORUS.   March on! Proceed!
     Let's check to see if any man is following in our tracks.
        Turn round and look!   480
     Pay close attention all the time; the rogues are every-
        where.
     Beware in case someone should creep behind and see
        we're women.

     While walking on, be sure to stamp the ground with
        both your feet.   *Strophe*
        What shame we all would have to face
     If ever our design should be exposed among our
        husbands.
        So stick together in close ranks,
        And keep your eyes peeled all around,
        This way and that, to left and right:
     We can't afford to see our plan collapse into disaster.
     Let's hurry on, there isn't far to go to reach the spot
     From which we first set out to make our way to the
        Assembly.   490
     Not far ahead you see the house belonging to our
        general,
     The woman who devised this plan that's won the
        citizens' votes.

     We've every reason, then, to start removing our
        disguise: *Antistrophe*
        We mustn't tarry, wearing beards,
     In case we're seen in full daylight and soon informed
        against.

So move across into the shade
Provided by this nearby wall,
And while still glancing round about
Convert yourselves, each one of you, into your female
state.
Act quickly now! I see our general coming down the
street.   500
She's on her way back home, of course, returning from
the Assembly.
Each one of us must hastily remove her shaggy beard:
These cheeks of ours have long been chafing under
this disguise.

[*The* CHORUS *members start to remove their beards and male clothes.*
Enter PRAXAGORA, *still dressed as a man.*]

PRAXAGORA. Well, women, what success we've had today!
Things have turned out exactly as we planned.
But now we must be quick, before we're seen:
Discard your cloaks, get rid of all men's shoes—
'Unloose the leather reins that draw so tight'.*
And, lastly, throw away your sticks. [*to* LEADER] But you,
Keep all these women in order, while I slip   510
Inside the house before my husband sees me,
And put this cloak back where I took it from,
As well as all the other things I borrowed.

LEADER [*pointing to beards, etc.*]. There! Everything is off. It's up
to you
To tell us how to implement your plans.
I know I've never met a shrewder woman.

PRAXAGORA. Don't leave; I'll need advice in carrying out
The office to which I've found myself elected.*
In the Assembly's noise and fury you proved your mettle.

[PRAXAGORA *approaches her house, but the door opens and* BLEPYROS
emerges. Soon afterwards, CHREMES *reappears down the street and starts*
to listen.]

BLEPYROS. Just *where* d'you think you've been, Praxagora?   520
PRAXAGORA. What's that to you?
BLEPYROS.   What's that to me? How cool!
PRAXAGORA. You surely won't accuse me of having a lover.
BLEPYROS. Not *one*, perhaps.

PRAXAGORA.   All right, you're free to check.

BLEPYROS. But how?

PRAXAGORA.   Why, smell my hair for trace of scent.

BLEPYROS. What? Can't a woman be fucked without some scent?*

PRAXAGORA. No, *I* can't—more's the pity.

BLEPYROS.   What made you, then,
   Slip out at dawn, and take my cloak with you?

PRAXAGORA. I was sent for, in the night, by a friend of mine
   Who was giving birth.

BLEPYROS.   Then why not tell me first,
   Before you left?   530

PRAXAGORA.   Instead of showing concern
   For the suffering mother?

BLEPYROS.   But *after* informing me.
   There's something suspicious here.

PRAXAGORA.   I swear there isn't.
   I left without ado: the woman's message
   Requested me to go without delay.

BLEPYROS. Then why not simply wear your very own cloak?
   You stripped off mine instead, left yours behind,
   And abandoned me to lie there like a corpse—
   You only forgot the wreath and funeral flask!*

PRAXAGORA. The air was chilly; you know I'm small and weak:
   I wrapped myself inside your cloak for warmth.   540
   But *you*, my husband, were lying all warm and snug
   When I left the house.

BLEPYROS.   And why did you need to take
   My *shoes* with you? And what about my *stick*?

PRAXAGORA. I thought I'd scare off muggers who'd steal the
      cloak.*
   I wanted to imitate *you* by stamping my feet
   And striking the ground with the stick as I walked along.

BLEPYROS. I suppose you know you've lost a bag of wheat,
   Which I could have bought with my pay for Assembly
      attendance?

PRAXAGORA. Never mind! The news is good—a baby boy!

BLEPYROS [*obtusely*]. The Assembly's had a baby?   550

PRAXAGORA.   The woman, of
   course!
   [*Casually*] But *has* there been an Assembly?

BLEPYROS.   There certainly
   has:
I mentioned it yesterday.
PRAXAGORA.   Oh, now I remember.
BLEPYROS. So you haven't heard the decision?*
PRAXAGORA.   No, certainly not.
BLEPYROS. Prepare yourself to hear some special news:
   They say the city's been handed over to *women*!
PRAXAGORA. To weave its clothes?*
BLEPYROS.   To be in charge!
PRAXAGORA.   Of what?
BLEPYROS. Of every single part of the city's existence.
PRAXAGORA. By Aphrodite! That mean's the city's future
   Is a happy one.
BLEPYROS.   Why's that?
PRAXAGORA.   For many reasons.
   No longer will people be free to harm the city.   560
   We'll put a stop to bribing of witnesses,
   As well as to informing—
BLEPYROS.   In heaven's name,
   Don't do this: don't deprive me of my living!*
CHREMES [*intervening*]. You really should allow your wife to
   speak.
PRAXAGORA. There'll be an end to mugging; an end to envy;
   An end to paupers walking round half-naked;
   An end to abuse; an end to harrying debtors.
CHREMES. Immense improvements, surely—if she's right!
PRAXAGORA [*to* CHREMES]. I'll give you proof. You'll soon be on my
   side,
   [*Pointing to* BLEPYROS] And even *he* won't contradict my
   claim.   570

[HALF-AGON: 571-709]

CHORUS.
   Now concentrate your mind! Rouse philosophical thoughts!*
      Your female friends depend on your intelligence.
        Amid prosperity that's shared by all
        Your eloquent tongue will glorify
   The citizens to whom you bring such countless benefits.

It's now or never—show your worth!
The city needs a brilliant new invention.
Make sure your plans
Are quite original in word and deed.
(This audience hates to see old stuff served up again!) 580

LEADER. Proceed at once, and get to grips explaining your
    intentions:
  To keep things moving quickly always pleases these
    spectators.
PRAXAGORA. Well now, I have no doubts about the merits of my
    case.
  But will the audience, that's my fear, accept my
    innovations,
  Instead of sticking with the old, familiar repertoire?
BLEPYROS. As far as innovation goes, you needn't be afraid:
  There's nothing we like better than abandoning tradition!*
PRAXAGORA. In that case, please don't interrupt or start to
    shout and heckle,
  Until you understand my scheme and hear it from my lips.
  My plan is that all property from now on must be *shared*.* 590
  We must abolish rich and poor, with one man farming acres
  While down the road another lacks enough land for his
    grave.
  Or one man owning many slaves, another owning none.
  I now decree that everyone must share the same resources.
BLEPYROS [*butting in*]. But *how* be 'shared'?
PRAXAGORA [*exasperated*].   You'd even be the
    first to eat the dung!
BLEPYROS. Well, isn't dung a thing we share?
PRAXAGORA.   So what? Don't
    interrupt!
  I was just about to tell you that the city's land and silver,
  As well as private property, will now belong to all.
  We women will use these common goods to feed the
    population:
  For *we'll* control expenditure, and budget circumspectly. 600
CHREMES. Suppose that someone has no land, but hidden
    property—
  Say, gold and silver coins?

PRAXAGORA.   He'll need to add them to the pool.
  He won't escape, unless he lies.
BLEPYROS.   But *that*'s what makes him
    wealthy!
PRAXAGORA. But even if he does, he'll be no better off.
CHREMES.   Why not?
PRAXAGORA. No one will suffer poverty. They'll all have quite
    enough
  Of bread and fish and cakes and clothes and wine and
    wreaths and chickpeas.
  So what's the use of hoarding wealth? That's what I'd like
    to know.
CHREMES. But as things stand it's *wealthy* folk who steal to
    boost their riches.
PRAXAGORA. That used to be the case, my friend, when previous
    laws applied.
  But once our lives are communist, withholding wealth
    won't pay.   610
BLEPYROS. Suppose that someone sees a girl, and wants to—
    poke her fire:
  He'd pay for her from private wealth, then once he'd slept
    with her
  He'd still enjoy the common goods.
PRAXAGORA.   But *sex* will now be free!
  For women too will all be shared—yes, both for making
    love,
  And also bearing anyone's child.
BLEPYROS.   But surely men will turn
  Exclusively to the prettiest ones; it's those they'll want to
    bang?
PRAXAGORA. But all the less attractive ones will sit beside the
    beauties.
  Before a man can take his pick, he'll lay a vile one *first*.
BLEPYROS. But once we older men have had it off with ugly
    women,
  Our cocks will surely start to droop before we reach the
    others?   620
PRAXAGORA. I don't suppose they'll fight for *you*; don't worry
    yourself at all.
BLEPYROS. Why not?

PRAXAGORA. Because such impotence is just your normal state!

BLEPYROS. Your plan makes sense on *women*'s side. You've made entirely sure

There won't be any holes unfilled. But what about the *men*?

Won't women shun the hideous ones, and go for handsome types?

PRAXAGORA. The lousy men will have to track the handsome ones each evening;

They'll watch their movements everywhere and keep them in their sights.

The women won't have access to the tall, attractive men

Until they've given pleasure to the little, ugly fellows.

BLEPYROS. Lysikrates' revolting nose will start to look quite pleased then! 630

PRAXAGORA. That's right. What's more, my plans are meant to favour common people.

They'll have a chance to cock a snook at swanks with signet-rings,

By getting in first and telling them, 'Please step aside and wait there:

I'll let you have your turn when *I've* completed all my business.'

CHREMES. But once we live as you describe, how ever will each person

Know who his children are?

PRAXAGORA. Why care? The children will consider

All men who've reached a certain age as being their own fathers.

BLEPYROS. That means that when they don't know who their father is, they'll throttle

Not one but all old men. As now they throttle their *actual* fathers!*

If parentage becomes unknown, they'll shit on all old men! 640

PRAXAGORA. But witnesses won't let it pass. Before, they didn't bother

When seeing others beaten up; but now, each time it happens,

They'll intervene in case it proves the victim's their own father.

BLEPYROS. The general plan is fine, no doubt. But what if
    Epikouros
  Or Leukolophos should come to me and call me 'Dad'? How
    dreadful!*
PRAXAGORA. I can think of something worse than that.
BLEPYROS.   Well tell
    me what it is.
PRAXAGORA. If Aristyllos *kisses* you and claims you as his father.
BLEPYROS. He'd get a thrashing, if he tried!
PRAXAGORA.   And *you* would stink
    of something!
  But *he* was born before our new decree came into force;
  You needn't fear his kiss at all.   650
BLEPYROS.   That's just as well for him!
CHREMES [*intervening*]. Now, who will work the land?
PRAXAGORA.   The slaves.
    And *your* concern will be
  To wait for evening shadows to fall, and then slip off to
    dinner.
CHREMES. And what about acquiring clothes? Another urgent
    question.
PRAXAGORA. You'll keep the ones you've got for now; we
    women will weave you more.*
CHREMES. I've one more question. What's the rule for fines
    incurred in law courts?
  How will they pay? It can't be right to use the common
    funds.
PRAXAGORA. There won't be any *need* for courts.
BLEPYROS.   You'll soon
    regret that statement!
CHREMES. That's my view too.
PRAXAGORA [*to* BLEPYROS].   Then tell me why the courts will
    still be needed.
BLEPYROS. For lots of reasons, patently! Let's take just one
    example:
  To deal with debtors who don't pay up.   660
PRAXAGORA.   And how will
    anyone *lend*,
  When all belongs to a common fund? It's clear he'd be a thief.
CHREMES. An excellent response!

BLEPYROS. But something else I'd like to
know:
What penalty will be imposed in cases of assault,
When after-dinner brawls occur. Let's hear you answer *that*.

PRAXAGORA. They'll forfeit some of the food they eat. When
punished in this way,
The price their belly pays will make them act with more
restraint.

BLEPYROS. Will no one ever turn to theft?

PRAXAGORA. What for, when all is
shared?

BLEPYROS. Won't muggers still steal cloaks by night?

PRAXAGORA. Not if you
sleep at home!
Such crimes will vanish from our streets, since none will
suffer want.
And if a mugging does occur, what reason for resistance?   670
The common fund will soon provide another, better cloak.

BLEPYROS. Won't people gamble still with dice?

PRAXAGORA. What *stake* would
be involved?

BLEPYROS. What style of life will you offer us?

PRAXAGORA. A life that's shared
by all.
I'll turn the city into one great dwelling-house for all;
You'll come and go just as you please.

BLEPYROS. And where will dinner
be served?

PRAXAGORA. I'll soon convert the law courts and the stoas to
this purpose.

BLEPYROS. But what will you use the podium for?*

PRAXAGORA. For bowls of
wine and water.
I'll also make the boys stand there for poetry recitals.
They'll sing the praises of the brave, and mention any
cowards.*
The cowards then will feel such shame they'll never dine.   680

BLEPYROS. How
splendid!
But where will you put the allotment racks?*

PRAXAGORA.   Where else? In
   the Agora.
They'll stand beside Harmodios,* dispensing supper tickets,
Till everyone is satisfied and knows his place for dinner.
The herald's voice will tell them which locations match
   their letters:
For some the Royal Portico, the one next door for others;
And others still will find themselves in the Barley-Market
   Stoa.*

BLEPYROS. It sounds as though they'll hardly starve!

PRAXAGORA.   They'll all
   receive their dinner.

BLEPYROS. But anyone who draws a blank will surely be ejected.

PRAXAGORA.
       Such things will not occur with us.
       We'll guarantee rich fare for all,   690
       So everyone, once nicely drunk,
       Will leave in a mood of revelry.
       And as they walk along the streets,
       The women will solicit them
       And call, 'Come here, inside this house.
       We've got a ripe young girl in here.'
       'No, here instead!' another shouts,
       As she leans her head from a window above.
       'I've a girl up here who's gorgeous and white;*
       But before you can have her you've got to sleep   700
       In *my* bed first!'
       Meanwhile all handsome adolescents
       Will be observed by ugly men
       Who'll say to them: 'Just hold on there!
       You're wasting your time if you rush ahead.
       The law now states explicitly
       It's the ugly ones who get first fuck.
       You'll have to stand outside and wait:
       Perhaps you ought to pass the time
       With a double-handed wank.'

So, are you both quite satisfied?   710

BLEPYROS.   Not half!

PRAXAGORA. Well, I'm now needed in the Agora,
   To receive all property that's brought along;

I'll take a fine-voiced heraldess with me.
I hold elected office, so that's my task;
And I've got to organize communal meals,
So *you* can have your first grand feast today.
BLEPYROS [*incredulous*]. The feasts will start immediately?
PRAXAGORA.   Of course!
   My second task is to ban slave prostitutes,
   Yes, all of them.
BLEPYROS.   What for?
PRAXAGORA.   It's surely clear.
   [*Pointing to* CHORUS] So *they* can have the best young men
      themselves.   720
   We don't want slave-girls looking beautiful
   And stealing sex away from free-born women.
   They're allowed to sleep with only fellow-slaves,
   And must let their pussies keep their shaggy state.*
                                          [*Starts to leave.*]
BLEPYROS. I think I ought to come along with you.
   I'd like to attract attention and hear men say:
   'Look, there's our lady-general's splendid husband.'
                        [*Follows off* PRAXAGORA *by a side entrance.*]
CHREMES. And I'll prepare my goods for the Agora:
   I need to check what property I've got.   [*Into house.*]

[CHORAL INTERLUDE]*

[CHREMES *reappears from his house: helped by slaves, he brings out objects
which he arranges like members of a ritual procession at the Panathenaic
festival.*]*

CHREMES. Come out here, sieve, and see you look your best;   730
   I've picked you out from all of my belongings
   As basket-carrier,* since your face is powdered
   By all those bags of flour you've polished off.
   Where's the girl who'll carry the stool?* You, cooking-pot,
   Come out. My word, you're black! You must have boiled
   The stuff with which Lysikrates dyes his hair.
   [*Putting the pot behind the sieve*] Stand next to her. And
      you come here, young maid.
   Now, you there, water-carrier, bring that pitcher;*
   Stand over here. And you, young girl musician,*

Come out: your singing's often woken me up   740
To send me out at dawn to Assembly meetings.
Come forward next, the one who carries the bowl.
Bring honeycombs, put olive branches there.*
Bring out the tripods too and flask of oil.
You can let the riff-raff come and join us now.*

[*Slaves bring out further miscellaneous pots and pans. As* CHREMES
organizes everything, the NEIGHBOUR *reappears along the street.*]

NEIGHBOUR [*musing to himself*]. To think of handing in my own
    belongings!
  It would ruin me! What an idiot I would be!
  It's out of the question, until I've found out more
  And watched the situation very closely.
  I've sweated and stinted to get my livelihood: 750
  I don't intend to lose it, like a fool,
  Before I learn precisely what's afoot.
  [*Noticing* CHREMES] You there! What's all this household stuff
    you've got?
  Have you brought it out because you're moving house,
  Or to pledge against a loan?
CHREMES.   No, certainly not.
NEIGHBOUR. Then why's it all lined neatly up like this?
  Don't tell me you're sending it off to public auction?
CHREMES. I'm about to carry it off to the Agora
  And hand it in to the city. That's now the law.
NEIGHBOUR. To hand it in?   760
CHREMES.   That's right.
NEIGHBOUR.   You've sealed your fate!
  You'll ruin yourself.
CHREMES.   'How come?
NEIGHBOUR.   How come? It's clear!
CHREMES. You mean I shouldn't carry out the law?
NEIGHBOUR. What law, you fool?
CHREMES.   The one that's just been passed.
NEIGHBOUR. That's just been passed! You really are quite crazy.
CHREMES. I'm crazy?
NEIGHBOUR.   Of course. There can't be anyone else
  Who's so naïve.
CHREMES.   For doing what I'm told?

NEIGHBOUR. You think that *sensible* people do what they're told?
CHREMES. I certainly do.
NEIGHBOUR.   No, only imbeciles!
CHREMES. You mean you won't give in your things?
NEIGHBOUR.   I'll wait,
　Until I see just what the majority do.   770
CHREMES. They're surely getting ready to take their goods
　And give them in.
NEIGHBOUR.   I'll believe it when I see it!
CHREMES. You can hear them saying so in the streets.
NEIGHBOUR [*ironically*].   No doubt!
CHREMES. They're vowing they'll take it all along.
NEIGHBOUR.   No doubt!
CHREMES. I hate your sceptical tone of voice.
NEIGHBOUR.   No doubt!
CHREMES. I'd like to see you blasted then!
NEIGHBOUR.   No doubt!
　D'you think that anyone sane will bring his goods?
　That's not the Athenian way. We only like
　To *take*, not give. In fact, we're like the gods.
　You only need to look at their statues' hands: 780
　For while we're praying they'll give us favourable gifts,
　They stand there stretching out an upturned hand
　And wait to *receive* a gift, not give us one.*
CHREMES [*turning away*]. Look, fellow, please leave me alone;
　　I've lots to do.
　I've got to fasten these things. [*to slave*] Now where's my
　　strap?
NEIGHBOUR [*incredulous*]. You're actually going to take them?
CHREMES.   Of
　　course I am!
　I'm tying these tripods, look.
NEIGHBOUR.   Such lunacy!
　Instead of holding back and waiting to see
　What others do, and only then—
CHREMES.   Do what?
NEIGHBOUR. Wait a little longer still, and play for time.   790
CHREMES. But what's the point?
NEIGHBOUR.   Suppose an earthquake happened,
　Or a lightning flash, or a cat went rushing past:*

They'd soon stop handing things in, you dunderhead!

CHREMES [*unmoved*]. A fine old mess I'd be in, if I couldn't find
   Any space to put my things!

NEIGHBOUR.   Is *that* your worry?
   There'll still be space in two days' time.

CHREMES.   Why's that?

NEIGHBOUR. I know the Athenians' ways: they're quick to *vote*,
   But they soon go back on all their resolutions.*

CHREMES. I tell you, they'll bring their goods.

NEIGHBOUR.   But what if they
      don't?

CHREMES. It's certain, they're bound to do it.   800

NEIGHBOUR.   But what if they
      don't?

CHREMES. The rest of us will *force* them.

NEIGHBOUR.   What if they're stronger?

CHREMES [*shrugging*]. I'll leave them to it.

NEIGHBOUR.   But what if they sell
      your goods?

CHREMES. Damnation on your head!

NEIGHBOUR.   But what if I'm damned?

CHREMES. I'll celebrate!

NEIGHBOUR [*incredulous*].
                     Do you *want* to take your goods?

CHREMES. I do, because I see my neighbours too
   Are taking theirs.

NEIGHBOUR [*ironically*].
                     I'm sure Antisthenes
   Will hand in his! I think he'd rather spend
   A whole month shedding a different load—his shit!*

CHREMES. Get lost!

NEIGHBOUR.   But will Kallimachos, chorus-trainer,
   Have something to give?   810

CHREMES.   Well, more than Kallias will!*

NEIGHBOUR [*exasperated*]. This fellow will let his property
      go to ruin!

CHREMES. What tosh!

NEIGHBOUR.   What tosh? You seem to be forgetting
   The Assembly's always voting for such decrees.
   Don't you know the one we passed on the price of salt?*

CHREMES. Of course I do.

NEIGHBOUR.   Or when we voted to use
   Bronze coinage—don't you recall?

CHREMES.   Not half! Those coins
   Were almost the death of me. [*reminiscing*] I sold some
      grapes
   And made my way, bronze coinage in my mouth,*
   To go and buy some grain in the Agora.
   Then just as I opened my sack, to have it filled,   820
   The herald shouted that henceforth no bronze coins
   Were legal tender: 'The currency's silver now.'*

NEIGHBOUR. And didn't we, only the other day, all swear
   We'd raise five hundred talents from the tax
   Euripides proposed as state-accountant?*
   At first we showered Euripides with praise.
   But when we thought again, it started to seem
   The same old story—another nasty tax.
   So then we all reviled Euripides!

CHREMES. But things are changing, friend. It used to be us,   830
   But now it's the *women* in charge.

NEIGHBOUR.   Which makes me wary
   In case they plan to piss all over me!

CHREMES. Enough of your nonsense! [*turning*] Slave, my
     baggage-pole.

[*As* CHREMES *watches his slave pick up his belongings, a female* HERALD
enters from a side entrance.]

HERALD. All citizens of Athens, attend to this!
   Come, hurry along to see our lady-general
   And find out how the lot has fallen out
   In assigning each of you to a dining hall.*
   The tables have been set up; they're standing laden
   With all the finest foods you could ever imagine.
   The couches are draped with rugs and coverlets.   840
   The wine is being mixed; the perfume-girls
   Are standing waiting. The fish is being grilled,
   The hares are on the spits, the cakes are baking,
   The garlands are being made, the nuts are roasting.
   The youngest women are boiling pots of soup.
   [*Suggestively*] Among them Smoios, garbed in *riding* gear,

Is cleaning the women's dishes—with his lips.*
Geron has turned up there in his dandy's clothes:*
He's cracking jokes with another 'young' companion,
And has thrown aside his usual shoes and cloak.   850
So come along! The slaves are waiting ready
To serve you bread: make sure your mouths are open!
NEIGHBOUR. I'll get along straight away. Why loiter here,
   Now that the city's established this new regime?
CHREMES. But where are you off? You've not surrendered your
      goods.
NEIGHBOUR. To dinner.
CHREMES.   The women won't let you, if they're wise,
   Until you hand in your goods.
NEIGHBOUR.   I will.
CHREMES.   But when?
NEIGHBOUR [*nonchalantly*]. I don't intend to make a fuss.
CHREMES.   You *what?*
NEIGHBOUR. I'm sure I won't be the last to hand things in.
CHREMES. You're really going to dine?   860
NEIGHBOUR.   I can't avoid it:
   We've got to give the city all possible help,
   If we've got good sense.
CHREMES.   But what if the women exclude you?
NEIGHBOUR. I'll charge right in, head-first.
CHREMES.   But what if they whip
      you?
NEIGHBOUR. I'll take them to court.
CHREMES.   But what if they laugh you
      down?
NEIGHBOUR. I'll stand by the door—
CHREMES.   And after that, what then?
NEIGHBOUR. I'll snatch the food from people who carry it in.
CHREMES [*dismissively*]. Make sure you turn up after me! [*to his slaves*]
      Sikon
   And Parmenon, pick up my worldly goods.
NEIGHBOUR. Now let me give you a hand.
CHREMES.   That *won't* be needed:
   I'm worried that when we reach the lady-general   870
   To deposit these things, you'll claim that some are yours.
                              [*Exit* CHREMES *with his slaves.*]

NEIGHBOUR. Well blast! I'm going to have to find a ploy
  To guarantee my property stays my own
  Yet I get my share of the common meals as well.
  [*Ponders*] Yes, surely that will work! I must be off
  To claim my dinner at once without delay.   [*Exits.*]

[CHORAL INTERLUDE]*

[*An ageing woman, hideously made-up in anticipation of the new sexual
communism, appears at one of the doors.*]

HAG^. What's keeping the men? They should have come long
  ago.
  And here I am, my face all plastered white,
  Standing by my door in this yellow chiffon dress.*
  I've nothing to do but hum myself a tune   880
  In the hope of having some fun by catching a man
  As he passes by. [*airily*] O Muses, come to my lips,
  And help me find a sexy Ionian song.
  [*She starts to hum, as the* GIRL *sticks her head out of a window next
          door.*]

GIRL. So you managed to slip out before me, then, you crone?
  You thought that while I wasn't around you might
  Pick all the *grapes* for yourself, and lure a man
  By singing. Well *I* shall sing a rival song!
  [*Ironically*] I don't suppose it's what the audience wants:
  But you never know, it might prove quite amusing.

HAG^ [*gesturing obscenely*]. That's what I think of you. Just   890
  disappear!
  [*To the piper*] Now, piper darling, take your instrument
  And play a tune that suits both you and me.

            [*The piper obliges with a sensual melody.*]

[*Singing*]   Anyone who wants a good time
                Ought to come and sleep with me.
                Young girls lack sophistication;
                Riper women know the tricks.
                If a man becomes my partner,
            True love will be his, for ever and a day:
                I'll not run off to another!

GIRL [*singing at the window*].   900

Young girls shouldn't be derided.
We have soft eroticism
All around our tender thighs
And upon our lovely breasts.
You, old depilated crock with painted face,
Only death could fancy!

HAG^A.　　May your orifice prove quite useless!
May you find you've got no fanny,
When you're ready to be laid!
When you're lying waiting to embrace your love,
May you find you've caught a *snake*!   910

GIRL [*to a different melody*].

Oh dear! Whatever will happen to me?
There's no sign of my boyfriend
Though I'm waiting all alone
(My mother's left the house):
What need is there to tell you any more?
[*To* HAG^A] I beg you, granny, go and fetch
A leather companion for yourself,
To give you *solitary* pleasure.*

HAG^A.　　Corrupted by Ionian lust,
You've got the itch, poor thing!
I think you'd use your tongue in Lesbian style.*   920
You needn't think you'll poach
My fun from me; you can't
Deprive me of my prime!   [*The music finishes.*]

GIRL. You can sing what you like, and slink out like a cat.
HAG^A. I'm making sure it's *me* they'll come to first.
GIRL. To attend your funeral! There's a new one, crone!
HAG^A. A new one!
GIRL.　　　　Well, old hags have heard them all.
HAG^A. It's not my age that will cause you pain.
GIRL.　　　　　　　　　　　　　　　　What then?
I suppose it'll be the look of your cosmetics?
HAG^A. Stop talking to me!   930
GIRL.　　　　　　And *you* stop lurking around!
HAG^A. Why should I? I'm singing a song for my lover's sake.
GIRL. A 'lover' of yours? He must be geriatric!
HAG^A. You'll find out soon, when he comes to pay a visit.

GIRL [*suddenly*]. Well here he comes at last!

HAG^A.   But not for you,
  You shrew!

GIRL.   O yes he is, you rotten cow!
  He'll show you soon enough. I'm going inside.

                           [*Leaves the window.*]

HAG^A. I'll go in too: my pride is greater than yours!

[*She steps back into the house. Enter a* YOUTH, *intoxicated, garlanded, and carrying a torch. He starts to sing in the style of a drinking-song.*]

YOUTH.   I long to sleep in my girlfriend's arms.
         If only I didn't have to bang
           An ugly harridan first!   940
         It's just too much, for a free-born man.

HAG^A [*reappearing, picking up the tune*].
          You'll soon regret, if you bang your girl!
         Old women are now *à la mode*.
          The law says come to *me*!
        It's only right, in democracy.

  I'm going to watch precisely what you do.   [*Steps back inside.*]

YOUTH. If only, gods, I found my girl alone!
  I've had some wine; my lust's now running strong.

GIRL [*reappearing at window*]. I've managed to trick that
  infernal little hag!
  She's gone away, believing I wouldn't come back.   950
  But here's the man we were talking about before.   [*She sings.*]

          Come here to me, come here to me,
          O love of mine, come here to me!
          Come close to me, and in my bed
          Resolve to spend the night with me.
          I feel a dizzy passion for
          The locks of hair upon your head.
          The pressure of a strange desire
          Is wasting all my life away.
          Release me, Eros, from this pain!
            Make sure this man
            Comes to my bed!

YOUTH [*answering*].
          Come here to me, come here to me,   960
          O love of mine, come down to me!

Rush down and open up the door,
Or I'll collapse and pine away.
I long to lie in your embrace
And wrestle with your buttocks.
O Aphrodite, I'm mad about her!
Release me, Eros, from this pain!
Make sure this girl
Comes to my bed!

Those words of mine can hardly show the force of love I feel.
O darling, please, I beg you now and plead with all my
heart: 970
Unlock the door and hold me tight!
It's for you I suffer so much!

O sweetheart dear, my golden treasure, Aphrodite's flower,
My honey-bee, my lovely Grace, O face of tenderness,
Unlock the door and hold me tight!
It's for you I suffer so much!

[*He starts to knock on the* GIRL's *door, as she leaves the window to come
down. But* HAGᴬ *emerges first.*]

HAGᴬ. You there! You must be knocking for me.
YOUTH.   Not likely!
HAGᴬ. You were *battering* on my door.
YOUTH.   I'm damned if I was!
HAGᴬ. Well *who*'ve you come to find, with that torch of yours?
YOUTH [*evasively*]. A chap who knocks around a lot.
HAGᴬ.   Who's that?
YOUTH. Well it isn't the fucker that *you* require, I'm sure!   980
HAGᴬ. I swear by Aphrodite, you've got no choice.
YOUTH [*ironically*]. This isn't the over-sixties' day, you know;
We've put your cases off till another time.*
It's the under-twenty girls I'm dealing with.
HAGᴬ. But, sweetie, that's how things once *used* to be.
They've changed; it's *us* you've got to satisfy first.
YOUTH. I can choose the piece I like—that's the rule of the
game.
HAGᴬ. You've had a free meal: we're playing a different game.
YOUTH [*turning*]. You're talking nonsense: I'm knocking on *this*
door here.
HAGᴬ. But not until you've knocked on *my* door first.   990

YOUTH. It's not your crumbling entry I'm looking for.

HAG^. I know you love me: you're just surprised to find
  I'm waiting at the door. So give me a kiss.

YOUTH [*ironically*]. But I'm terrified of your lover, my dear.

HAG^.   Who's
  that?

YOUTH. That brilliant artist.

HAG^.   I don't know who you mean.

YOUTH. The one who paints white oil-flasks for the dead!*
  You'd better go, before he sees you here.

HAG^. I see your aim.

YOUTH.   And I see yours, all right!

HAG^. By Aphrodite, who picked me out at birth,
  I'll never let you go.   1000

YOUTH.   You're mad, old crock!

HAG^ [*pulling*]. Just stop this twaddle! I'll get you into bed.

YOUTH [*to audience*]. Why bother to buy those hooks we use in
  wells,
  When a bent old crone could be lowered down instead
  To lift the buckets of water up to the top?

HAG^. Stop mocking me, cruel thing! You'll follow me.

YOUTH. You can't compel me—you haven't paid the city
  The tax that has to be paid on property transfers.*

HAG^. By Aphrodite! you've got to come with me:
  It's men of your age I like to take to bed.

YOUTH. But women as old as you I find repulsive!   1010
  You haven't a hope of persuading me.

HAG^ [*producing a document*].*   But *this*
  Will leave you no choice.

YOUTH.   What's that supposed to be?

HAG^. A decree which says you're obliged to pay me a visit.

YOUTH. Well read out what it actually says.

HAG^.   I shall.
  'The women hereby decree that should a young man
  Desire a young girl, he may not bang with her
  Until he knocks an older woman first.
  But if he refuses, and still desires the girl,
  The law entitles all the older women
  To drag him where they want—and by the knob!'   1020

YOUTH. Oh no! It sounds exactly like Prokroustes!*

HAGᴬ. We've now got *women*'s laws to be obeyed.

YOUTH. But what if one of my demesmen or my friends
   Should come and bail me out?*

HAGᴬ.   No *man*'s allowed
   To handle large sums of money any longer.*

YOUTH. Does the law permit excuses?

HAGᴬ.   No dodging's allowed.

YOUTH. I'll claim I'm a merchant: they get exemption.*

HAGᴬ.   Like hell!

YOUTH. So what must I do?

HAGᴬ.   Just follow me here inside.

YOUTH. Do I have no choice?

HAGᴬ.   The compulsion's absolute!

YOUTH [*melodramatically*]. In that case, lay a funeral bier for
      me: 1030
   Throw down the herbs and spread the broken twigs;
   Prepare the ribbons, and fetch the flasks of oil;
   And place the water-jug outside my door.*

HAGᴬ. You've also got to buy a garland for *me*.

YOUTH. Provided it's made of wax—to put on your tomb.
   I expect you to crumble to pieces before my eyes.

[HAGᴬ *starts to pull him into the house, just as the* GIRL *appears at the
                        next door.*]

GIRL. And where are you dragging him off?

HAGᴬ.   In here: he's mine.

GIRL. You won't, if you've got any sense. He's far too young
   To go and sleep with you: you're old enough
   To be his *mother*, instead of a wife for him.   1040
   If you older women should implement this law,
   You'll make the city swarm with Oedipuses!*

                          [*She snatches the* YOUTH.]

HAGᴬ. You loathsome creature! You've made up this excuse
   From envy. I'll soon revenge myself on you. [*Rushes into house.*]

YOUTH. By Zeus the Saviour! I owe my life to you,
   My darling, for getting me out of that old crone's clutches.
   I'll pay you back tonight for this piece of help:
   [*Lewdly*] Your reward will be something rather long and thick.

[*As the* GIRL *takes the* YOUTH *towards her house, the even more hideous*
   HAGᴮ, *with a large ruddy face, appears from another door.*]

HAG^B [*to* GIRL]. Hey you! I'll have you know you're breaking
    the law
  By dragging him off: it says in black and white   1050
  He must come to *my* bed first.
YOUTH.   Oh what a fate!
  What hole did *you* crawl out of, foul-faced bag?
  This monster's more appalling than the last!
HAG^B [*grabbing* YOUTH]. You'll come with me!
YOUTH [*to* GIRL].   You've got to
    intervene:
  She's dragging me off.
HAG^B.   But you're being dragged away
  By the law, not me.
YOUTH.   It's a spook who's tugging me off!
  She looks like a large, inflamed, and bloody blister.
HAG^B. Just follow *me*, you coward, and stop your drivel.
YOUTH [*desperately*]. Please give me a chance to go and relieve
    myself:
  I need to try to recover my self-composure.   1060
  Otherwise you'll see my fear will soon produce
  A yellow substance.
HAG^B.   Don't worry! You'll shit indoors.
YOUTH. Not half! I fear I'll never be able to stop.
  [*Changing tack*] Please let me go: I'll provide two sureties
  To cover my bail.
HAG^B [*dragging him*]. Don't bother.

[HAG^C, *with a face of death-like whiteness, bursts from another door and*
      grabs the YOUTH. *who does not at first see her face.*]

HAG^C.   And where d'you think
  You're going with her?
YOUTH.   Me, 'going'? I'm being abducted!
  Whoever you are, I wish you all the best:
  You've saved me from disaster. [*Sees* HAG^C's *face*] O Herakles!
  O Pan! O Korybantics! O Dioskouroi!*
  This monster's more grotesque than the one before.   1070
  Please tell me just what kind of thing you are.
  Perhaps a monkey plastered with white cosmetics?*
  Or a crone who's come back up from the land of the dead?
HAG^C [*tugging*]. Enough of your gibes! Now follow me in.

HAG^B [*likewise*].   No, *me*!

HAG^C. I'll never release my grip.

HAG^B.   But nor will I.

YOUTH. You'll tear me down the middle, you hideous sluts!

HAG^B. It's *me* the law requires you come to first.

HAG^C [*proudly*]. No, not if an uglier woman presents a claim.

YOUTH. But once I've been destroyed by you two women,
  How will I ever reach that lovely girl?   1080

HAG^C. That's your affair: this takes priority.

YOUTH. But which one gets laid first, if I want to escape?

HAG^B. Once more, it's *me*.

YOUTH [*pointing to* HAG^C]. Then *she* should let me go.

HAG^C [*still tugging*]. It's *me* you come to first.

YOUTH [*pointing to* HAG^B].   If *she* lets go.

HAG^B. I'm damned if I'll let you go!

HAG^C.   And so am I!

YOUTH. Thank goodness you don't run ferry boats.

HAG^B.   Why's that?

YOUTH. You'd sever your passengers' bodies right down the
  middle!

HAG^B. Shut up and come in here.

HAG^C.   No, into *here*.

YOUTH. It's clear Kannonos' law is still in force:*
  I'm going to have to fuck 'while held in fetters'.   1090
  How on earth can I row with both my oars at once?

HAG^B. You'll manage all right, once you've eaten a dish of
  onions.*

YOUTH. Destruction's close! She's dragged me to the door
  And almost in!

HAG^C [*to* HAG^B].   It won't make any difference:
  You'll pull me in as well.

YOUTH.   No, anything else!
  One monster's bad enough: I can't face two.

HAG^C. I'm clinging, whether you want me to or not!

YOUTH. Calamitous plight! To have to fuck this cow
  Right through the night, and through the day as well,
  And then, once free of her, to have to deal   1100
  With a toad whose cheeks are white as a funeral urn!*
  What a ghastly life—a god-forsaken life!
  Preserve me, Zeus! I face annihilation

If I'm going to be penned in with beasts like these!
[*To audience*] There's one thing, though; if my ship should
    founder here,
While being piloted by this pair of tarts,
You can place my grave right by the harbour mouth
[*Points to* HAG^c] And stick this hag on top of the monument:
Just coat her in pitch, and fasten down her feet
By pouring molten lead around her ankles;   1110
Then put her on top of the tomb—instead of an urn!*

[HAG^B *pulls him indoors, with* HAG^c *continuing to hold on. Along the
street, in very tipsy condition, comes a female* SERVANT *belonging to*
                        PRAXAGORA.]

SERVANT. How happy the people of Athens! How lucky am I!
    And happiness sublime is Praxagora's!
    [*To* CHORUS] The same is true of you women there round
        the door,
    And all you neighbours, as well as the locals here,
    And finally me myself, a slave attendant,
    Whose head is drenched in lovely fragrances.
    They smell so fine! But a better bouquet still
    Is the one that comes from jars of Thasian wine:
    It fills your head long after you've drunk the wine,   1120
    While other bouquets quickly fade away.
    Yes, Thasian wine's the best—the very best.
    Pour it me neat!* It'll keep us happy all night,
    If we choose the jar that has the best bouquet.
    Come, tell me, women, I need to find the master—
    Or rather, find the husband of my *mistress*!
LEADER. If you stay where you are, I think you'll soon find out.

[BLEPYROS *himself comes along the street, carrying a torch and escorted
                by dancing-girls.*]

SERVANT. You're right, he's here; and on his way to dinner.
    O master, what felicity is yours!
BLEPYROS. What, me?   1130
SERVANT.   Yes, you: there isn't a happier man.
    For how could anyone know superior fortune?
    Of thirty thousand citizens, maybe more,*
    You're the only one who's still got dinner to come.
LEADER. You've certainly made him sound a happy man!

SERVANT. But where are you heading for now?

BLEPYROS.   I'm off to dinner.

SERVANT. You're going to be the very last of all.
    Your wife had already told me to come and find you,
    And take you along in company with these girls.
    There's Chian wine still left for you to drink,
    With other good things too. So hurry along,   1140
    And if there are any spectators who like the play,
    Or any judges who don't feel ill-disposed,
    They should go with you. The entertainment's free!

BLEPYROS. But why not issue a generous invitation
    To *everyone*? Show hospitality rich
    To old men and young, and even to little boys.
    The dinner's prepared and waiting on the table
    For one and all—at least, back in their homes!*
    It's time for me to hurry to dinner myself.
    I've got my torch here ready to light the way.   1150

LEADER. What's keeping you? You should be getting along,
    And taking these girls. But while you're making your way,
    I'll sing a little song for dinner-time.
    I want to give the judges some advice.*

    [*Declaiming*] *Clever* judges ought to vote for me—because
        I'm clever too!
    Those who like a hearty laugh should vote for me—I give
        them laughs.
    On reflection, I suggest that *every* judge should vote for me!
    Don't allow the order of the plays to shape your attitudes.*
    I've been first, but just remember, when you come to place
        your votes,
    Not to break the oath you took, but judge us all
        impartially.   1160
    Don't behave like courtesans—you know the lousy type I
        mean:
    Those whose memories don't extend beyond the last affair
        they had.

CHORUS [*starting to dance*]. Oh! Oh! Now's the time,
    Let's begin to kick our legs and start to dance along the
        street.
    Dinner waits, my women dear. [*to* BLEPYROS] And you too,
        friend, should join the dance

In the Cretan style we set.*

BLEPYROS.   Yes, absolutely, here I go!

CHORUS [*singing*].

>   Lithe and agile, stamp the rhythm with your legs.
>   Think of what's coming:

>>   [*Singing the following sentence without drawing breath*]*
>   Slices of salt-fish and shark-fish and dog-fish and
>   Pieces of mullet with pickled accompaniments,   1170
>   Dripping with silphium,* honey, and olive oil,
>   Thrushes and blackbirds and pigeons and ringdoves and
>   Chicken and roast lark and sumptuous wagtail and
>   Fillets of hare-meat in alcohol sauces.
>   Now you've heard the list of dishes,
>   Run along swiftly and pick up your plate.
>>   When you've got it, don't delay:
>>   Find some—porridge to fill you up!*

[*Exit* BLEPYROS *with dancing-girls, followed by the frolics of the celebrating* CHORUS.]

>>   Guzzling's under way by now!
>>   Lift your legs up! Shout for joy!   1180
>>   Off to dinner! Shout for joy!
>>   Hurray, hurrah! We'll win the prize!
>>   Hurray, hurrah! Hurray, hurrah!

Wealth

INTRODUCTION

Wealth is Aristophanes' last surviving comedy, having been produced in 388 (festival unknown) towards the end of the playwright's life.[1] The relationship of the play which we have to
another with the same title produced by Aristophanes twenty years
earlier, in 408, is extremely obscure; but we can be confident that
the differences must at any rate have been extensive, and it is safe
to assume that the text we read was substantially created for the
production of 388. Since *Wealth* has been widely neglected in modern
times, and is now standardly dismissed as the weakest of the eleven
extant comedies, it may come as a surprise to some readers to discover that for a long time it was by far the most commonly read
Aristophanic play. This was probably already the case in later antiquity, and was certainly so in the Middle Ages, when *Wealth* existed
in many more manuscripts than any other of the poet's comedies.
This relative popularity was sustained after the advent of printing.
In England, for example, four of the nine translations made from
Aristophanes before the end of the eighteenth century were of this
play.[2] There can be no doubt that the main reason for this standing was a pair of factors: one, a scenario which is ostensibly
moral(istic) in its idealistic marrying of social justice with material
prosperity; the other, a reduction in the topical elements which,
even in antiquity itself, often proved a stumbling-block for readers
not entirely *au fait* with the fine detail of classical Athenian life and
culture.

There is plausibility in the supposition that it is precisely these
same factors which have led many modern critics and readers to
find the play somewhat dull and lacking in comic vigour. Such a
judgement, however, is in itself unlikely to advance our understanding of why the work is as it is, or of what kind of interest it
might have held for its original audience. Like *Assembly-Women*,

[1] After *Wealth* only two more of Aristophanes' comedies were staged in his lifetime, *Aiolosikon* (produced by his son Araros) and *Kokalos*: further details will be
found with the selection of fragments in volume iii of this translation. There is no
firm evidence for the date of the poet's death, which is generally assumed to have
occurred around 385.

[2] *Wealth* was also the first Aristophanic play to receive a production in England,
at Cambridge in 1536: see the general Introduction, 'Aristophanes and Posterity'.

Wealth exhibits structural and theatrical features which make it, in terms of the periodicization originally worked out by Hellenistic scholars, transitional between Old and Middle Comedy. Particularly salient in this respect are, first, the greatly diminished role of the chorus (largely restricted, in *Wealth*, to a rather loosely connected parodos, 253–321, and some later interlude songs[3]), which carries with it a fading of the formal elements typical of Old Comedy; and, secondly, the downplaying of the protagonist to a role which is no longer a central and driving source of dramatic energy. It is to the protagonist, Chremylos, that we might usefully turn first, for he represents—both in what he is and in what he is not—a kind of nodal point in the work's comic conception.

By the standards of all the earlier plays, Chremylos might well be thought to be an anaemic character. He scarcely approaches the inventiveness, the daring, or the exuberance of other protagonists. But that, we need to realize, is precisely the point. As a sombre, weary old man, he is disillusioned with his experience of the world. He has tried to lead a good life himself, but has reached the sad conclusion (long familiar, not surprisingly, to Greek moralists) that justice and material prosperity rarely go together (28 ff.). Unlike Peisetairos and Euelpides in *Birds*, his disenchantment is not self-centred or driven by infantile fantasizing. It has a clear social basis to it, as well as being rooted in fatherly concern for the prospects of his son. Twice in the opening scene we hear him refer to this son (who, incidentally, is never again mentioned in the play[4]), both times with a hint of pathos. At 35, just after lamenting that his own 'miserable life' is almost over, he tells Karion that he went to Delphi 'for the sake of my son—my only son'. Subsequently, when inviting Wealth into his house, he tells the god that he loves his son 'more than the world—apart from *you*' (251). This humorous twist leaves the status of Chremylos' paternal feelings intact, and contributes to his characterization as someone whose motives are far from egocentric. Nothing later in the play substantially changes that impression.

It is paradoxically significant that the early view we get of Chremylos is of someone rather *ordinary*—a person whose feelings, whose situation, and, not least importantly, whose reaction to his

---

[3] For interlude songs see, ?321/2, 626/7, 770/1, 801/2, and my note at *Assembly-Women* 729/30.

[4] Hermes' reference to the family's 'infants' at 1104 is comically immaterial.

situation are all compatible with the conditions of contemporary Athenian social life. Unlike, say, Trygaios with his dung-beetle in *Peace*, who sets out to confront Zeus himself on Olympos, or the two old men in *Birds*, who attempt to find entry into the world of myth, Chremylos does nothing out of the ordinary in going to consult Apollo's oracle at Delphi. In the Greek world, many individuals resorted to oracles to seek guidance in the pressing problems of their lives. The liberation which starts to open up for Chremylos when he receives his response from Apollo is the result not of his own creative endeavour but of the oracle itself. In all of Aristophanes' other surviving comedies the germinal idea of the plot derives from one of the central human characters, usually the protagonist him/herself. But in *Wealth* it stems from an external and divine agency. Aristophanes models this starting-point on an established, mythical story pattern,[5] but he neither gives nor needs a dramatic reason for doing so. The effect of this, however, is to scale down Chremylos into a much more mundane and passive figure than most earlier protagonists. It is true that Chremylos still has to produce an idea of his own to take advantage of the opportunity presented to him by Apollo, and in doing so he reminds us momentarily of Peisetairos in *Birds*. When he hears that Wealth's blindness is due to Zeus's malice towards men, he comes up with a scheme for restoring the god's sight and is even prepared to think in terms of challenging Zeus himself:

> D'you think that even Zeus's tyrannous power,
> With all its thunderbolts, is worth a trifle,
> If *you* should see again for even a while?

$$(124-6)$$

But this is hardly more than a flicker of the old-style boldness and initiative of an Aristophanic protagonist. In what eventually ensues, there is a kind of gap between the practical reality of what Chremylos himself does (taking Wealth, in established fashion, for a religious cure at Asklepios' shrine), and the social-cum-moral transformation which is allegorized in Wealth's recovery of vision.[6]

[5] The oracle given to Xouthos in Euripides' *Ion* (534-6) provides a pertinent parallel.

[6] Although the idea of Wealth's blindness was traditional, Wealth was not normally thought of or personified as an old man; indeed, the status of a young child, usually of Demeter, was more common. Aristophanes has chosen the old-man persona so as to create an image of decrepitude which is susceptible to the familiar comic process of reinvigoration.

Chremylos, we could say, never rises above the quotidian, even when the comic fantasy takes off.

There is a sense in which one would be justified in questioning whether Chremylos is the play's protagonist at all. Comic attention, at any rate, is more or less divided between him and his slave, Karion, from the very start.[7] In earlier plays we find slaves, sometimes in pairs (*Knights*, *Wasps*, *Peace*), who have initial prominence but subsequently vanish. Xanthias in *Frogs* has a more sustained role, since he remains with Dionysos up to the parabasis and reappears in the first scene after it. But only Karion remains for the entire play and continues to have a central part in the action. In surveying the comedy's outline, we can see Aristophanes aiming at a kind of counterpoint, of the sort which later became so usual in New Comedy, between the relatively serious master and the roguish slave. After combining them in the opening scene, he devotes the parodos (253–321) to Karion's banter and indecent frolics with the chorus, then shifts to the more sober conversation between Chremylos and Blepsidemos, which leads into the (half-)agon with Poverty. Thereafter there is a virtual alternation between the two characters. Karion serves as comic messenger reporting back from Asklepios' shrine, in a scene which again foregrounds an earthier style of humour (627–770); Chremylos returns with Wealth (771–801); and each of them in turn comes out of the house to deal with visitors, Karion meeting the Just Man and Informer (802–958), and later the quasi-servile Hermes (1097–1170), while Chremylos confronts the Old Woman and her former gigolo (959–1096) and, finally, the Priest (1171 ff.).

As the pattern of alternation in the later scenes makes particularly evident, the effect of the master–slave counterpoint in *Wealth* is to distribute between two characters the functions and qualities which in most of the earlier plays were attached to the single protagonist. While Chremylos, as I have emphasized, is rather bland and even sombre, though still nominally responsible for creating the conditions which lead to Wealth's redistribution, Karion is a much livelier, more thrusting comic persona,[8] and in the second half of the play he is at least equally responsible for exploiting or manipulating the results of the new state of affairs. In particular, his dia-

---

[7] We cannot be certain that the theatrical 'protagonist' (*prôtagônistês*, the leading actor in a performance) would have played Chremylos rather than Karion.

[8] Though even he is not without touches of moralism: see e.g. 48–50, 158–9.

logue with Hermes may remind us of Trygaios' meeting with the
same god in *Peace*, or of Peisetairos' encounters with Iris,
Prometheus, and the gods' embassy in *Birds*. But the notable difference is that the colourful mixture of self-confidence, jocular familiarity, and mischievous irreverence shown by those protagonists in
their dealings with deities (and others) is now exhibited by a slave-
character who is allowed a free rein in usurping the position which
might be expected to belong, by both social and comic logic, to his
master.

The centrality of Karion to *Wealth* looks forward, from our perspective of hindsight, to the trickster slaves who were to become so
important in the plots of New Comedy. Its significance within the
play itself can be read as ambiguous, since Karion's role simultaneously preserves elements of typical Aristophanic scurrility while displacing these elements away from a protagonist who can thereby
be characterized in terms more suitable, by approximately realistic
criteria, for his age and class. This is not the only respect in which
Wealth is a hybrid comedy, suspended to some extent between different species and tones of humour: the same point can be observed,
for example, in the coupling of a framework of quasi-mythological
allegory with the plain social ambience of house, street, and neigh-
bourhood. In general, of course, such juxtapositions are entirely
characteristic of Aristophanes' work, but in the case of *Wealth* we
may feel that anomalies and uncertainties in the play's conception
are left to an unusual extent unresolved. To pursue this question a
little further, we need to integrate a view of Chremylos, along the
lines already sketched, with a broader account of the work's thematic shape.

Like some other protagonists, such as Dikaiopolis in *Acharnians* or
Peisetairos in *Birds*, Chremylos is originally motivated both by a
sense of his personal plight and by a general dissatisfaction with the
state of things (28 ff.). But I earlier stressed that, unlike them, he
neither aspires to nor achieves an egotistical aggrandizement.[9] The
interplay between protagonist and city is here more delicately

---

[9] It is true that Chremylos expresses an ostensibly selfish and amoral desire for
wealth at 230-3, but this is only a momentary aberration from the moral emphasis
which otherwise pervades his point of view in the opening scene. Some critics, however, have read this as part of a pervasive irony in the work: see H. Flashar, 'The
Originality of Aristophanes' Last Plays', Eng. trans. in Segal (ed.), *Oxford Readings*,
314-28.

poised, as in *Lysistrata* or *Assembly-Women*, though, unlike the
heroines in those two plays, Chremylos does not so much execute
a grand plan to change the city as exact a promise from Wealth to
do so. The transformation which he later experiences is one which
certainly brings him personal wealth, but in the context of an overall change in economic conditions. Yet Chremylos' relationship to
Wealth, after the return from Asklepios' shrine, is the subject of
some ambiguity. Because Wealth comes back from the shrine to
Chremylos' house, and because those who feel either pleased (like
the Just Man) or aggrieved (like the Informer) with Wealth come to
the house in the expectation of finding him there, the impression is
created that Chremylos is in control of Wealth. But any resemblance
to, say, *Acharnians*, where peace becomes the private property of
Dikaiopolis (a wine, an elixir, an ointment) which others seek to
obtain from him, is superficial, since the visitors to the house are
direct testimony to the fact that Wealth's restored vision has (allegorically) caused changes in everyone else's life as well. Besides, the
end of the play unequivocally announces that Wealth will be per-
manently installed not in Chremylos' house but on the Akropolis
itself (1191-3), thus symbolizing the idea that the entire city will
benefit from the new dispensation allegorized by Wealth's recovered
sight. From that point of view, the protagonist finally emerges as a
kind of civic benefactor, and his personal gains, rather than being
egotistically or privately celebrated, are harmoniously blended with
the good of Athens as a whole.[10]

But that leads us on to a further question, which has been much
discussed in criticism of the play: who exactly profits from Wealth's
restored sight? Chremylos had originally complained that, as things
are, the evil prosper while the good endure hardship. A symmetrical reversal of this, which is what is anticipated explicitly at 95-7,
would align economic success with moral probity. This conception
is reiterated at several later points, including 495-6, 630, 751-9,
and is of course the premiss of the scene involving the Just Man and
the Informer. On the other hand, Chremylos anticipates a different
kind of outcome when, at 496-7, he suggests that Wealth's recovery of vision will have the effect of ensuring 'that *everyone* turns
good (and rich!)'. In other words, why would anyone choose *not* to
be 'good', if doing so could guarantee prosperity? This implication

[10] At 463 Chremylos even claims, in passing, a pan-Hellenic dimension to his
enterprise; the universalist overtones of e.g. 490, 498, should not be pressed.

easily shades into the motif of the universal provision of wealth (cf. *Assembly-Women*), and that notion is precisely what Poverty argues against at 510 ff., what the Informer seems to have been envisaging (cf. 864–5), and what both Hermes (1113–16) and the Priest of Zeus (1173 ff., esp. 1178) imply has happened by their remarks about the cessation of religious sacrifices.[11] Although the dominant impression created by the later scenes of the play is the enrichment of the 'decent' at the expense of the wicked, Aristophanes is happy to allow some elision between this idealistic result and the sheer dream, with its echoes of Golden Age myths, of new-found, inclusive affluence for one and all.

In this connection it may be worth glancing at a scene that has often troubled those who look for some sort of moral coherence in the play. When the Old Woman comes to complain to Chremylos that she has been deserted by the Young Man who was her gigolo, it becomes clear that the latter has escaped from the poverty which induced him to provide a sexual service in return for gifts. The woman becomes the butt of some cruel gibes from Chremylos, who is more scurrilous in this scene than anywhere else in the play. Does he regard the woman as at fault, because of sexual shamelessness, and the Young Man as innocent? His remarks at 1003–5 and 1023–4 seem to chime with this interpretation, which would be strengthened if we could assume that the woman represents an ageing, wealthy courtesan who has lost the charms to attract men.[12] Yet at the very end of the play Chremylos tells her that he has persuaded the Young Man to return to her (1200–1), and this looks like an acknowledgement that a kind of comic sympathy for her is possible after all (cf. 1071–5). Moreover, unlike the earlier scene with the Just Man and the Informer, it is never implied that the Young Man's new wealth is matched by the Old Woman's impoverishment. This helps to confirm that, despite the social debasement

---

[11] This last point vindicates Chremylos' claim at 124–6 and 133. A further passage which may imply universal wealth is 760–3, but that is best understood as addressed towards the chorus (cf. 627–30).

[12] Nothing in the scene allows us to decide whether the woman is of citizen status; but the parallelism with the Hags in *Assembly-Women* shows that this is not out of the question. Cf. also the motif of a man abandoning a former female lover at Lysias 1.15, but there (unlike here) adultery was allegedly involved. It is possible that the theme of a woman abandoned by her lover owes something to mime (cf. my Introduction to *Assembly-Women*, n. 13): see the related motifs at Theokritos 2.4–6, 155–8.

involved in her predicament, the woman is not a convincingly moral target but a convenient stooge for the kind of licentiously physical and sexual humour which the traditions of the genre had encouraged.

This episode tends, therefore, to reinforce the conclusion that the plot of *Wealth* hardly rewards a robustly moral reading: there is too much comic ambiguity, and too little consistency of dramatic premisses, for that. If we ask where the focus of the play's potential appeal to an Athenian audience lies, we should concentrate on the social background and the mentality of the protagonist. Chremylos is a small to middling farmer, a loose category which probably embraced a substantial proportion of Athenian citizens; we may be meant to think of him as at the poorer end of the economic bracket for hoplites (cf. 450–1), and perhaps as having once been better off than he is now (cf. 221). But what matters most about him is not the exact sociological detail of his status but the view of the world which is associated with his way of life. For Chremylos, as for Blepsidemos and the chorus, making a living from the land is not easy, and there is never enough of a surplus to lift altogether the fear of hardship.[13] It is easy for such people to look around and believe that most of those wealthier than themselves owe their property to dishonesty of one kind or another, especially, perhaps, those who do not have to work the land themselves. That is the kind of grumbling note which Chremylos strikes at the outset (28 ff.), and it is enough to mark his outlook as stemming from a certain kind of hardened, embittered cynicism.

The comic impetus of *Wealth* is one which invites an implicit sympathy with Chremylos' point of view and a corresponding enjoyment of the new riches which come to him and to those like him (cf. 627–30). Sympathizing in a general way with good characters who prosper is easy, and an archetypally comic experience; but Aristophanes complicates the nature of such sympathy by confronting Chremylos (and Blepsidemos), in the half-agon, with a character whose objections to his plans for Wealth interestingly draw on what look like the values of his own social class. In the first place, Poverty—whom some critics wrongly describe as a 'goddess'—essentially *is* the small farmer's (as well as the artisan's) way of life; she stands, as she herself emphasizes, not for outright penury

---

[13] Chremylos' status, and the hardship which goes with it, is first indicated at 218–26.

but for the toughness which goes with the countryman's virtues of hard work and parsimony (551-4):

> No, what you've said is never true of the life which *I* deliver.
> A beggar's life is the one you mean, a life without possessions.
> The poor man's life, admittedly, is full of thrift and labour:
> He never has a thing to spare—but he never goes short, either.

This is an attempt to put a positive gloss on the kind of existence which Chremylos leads, and which he himself characterizes as intolerably miserable. Yet Poverty's arguments bring him face-to-face, to a considerable degree, with an image of his own mentality. Her suggestion that she makes people both physically and morally tougher, through the discipline of hard work, is complemented by the allegation that the rich are decadent and corrupt (557-78). The strength of this case is that it tallies with Chremylos' original dissatisfaction with life (28-31), which he reiterated at the start of the agon itself (500-4). Poverty and Chremylos appear to agree, at bottom, that in the present way of the world virtue and material prosperity do not consort with one another.[14]

The agon of *Wealth* is unique among the surviving plays of Aristophanes in confronting the protagonist with opposition which is not so much an external impediment as a reflection of his own psychology. How, then, can the debate be resolved? In a sense, it cannot. Chremylos never produces a cogent refutation of Poverty, and the disagreement between them degenerates first into a burlesque of religious considerations, in the question of whether Zeus himself is really rich (579-91), and then into a typically comic victory through abuse and violence, as Poverty is hounded away (598-612). Psychologically, Chremylos has 'won' the agon only by banishing any fear of the moral degeneration that abundant wealth might bring with it.[15] Comically, the pleasures which wealth makes possible have proved too powerful for the inhibitions and negative sentiments voiced by Poverty, even though, as the rest of the play will confirm, Chremylos is hardly the person (unlike a Dikaiopolis or Peisetairos) to indulge these pleasures at the expense of moral

[14] This is also the view expressed, with cynical robustness, by Plato's Thrasymachos in book 1 of the *Republic*: see esp. 343d, 'the just man everywhere comes off worse than the unjust'.

[15] Such fear had, after all, been emphatically expressed by Wealth himself at 107-11.

scruples. It is probably fair to say that the agon of *Wealth* serves a more ambiguous dramatic function than any other in Aristophanes. While opening up the way for the protagonist's success, it casts doubt on the idealistic, 'Golden-Age' fantasy that riches for all would be an unqualified blessing,[16] and it thereby makes it hard for the play to proceed with the kind of untroubled hedonism which had been typical of Old Comedy. But then again, as the character of Chremylos and the idea (though imperfectly maintained, as we earlier saw) of a *moral* redistribution of wealth both make clear, such hedonism was no longer Aristophanes' goal in this work.

Wealth, it seems reasonable to conclude, represents not just a falling-away of Aristophanes' earlier powers, but a partial experiment in a new style of humour. As such, it can legitimately be labelled as Middle rather than Old Comedy, even though the use of such terminology only acknowledges and does not explain what is at issue. The core of the changed ethos which the play manifests can best be described as a movement away from the rich Athenian particularity, the abundance of local texture and colour, which was the hallmark of fifth-century plays and of Old Comedy more generally. In its place comes a greater reliance on broadly categorized types of character and on a scenario which is significantly Athenian only in a few respects. Whereas a play such as *Wasps* depends on all the specificities of the Athenian judicial system, the social and moral categories which permeate the setting and concerns of *Wealth* are essentially those of rich versus poor and good versus bad. As such, the comedy appears to float relatively free of Athens of the 380s, and requires much less historical exegesis than any other surviving Aristophanic play in order to be made intelligible to cultures remote in time and place from the classical Athenian polis. Superficially at least, *Wealth* possesses the uncomplicated directness, the pure transparency, of a comic fable, and that is surely the chief reason both for the appeal which it long exercised during periods at ease with overt moralizing, and equally for the dissatisfaction which it tends to produce on the jaded palates of modern readers.

---

[16] Poverty's argument at 510 ff. can be understood as a realistic economic rebuttal of Chremylos' instinctive but unreflective utopianism: Poverty is making the point that true wealth cannot merely be equated with money, given the continuing need (which fantastic utopianism ignores) for economic *production*.

WEALTH

Speaking Characters

KARION: slave of CHREMYLOS
CHREMYLOS: elderly, hard-up Athenian farmer
WEALTH: Ploutos, blind god of wealth
CHORUS: of farmers, the class to which CHREMYLOS belongs
BLEPSIDEMOS: friend of CHREMYLOS', and socially similar
POVERTY: personification of economic hardship
WIFE: of CHREMYLOS
JUST MAN
INFORMER: blackmailer and bringer of malicious prosecutions
OLD WOMAN
YOUNG MAN: former gigolo to the OLD WOMAN
HERMES: defector from the gods
PRIEST: of Zeus the Saviour

Silent Characters

CHILD: of the JUST MAN
WITNESS: accompanying the INFORMER
Various SLAVES

[*The scene is a street in Athens; the single door in the stage building will become that of* CHREMYLOS' *house. A blind old man, extremely decrepit and shabbily dressed, stumbles on from a side entrance. He is followed by another old man with his slave, both wearing laurel wreaths; the slave carries a small joint of meat.*]

KARION [*towards audience*]. In the name of all the gods, how
    hard it is
To be the slave of a master who's quite insane!
Suppose the servant offers some good advice,
But his master thinks his views should be ignored.
When things go wrong, the slave himself still suffers!
His fate is such he doesn't have control
Of even his body: his purchaser has full rights!*
That's how things are. But now it's Loxias,
[*Mock-formally*] 'Who issues oracles forth from tripod
    golden',*
I want to criticize, and with good reason.   10
He has the skills, they say, of doctor and prophet,
Yet sent my master away quite raving mad—
This master here who's following someone blind,
Which stands all common sense right on its head.
It's us with sight who ought to lead the blind,
But *he* keeps following here, and makes me too;
Yet when I ask him questions, he stays quite mum.
[*To* CHREMYLOS] Well *I've* got no intention of staying silent,
And if you don't explain just what we're doing,
I'll cause you, master, all the trouble I can.   20
You'll never dare to beat me, not while I'm wreathed.*
CHREMYLOS. That's true—I'll remove the wreath! You'll suffer
    all right,
If you make a nuisance.
KARION.   Oh pish! I won't give up
Until you tell me exactly who this is.
[*Wheedling*] I've got your interests at heart, that's why I'm
    asking.
CHREMYLOS. I'll let you into the secret; I trust you most
Of all my slaves—well, trust you to *steal* the most!
[*Earnestly*] I've always been a pious and honest man,
And yet I've never prospered.
KARION.   How well I know it!

CHREMYLOS. I've watched while others got rich—like temple-
    robbers,   30
    Politicians, informers, and other rogues.
KARION.   Too true!
CHREMYLOS. That's why I decided to go and consult Apollo.
    It wasn't to help myself: my miserable life
    Is almost over now; my force is spent.
    I went for the sake of my son—my only son—
    To find out whether he ought to change his ways
    And become a scoundrel, a good-for-nothing crook.
    [*Bitterly*] That seems the way to find success in life!
KARION [*melodramatically*]. 'What spake, then, Phoibos' voice
    from sacred wreaths?'*
CHREMYLOS. You'll hear. The god's response was loud and clear: 40
    He urged me when I got outside the shrine
    To attach myself to the very first passer-by
    And persuade him make the journey home with me.*
KARION. And who was the very first person you met?
CHREMYLOS [*pointing to* WEALTH].   Why, *him*.
KARION. Well don't you grasp what the god was trying to
    say?
    It's abundantly clear, you blithering fool, he meant
    Your son should lead the life that's normal in Athens!
CHREMYLOS. What makes you sure of this?
KARION.   It's quite apparent.
    Why, even the blind could see it! Success these days
    Is gained by leading a good-for-nothing life.   50
CHREMYLOS. That can't be what the oracle's hinting at.
    It must be something deeper. But if this man
    Would tell us *who* he is and what's his reason
    For coming all the way back home with us,
    We'd soon find out just what the oracle means.
KARION [*brusquely, to* WEALTH]. Look here, are you going to tell
    us who you are
    Or must I force it out? Come on, be quick!
WEALTH. My answer is: just go and boil your head!
KARION [*to* CHREMYLOS]. Did you understand?
CHREMYLOS.   He said it to you,
    not me!
    It serves you right for asking in such crude style.   60

[*To* WEALTH, *ingratiatingly*] I'd be obliged, as a man who
  keeps his word,
If you'd answer the question.
WEALTH.   To hell with you as well!
KARION [*ironically*]. Well there you have your omen from the
  god!
CHREMYLOS [*shaking* WEALTH]. My patience is running out, I'm
  not amused.
KARION [*grabbing him*]. Reveal your name, or you'll come to a
  nasty end!
WEALTH. Please leave me in peace, whoever you are.
CHREMYLOS.   No hope!
KARION. Then let me execute my threat first, master;
  I'll make him come to a nasty end, all right.
  I'll carry him off and leave him on top of a cliff.
  From there he's bound to fall and break his neck!   70
CHREMYLOS. Yes, take him quickly.
WEALTH.   No, don't!
CHREMYLOS.   Then will you speak?
WEALTH. But if you learn my identity, I'm sure
  You'll make me suffer and never let me go.
CHREMYLOS. I promise we'll let you go, if it's what you
  want.
WEALTH. Then take your hands off now.
CHREMYLOS.   Right, there you are.
WEALTH. Now listen. It seems I've really got no choice:
  I'll have to reveal what I wanted to keep concealed.
  My name is Wealth.
KARION.   You rotten, filthy swine!
  You're *Wealth*, and yet you didn't want us to know?
CHREMYLOS. But *are* you Wealth—in such a miserable state?   80
  I beg you, by every god whose name I know,
  By Zeus himself: are you *really* Wealth?
WEALTH.   I am.
CHREMYLOS. The god himself?
WEALTH.   His *very* self.
CHREMYLOS.   Then why
  D'you look so grimy?
WEALTH.   I've been with Patrokles,*
  Who's never had a wash his whole life long.

CHREMYLOS. But tell me how you sank as low as that.
WEALTH. It's Zeus's work, and done from malice to men.*
   When I was a growing lad, I took a vow
   That I'd only visit the homes of the just and wise
   And decent folk. So Zeus then made me blind,   90
   To stop me knowing precisely who they were.
   That's how much malice he feels towards the good!
CHREMYLOS. How *can* he, when it's only the good and just
   Who honour him?
WEALTH.   I quite agree.
CHREMYLOS.   Well, look:
   Suppose you had your sight back, as before,
   Would you keep away from the bad?
WEALTH.   I can promise you that.
CHREMYLOS. And would you visit the just?
WEALTH.   I certainly would:
   It seems so long since I last set eyes on them.
KARION. I bet! That's true of me, and I can *see*!
WEALTH [*turning*]. Well let me go: you know my story now.   100
CHREMYLOS. But now we want to keep you all the more.
WEALTH. I told you so. I said you'd cause me trouble,
   The pair of you.
CHREMYLOS.   But please, I beg you, listen,
   And don't abandon me: you'll never find
   A man with a better character than mine.
KARION. Quite right, there's no one better—except myself!
WEALTH. But everyone says that. Yet when they get
   Their hands on *me*, and find themselves grown rich,
   They overrun all limits with their vice.
CHREMYLOS. That's how things are; but *some* of us aren't bad.   110
WEALTH. Oh yes you are, without exception!
KARION [*menacingly*].   Watch it!
CHREMYLOS. But let me just describe the advantages
   You'll soon derive from staying here with us.
   [*Hesitantly*] I think, I think—may heaven assist my hope—*
   I could rid you of this ailment in your eyes
   And give you back your sight.
WEALTH.   No, please don't try!
   I've got no wish to see again.
CHREMYLOS.   You've not?

KARION. A desperate case! He'll clearly never change.

WEALTH. Your plan's sheer folly: suppose that Zeus finds out.
  He'd make my life a misery.   120

CHREMYLOS.   Doesn't he *now*,
  When he leaves you stumbling aimlessly around?

WEALTH. Perhaps. But I know I'm scared to hell of him.

CHREMYLOS. You're *what*, you coward? And you of all the gods!
  D'you think that even Zeus's tyrannous power,
  With all its thunderbolts, is worth a trifle,
  If *you* should see again for even a while?

WEALTH. Don't mention that, you scoundrel!

CHREMYLOS.   Please stay calm!
  I'll give you proof that *you* hold greater power
  Than Zeus himself.

WEALTH.   What, me?

CHREMYLOS.   I swear it's true.
  To start with, why is Zeus the king of gods?   130

KARION [*butting in*].
  Because of money—he's got the most.

CHREMYLOS.   Right then:
  Now *who*'s the one supplying the money?

KARION [*pointing to* WEALTH].   It's *him*.

CHREMYLOS. And isn't he also the reason men worship Zeus?

KARION. Quite right! They ask for wealth when saying their
    prayers.

CHREMYLOS. So *he*'s the cause of all these things. He'd soon
  Put stop to them as well, at will.

WEALTH.   How's that?

CHREMYLOS. No one at all would sacrifice an ox,
  Or even a barley-cake, or anything else,
  Without your help.

WEALTH.   But why?

CHREMYLOS.   They couldn't acquire
  The wherewithal to buy these things, unless   140
  You gave them money yourself. So even Zeus,
  If he causes trouble, could be destroyed by you.

WEALTH. Is it true that I'm the reason they worship Zeus?

CHREMYLOS. What's more, it's you who brings about the things
  That people think desirable and fine.
  In everything it's clear that money talks.

KARION. I'll vouch for that myself! A free man once,
  I've now become a slave—for a piffling debt.*
CHREMYLOS. I've heard Korinthian courtesans don't notice
  If someone poor should make a pass at them.   150
  But once a wealthy man comes on the scene,
  Without delay they thrust their arse at him.
KARION. And *boys*, I've heard, behave in just that way.
  The lovers themselves don't matter, it's just the money!
CHREMYLOS. But not the *good* ones, only the prostitutes.
  The good ones never ask for money.
KARION.   Then what?
CHREMYLOS [*ironically*]. Perhaps a pedigree horse, or hunting
    dogs!
KARION. No doubt they feel ashamed to ask for money,
  And dress their vices up with pretty words.*
CHREMYLOS [*to* WEALTH]. All crafts, and every kind of human skill,   160
  Have been devised with only *you* in mind.
  It's true of those whose trade is making shoes;
  The bronzesmiths, and the carpenters as well;
  The goldsmiths who obtain their gold from you—
KARION. And don't forget the muggers and burglars too!
CHREMYLOS. The fullers—
KARION.   *And* the cheating clothiers too!
CHREMYLOS. The tanners—
KARION.   *And* the onion-sellers too!
CHREMYLOS. And adulterers are tortured to squeeze out *you*.*
WEALTH. What a fool I've been! I never knew these things.

[KARION *continues to address his remarks to* CHREMYLOS, *while the latter
                speaks to* WEALTH *himself.*]

KARION. It's money that makes the Persian king so proud,   170
  And money that makes the Assembly meet in Athens.*
CHREMYLOS. And don't you think it's *you* who fills the triremes?*
KARION. And doesn't he feed Korinthian mercenaries?
  Won't Pamphilos feel pain because of *him*?
CHREMYLOS. And the needle-maker too,* with Pamphilos!
KARION. Isn't *he* the cause of all Agyrrhios' farts?*
CHREMYLOS. And aren't Philepsios' fictions due to you?*
  It's surely for you we're allies now with Egypt?*
  Why else does Laïs love Philonides?*

KARION. Timotheos's tower—*   180
CHREMYLOS [*cutting* KARION].   Fall on your head!
  [*To* WEALTH] Yes, everything that's done is done for *you*.
  It's you and you alone who lie behind
  The bad things and the good, be sure of that.
KARION. That's certainly true in war: the winning side
  Is always the one with *him* in good supply.
WEALTH. Can *I* do all these things, and single-handed?
CHREMYLOS. Of course you can, and many more besides.
  No one has ever had their fill of you.
  With every other thing, men have a surfeit:*
  With love—   190
KARION.   Or bread—
CHREMYLOS.   Or music—
KARION.   Or sweet desserts—
CHREMYLOS. Or honour—
KARION.   Or cakes—
CHREMYLOS.   Or manliness—
KARION.   Or figs—
CHREMYLOS. Prestige—
KARION.   Dry bread—
CHREMYLOS.   Or generalship—
KARION.   Or soup.
CHREMYLOS. But no one's ever had too much of *you*.
  If someone's wealth should rise to thirteen talents,
  He sets his sights the more on sixteen talents.*
  And if he gets to that, he aims at *forty*:
  He swears that life's intolerable with less!
WEALTH. I'm quite convinced by what you've both been saying.
  There's just one worry still on my mind—
CHREMYLOS.   What's that?
WEALTH. I *must* make sure the power you say I have   200
  Remains in my control, not someone else's.
CHREMYLOS. How timid you are! Of course it's always said
  That wealth's a craven thing.
WEALTH.   That isn't true:
  It's just a slander started by a burglar
  Who found my house had nothing for him to take,
  Because my goods were all locked safely up.
  So then he called my prudence cravenness!

CHREMYLOS. You need have no concern at all. If only
  You'll lend yourself wholeheartedly to my plan,
  I'll give you eyesight sharper than Lynkeus had!* 210
WEALTH. But how will you manage that? You're just a mortal.
CHREMYLOS [*solemnly*]. I've got high hopes because of Phoibos'
    words
  'When he shook his laurel-tree and spoke to me.'*
WEALTH [*alarmed*]. You mean *Apollo* knows this too?
CHREMYLOS.   He does.
WEALTH. Beware—
CHREMYLOS.   Don't worry at all, my friend; it's safe.
  Please rest assured, if I have to fight to the death
  I'll carry through my plan.
KARION.   Can *I* help too?
CHREMYLOS. We'll gather lots of other allies too,
  The honest folk who're always short of food.
WEALTH. Good grief! They sound a sorry bunch of allies. 220
CHREMYLOS. Not once they find themselves grown rich again!
  [*To* KARION] Now run along at once—
KARION.   To do just what?
CHREMYLOS. To summon my fellow-farmers—the ones you'll find
  Out in the fields, all toiling the day away.
  I want each one of them to come along
  To get his share of what Wealth has for us.
KARION. I'm off. But fetch out one of the slaves from there
  To take this joint of meat inside the house.*
CHREMYLOS. Leave me to deal with that. Get running along.
       [KARION *puts down the joint and rushes off by a side entrance.*]
  Now, Wealth—the most distinguished of all the gods— 230
  Please enter my house with me: this is the place
  Which *you* must fill with riches to the roof
  This very day—by honest means or foul!
WEALTH. But I loathe it every time I have to go
  Inside a house I haven't been in before:
  It's never yet done me one little bit of good.
  If I find myself inside a miser's house,
  He digs a hole and buries me in the ground.
  Then if a decent friend of his comes round,
  And asks to borrow a tiny amount of cash, 240
  He swears he's never set eyes on me at all!

But if I enter the house of a libertine,
I'm gambled away on whores and dicing games:
In no time at all I'm thrown back naked outdoors!
CHREMYLOS. It's because you've never known anyone in-between.
  Now *that*'s the sort of person I am myself:
  I'm as fond of being frugal as anyone else,
  But I'm also fond of spending, when times are right.
  [*Taking* WEALTH's *arm*] Let's go indoors. I'd like to introduce
     you
  To my wife and only son: the son I love   250
  More than the world—apart from *you.*
WEALTH.   I'm sure!
CHREMYLOS. It's only right to tell the truth to you.

[CHREMYLOS *picks up the joint of meat and leads* WEALTH *into his house.*
After a short pause, KARION *reappears, leading the* CHORUS *of farmers, who*
                        hobble on sticks.]

                    [PARODOS: 253-321]

KARION. O you who, like my master, feed yourselves on leaves
     of thyme-plants,
  His friends and fellow-demesmen all,* and lovers of hard
     labour,
  Now hurry along, don't tarry there: we haven't time to
     loiter.
  The situation's critical: your help is needed promptly.
LEADER. You must have seen that all along we've made the
     keenest progress,
  As much as anyone could expect of old and feeble men.
  Perhaps you think I ought to *run*, before I've heard you tell
     me
  The reason why your master wants to summon me to his
     house.   260
KARION. Well didn't I tell you long ago? You ought to listen
     harder.
  My master says there's now a chance for all of you to change
  Your cold and harsh conditions of life for something much
     more pleasant.
LEADER. But what's this message all about? And what's he got
     for us?

KARION. I'll tell you, then, you nasty things: he's brought an
old man home,
A dirty, stooping, wrinkled wretch, who's bald and
toothless too.
What's more, I'll swear by heaven above he's circumcised
as well!*

LEADER [*ironically*]. Well what a find of gold that sounds! Do
please repeat the news!
The asset which you've just announced seems ready for a
coffin!

KARION. It's senile fools like *you*, I think, who ought to be in
coffins!   270

LEADER [*suspicious*]. D'you think you'll get away scot-free with
playing tricks on me?
It's fortunate I've got this stick: I'll use it on your back!

KARION. But why should you suppose that I'm a trickster
through and through?
And don't you even think I might be telling you the truth?

LEADER. The rascal's got real arrogance! Your shins will soon
be smarting.
A beating and a spell in chains is clearly what you're after!

KARION. And *you* should draw your jurors' pay—while lying
in your coffins!
You'd better hurry off at once; your ticket's one for Charon!*

LEADER. I'd like to see you break your neck! You're such a low-
born scoundrel.
You jeer at us, and yet you won't reveal why we were sum-
moned.   280
We left our work to struggle here; we thought the call was
urgent.
We didn't even stop to pick the thyme-plants as we walked.

KARION. All right, I'll let the secret out: my master's brought
back home
The god of wealth himself! He's going to make you wealthy
men.

LEADER. You mean it's really possible for *us* to grow quite rich?

KARION. You might become new Midases*—you just need ass's
ears!

LEADER. I'm absolutely overjoyed. I feel such sheer delight
I've simply got to dance—provided what you say is true.

[KARION, *followed by the* CHORUS, *breaks into a burlesque song and dance, mimed out with suitably vulgar movements and phallic gestures.*]

KARION.

What's more, I'd like to join with you—o thrum-de-
thrum*—as Cyclops.   290
Yes, that's the role I'm going to play; I'll swing my
feet like this
And lead your dance. [*as Cyclops to his animals*] Ahoy
there, young ones, echo all my cries,
While bleating songs of little sheep
And foully stinking goats.
Come after me, with pricks skinned back. You goats
will have your breakfast!

CHORUS.

Well, we in turn will counter you—O thrum-de-thrum
—old Cyclops.
We'll bleat away because we've found you feeling
rather peckish.
Your knapsack's full of veg and herbs you've picked up
growing wild.
You lead your sheep, with head all sore
From last night's wine. You'll soon lie down,   300
And as you sleep a burning stake we'll seize and make
you blind!*

KARION.

And now I'll change to Circe's role,* the witch who
mixes potions.
She once persuaded all the comrades of—Philonides,
To act like boars, somewhere in Korinth,
And eat up kneaded shit which she prepared for them
herself.
I'll act the story out in full,
While you must grunt along with great delight
And follow your mother, piglets!

CHORUS.

Now you're assuming Circe's role, the witch who
mixes potions,

We'll catch you while you're casting spells and soiling
    all those comrades.   310
      Let's pick you up 'with great delight'
And doing as Odysseus did let's hang you by the—
    bollocks!
      We'll rub your nose in shit, you goat;
    Like Aristyllos, gaping, you'll then say:
      'Just follow your mother, piglets!'

KARION.
    Hoy, that's enough of all this mirth; it's time to end
    our jesting.
      Now you must change to other ways,
      While I shall sneak inside the house
      To see if I can filch some food,
      Yes, bread and meat, from master's store,   320
    And spend the whole day long laid out in sluggish
    gluttony.

[*Into house, as the* CHORUS *continues with a short routine.* After they
    have finished,* CHREMYLOS *enters from the house.*]

CHREMYLOS. I'd wish you all 'good day', my fellow demesmen,
  If it weren't becoming old-fashioned and rather stale.
  You're welcome, all the same: I'm glad you hurried
  And turned up promptly here without demur.
  I hope you're going to prove my true supporters
  And help me give protection to the god.
LEADER. Yes, count on me! I'll show some warlike spirit.
  You don't suppose that just to get three obols
  We push and shove at every Assembly meeting,*   330
  Yet wouldn't want our hands on Wealth himself!
CHREMYLOS [*pointing*]. But look who's coming along; it's
    Blepsidemos.
  He's striding down the street with urgency:
  It's clear he must have heard what's happened here.

        [*Enter* BLEPSIDEMOS, *musing to himself.*]

BLEPSIDEMOS. What on earth's being going on? How's Chremylos
  Got rich, then, overnight? It can't be true.
  And yet the rumour's spreading round the town;
  The barbers' shops* were buzzing with the story

Of how the man's grown wealthy overnight.
What's more, I'm quite surprised that some success   340
Induces him to summon all his friends.
That's not the normal practice in these parts!*
CHREMYLOS [*aside*]. I won't dissemble: I'll tell him all the facts.
　Ah, Blepsidemos, affairs are looking up.
　As one of my friends, you'll have a share yourself.
BLEPSIDEMOS. Are the rumours true, you've become a wealthy
　man?
CHREMYLOS. Not yet; it's imminent—if god proves willing.
　There's just, yes just some risk in the whole affair.
BLEPSIDEMOS. What sort of risk?
CHREMYLOS.　　　　　　　　Well—
BLEPSIDEMOS.　　　　　　　　　　　Spit it out straight away.
CHREMYLOS. If we succeed, prosperity's ours for good.   350
　But if we fail, our lives will be wiped out.
BLEPSIDEMOS. It sounds as though your ship's got dodgy cargo!
　I don't like this at all. Such sudden wealth
　Combined with fear of what might be in store:
　There must be something rotten behind it all.
CHREMYLOS. What sort of thing?
BLEPSIDEMOS.　　　　　　　　Well, maybe a case of theft.
　Perhaps you've filched some valuables from Delphi,
　From the god's own shrine, and now you're feeling guilty.
CHREMYLOS. Preserve us, lord Apollo! What a lie!
BLEPSIDEMOS. Just stop this bluster, friend. I *know* it's true.   360
CHREMYLOS. How dare you even think of such suspicions!
BLEPSIDEMOS. Oh dear, there's no one honest alive these days.
　The only thing they care about is lucre.
CHREMYLOS. I really think you're going right off your head.
BLEPSIDEMOS. He's changed so much: he's not the man I knew.
CHREMYLOS. I swear by heaven, you're going quite raving mad.
BLEPSIDEMOS. Why, even the look in his eyes seems shifty now:
　That shows he must have committed some sort of crime.
CHREMYLOS. I understand your prattle: you want a share
　Of anything I've stolen.   370
BLEPSIDEMOS.　　　　　　A share? Of what?
CHREMYLOS. It's not like that at all: you've got it wrong.
BLEPSIDEMOS [*sardonically*]. Perhaps you didn't steal but *robbed*.
CHREMYLOS.　　　　　　　　　　　You're crazy!

BLEPSIDEMOS. You claim you haven't been taking anyone's
    goods?

CHREMYLOS. I certainly haven't.

BLEPSIDEMOS.   I can't believe his nerve!
  What can one do? He won't admit the truth.

CHREMYLOS. You've brought a charge before you've learnt the
    facts.

BLEPSIDEMOS [*changing tone*]. I'd like to help, old thing, for a
    modest sum.
  Before the information's public knowledge,
  I'll gag the politicians' mouths with—cash.

CHREMYLOS [*ironically*]. Oh yes, I'm sure you'd prove your
    friendship then.   380
  You'd spend a sum, then charge four times as much!

BLEPSIDEMOS. I'm looking at someone who'll end up sitting in
    court
  And pleading for mercy, holding a suppliant branch
  With wife and children by his side.* They'll look
  Like 'Herakles' family' painted by Pamphilos.

CHREMYLOS. You've got it all wrong, you fool. I'm going to see
  That only the good get rich.

BLEPSIDEMOS [*ironically*].   What's that you say?
  Have you stolen as much as *that*?

CHREMYLOS.   Such impudence!
  You'll be my ruin.   390

BLEPSIDEMOS.   You'll ruin yourself, more like.

CHREMYLOS. I won't, you loathsome wretch, so long as I have
  My Wealth.

BLEPSIDEMOS.   What wealth?

CHREMYLOS.   I mean the god himself.

BLEPSIDEMOS. But where?

CHREMYLOS.   Indoors.

BLEPSIDEMOS.   Which house?

CHREMYLOS.   Mine.

BLEPSIDEMOS.   *Yours?*

CHREMYLOS.   That's right.

BLEPSIDEMOS. To hell with you! You've Wealth indoors?

CHREMYLOS.   I swear!

BLEPSIDEMOS. You're telling the truth?

CHREMYLOS.   I am.

BLEPSIDEMOS.   The absolute truth?

CHREMYLOS. I swear by Poseidon.

BLEPSIDEMOS [*suspiciously*].   You mean the god of the sea?

CHREMYLOS. If there's any other Poseidon, I'll swear by him!

BLEPSIDEMOS. Well, why have you not sent Wealth to visit your
     friends?

CHREMYLOS. Things haven't yet reached that stage.

BLEPSIDEMOS.   What stage
     d'you mean?

     The time for sharing?   400

CHREMYLOS.   That's right. For first—

BLEPSIDEMOS.   Well, what?

CHREMYLOS. The two of us must make him see.

BLEPSIDEMOS.   Make who?

CHREMYLOS. Make *Wealth* somehow get back his former sight.

BLEPSIDEMOS. Is he really blind?

CHREMYLOS.   I swear by heaven he is.

BLEPSIDEMOS. No wonder he's never set foot inside my house.

CHREMYLOS. But if the gods are willing, he'll visit you now.

BLEPSIDEMOS. Well surely we ought to fetch a doctor round.

CHREMYLOS. What doctors are there these days in the city?
     They earn no fees, and no one wants to practise.

BLEPSIDEMOS [*turning to audience*].
     Let's look for one.

CHREMYLOS [*likewise*]. I can't see any.

BLEPSIDEMOS.   Nor I.

CHREMYLOS. Then here's a better idea. I planned before   410
     To take him off to the shrine of Asklepios
     And make him sleep there.

BLEPSIDEMOS.   Yes, the perfect plan!
     Don't wait a moment longer; it's time for action.

CHREMYLOS [*turning*]. I'm going.

BLEPSIDEMOS.   Good, hurry along.

CHREMYLOS.   That's what
     I'm doing.

[*Before* CHREMYLOS *can go inside,* POVERTY *rushes on from a side entrance.
     At the sight of her pallid, severe appearance both men cower.*]

POVERTY [*portentously*]. What shameless, heinous crime are you two
     plotting,

What daring deed, you miserable puny men?
Don't try to flee from me, stay there!
BLEPSIDEMOS. Oh help!
POVERTY. I've come to grind your bones into the dust.
The deed you dare is one which breaks all laws.
No other person—no, not god nor man— 420
Has ever done the same. Your fate is sealed.
CHREMYLOS. But who are *you*? Your face is deathly white.
BLEPSIDEMOS. Perhaps she's a Fury out of some tragedy;
Her eyes have got that frenzied, tragic look!*
CHREMYLOS. But she's got no torches.
BLEPSIDEMOS.   She's done for, in that case.
POVERTY. But who do you *think* I am?
CHREMYLOS.   A hostel-keeper,
Or maybe a market-seller. That would explain
This unprovoked attack and your raucous voice!*
POVERTY. What, 'unprovoked'! In view of your dastardly deed
In trying to have me thrown off all the land? 430
CHREMYLOS. Thrown off the land? Why not thrown down the
    pit?*
But you should have told us who you are at once.
POVERTY [*solemnly*]. I'm one who'll punish you both this very
    day
For setting out to obliterate me from here.
BLEPSIDEMOS. She's surely not the barmaid round the corner,
The one who always serves me up short measure?
POVERTY. I'm *Poverty*, who's lived here all these years.
BLEPSIDEMOS [*turning*]. We need divine protection! Let's escape!
CHREMYLOS. Hey, what's the matter? You snivelling, cowardly
    dog,
Don't run away! 440
BLEPSIDEMOS.   I certainly will!
CHREMYLOS.   No, don't!
Are a pair of men to flee from just one woman?
BLEPSIDEMOS. She's no mere woman; she's *Poverty*, you ass!
There's no more destructive creature in all the world.
CHREMYLOS. Please stay, I beg you, stay!
BLEPSIDEMOS.   It's out of the question.
CHREMYLOS. Please listen. Just think of what we'll both be
    doing—

I can't imagine anything worse at all—
If we run away, deserting the god in there,
And put up no fight because we're afraid of *her*.
BLEPSIDEMOS. But how can we fight? What weapons or force
    would work?
We haven't got a breastplate or a shield: 450
This vile old woman has made us pawn them all!*
CHREMYLOS. Don't worry. I'm confident this god alone
Can vanquish all this woman's evil ways.
POVERTY. You've got the gall to grumble still, you *scum*,
When I've caught you both red-handed in your crime?
CHREMYLOS. But why, you vicious old beast, d'you hurl abuse
At people who've never done you any harm?
POVERTY. No harm! You mean to say you don't believe
You injure *me* at all when you attempt
To have Wealth's sight restored?   460
CHREMYLOS.   What's that to you,
If what we do brings good to all mankind?
POVERTY. And what's this 'good' you'd find?
CHREMYLOS.   You want to know?
Well, first of all, ejecting *you* from Greece!
POVERTY. Ejecting me! And what do you imagine
Would cause more human woe than that?
CHREMYLOS.   More woe?
Abandoning our plans would do just that.
POVERTY. But listen: I'm ready to argue the issue with you,
Right here and now. Then if I'm able to prove
That *I* alone am the cause of all that's good,
That *I'm* the one who makes your lives worth living—   470
Well, if I fail, you can do what you like with me.
CHREMYLOS. You dare to make such claims, repulsive hag?
POVERTY. I'm right as well, be sure. I'll easily show
You're making such a catastrophic error
If you plan to turn the just into the rich.
CHREMYLOS. This woman's head belongs in a pillory-block!
POVERTY. Don't rave and shout before you've heard me speak.
CHREMYLOS. But who could stop himself from shouting out
At words like yours?
POVERTY.   A rational man, that's who!
CHREMYLOS. Now if you lose the case, what penalty then   480

Can I impose?

POVERTY.   Whatever you like.

CHREMYLOS.   Superb!

POVERTY. But you two suffer the same, if *I'm* the winner.

CHREMYLOS [*to* BLEPSIDEMOS]. D'you think that twenty deaths
    would be enough?

BLEPSIDEMOS. For her—but two will quite suffice for us.

POVERTY. And it's only what you'll both deserve. For how
    Could anyone think my arguments unjust?

[HALF-AGON: 487-618]*

LEADER. It's time for you to put your case; you'd better make it
    clever.

    You need to win the argument and offer no concessions.

CHREMYLOS. I'll start with what I'm sure is clear to any thinking
    person,

    That in a world where justice ruled, the good would be
    successful,   490

    But for all evil, godless men the opposite would hold.

    Well that's a thing we long to see; we think we've now
    discovered

    A splendid, noble stratagem for bringing it about.

    If Wealth should once regain his sight and cease to wander
    blindly,

    He'll make his way, and once for all, to people who are
    good,

    While evil, godless men he'll shun. And that will then
    ensure

    That *everyone* turns good (and rich!)—they'll all become
    god-fearing.

    But who could find a greater boon than this for human
    beings?

BLEPSIDEMOS. No one at all; I'll vouch for that. Don't bother
    asking *her*, though.

CHREMYLOS. Now just consider how we humans live as things
    are now.   500

    Who could deny it's lunacy—in fact, outright dementia?

    For many men grow wealthy though they're rotten to the
    core.

Injustice lets them pile it high. Yet many decent folk
Still struggle through life and almost starve: [*to* POVERTY]
   it's *you* they can't escape.
[*To* BLEPSIDEMOS] That's why I say if Wealth could see, and
   put a stop to *her*,
There couldn't be a finer way to help the human race.
POVERTY. You've lost your wits, the pair of you. What gullible
   old codgers!
You match each other perfectly—in nonsense and in folly.
If all your wants were satisfied, I swear you'd think things
   worse.
Suppose that Wealth regained his sight and shared himself
   around,   510
You'd find that every art and craft would promptly disappear.
And once they've gone do you believe that anyone will want
To manufacture metalware or ships or clothes or cartwheels?
And what of making shoes or bricks, or washing clothes,
   or tanning?
[*Loftily*] And who will choose to till the loam and reap
   Demeter's produce,*
Once idleness can be preferred and all these things ignored?
CHREMYLOS. I've never heard such utter bosh! Those tasks
   you've just described
Will all be carried out by *slaves*.
POVERTY.   But how will slaves be found?
CHREMYLOS. We'll purchase them with cash, of course!
POVERTY.   But who
   will want to *sell* them,
When no one needs to earn the cash?   520
CHREMYLOS.   Thessalians love their
   profits:*
The traffickers will bring the slaves from kidnappers at
   home.
POVERTY. But why on earth will *anyone* still want to kidnap
   slaves,
If what you said before is true? Once everyone is rich,
There won't be any reason left to take such deadly risks.
Without a slave you'll need to plough and dig and toil
   yourself,
Which means you'll have a *harder* life.

CHREMYLOS.   Oh go and stew yourself!

POVERTY. What's more, you'll never sleep in bed, for who will
    build the bedsteads?

  Or lie upon luxurious quilts, for who, once rich, will weave
    them?

  There won't be scents whose precious drops can grace the
    brides you marry,

  Nor fine, embroidered, coloured robes to drape around their
    bodies.   530

  So what will be the use of wealth, if all these things are
    lacking?

  But while it's *me* who lives with you, you have your needs
    provided.

  I sit beside the artisan and rule his whole existence,

  Compelling him through neediness to forge his livelihood.

CHREMYLOS. What benefits can *you* provide? Just chilblains from
    the bathhouse,*

  And houses crammed with hungry kids and ageing female
    in-laws.

  I haven't even mentioned yet the lice and gnats and fleas,

  Whole swarms of them which irritate by whining round
    our heads.

  They wake us up with messages: 'Get up, or else you'll starve!'

  And, furthermore, while you're around, it's rags we wear
    not cloaks.   540

  We sleep on bug-infested mats, and toss and turn all night.

  Instead of blankets all we have are seedy coverlets.

  Instead of pillows for our heads, we rest on lumps of stone.

  We eat no bread, just mallow shoots, and mangy radish
    leaves.

  We own no stools but have to sit on broken wine-jar tops.

  And for a kneading-trough we use a pot that's cracked in
    half.

  [*Sarcastically*] I think I've done enough to show how many
    gifts you bring us!

POVERTY. That's not my life you've just described, but only that
    of *beggars*.

CHREMYLOS. But beggary and poverty are like a pair of sisters.

POVERTY [*ironically*]. No doubt you think Dionysios is just like
    Thrasyboulos!*   550

No, what you've said is never true of the life which *I*
  deliver.
A beggar's life is the one you mean, a life without
  possessions.
The poor man's life, admittedly, is full of thrift and labour:
He never has a thing to spare—but never goes short, either.
CHREMYLOS. Demeter, goddess of the crops! A blissful life it
  sounds:
  He toils and shows unending thrift, yet can't afford a burial!
POVERTY. Just jibes and jests—that's all you have! No serious
  arguments.
  You overlook that I produce far better men than Wealth
  does,
  In intellect and body too. With *him* it's gout they suffer,
  And bloated bellies, fat legs too—yes, rank obesity.   560
  With *me* they're lean, with wasp-trim waists; in war they
  sting their foes.*
CHREMYLOS. Perhaps it's just by starving them you turn them
  into wasps!
POVERTY. I'll now proceed to make you see, where virtue is at
  issue,
  That *mine*'s a life of self-restraint, while Wealth produces
  violence.
CHREMYLOS [*ironically*]. Of course, it's highly self-restrained to
  steal and burgle houses!
POVERTY. Consider, then, all over Greece, the ways of politicians.
  While poverty is all they have, they treat their cities justly.
  Yet once they've filched the public funds, their justice
  disappears:
  They plot against the masses then and try to harm the
  people.   570
CHREMYLOS. For once you've told the honest truth, despite
  your nasty tongue.
  But don't expect reward for that; you still deserve to
  suffer
  For putting forward arguments in hope that you'll
  persuade us
  That poverty, not wealth, is good.
POVERTY.   But why not, then,
  refute me,

Instead of all this flailing rant?

CHREMYLOS. Well, why do people *shun* you?

POVERTY. Because I try to make them good. It's just the same
with children:

Their fathers wish the best for them, yet still their children
shun them.

It shows how very hard it is to recognize true justice.

CHREMYLOS. Perhaps you'll claim that Zeus himself can't
recognize good standards.

For *he* believes in having wealth—   580

BLEPSIDEMOS [*gesturing*]. While sending *her* to us!

POVERTY. What prehistoric, senile fools! Your wits are blind
with folly!

No, Zeus himself is truly poor; I'll give you ample proof.

If Zeus had wealth, then tell me why one year in every
four

He brings together all the Greeks to hold Olympic games,

Yet when the winners are announced he gives them
wreaths of olive?

He ought to give them wreaths of *gold*, if wealth were his
in plenty.

CHREMYLOS. No, surely this just goes to prove how much he
values wealth.

He's parsimonious, that's the point, and doesn't like to
squander:

He gives the winners worthless wreaths, and keeps his
wealth himself.

POVERTY. The shame of that would be far worse than poverty
itself,   590

If Zeus was rich yet still behaved with grasping selfishness.

CHREMYLOS. May Zeus give *you* an olive wreath—to decorate
your corpse!

POVERTY. Such impudence, to keep denying that all of life's
good things

Are yours because of Poverty!

CHREMYLOS. Let *Hekate*, then, tell us

Which of the two is preferable—great wealth or constant
hunger.

She'll tell you that each month the rich send dinner to her
shrines,

While all the paupers stand around to snatch the food away.
[*Gesturing aggressively*]
So stop your grousing. Just get lost!
We've heard enough from you.
No matter what, you *won't* persuade.   600

POVERTY [*loftily*].
'O city of Argos, hear his words!'*

CHREMYLOS.   Call Pauson next—he dines with you.*

POVERTY.   What grief, what suffering waits for me?

CHREMYLOS.   To hell with you! And make it sharp!

POVERTY.   Where in the world do I belong?

CHREMYLOS.   The place for you is a pillory:
And that's long overdue!

POVERTY.   I swear you'll summon me back one day
To live with you again.

CHREMYLOS.   We'll wait and see. For now, get lost!   610
The life I want is a life of wealth,
And *you* can go and hang yourself!   [POVERTY *exits.*]

BLEPSIDEMOS.   Three cheers for that! It's now my wish
To hold a feast with all my sons
And with my wife. I want a bath,
Then when I come out gleaming clean,
The artisans and Poverty
Will hear a rasping fart!

CHREMYLOS. That blasted woman's gone away at last!
It's time for you and me to take the god   620
And make him lie within Asklepios' shrine.

BLEPSIDEMOS. Let's go at once, in case some other nuisance
Should come along and spoil our splendid plans.

CHREMYLOS [*shouting in*]. Hoy, Karion! Bring out the bedding now,
And bring out Wealth himself with all due care,
As well as all the other things we've packed.

[KARION *appears with* WEALTH, *while other slaves carry bedding and various baggage. With* CHREMYLOS *and* BLEPSIDEMOS, *the procession makes its way off-stage by a side entrance.*]

[CHORAL INTERLUDE]*

[*It is now the following day.* KARION *rushes on, returned from the shrine.*]

KARION [*excited*]. Old men, who used to dunk your scraps of
  bread
  In bowls of soup at Theseus' festival,*
  What fortune, what felicity is yours
  And that of all who share your moral ways!   630
LEADER. Come on then, tell us the news about your friends.
  It's clear you've something wonderful to report.
KARION. My master's now won perfect happiness!
  Yet Wealth is happier still: no longer blind,
  [*Loftily*] 'His sight has been restored, his eyes made clear,
  Thanks to Asklepios' kindly healing art.'*
CHORUS [*singing*]. Cause for joy! Cause for acclaim!
KARION [*cheekily*]. Yes, joy's the thing—but *you* can take it or
  leave it.
CHORUS [*still singing*].
                My voice will acclaim Asklepios,
                Blessed in his sons, a light for all mankind.   640

  [*The noise of celebration brings out the* WIFE *from the house.*]

WIFE. What's all the shouting here? Has someone brought
  Good news? That's what I've long been hoping for,
  Sitting indoors and waiting for him to come.
KARION. My mistress, quickly, quickly, fetch some wine,
  To drink a toast (I know you like a tipple):*
  I bring you every good thing in the world.
WIFE. Well, where's it all?
KARION.   You'll hear about it soon.
WIFE. Then hurry up and tell me what you mean.
KARION. Then *listen*, while I make a full report.
  You need to hear a blow-by-blow account.   650
WIFE. But blows aren't what I want to hear.
KARION.   But surely
  You want to hear the happy news?
WIFE.   Yes, *that*!
KARION [*drawing breath*]. As soon as we arrived there at the
  shrine,*
  Bringing along that most unhappy figure
  Who's *now* the happiest person in the world,
  We led him to the seashore straight away
  Then had him washed.

WIFE [*sarcastically*].   How happy he must have been,
  A poor old man immersed in freezing water!
KARION. We then approached Asklepios' sacred precinct.
  And when our sacrificial cakes had burnt   660
  Upon the altar, 'oiling Hephaistos' flame',*
  We made Wealth lie straight down, as was in order,
  While each of us laid out a mat as well.
WIFE. Were others there who needed a sacred cure?
KARION. Yes, one was Neokleides, who's rather blind
  Yet steals with more success than those with sight.
  And many others too, with every kind
  Of sickness. Then the temple-servant came,
  To snuff the lamps and urge us all to sleep.
  He said that any noise should be ignored;   670
  So there we lay, all keeping to our places.
  I found I couldn't get to sleep at all.
  A pot of porridge was starting to drive me mad:
  It lay close by the head of a nasty hag;
  I felt a craving to crawl and guzzle it up.
  I looked across and saw the temple-priest
  Was filching all the pastries and the figs
  That lay on the sacred table.* After that
  He made his way round all the altars there,
  To see if any cakes were left unburnt.   680
  He popped them all—*religiously*, of course—
  Into a bag. So thinking such things pious,
  I went and helped myself to the pot of porridge!
WIFE. Unholy man! Did you have no fear of the god?
KARION. Not half I did—I feared that crowned with wreaths
  He'd manage to get to the pot before I could!
  I took my cue from what the priest had done.
  Well, when the old hag heard me start to move,
  She stretched her hand. So naturally I *hissed*,
  And sank my teeth, like snake's fangs, in her flesh.*   690
  At once she drew her hand back in again,
  Curled herself up and lay all motionless—
  So scared she gave a stinking, cat-like fart!
  That left me free to slurp up lots of porridge;
  Then, when I felt full up, I lay back down.
WIFE. But didn't Asklepios come?

KARION.   He hadn't come yet.
But soon I did a *very* amusing thing.
The god himself was just approaching, when
My bloated belly produced a massive fart.

WIFE. He must have felt disgust at you at once!   700

KARION. He didn't. Iaso, walking with him, blushed,
While Panakeia held her nose and turned.*
I must confess my farts don't smell like incense!

WIFE. And Asklepios himself?

KARION.   Oh, utterly blasé.

WIFE. You mean to say the god is really *vulgar*?

KARION. Not vulgar, no—he just eats shit.*

WIFE.   How shocking!

KARION. Straight after this I covered my head right over.
I felt afraid as *he* went round the room
And checked each person's malady, one by one.
After that a slave brought forward various things: 710
A mortar made of stone, a pestle, a box—

WIFE. Of stone, you said?

KARION.   No, not the *box*, of course.

WIFE. And how did you manage to see, you rotten scoundrel?
You said you covered your head.

KARION.   I managed to peep
Through one of the many holes torn in my cloak.
[*Resuming*] Now, first of all he turned to Neokleides
And started to grind ingredients for a poultice.*
He put three heads of garlic in his mortar
Then mixed in fig-juice rennet, and squill as well.
Next, once he'd soaked it all in acrid vinegar,   720
He turned the eyelids out and smeared them both
To make it sting the more. But Neokleides
Screamed out and tried to flee. The god just laughed:
'Stay there and keep the poultice on your eyes;
I'll put a stop to all your Assembly pranks.'

WIFE. What a shrewd and pro-Athenian god he is!

KARION. After that he went and sat down next to Wealth.
The first thing that he did was touch his head,
Then picking up a piece of spotless linen
He wiped it round his eyelids. Panakeia   730
Wrapped round his head and right around his face

A purple cloth. The god then clicked his tongue,
And from the temple slid a pair of snakes
Immense in size.

WIFE.   O merciful gods above!

KARION. They both slipped silently beneath the cloth
And licked his eyelids round, it seemed to me.
[*Cheekily*] And sooner than you'd drink a gallon of wine,
My mistress, Wealth stood up, his sight restored!
I felt quite overjoyed and clapped my hands
And woke the master up. At once the god   740
Just disappeared, with his snakes, inside the temple.
You can't imagine how the rest of us
Then spent the whole night long embracing Wealth,
Quite wide awake until the new dawn broke.
And *I* acclaimed Asklepios the most
Because he gave Wealth back his sight so soon
But blinded Neokleides more than ever!

WIFE. How great your power, O lord Asklepios!
But tell me, where's Wealth now?

KARION.   He'll soon be here.
He's been held up by crowds along his route.   750
For those who in the past led moral lives,
But still stayed poor, were now so overjoyed
They came to shake his hand in gratitude.
And as for those whose wealth and means were great
But not acquired in very honest ways,
They now wore frowns and scowls upon their faces.
The others, though, processed behind in garlands.
They laughed and chanted hymns: the rhythmic beat
Of old men's feet rang out as all marched on.
So come, let everyone with one accord   760
Lift up their legs and join the happy dance!
You'll never again come home to hear the news
That all your grain's used up, your sacks are empty.

WIFE. In Hekate's name, this news of yours deserves
A special reward: I'll hang around your neck
A string of fresh-baked loaves.*

KARION.   Then don't delay,
The men will soon arrive back home as well.

WIFE. I'll hurry inside and fetch a tray of sweets

To shower over Wealth's new-purchased eyes.*   [*In.*]

KARION. While I'll go back to meet them as they come.   770
               [*Off by the same side entrance by which he entered.*]

[CHORAL INTERLUDE]*

[*Enter, from a side entrance,* WEALTH, CHREMYLOS, *who is shaking off some
                    well-wishers, and* KARION.]

WEALTH. I offer worship first to the sun above,
   And next to the famous soil that Pallas guards
   With all of Kekrops' land which made me welcome.*
   I feel ashamed of what I used to suffer.
   To think of those I lived with, unawares,
   While shunning in my ignorance the folk
   Who merited my company! How dire!
   In both respects my life was all awry.
   But now I'll have these things reversed again
   And show the world in future I never meant   780
   To give myself to all those evil people.

CHREMYLOS. Well hang it all! It's difficult dealing with friends—
   The sort who appear as soon as you have success.
   They jostle around and knock you on the shins,
   Each one displaying goodwill with lots of show.
   Has *anyone* failed to greet me? In the market
   I was hemmed right in by crowds of old men there.

[*The* WIFE, *carrying a tray of sweetmeats, comes out to welcome the
         party, turning first to* CHREMYLOS *and then to* WEALTH.]

WIFE. O dearest, welcome home! [*to* WEALTH] And you too,
       greetings!
   Now, let's observe tradition: I have to hold you
   And shower this food all over you.   790

WEALTH.   No, don't!
   At the moment when I cross your threshold here
   For the very first time since getting back my sight,
   You shouldn't be bringing things out, but taking them in!

WIFE. You mean you won't accept these sweetmeats here?

WEALTH. I will, but at your hearth—that's true tradition.
   [*Gesturing at the audience*] That way we'll soon avoid the
       usual nonsense.

It's rather infra dig for our director
To toss out figs and sweets to these spectators
And bribe them in that way to raise a laugh.*
WIFE. I quite agree: [*pointing*] look there at Dexinikos*   800
   Who's standing up already to snatch the figs.

                                        [*All into the house.*]

[CHORAL INTERLUDE]*

[*Enter* KARION *from the house, rubbing his eyes.*]

KARION [*to the audience*]. Well, gentlemen, prosperity is *sweet*,
   Especially when no money leaves the house!
   A heap of goods has piled up in our house,
   And not a single one's ill-gotten gain.
   I'll tell you what's so nice about great wealth.
   The meal-tub's brimming with gleaming barley grain;
   The vats are brimming with dark and fragrant wine;
   Our coffers are crammed with gold and silver coins;
   You wouldn't believe how much we've stored away.
   The well's awash with olive oil; the flasks   810
   Are full of scent, the cupboards upstairs with figs.
   Our saucers, dishes, and pots have turned to bronze;
   Our plates, which used to be such grimy things,
   Have turned to highly polished silverware.
   Our oven's changed from bricks to ivory.
   We slaves sit playing games with golden sovereigns,
   And now we've got so used to luxury
   We wipe our bums on garlic, not on stones.
   Right now the master's standing garlanded
   To sacrifice a pig, a goat, a ram.   820
   The smoke was far too much for me; it stung
   My eyes: that's why I came out here just now.

[*Enter, from a side entrance, the* JUST MAN, *accompanied by a* CHILD
         carrying a tattered cloak and an old pair of shoes.]

JUST MAN. Come along, come along, my child. Let's see the god.
KARION. Hello, what's going on here? Who's this I see?
JUST MAN. A man once downcast, now no longer so.
KARION. It's clear, I see, you're one of the decent folk.
JUST MAN. That's right.

KARION.   Well what d'you want?

JUST MAN.   To see the god.

For he's the one I owe my fortune to.
My own inherited wealth was sufficient at first,
So I used to lend some help to needy friends,   830
Believing that this was a useful way to act.

KARION. I suppose you quickly found your money ran out?

JUST MAN. Precisely so.

KARION.   And your life was then downcast?

JUST MAN. Precisely so. I used to think I'd find
That friends who'd come to seek my help before
Would lend support in turn if *I* should ask.
They shunned me, though, and didn't want to know me.

KARION. I bet they even sneered.

JUST MAN.   Precisely so.

My cash dried up; my life lay all in ruins.
But now that's changed. And that's the reason why   840
I've come to pay the god my due respects.

KARION. But what's this ragged cloak, in heaven's name,
This child of yours is carrying. Please explain.

JUST MAN. This cloak's a votive offering to the god.

KARION. Perhaps it's what you wore for the Greater Mysteries?*

JUST MAN. No, that's what I wore while freezing to death for
    years!

KARION. And the shoes?

JUST MAN.   Yes, these shared all my winters too.

KARION. Are *they* an offering too?

JUST MAN.   They certainly are.

KARION [*ironically*]. Delightful gifts you've brought to give the god!

[*Enter, from a side entrance, an* INFORMER,* *accompanied by a* WITNESS.]

INFORMER [*melodramatically*]. How cursed I am! I'm doomed
    and woebegone!   850
Cursed three times over—four times, even five!
Twelve times, I say—*ten thousand times*, alas!
I've drained life's bitter cup, the dregs and all.

KARION. Preserve us from a plague, o merciful gods!
I wonder what affliction's struck this man.

INFORMER. What torment could be greater than I suffer?
Stripped as I've been of everything I owned

Because of this wretched god, whose eyes I'll blind
Once more, unless my legal ploys desert me.

JUST MAN [*to* KARION]. I'm fairly sure I know what's happened
    here.   860
This man has clearly fallen into hardship:
He must have been a nasty bent old coin.

KARION. If that's the case, I hope he rots to death!

INFORMER [*noticing* KARION]. I'd like to know that fellow's where-
    abouts
Who promised he'd turn us all to wealthy men
As soon as his eyes could see again. Yet now
He's brought down rack and ruin on *some* of us.

KARION. But who's he done this to?

INFORMER.   To *me*, right here.

KARION. So *you* were one of the nasty criminal class?

INFORMER. How dare you—you and your scummy friends in
    there!   870
It must be *you* who've stolen my possessions.

KARION. Well, holy snakes, we face a whirlwind here!
This informer clearly means to gorge himself.

INFORMER [*to* KARION]. I want you taken at once to the Agora.
We'll soon extract confession of your crimes
Through torture on the wheel.*

KARION.   Just try it, then!

JUST MAN. By Zeus the Saviour, what a benefactor
The whole of Greece has found, if Wealth intends
To make informers die a painful death!

INFORMER. How dare you jeer! So *you*'re involved as well.   880
[*Inspecting him*] Now where did you get this cloak? It's not
    the same
Old rags I saw you wearing yesterday.

JUST MAN [*raising a hand*]. I'm not afraid of *you*: this ring
    protects me;
I bought it for a drachma from Eudamos.*

KARION. But nothing will help prevent informers' bites!

INFORMER. This is a case of wanton verbal abuse.*
You jeer, but haven't explained just what you're up to:
Some crooked purpose clearly brings you here.

KARION [*aggressively*]. Too true, as far as you're concerned, you'll
    see!

INFORMER. You're going to feast on money you stole from *me*.   890
JUST MAN. I really hope that you and your witness here
   Will burst your guts!
KARION.   But make them *starving* guts!
INFORMER. D'you still deny my claim, you stinking thieves?
   You're cooking fish and roasting joints in there.
                 [*He smells round the door with loud, dog-like sniffings.*]
   Hh-hh, hh-hh, hh-hh, hh-hh, hh-hh.
KARION. Have you caught a smell?
JUST MAN.   Perhaps he's caught a *cold*,
   He's wearing such a short and tattered cloak!
INFORMER. O gods above, should such things be endured?
   That *they* should hurl abuse at *me*! What shame
   For a decent, patriotic man to suffer!   900
JUST MAN. A patriot, *you*, and decent!
INFORMER.   Yes, like no other.
JUST MAN. Then let me ask you something.
INFORMER.   Ask what you like.
JUST MAN. D'you live by farming land?
INFORMER.   You think I'm mad?
JUST MAN. Then trading overseas?
INFORMER [*slily*].   I sometimes claim so.*
JUST MAN. Well, did you learn a craft?
INFORMER.   No, certainly not.
JUST MAN. Then how have you managed to live without a job?
INFORMER [*self-importantly*]. I *oversee* all public and private
      business.
JUST MAN. But what gives *you* the right?
INFORMER.   I'm free to do it.
JUST MAN. How dare you claim you're decent, you petty crook,
   When you're loathed for doing what's no concern of yours? 910
INFORMER. Is it no concern of mine, you bird-brained fool,
   To serve my very own city with all my might?
JUST MAN. So meddling in others' affairs is public service?
INFORMER. That's *not* what I do: I support the rule of law
   And help to catch the people who transgress.
JUST MAN. But isn't that why the city appoints the jurors,
   To enforce its laws?
INFORMER.   But who's to bring the charges?
JUST MAN. Anyone who wants.*

INFORMER.   Well *that*'s just who I am.
  Which proves the city's business depends on me.
JUST MAN. Well, if that's so, the city's in rotten hands.   920
  [*Changing tone*] But wouldn't you really prefer a peaceful
    life,
  With nothing to do?
INFORMER.   That sounds like being a sheep,
  If you mean a life without a proper purpose.
JUST MAN. But won't you change your mind?
INFORMER.   I wouldn't do that
  For Wealth himself—or all Kyrene's assets.
KARION [*aggressively*]. Remove your cloak at once!
JUST MAN.   He's talking
  to *you*.
KARION. And then your shoes.
JUST MAN.   He's talking to you again.
INFORMER [*defiantly*]. I dare you all to lay a hand on me—
  Anyone who wants.
KARION [*mimicking him*].

                'Well *that*'s just who I am.'   [*He attacks.*]
INFORMER. Help! Help! They're robbing my clothes in broad
  daylight.   930
KARION. I'll teach you to make a living from others' business.
INFORMER [*to the* WITNESS]. You see what he's doing? I'll need you
  to testify.   [*The* WITNESS *runs off.*]
KARION. So much for that witness of yours! He's turned and fled!
INFORMER. Help! Help! They've got me trapped.
KARION.   Ah, starting to
  scream?
INFORMER. Help! Help! I say.
KARION [*to the* JUST MAN].   Please give me that ragged cloak
  To wrap around this dastardly informer.
JUST MAN. No, don't: it's vowed already to Wealth himself.
KARION. What better place to put this dedication
  Than round a vicious criminal just like this?   [*Drapes him.*]
  Not Wealth, at least; for he needs *lordly* clothes.   940
JUST MAN. And what's to be done with the shoes, just tell me
  that?
KARION. I'll fix them on his face, like this; that's how
  They nail their offerings up on olive trees.*

[*He attaches the shoes.*]

INFORMER [*breaking free*]. I'm getting out of here! I recognize
  I haven't a chance against you two. But once
  I find a partner, no matter how weak, I'll take
  This mighty god of yours to court today
  For making a blatant attempt, and all alone,
  To undermine democracy, without
  Persuading the people's Council or Assembly.   [*Exits.*]   950
JUST MAN [*calling after him*]. Oh, since you're going away in
      that gear of mine,
  I recommend you hurry straight to the baths
  And stand in prime position to warm yourself:*
  That's where I kept my station in the past.
KARION. I bet the bathman grabs him by the balls
  And drags him straight outside! He'll recognize
  What a nasty, bent old coin he's dealing with.
  Let's go inside, to let you worship Wealth.

[*Both go into the house. As they do so, there enters, from a side entrance,
a large and hideous* OLD WOMAN, *highly made-up and accompanied by a
slave who carries some food.*]

OLD WOMAN [*affectedly*]. Am I right in thinking, old gentlemen,
      I've found
  The house which belongs to this new god who's arrived?   960
  Or has my journey proved to be mistaken?
LEADER [*imitating her*]. Please rest assured that this is his very
      door,
  Young girl—for that's the age your *speech* suggests!
OLD WOMAN. Oh good, I'll knock and find out who's inside.

          [*Before she can do so,* CHREMYLOS *comes out.*]

CHREMYLOS. No need for that; I'm coming out anyway.
  Let's hear at once the reason you've paid a visit.
OLD WOMAN [*confidentially*]. My dearest friend, I've *suffered*
      beyond belief.
  Since the very day this god got back his sight,
  He's made my life just *too* unbearable.
CHREMYLOS. What's wrong? You're surely not another of
      those*—   970
  A *female* informer?
OLD WOMAN.   No, no, of course I'm not.

CHREMYLOS. You didn't commit offences involving—drink?*

OLD WOMAN. You're poking fun; but *I've* been torn to shreds.

CHREMYLOS. Then tell me straight away what's cut you up.

OLD WOMAN. Well, listen. I used to have a young boyfriend—
Utterly poverty-stricken, but *really* handsome.
And decent too. [*Coyly*] Whatever I asked of him,
He always tried to gratify my needs.
So I, in turn, gave every help to him.

CHREMYLOS. Now, what requests did he tend to make of you?   980

OLD WOMAN. Not much: he always felt so *terribly* shy.
He'd ask, perhaps, for twenty silver drachmas
To buy a cloak, and eight to spend on shoes.*
He'd urge me buy small dresses for his sisters,
Or a little shawl as a present for his mother.
And maybe four months' rations of wheat as well.

CHREMYLOS [*ironically*]. What *very* modest requests, I quite agree.
It's clear that, as you said, he felt so shy.

OLD WOMAN. What's more, he stressed it wasn't greed at all
That made him ask, but only pure affection.   990
[*Sentimentally*] He wanted that cloak to make him think of
me.

CHREMYLOS [*mimicking*]. He must have been so *terribly* much in
love.

OLD WOMAN. But now the filthy swine has changed his tune.
Something's gone wrong: he's quite a different person.
A while ago I sent him round this cake
Together with all the sweetmeats on this plate,
And added a message as well, to let him know
I'd pay a visit tonight.

CHREMYLOS.   And what did he do?

OLD WOMAN. He sent me back this *wedding*-cake—but saying
He never wanted to see my face again!   1000
On top of that he sent a further message:
'Long, long ago Milesian men were brave.'*

CHREMYLOS. I can tell he always had some moral scruples.
Now that he's rich, he's gone off lentil soup.*
In the past, when poor, he couldn't afford to choose.

OLD WOMAN. Well, in the past he never missed a day:
He always came and knocked on *my* front door.

CHREMYLOS. Perhaps he hoped he'd find you dead?

OLD WOMAN. How can you!
He loved to hear my voice.

CHREMYLOS. To get your money!

OLD WOMAN. I swear that when he saw me feeling sad, 1010
He'd sweetly say, 'My little duck, my dove!'

CHREMYLOS. And then, perhaps, he'd ask for money for shoes!

OLD WOMAN. Once, during the Greater Mysteries at Eleusis,
Because some man had ogled me on my wagon*
It made my boyfriend beat me up all day.
That shows how far the young man's jealousy went.

CHREMYLOS. He didn't want to share his *food*,* it seems.

OLD WOMAN. He told me I had a lovely pair of hands.

CHREMYLOS. Especially when they held out twenty drachmas!*

OLD WOMAN. He claimed I had such sweetly fragrant skin. 1020

CHREMYLOS. Yes, probably when you poured out Thasian wine!

OLD WOMAN. He said my eyes gave such a melting look.

CHREMYLOS. This fellow was shrewd, all right. He found a way
To consume the wealth of an old, lascivious sow!

OLD WOMAN. It's wrong, my friend, for the god to cause such
things
While claiming he's on the side of those who suffer.

CHREMYLOS [*softening*]. Well what should he do? He'll act on
your instructions.

OLD WOMAN. It's only right that the god should make this man
Repay me for the generous things I did.
It's surely wrong that *I* should be the loser. 1030

CHREMYLOS [*suggestively*]. Well didn't he give you recompense
each night?

OLD WOMAN. He said he'd never abandon me in life.

CHREMYLOS. What's wrong? He now just thinks of you as dead.

OLD WOMAN. I almost *am*, dear friend, from pining away.

CHREMYLOS. It looks to me like a case of *rotting* away!

OLD WOMAN. I've grown so thin, I'd slip through a ring, you
know.

CHREMYLOS. Provided the ring were the size of a carriage
wheel!

OLD WOMAN. Oh look, here comes the boy approaching now,
The one I've been complaining about to you.
It looks as though he's *en route* to attend a revel. 1040

CHREMYLOS. It does: he's carrying garlands as well as a torch.

[*Enter, from a side entrance, a rather drunk* YOUNG MAN, *brandishing a torch and garlands. He sees the* OLD WOMAN.]

YOUNG MAN. How nice to see you!

OLD WOMAN [*to* CHREMYLOS].   What's that?

YOUNG MAN.   My ancient friend,
  Your hair has greyed so quickly; I'm quite amazed.

OLD WOMAN. I can't endure abuse like this much longer!

CHREMYLOS. It sounds like ages since your last encounter.

OLD WOMAN. I beg your pardon! He saw me yesterday!

CHREMYLOS. If so, then his is a rather unusual case:
  Intoxication makes his eyesight *better*.

OLD WOMAN. That's quite untrue: he's just a loutish brute.

YOUNG MAN [*approaching her*]. O all ye gods who care for ancient
      things!   1050
  What a vast collection of wrinkles in just one face!

OLD WOMAN. Please keep your torch away from me!

CHREMYLOS.   She's right.
  It would only take a single spark from that
  To ignite her like a dry old olive branch.*

YOUNG MAN [*coaxing*]. Would you like some sport, for old time's
      sake?

OLD WOMAN [*startled*]. But *where?*

YOUNG MAN. Right here; I'll give you nuts.

OLD WOMAN.   What game d'you
      mean?

YOUNG MAN. It's 'Guess the —— *teeth*'!*

CHREMYLOS.   O let me have first go.
  I'm sure I know the answer—just three or four.

YOUNG MAN. You've lost the bet: she possesses a single molar!

OLD WOMAN. You horrible man, you must have lost all shame   1060
  To pour such bilge all over me in public.

YOUNG MAN. Pour what? A washing-down would do you good.

CHREMYLOS [*inspecting her*]. I don't agree; she's tarted up for
      sale.
  If someone washed this white cosmetic off,*
  You'd see the seedy remnants of her face.

OLD WOMAN [*to* CHREMYLOS]. I can see that age has made you
      lose all shame.

YOUNG MAN [*leering*]. Perhaps he *fancies* you and means to touch
  Your tits, because he thinks I haven't noticed.

OLD WOMAN [*to* CHREMYLOS]. In Aphrodite's name, keep off, you
    swine!

CHREMYLOS. In Hekate's name, I *would* be mad to touch you!*   1070
  [*Changing tone*] But look here now, young man, I won't
  allow
  Your loathing for this girl.

YOUNG MAN.   I dote on her!

CHREMYLOS. But she makes complaints about you.

YOUNG MAN.   What
    complaints?

CHREMYLOS. She claims you treat her badly and sometimes say
  'Long, long ago Milesian men were brave.'

YOUNG MAN [*confidentially*]. I'll let you have her without a
    fight.

CHREMYLOS. You'll *what*?

YOUNG MAN. I'll show your seniority due respect. You see,
  I'd never have made a younger man this offer.
  You're welcome to have the girl and take her away.

CHREMYLOS. Ah, *I* can see your ploy: you no longer think   1080
  She's good enough for you.

OLD WOMAN.   He must be stopped!

YOUNG MAN. I've no desire to keep up any connection
  [*Gestures at audience*] With a woman whose been well shagged
    by thirteen thousand!*

CHREMYLOS. It's now too late to try to change your mind:
  You chose to drink the wine, so drain the dregs.

YOUNG MAN. These dregs are ancient, though, and rancid too.

CHREMYLOS. Then simply use a filter to cut them out.
  Come on inside.

YOUNG MAN.   I'd certainly like to come
  And dedicate these garlands to the god.

OLD WOMAN. And *I've* got something to say to Wealth as well.   1090

YOUNG MAN [*turning*]. Then *I'm* not going inside.

CHREMYLOS.   You needn't
    worry:
  She isn't going to rape you.

YOUNG MAN.   That's just as well.
  I've tarred this vessel's underbelly enough.*

OLD WOMAN. Get into the house: I'll follow you right behind.

                                  [*Both in.*]

CHREMYLOS. Great Zeus above, this hag won't let him go.
　　She clung to the boy just now with a limpet's grip!

[CHREMYLOS *follows them into the house. Enter, from a side entrance,* HER-
MES, *who timidly knocks on the door then backs away.* KARION, *with a cup
in his hands, looks out.*]

KARION. Well who's this knocking this time? [*Looks around*]
　　What's going on here?
　　No one around, it seems. Perhaps this door
　　Is squeaking away for nothing, and wants a kick. [*Turns to
　　　go in.*]
HERMES. Hey, Karion, wait a minute!   1100
KARION [*coming back*].　　　　　Now you there, tell me,
　　Was it you who thumped so loud on the door just now?
HERMES [*disingenuously*]. Oh no, I was *going* to knock—you
　　　came out first.
　　Please hurry and call your master out at once,
　　Then tell his wife and children to come out too,
　　Then tell the slaves, and then the dog as well,
　　And then yourself—and then the family pig.
KARION. But what's this all about?
HERMES.　　　　　　　　It's Zeus, you rogue:
　　He wants to mash you all up in a dish,
　　Then throw the lot of you down the criminals' pit.*
KARION. Cut out the tongue to reward this herald's news!*   1110
　　But why does Zeus propose to do these things?
HERMES. Because you've done the most outrageous deeds.
　　For ever since Wealth recovered his sight afresh,
　　We gods have had no incense, laurel, or cakes,
　　No sacrificial victim of any kind—
　　No nothing at all.*
KARION.　　　　　And that's your future too.
　　It serves you right for treating us humans badly.
HERMES. The *other* gods don't matter so much to me.
　　But I myself am wasting away.
KARION [*taking the point*].　　I see.
HERMES. Before, the female tavern-keepers spoilt me.   1120
　　At dawn I'd get wine-flavoured cakes and honey,
　　And figs as well—the perfect diet for Hermes.
　　[*Gestures to sky*] But now I sit upstairs, all famished and idle.

KARION. And quite right too! Despite these treats you got,
　You sometimes caused us harm.
HERMES [*self-pityingly*].　　　　　What grief I feel,
　What grief for the cakes they baked on the fourth of the
　　month!*
KARION [*mock-tragically*]. 'You pine and call in vain for one
　now gone.'*
HERMES. What grief for the legs of ham that I used to eat!
KARION. You can *ham* away as much as you like out here.
HERMES. What grief for the steaming innards I used to eat!　　1130
KARION. It sounds as though your *innards* are causing pain.
HERMES. What grief for the cups of full-bodied wine I drank!
KARION [*offering his cup*]. Why not just drink this down, and
　then skedaddle?
HERMES [*wheedling*]. You'd surely help an old and trusted
　friend?
KARION. Provided the help you want is mine to give.
HERMES. Suppose you fetch me out a well-baked loaf
　To soothe my hunger. And bring a joint as well
　From the sacrifice inside.
KARION.　　　　　　　　　I can't do *that*!
HERMES. But when you used to filch your master's food
　I always helped to save you from detection.　　1140
KARION. But only since you took a share, you cheat!
　A well-baked pastry always came your way.
HERMES. But even *that* you usually ate yourself!
KARION. Well I was the one who had to take the whipping
　Whenever my mischief got me into trouble.
HERMES. Don't bear a grudge—accept an amnesty.
　I beg you, by the *gods*, please give me a home.
KARION. You'll really abandon the gods and stay down here?
HERMES. Of course: conditions with you are so much better.
KARION. Are you sure defection's quite the proper thing?　　1150
HERMES [*sententiously*]. 'One's homeland is wherever one feels
　at home.'*
KARION. What *good* will you be to us, if you stay down here?
HERMES. You can stand me by the door, as 'god of the hinge'.*
KARION. As 'god of the hinge'? We don't want *twisters* here!
HERMES. Then 'god of merchandise'.
KARION.　　　　　　　　　We're wealthy now:

What need to keep a Hermes who's a tradesman?

HERMES. In that case, 'god of deceit'.

KARION.   That's out of the question.

[*Sententiously*] 'Our lives eschew deceit; our ways are
    honest.'*

HERMES. Then 'god who acts as guide'.

KARION.   But Wealth can see:

We won't be needing a guide here any longer.   1160

HERMES. Then 'god of the games'. Now surely you can't object.

Poetic contests, athletic competitions—

To fund such things is a perfect use for wealth.*

KARION. How very convenient, having so many titles!

This god's invented a special way of life.

It's not surprising that those on jury service

Contrive to get their names on several lists.*

HERMES. Shall I go inside, on the terms agreed?

KARION.   All right.

But I want you to go to the well and wash some tripe,

To prove your servile status straight away.   1170

[KARION *follows* HERMES *indoors. A few seconds later, a* PRIEST *appears from
a side entrance.*]

PRIEST [*to* CHORUS]. I need precise directions to Chremylos' house.

[*The door opens and* CHREMYLOS *himself comes out.*]

CHREMYLOS. Well what's the matter, my friend?

PRIEST.   A pile of trouble.

Since the time this Wealth of yours acquired his sight,

My life's been blighted by famine. I've nothing to eat,

Despite my post as priest of Zeus the Saviour.

CHREMYLOS. Then tell me, in heaven's name, the reason for
    this?

PRIEST. All sacrifice has ceased.

CHREMYLOS.   But what's the cause?

PRIEST. The cause is universal wealth. Before,

When wealth was scarce, a merchant, say, would come

To sacrifice in thanks for crossing the seas.   1180

Or someone would come in thanks for being acquitted.

As priest I often joined in the feasting too.

But now the temple's empty. Nobody comes—

Except the many who need to defecate.*

CHREMYLOS [*facetiously*]. And don't you take your share of what
    they leave?

PRIEST. So *I* shall abandon Zeus the Saviour too:
    I want to come and join your new cult here.

CHREMYLOS. Don't worry. I think you'll find that all is well.
    For Zeus the Saviour too is here inside:
    He decided to come himself.   1190

PRIEST.   Then what could be better?
                                          [*Approaches the door.*]

CHREMYLOS. But stay out here. We're just about to go
    To dedicate Wealth where once he stood before,
    As guardian of Athena's treasury vault.*
    [*Calling in*] Ignite the torches and bring them out. [*to* PRIEST]
    It's time
    For *you* to lead the god's torch-lit procession.

PRIEST. I shall, with pleasure.

CHREMYLOS [*calling again*].   Please call out Wealth himself.

      [*The first figure to appear at the door is the* OLD WOMAN.]

OLD WOMAN. And what about me?

CHREMYLOS.   Oh, *you* can carry these pots,
    The ones for Wealth's new shrine, on top of your head.*
    Look solemn, now. Your dress looks bright enough.*

OLD WOMAN. But what about my problem?   1200

CHREMYLOS.   You'll find it's solved.
    Your boyfriend's going to pay you a visit tonight.

OLD WOMAN. Well if you guarantee he's going to come,
    I'm happy to carry these pots for your procession.
                             [*She lifts them onto her head.*]

CHREMYLOS [*observing her*]. That makes the situation rather odd;
    I've never seen anything quite like this before.
    With other pots the scum lies on the top;
    But here the pots themselves stand on the scum!

[WEALTH *appears, followed by other members of the household, including*
    KARION. *The* PRIEST *leads off the procession by a side entrance.*]

LEADER. This clearly is no time for hanging round. We'd better
    follow.
    We'll take position at the rear, and sing as we proceed.

[*The* CHORUS *completes the procession, accompanying it with appropriate*
    chants of celebration.]

EXPLANATORY NOTES

The Explanatory Notes are chiefly designed to provide concise guidance to historical and other details which might puzzle a modern reader. For three of the four plays in this volume, fuller information about most points can be found in the Oxford commentaries which are cited in the Select Bibliography.

Fragments of lost tragedies are cited from the following works:

Nauck   A. Nauck (ed.), *Tragicorum Graecorum Fragmenta* (2nd edn., Leipzig, 1889)

TrGF   *Tragicorum Graecorum Fragmenta*, ed. B. Snell *et al.* (Göttingen, 1971–).

Play titles are abbreviated as follows:

A.	*Acharnians*
AW	*Assembly-Women*
B.	*Birds*
C.	*Clouds*
F.	*Frogs*
K.	*Knights*
L.	*Lysistrata*
P.	*Peace*
W.	*Wasps*
We.	*Wealth*
WT	*Women at the Thesmophoria*

BIRDS

17–18 *jackdaw . . . three*: the 'son of Tharreleides' is unknown; the joke might convey a gibe about size or noisiness. There were six obols in a drachma, which was a day's wages in the later fifth century for certain jobs; three obols was the daily rate of remuneration for jurors (note on *L*. 625). The prices given are presumably high.

   28 *join the crows*: the Greek expression, lit. 'to the ravens' (often translated 'to the crows'), is a slang equivalent of 'go to hell!'. Euelpides puns on the literal sense.

   31 *Sakas*: the term, applied by Greeks to certain Scythian peoples, is apparently a satirical nickname (implying foreign birth) for the minor tragic poet Akestor (cf. *W*. 1221).

   41 *sit in the courts*: the Athenians sometimes mocked the extensiveness

of their legal system, which involved a panel of 6,000 jurors, as an addiction to law courts and jury service: cf. 109, and e.g. *C.* 207–8, *P.* 505.

43 *basket . . . wreaths*: all three items suggest a prospective sacrifice, to the gods of a new-found city; cf. my Introduction to the play.

57 *yoo-hoo*: Euelpides uses what in Greek is the usual call of 'Slave!' when knocking on a house door; its sound allows wordplay with the noun for hoopoe.

68 *Phasis*: a river South of the Black Sea (modern Georgia), after which the pheasant (Gk. *phasian(ik)os*) was named; for pheasants, cf. *C.* 109.

71 *cock-fight*: the loser of a cock-fight could be called 'slave'; for this popular sport, cf. e.g. 759, 1365–6.

76 *Phaleron*: the old harbour of Athens, before the building of the Peiraieus; small fish were an Athenian favourite (cf. *A.* 901–2).

94 *What . . . crest*: the line has overtones of tragic formality of diction; cf. 993–4, *WT* 136–40, *F.* 47.

95 *twelve gods*: the major Olympians, who formed a kind of extended divine family; cf. *K.* 235.

101 *tragic plays*: Sophokles (*c.*496–406) had treated the gruesome story of Tereus and Prokne (see Index of Names) in his *Tereus*, though he is unlikely to have shown Tereus on stage as a hoopoe; cf. my Introduction to the play.

102 *bird or—peacock*: a similar joke pattern occurs at 1203 and at e.g. *L.* 982; the reference to peacocks reflects their exotic status as a still recent import from Persia (cf. 269, 885, *A.* 63).

108 *triremes*: the warships of Athens's large and expert navy, her greatest military asset; the previous summer a large number of triremes had set sail on the Sicilian expedition (Thucydides 6.30–1). Cf. *L.* 173.

109 *jurymen*: cf. n. on 41.

112 *What venture . . . here*: the line, like a number of Tereus' utterances, has a stylistic elevation which echoes his tragic associations (100–1).

126 *Aristokrates*: probably the Aristokrates who, among other things, served as general the year after this play (Thucydides 8.9.2); but there were others of the same name.

142 *squeeze his balls*: a hedonistic inversion of normal paternal concern (cf. Plato, *Symposium* 183c) over the homosexual seduction of a son.

145 *Red Sea*: for the Greeks this term covered the whole Arabian gulf.

146 *galley*: the 'Salaminia', one of two official galleys; it had been used to serve a summons on Alkibiades the previous summer, in connection with the scandals—mutilation of the herms (cf. *L.* 1094) and

profanation of the Mysteries—which preceded the sailing of the fleet to Sicily (Thucydides 6.52).

149–51 *Lepreon . . . Melanthios*: Lepreon, a town in the West Peloponnese, prepares for the gibe at Melanthios, a minor tragic poet previously mocked at *P.* 801 ff., 1009 ff.

152–4 *Opountians . . . gold*: Opous, in Lokris (South-east central Greece), prepares for the gibe at Opountios, whose nature remains obscure; whether 'one-eyed' in the further joke at 1294 should be taken literally is uncertain. A talent (= 6,000 drachmas, cf. n. on 18) is wealth beyond the level of ordinary people.

161 *bridegroom's life*: probably a proverbial expression; the preceding plants all had associations with weddings.

174 *You . . . words*: a quasi-tragic line.

186 *Melos*: the reference (see Index of Names) lends Peisetairos the ruthlessness of an Athenian imperialist, despite his desire to escape the city; cf. my Introduction to the play.

203 *nightingale*: Prokne (see Index of Names).

212 *Itys*: son of Tereus and Prokne (see Index of Names).

275 *'of colour rare'*: a phrase quoted or adapted from Sophokles (*Tyro* fr. 654, *TrGF* IV).

277–8 *Mede . . . camel's help*: the Medes were a near-eastern people related to the Persians; for Medes and camels, cf. e.g. Herodotos 7.83.2.

282–3 *families . . . Hipponikos*: it was common for male Athenian names to pass down two generations at a time; thus the grandfather of Kallias (see Index of Names) was also Kallias, and both his father and son were called Hipponíkos.

291 *crested*: as in English, the Greek *lophos*, 'crest', can refer to birds, helmets, and hills. The joke switches between these; see Index of Names, 'Karians'. Races in armour were a recognized athletic competition.

296 *entrance*: a meta-theatrical reference to one of the theatre's side entrances; see Introduction, 'Stage Directions'.

300 *Sporgilos*: we know nothing else about this barber; his name may anyway have been that of a bird (meaning ?sparrow).

301 *owl to Athens*: 'to bring owls [Athena's bird: cf. 516] to Athens' meant the equivalent of 'carrying coals to Newcastle'.

324 *lovers*: Thucydides 2.43.1 famously depicts Perikles enjoining the Athenians to be 'lovers' of their city; cf. 1279, *A.* 142–4, *K.* 732.

342 *pecked out*: cf. 1613, with 583 for the reality alluded to.

353 *taxiarch*: the infantry commander of each of the city's ten tribes; next in command after the generals.

358 *No owls*: because Athena's bird (cf. 516) would never attack the products of potters, Athena's craftsmen.

368 *my wife*: the Athenian Prokne (see Index of Names).

395 *Kerameikos cemetery*: the Kerameikos area (lit. 'Potters' district', hence a pun with 386 ff.), outside the city walls on the North-west side, was the location of Athens's largest burial ground; war dead could be buried there (cf. Thucydides 2.34).

399 *Birdsnest Creek*: the Greek names the Peloponnesian town of Orneai (punning on *ornea*, 'birds'); there had been an abortive Athenian siege of it about a year previously (Thucydides 6.7.1-2).

402 *soldiers' arms*: the birds' aggression and anger are their 'weapons', to be grounded, in hoplite (infantry) style, during the suspension of hostilities.

430-1 *sophist . . . subtle*: on the importance of this description, see my Introduction to the play.

441 *cutler*: we do not know whether the racy story in question was an animal fable or a scandalous anecdote about a contemporary.

445 *vote for us*: although the judges numbered ten, only the first five of their votes (drawn randomly) counted; the following line indicates the unsurprising possibility that the audience as a whole might influence the outcome (see Plato, *Laws* 659a, 701a). Cf. 1101 ff., *AW* 1154 ff.

450 *noticeboards*: call-up lists appeared on official noticeboards in the Agora; cf. *P.* 1179-84.

464 *Is dinner . . . ?*: throughout the agon Euelpides plays a traditional buffoon's role.

469 *Kronos and the Titans*: Kronos was father of Zeus and ruler of the pre-Olympian gods known as Titans; cf. my Introduction to the play.

472 *Aesop said*: this particular fable is not preserved.

476 *headland*: the Greek puns on the Athenian place name Kephale (lit. 'head'), the location of a large cemetery.

485 *'Persian bird'*: this term for the cock reflects its original introduction into Greece from Persia; cf. 833. Dareios and Megabazos are Persian names, the former that of two earlier kings, the latter of various aristocrats.

487 *headdress all erect*: the Persian king wore a peaked cap.

491 *lathe . . . craftsmen*: an instance of a sesquipedalian Aristophanic compound; cf. *L.* 457-8, and, for the extreme case, see n. on *AW* 1168.

494 *naming-day*: babies were formally named at a feast held on the tenth day after birth; cf. 922.

501 *obeisance to the kites*: the first appearance of the kite, taken as harbinger of spring, was sometimes greeted, no doubt especially by country people, by rolling over on the ground.

503 *swallowed a coin*: Athenians sometimes carried small change in their mouths; cf. *AW* 818, *W.* 609, 791.

507 *pricks to work*: Euelpides reinterprets an obscene expression (perhaps
a soldiers' 'jocular reveille call', as Dunbar suggests), alluding in the
process to the near-eastern practice of circumcision.

512 *Priam held a bird*: the king of Troy might be depicted in the tragic
theatre carrying a sceptre with a bird on its top.

515 *eagle on his head*: in fact Zeus' eagle seems never to have
been depicted on his head; if this is not a humorous allusion to
real birds alighting on statues (cf. n. on 1115), we should perhaps
take Peisetairos to be blustering, as in so much else of what he
says.

516 *owl . . . goshawk*: the owl was often linked with Athena, e.g. appearing with her on Athenian coins (see 1106); cf. 301, 358, and
Theophrastos, *Characters* 16.8. We know of no image of Apollo with
a goshawk; but cf. the hawk simile at *Iliad* 15.237.

521 *swindle*: Lampon (see Index of Names) is cast as a charlatan, but
Greeks really did sometimes swear by animals.

534 *silphium*: a pungent, fennel-type herb, imported from Kyrene (see
Index of Names), whose juice was used as seasoning in Greek cooking; cf. 1579 ff., *AW* 1171.

552 *Babylon . . . bricks*: the walls of Babylon had been described by
Herodotos 1.178–9; cf. n. on 1126–9.

553 *Giants*: see n. on 824–5.

556 *ban the gods*: cf. 188–92 for Peisetairos' earlier adumbration of such
an idea.

559 *Alkmene . . . Semele*: Alkmene, mother of Herakles by Zeus; Alope,
mother of Hippothoön by Poseidon; Semele, mother of Dionysos by
Zeus.

564 *fit . . . features*: in the following lines, the coot's Greek name, *phalêris*,
plays on 'phallus', and 'barley' has the slang meaning of penis;
ducks are aquatically apt for the god of the sea; gulls are symbols of
the gourmand (cf. *K.* 956, with *B.* 1583 ff. for Herakles the glutton);
'king' was an existing nickname of the wren, whose Greek name
forms a pun with 'uncastrated' in the next line.

575 *quivering dove*: the phrase is applied to Iris in the Homeric *Hymn to
Apollo* 114; cf. *Iliad* 5.778 (Hera and Athena).

576 *wingéd lightning-bolt*: the phrase is reminiscent of elevated poetry.

584 *pay him*: in the way human doctors were paid; perhaps also in the
way in which people paid fees to his oracle at Delphi.

609 *five . . . crow*: the phrase is adapted from a lost poem by Hesiod (fr.
304, R. Merkelbach and M. L. West (eds.), *Hesiodi Fragmenta Selecta*
(Oxford, 1970)).

645 *Krioa*: a real Athenian deme (exact location unknown), one of the
*c.*140 local districts into which Attika was divided from the late sixth

century; membership of a deme was part of citizenship and was inherited.

652-3 *fox . . . eagle*: the latter fed the former's cubs to its young; the fox, lacking wings (like Peisetairos), was unable to take revenge.

656-7 *Xanthias . . . Manodoros*: two common slave-names at Athens. Some editors think that Peisetairos and Euelpides had this pair of slaves with them at the start of the play. I prefer to see the names as a humorous reflection of Peisetairos' transfer of human habits to the bird world (cf. 1311).

672 *skewers*: the joke probably refers to the performer's double reed pipes (*auloi*: cf. n. on 861).

692 *Prodikos*: fifth-century rhetorician and sophist, known to have speculated about the origins of religion. In what follows the chorus presents a cosmogony of the kind most familiar from Hesiod's *Theogony*, esp. lines 116 ff.

695 *from wind*: a hen's unfertilized eggs were called 'wind-eggs'; Aristophanes comically elevates the term to a new cosmogonical significance.

707 *lovers' gifts*: for the practice of gift-giving by men to their younger homosexual partners, see *We.* 153-9; normal anxiety about physical seduction was (obliquely) reflected in the humour of 137-42.

712 *Orestes*: apparently a nickname for a footpad or mugger (cf. n. on 1491-3, with *A.* 1166); it is not clear whether an individual or a type is meant.

719 *augury*: 'bird' was sometimes used in Greek to mean 'omen'.

734 *birds' milk*: an expression for sybaritic luxury; cf. 1673 and *W.* 508.

746 *Mountain-mother*: Kybele; see n. on 876.

748-51 *Phrynichos . . . music*: Phrynichos was a tragic poet, active in the first quarter of the fifth century and apparently remembered mostly for his choruses (cf. *W.* 220, 269-70, *F.* 1299-1300).

759 *spur . . . fight*: an allusion to cock-fighting; cf. n. on 71. For birds' treatment of their fathers, see 1347 ff.

763 *Philemon's clan*: Philemon may be another Athenian accused of foreign origins; alternatively, the name may have Phrygian associations (cf. the mythological Philemon, e.g. Ovid, *Metamorphoses* 8.631 ff.). We know nothing of Spintharos.

766-8 *son of Peisias . . . partridge-artifice*: the target of this passage cannot be securely identified. The 'exiles' are probably those accused of the mutilation of the herms (*L.* 1094 with n.) or the profanation of the Mysteries in 415. Partridges are known for various forms of devious behaviour, including pretence of injury to distract hunters from their young (cf. 1292-3).

774 *Hebros*: a Thracian river which runs into the north-east Aegean.

789 *watch the comedies*: the apparent implication (disputed by some) is that at this date the City Dionysia was organized to allow performances of tragic trilogies in the mornings, individual comedies in the afternoons.

790 *Patrokleides*: possibly the political figure known from e.g. Andokides, *On the Mysteries* 73; but we cannot reconstruct the motive for the scatological imputation against him.

794 *Council seats*: prime seating was reserved for members of the Council (500 in all, see Index of Names); cf. *P*. 887, 906.

800 '*red horse-cock*': an Aischylean phrase (fr. 134, *TrGF* III), referring to a hybrid creature used as a ship's emblem; cf. *F*. 932–5. It here suits the supposedly arrogant Dieitrephes (see Index of Names), preening himself on his rise from phylarch (officer of a tribal division of the cavalry) to hipparch (one of its two or three supreme commanders).

808 *Shot . . . feathers*: Aischylos, *Myrmidons* fr. 139.4–5 (*TrGF* III), where Achilles had compared his fatal loan of armour to Patroklos with the story of an eagle killed by an arrow bearing its own feathers.

822–3 *Theogenes . . . Aischines*: on Theogenes, see the Index of Names; Aischines is not otherwise identifiable.

825 *Giants*: the prodigious offspring of Heaven and Earth (see Index of Names) who fought a cosmic battle, the gigantomachy (common in Greek art, including the east metopes of the Parthenon), against the Olympian gods; the site of Phlegra was disputed. Peisetairos burlesques the myth by treating it as a case of inflated fiction.

828 *Polias*: 'Guardian of the city', cult title of Athena in her role as ancient goddess of the Akropolis and patroness of Athens.

833 *Persian bird*: see n. on 485.

835 *war-god's chick*: the phrase, lit. 'chick of Ares', may have arisen (humorously) from cock-fighting; cf. n. on 71.

842 *the bell*: bells were sometimes rung as part of the procedure of sentry duty; cf. 1160 and Thucydides 4.135.1.

857–8 *Chairis*: a Boiotian pipe-player, mocked elswhere for supposed musical incompetence (cf. *A*. 16, 866, *P*. 951); this is probably meant as a gibe by the chorus at the actual pipe-player, or conceivably Chairis himself was the performer (O. Taplin, *Comic Angels* (Oxford, 1993), 106).

861 *raven . . . piper's cheek-band*: the leather cheek-band was worn round the head by musicians to help hold a pair of reed pipes (*auloi*) in position; cf. *W*. 582. 'Raven' may just be an insult at the supposedly unpleasant sounds being produced; or the procession may have contained a raven-piper.

864 *Hestia*: goddess of the hearth, often addressed at the start of prayers.

868 *Sounion's . . . lord*: the hawk usurps the site of Poseidon's temple at Sounion, the headland at the southern tip of Attika.

869 *Pytho and Delos*: Pytho was a traditional name for Delphi (see Index of Names) and its territory; the island of Delos, birthplace of Apollo, was sacred to the god; Leto, in the next line, was mother of Apollo. Swans were associated with Apollo as god of song (cf. 769–72).

876 *Queen . . . Kleokritos*: Peisetairos picks up the Priest's allusion to the 'Great Mother' goddess (or Mountain-mother, 846), Kybele, whose ecstatic rites, engaged in by Korybantics (see Index of Names), were derived from Anatolia. Kleokritos is the butt of a joke about (ostrich-like) obesity (cf. *F.* 1437), but if he is the same man as the Archon of 413/412 he must have been a respectable figure.

880 *the Chians*: in appreciation of the loyalty of Chios (see Index of Names) as an ally, Athens had added the phrase 'and for the Chians' to official prayers for the city's well-being.

910 *Homer's phrase*: in fact the poet has produced a compound of two different epic expressions.

918–19 *dithyrambs . . . Simonides*: dithyrambs were poems performed by choruses of fifty, in honour of Dionysos; cf. Kinesias at 1372 ff., esp. 1388. Simonides (*c.*556–468) composed many dithyrambs, as well as works, some of them commissioned by rich rulers (the Poet is dropping hints), in several other genres.

922–3 *few days . . . naming-day*: see n. on 494; for the incidental reference to the passage of dramatic time, cf. *L.* 881.

926 *Come, father . . .* : the poet borrows phrases from the lyric poet Pindar (518–438), including an address to Hieron, tyrant of Syracuse, who in 476/5 established a new city near, and named after, Mount Aitna (Etna) in Sicily.

939 *Pindaric utterance*: the poet returns to the source of some of his earlier snatches (n. on 926).

941–5 *Among . . . to you*: the poet stitches together two further extracts from Pindar.

962 *Bakis*: apparently a quasi-generic (and non-Greek) title for certain oracular sources; cf. *K.* 123 ff., *P.* 1071, and e.g. Herodotos 8.20.

968 *between Korinth and Sikyon*: adjacent territories in the north-east Peloponnese (cf. Index of Names, 'Korinth'), with no in-between; the phrase, which occurs in real oracles, is therefore paradoxical, and came to mean 'nowhere'.

971 *Pandora*: 'giver of all gifts'; here an earth-goddess rather than the 'first woman' of e.g. Hesiod, *Works and Days* 59 ff.

988 *Diopeithes*: a political and religious figure, comically accused of corrupt manipulation of oracles and the like (cf. *K.* 1085); for Lampon, see Index of Names.

993–4 *What aim . . . journey*: for the style of questioning, see n. on 94.

  998 *Kolonos*: the name both of an Athenian deme (cf. Sophokles' *Oedipus at Kolonos*) and of a region of the city close to the Agora. It is uncertain which is meant here, or why; one possibility is that Meton (see Index of Names) had erected a sundial in one of these places. In any case, the line is pointedly bathetic.

1001 *baking-lid*: a parody of the kind of analogies sometimes used by Greek scientists; cf. *C.* 96 for the same point.

1009 *Thales*: of Miletos, the earliest of Greek scientist-philosophers (active *c.*600), hence a byword for intellectual distinction (cf. *C.* 180).

1021 *consuls*: the Inspector, an official sent by Athens to enforce imperial regulations on her allied cities, asks for the whereabouts of *proxenoi*, local citizens who held semi-official responsibility for looking after the interests of Athens.

1028 *Pharnakes*: a Persian satrap; the Inspector boasts about his supposed diplomatic importance, at a time when we know that there were divisions between the governors of the Persian empire.

1032 *urns*: voting-urns for a law court; it is implied that the Inspector has come to make legal arrangements for the new city, though his carrying of the urns is an absurdity.

1035 DECREE-SELLER: we have no other evidence for this type of person, who may be a hyperbolic burlesque on Athenian political life; cf. n. on 1289.

1040–1 *the people . . . Olophyxos*: the wording is close to known Athenian imperial decrees; see esp. the so-called Coinage Decree, translated in C. W. Fornara, *Archaic Times to the End of the Peloponnesian War* (Cambridge, 1983), 105. Olophyxos was a small Athenian ally in north Greece: it is chosen here not for official logic but for the sake of a pun in the Greek.

1046–7 *I summon . . . assault*: it was an important feature of the Athenian legal system that cases involving inhabitants of allied cities were heard at Athens itself; cf. 1424–5, 1453–60.

1052 *ten thousand drachmas*: a huge sum, more than one-and-a-half talents (1 talent = 6,000 drachmas; see n. on 18); but this figure is known as the penalty cited for transgression of certain Athenian decrees.

1054 *crap on pillars*: the Decree-Seller accuses Peisetairos of befouling official inscriptions; the allegation is probably of political subversiveness, though such behaviour might sometimes have occurred for more banal reasons; cf. *We.* 1184, *F.* 366.

1073–5 *Diagoras . . . reward*: Diagoras was an intellectual and poet who had probably become notorious for the expression of impious views (cf. *C.* 830), though we cannot be certain that he had been outlawed in the precise terms suggested here. The passage parodies the custom of official proclamations at the City Dionysia; if a decree offering rewards for killing Athenian tyrants was still issued at this date, it was a relic of past times (but see note on *L.* 619 for continuing Athenian fears of tyranny). A talent would be a large reward: see n. on 154.

1079–83 *sells . . . net*: the passage pictures perfectly normal activities of a bird-catcher/seller, equivalent to those of, say, butchers; an Athenian audience would regard them as 'cruel' only from the birds' fictionally anthropomorphized perspective.

1084 *breeding birds*: rich Athenians sometimes kept aviaries and bred various species of birds as pets, for display (e.g. peacocks), or for such purposes as cock-fighting; see e.g. Plato, *Republic* 5.459a, Theophrastos, *Characters* 21.6.

1103 *if they vote*: see n. on 445.

1104 *Paris*: the Trojan shepherd chosen as judge of the 'beauty contest' between Athena, Hera, and Aphrodite; he was offered gifts by all the goddesses, and his reward for choosing Aphrodite was Helen.

1106 *Owls of silver*: Athenian coins (see n. on 516); Laurion, in south Attika, was the site of Athens's silver mines.

1115 *statues have*: Greek statues regularly had bronze disks on small spikes over their heads, as protection from bird-droppings.

1126–9 *braggarts . . . Wooden Horse*: perhaps a parody of the claim at Herodotos 1.179.3 that the wall of Babylon (cf. 552) was large enough for a four-horse chariot to be driven round it; but cf. also Thucydides 1.93.5. Proxenides, alleged braggart, is mentioned also at *W.* 325; for Theogenes, see the Index of Names.

1136–7 *cranes . . . stones*: it was popularly believed that cranes swallowed stones as a kind of ballast for their high flights; cf. 1428–9.

1147 *What . . . feet*: a line in tragic style, with 'feet' substituted for 'hands' (adesp. fr. 46, *TrGF* II), which seems to have had a quasi-proverbial status.

1150 *their tails*: my translation imports the idea of 'tails'; it is hard to make sense of the Greek at this point.

1155 *woodpeckers*: actually the Greek may mean 'pelicans', whose name sounded similar to the word for 'axe'.

1160 *ring the bell*: see n. on 842.

1175 *Outrageous . . . malefaction*: the line is in tragic style; there are other overtones of tragic messenger scenes in the context.

1197–8 *deity . . . ear*: the chorus-leader speaks in tragic fashion, in preparation for Iris' appearance on the 'machine', which was especially associated with divine epiphanies in tragedy; cf. my general Introduction, 'Stage Directions'.

1203 *ship—or helmet*: the absurd question (cf. 102) probably depends on features of Iris' appearance—perhaps oar-like flapping wings, or a billowing dress, and a prominent traveller's hat.

1204 *official galley*: see n. on 146.

1232-3 *To slaughter . . . fumes*: Iris uses the language of elevated poetry.

1238 ff. *Avoid . . .* : the whole of this speech of Iris' is a cento of tragic phrases and idioms.

1247-8 *Amphion's . . . fire*: at least part of these two lines comes from Aischylos' lost *Niobe* (fr. 160, *TrGF* III). Amphion was husband of Niobe; their children were destroyed by Apollo and Artemis after Niobe had boasted that she was as happy as their mother, Leto.

1252 *Porphyrion*: leader of the Giants in their rebellion against the Olympians; see n. on 824-5.

1255 *screw you*: see my Introduction to the play for the satyric character of this threat of rape.

1279 *lovers*: see n. on 324.

1281-3 *Spartan ways . . . message-sticks*: Spartans typically wore longer hair and less trimmed beards than Athenians; see *L.* 279, 1072, *W.* 476-7. Athenians readily thought of them as ruggedly unconcerned for physical hygiene etc. (cf. *L.* 280), hence the association with the reputedly unkempt Sokrates. More factually, Spartans carried messages on leather or papyrus wrapped around a stick; cf. *L.* 991.

1289 *decrees*: it seems that copies of laws/decrees were sometimes for sale in the Athenian Agora; a later comic passage, Euboulos fr. 74, may allude to the same detail. Cf. n. on 1035.

1291 ff. *names of birds*: we do not know the point of every joke in the following catalogue. We cannot securely identify the 'tavern-keeper' (for his partridge-like limp, see n. on 768) or Menippos ('Swallow' probably implies foreign birth: cf. n. on 1681). For Opountios, see 154. Lykourgos was a member of a rich Athenian family which probably had Egyptian connections (hence 'Ibis'). Syrakosios was a democratic politician, here mocked for the sound of his oratorical voice. Meidias may also have been a politician, but the present joke plays on a taste for the sport of quail-tapping (which involved, among other things, flicking the birds on the head in order to try to make them flinch). For others, see the Index of Names.

1311 *Manes*: a common slave-name, of Anatolian origin, at Athens; cf. 656-7 and *L.* 908.

1337-9 *O for . . . swell*: taken, in part at least, from Sophokles' lost *Oinomaos* (fr. 476, *TrGF* IV).

1348 *It's fine . . . fathers*: cf. 757-9, and see *C.* 1427-9 for an equivalent use of this 'argument from nature' (a type common in contemporary intellectual debate) by another rebellious young man.

1354 *on boards*: like the ancient laws of Drakon and Solon at Athens (cf. Aristotle, *Constitution of the Athenians* 7.1).

1362-3 *What's more . . . boy*: the two lines are modelled on verses 27–8 by Theognis, sixth-century elegiac poet from Megara.

1365 *cock's spur*: cf. 759.

1373 *I fly . . . light*: an extract from a love-song by the sixth-century lyric poet Anakreon (D. L. Page (ed.), *Poetae Melici Graeci* (Oxford, 1962), fr. 378).

1385 *preludes*: elaborate introductions to dithyrambs (see n. on 918); they probably took a semi-improvised form and particularly exemplified the 'airily' inflated language, including many compound words, which was by this date especially associated with the genre; cf. *C.* 333-8, *P.* 828-31.

1405-7 *train . . . tribe*: official competitions for dithyrambic choruses were organized according to the ten official tribes of Athens; costs were defrayed by rich citizens serving as *chorêgoi*: Leotrophides is one such, apparently chosen here because known to be as physically slight as Kinesias himself.

1410-11 *Who are . . . swallow*: the Informer adapts the start of a song by the lyric poet Alkaios (born *c.*620) from Lesbos (E. Lobel and D. Page (eds.), *Poetarum Lesbiorum Fragmenta* (Oxford, 1955), fr. 345).

1423 *profession*: the idea is intrinsically satirical; the term 'informer' was strictly opprobrious, referring to anyone suspected of manipulating the Athenian legal system for personal gain. Cf. the informers at *A.* 818 ff., 910 ff., *We.* 850 ff.

1429 *stones*: see n. on 1137.

1440 *barbers' shops*: as in eighteenth-century London, these were recognized meeting-places in Athens; cf. *We.* 338.

1463 *Korkyra*: modern Corfu; Korkyrean leather whips were semi-proverbial. Peisetairos 'puns' visually on the use of a whip to operate a spinning-top (cf. J. Boardman, *Athenian Red Figure Vases: The Classical Period* (London 1989), ill. 108).

1470-81 *Many . . . shields*: see the Index of Names, 'Kleonymos', for the various satirical suggestions conveyed by the song.

1491-3 *Orestes . . . side*: the conclusion runs together the different threats posed by Orestes, son of Agamemon (subject of religious 'hero'-cult after his death), whose powers include the ability to inflict paralytic strokes, and Orestes the footpad (see 712).

1494 *parasol*: see my Introduction to the play, with n. 11.

1500 *Oxen-loosing hour*: Prometheus echoes a Homeric phrase (e.g. *Iliad* 16.779) denoting late afternoon.

1522 *down*: in a normal geographical context the Greek adverb could

1529 *Triballians*: the name belonged to a Thracian tribe who became a byword at Athens for extreme savagery.

1541 *three obols*: the increasingly ludicrous list culminates in a reference to the daily payment made to serving jurymen (n. on *L.* 625).

1551 *basket-carrier*: girls, usually chosen from leading Athenian families, who carried sacred baskets on their heads in religious processions, including the Panathenaia; cf. *A.* 242, *L.* 646, 1193, *AW* 732. They were evidently sometimes accompanied by attendants carrying parasols.

1552 *stool*: a basket-carrier would also have an attendant carrying a stool for her to sit on; cf. *AW* 734.

1553 *Shadow-footers*: an imaginary people, supposed to live near the equator and to possess feet large enough to be used as parasols.

1553-64 *near the land . . . 'the bat'*: the song humorously evokes both Odysseus' view of the Underworld in *Odyssey* 11, and Aischylos' lost play, *Psuchagogoi* ('Ghost-Raisers': fr. 273a, *TrGF* III), in which spirits of the dead were called up through sacrifice at the side of a lake. Souls in Hades are specifically compared to bats at *Odyssey* 24.6.

1569 *Laispodias*: an Athenian general who supposedly wore his cloak draped low.

1579 *silphium*: see n. on 534.

1585 *democratic birds*: the idea implies faction (oligarchic vs. democratic) of the kind widely familiar in contemporary Greek politics; at the same time it paradoxically ascribes democracy to a situation which appears to be more like despotic rule by Peisetairos himself; cf. my Introduction to the play.

1611 *swears by raven*: cf. 520 and 1335.

1620 *'The gods are patient'*: a proverbial sentiment.

1652 *foreign mother*: a comic allusion to the fact that Herakles' mother, Alkmene (558), was a *human* seduced by Zeus.

1653-4 *heiress . . . legitimate sons*: Peisetairos talks in the terms of Athenian law, which made special provisions for 'heiresses', i.e. daughters of fathers who left no legitimate male heirs. An heiress' nearest male relative would sometimes be the beneficiary of the situation—and Athena's would be Poseidon (Zeus' brother)!

1660 *Solon's law*: the Athenians regarded Solon (*c.*640–560) as their greatest lawgiver (cf. *C.* 1187); while not all laws ascribed to him were necessarily his, the present one may be (and the quotation, in any case, is from a genuine and old statute on intestacy).

1669 *phratry*: a notional kinship group, lit. 'brotherhood', whose meetings were accompanied by cult practices; the son of an Athenian citizen was introduced into a phratry as a sign of legitimacy.

1673 *birds' milk*: see 734.

1681 *swallows*: the twittering of swallows was a common symbol of barbarian speech (cf. *F.* 681).

1694 ff. *Antistrophe*: despite the separation, this forms a strophic pair (see Introduction, 'Formality and Performance') with the *strophe* at 1553 ff.

1695 *water-clock*: the Greek puns on two meanings of the word *klepsydra*, one the Athenian spring (see Index of Names), the other the term for a water-clock used to time law-court speeches.

1696 *Nasty beasts*: the chorus sings satirically of those who specialize, whether as advocates or teachers of rhetoric, in the business of forensic speech-making. It is a final glimpse of the Athenian legal world from which Peisetairos was originally fleeing (40-1, 109-116).

1701 *Gorgias, Philippos*: Gorgias (*c.*483-376) was a famous Sicilian sophist and teacher of rhetoric, Philippos apparently one of his associates (cf. *W.* 421).

1705 *tongues*: it was common to cut out the tongue of a sacrificial victim and give it, as a special delicacy, to the priest or some other suitable recipient; cf. *P.* 1060, *We.* 1110, and Homer, *Odyssey* 3.332.

1734 *Fates: Moirai*, traditionally associated with apportioning a person's lifespan; but they also had associations with marriage. The wedding-refrain is traditional (cf. *P.* 1332 ff.).

LYSISTRATA

1-3 *Now, if . . . tambourines*: Lysistrata implies that women are irrepressible devotees of ecstatic/sensual cults; 'Bacchic' refers to worship of Dionysos (see Index of Names). For tambourines, or small drums, cf. 388 and *W.* 119.

8 *arching eyebrows*: there may be a clue here to the appearance of Lysistrata's mask; see n. 9 to my Introduction to the play.

12 *And so we are*: Kalonike, typically as it turns out, seems to endorse (male/comic) stereotypes of female weakness.

16 *hard for women*: the respectable norm for Athenian women—though variously qualified in practice—was a life spent predominantly in the house; certain religious festivals (cf. 1-3) were a salient exception.

36 *eels*: Boiotian eels, from Lake Kopaïs, were a well-known delicacy; cf. 702, and e.g. *A.* 880 ff. The war made them harder to obtain.

42 *'What . . . achieve?'*: the line is in tragic style, though probably not a quotation.

59–60 *Salamis . . . ride*: sailors from Salamis (see Index of Names), and here by extension their wives, acquired a popular/comic reputation for sexual lustiness; Greek terms for sailing, riding, driving, etc., are often used for sexual innuendo: cf. ?411, AW 37–9, and e.g. W. 501.

62 *Acharnai*: the largest of Athenian demes (see note on B. 645); situated north of the city, it was especially vulnerable to Spartan ravages of Attika, including those from Dekeleia (see Introduction to the play): Lysistrata expects the women of this district to be eager for peace. Cf. Aristophanes' own *Acharnians*.

64 *a drink*: an instance of the comic leitmotif of women's bibulousness; cf. 114, 195 ff., 395, 465–6, AW 14–15, 132, We. 645, 737, 972.

67–8 *Anagyrous . . . stink*: Anagyrous, in south-west Attika, was noted for a fetid plant which grew in its swamps; this gave rise to expressions roughly equivalent in type to 'raise a stink'.

79 *ravishing*: Lampito matches the Athenian notion of Spartan women as athletic; cf. e.g. Xenophon, *Constitution of Sparta* I 4, Euripides, *Andromache* 595–600.

81 *By the Twins*: a characteristic Spartan oath by Kastor (see Index of Names) and his brother; cf. 86, 90, 142, 983, 1095, etc.

89 *trimmed*: Greek women often depilated or trimmed their pubic hair, either by plucking (as here, cf. 151) or singeing (n. on 828); comedy implies that the practice was meant to please male preferences for visible, youthful pudenda (cf. F. 516).

91 *'choice piece'*: although the Korinthian is a wife, the humour probably plays on Korinth's reputation for producing courtesans and prostitutes (cf. We. 149).

103 *Eukrates*: a typically Aristophanic 'sting-in-the-tail' joke; the name of Eukrates, apparently a military commander (though not identifiable for certain), is substituted for that of a Thracian place name.

110 *synthetic relief*: Miletos (see Index of Names) had a name, in comedy at least, as a producer of dildoes; cf. 158, AW 916.

112 *By the two goddesses*: Demeter and her daughter Persephone; for this characteristically female oath, cf. AW 155.

127 *'What means . . . flow?'*: a line in quasi-tragic style.

139 *sex and intrigue*: the Greek expression, lit. 'Poseidon and a skiff', alludes to the story (treated by Sophokles in his *Tyro*) of Poseidon's seduction of Tyro and the exposure of twin babies in a skiff. Lysistrata refers more generally to tragedies about heroines such as Phaidra; see the charges against Euripides at F. 1043–51.

151 *triangles of hair*: see n. on 89.

155–6 *Menelaos . . . sword*: the story, concerning Menelaos' inability to kill his wife after the capture of Troy, is found at Euripides, *Andromache* 629–32.

158 *try self-abuse*: the Greek phrase, lit. 'flay a flayed dog', probably refers to the use of leather dildoes (cf. 109). We do not know whether this Pherekrates is the comic poet of that name, active *c.*440–420.

163 *forcing us*: cf. a husband's sentiment at *AW* 471.

169 *duplicitous guile*: Lampito inadvertently confirms the Athenian image of Spartans as inveterately perfidious; cf. 629, 1270, *A.* 307–8, *P.* 1063–8.

170–1 *And who . . . negotiations?*: Lampito's loaded question reflects a situation in which popular support for peace in Athens was probably low.

173–4 *triremes . . . funds*: ships and money. Triremes (cf. *B.* 108) were fitted with sails as well as oars. Athena's treasury was in a building on the Akropolis (cf. *We.* 1192–3); about a year before this play the Athenians had decided to draw on their financial reserves and build new ships (Thucydides 8.15.1, cf. 2.24.1).

189 *over a shield*: a reminiscence of Aischylos, *Seven Against Thebes* 42 ff.

192 *white horse*: such a victim was probably more typical of Scythian sacrifice (see e.g. Herodotos 1.216.4); but there may be sexual innuendo here.

197 *water*: unmixed wine was not regularly drunk (though used for toasts); it is associated with decadent barbarians (e.g. *A.* 75), slaves (*K.* 85–7, *AW* 1123), revelling heroes (*A.* 1229), the vulgar (*K.* 354), and, as here, the bibulous women of comic imagination (*AW* 227).

203 *Persuasion*: actually a deity, often cited in erotic contexts and long associated with Aphrodite, with whom she shared a shrine on the Akropolis.

231 *lioness position*: lit. 'lioness [*sc.* handle] on a cheesegrater'; the position is frequently depicted in erotic vase-paintings. For the contrasting position in the previous line, cf. *AW* 265.

246 *help them . . . gates*: on this change of direction, cf. my Introduction to the play.

270 *wife of Lykon*: Rhodia, who was the subject of sexual slurs in comedy. Lykon was a well-to-do Athenian (cf. *W.* 1301), possibly politically active, though probably not the same man as the accuser of Sokrates.

275 *leave unscathed*: Kleomenes, king of Sparta, had tried to stifle the nascent Athenian democracy by force in 508; he left after a two-day occupation of the Akropolis: see Herodotos 5.72, and my Introduction to the play.

280 *six full years*: the old men caricature the idea of Spartan hardiness, for which cf. e.g. *B.* 1281–2.

284 *Euripides*: Euripides (see Index of Names) the 'misogynist'—a comically distorted extrapolation from his plays—was the focus of Aristophanes' very next play, *Women at the Thesmophoria*, produced just two months after *L.*; cf. also 368–9.

285 *Marathon*: the reference (see Index of Names), taken literally, would make these veterans around a century old; for archetypal 'Marathon-fighters' see *A.* 181, *W.* 711.

299 *Lemnos*: north-east Aegean island with a volcanic history; hence proverbially associated with fire and its god, Hephaistos.

313 *generals now in Samos*: several generals were currently with the fleet at the island of Samos in the east Aegean, and indeed conspiring to turn Athens to oligarchy: see Thucydides 8.27 ff. But the reference may express a simple cynicism on the part of old soldiers.

344 *Gold-crested*: a reference to the golden diadem on the archaic olive-wood statue of Athena (262).

347 *Tritogeneia*: an old, formal title of Athena's (e.g. Homer, *Odyssey* 3.378); its meaning is obscure (possibly 'true-born').

360 *Boupalos*: sculptor (real or fictitious), butt of the sixth-century iambic (satirical) poet, Hipponax of Ephesos, who threatened violence against him.

368–9 *Euripides . . . woman*: see n. on 284.

380 *a juror*: the remark depends on the (comic) stereotype of jurors as typically vindictive as well as old, like the wasp-jurors of *W.*; cf. 624–5.

381 *hair on fire*: probably a traditional element of 'pantomime' comic violence; cf. 1217–18.

387 COMMISSIONER: one of a special board, first of ten and subsequently of thirty, set up by the Athenians in 413/412 to streamline the city's bureaucratic and financial procedures; see Thucydides 8.1.3.

388–9 *tambourines . . . Adonis*: the Commissioner thinks of women, as Lysistrata herself complained at the start (1–3), as addicted to religious rites of the ecstatic, sensual variety; for Sabazios, see the Index of Names. Adonis, a Cypriot youth beloved of Aphrodite and victim of an untimely death, was the subject of a women's vegetation cult which involved rooftop gardens. In what follows, Demostratos' wife is imagined on a house close to the Pnyx.

392 *fleet to Sicily*: the Commissioner evokes (fairly fancifully) one of the Assembly meetings which preceded the great Sicilian expedition of 415; see Thucydides 6.8–32. Demostratos was a member of a notable Athenian family, but we know little of his politics.

394 *Zakynthos*: island close to north-west Peloponnese, an ally of Athens; for its (subsequent) contribution to the Sicilian expedition, see Thucydides 7.31.2

422 *new oars*: this fits the earlier idea (173–4) that Athens is committed to using its financial reserves to rebuild a large navy.

435 *Artemis*: the oath by an archer-goddess is ironically apt; it starts a comically heightened sequence of women's oaths (439, 443, 447).

439 *Pandrosos*: a daughter of Kekrops, the legendary first king of Athens; she had a shrine on the north side of the Akropolis.

443 *Phosphoros*: lit. 'light-bringer', a title of Artemis or Hekate; both had enclosures near the west end of the Akropolis.

457–8 *market . . . wives*: comedy exploits the idea that working women of the types mentioned were typically aggressive harridans; cf. *F.* 549 ff., 857–8, *We.* 426–7. See n. on *B.* 491 for Aristophanic comic compounds.

495 *hold the purse strings*: cf. the same argument in Praxagora's mouth at *AW* 211–12.

513 *peace inscription*: a reference to the decision taken in 418 to renounce the Peace of Nikias (of 421) and renew hostilities with Sparta; cf. Thucydides 5.56.3.

520 *'Just leave the war to menfolk.'*: a phrase found at *Iliad* 6.492 (Hektor to Andromache) and 20.137 (Poseidon to Hera); the husband's voice might be heard as that of a posturing, would-be 'hero'. For the political interests of Athenian women, see my Introduction to the play, n. 16.

530 *veil*: respectable women would often be veiled in public.

537 *hitch . . . wool*: a woman might hitch up her clothes for wool-working; cf. *AW* 93–4, with the vase-painting illustrated in J. Boardman, *Athenian Red Figure Vases: the Archaic Period* (London, 1975), pl. 293. Bean-chewing was presumably for concentration, though elsewhere it is especially associated with rustics (690, *K.* 41).

554 *Lysimache*: this female name, like 'Lysistrata' itself, means 'war-breaker'. Since the contemporary priestess of Athena Polias had this name, some have seen here a reference to her; but the case for this is very weak. Neither here nor in the similar passage at *P.* 992 does the point depend on anything other than the name's etymology; and we have absolutely no reason to connect the priestess to the idea of peace.

560 *Gorgon-shield*: a Gorgon's head was a common emblem on military shields; cf. *A.* 574, 1095, *P.* 561.

578 *In quest for power*: Lysistrata's language alludes to political 'clubs' and groupings, some but not all of which had oligarchic leanings (cf. Thucydides 8.54.4 for events of 411, and, more generally, Plato, *Republic* 2.365d3); but the whole passage relies on a sweep of political 'cleaning-up' which does not lend itself to close analysis. See my Introduction to the play.

580–2 *everyone . . . Athens*: Lysistrata's proposal—ostensibly (though very
fuzzily) for a profuse extension of Athenian citizenship—is as extravagantly unrealistic as it is sentimental.

597 *sits and waits*: many if not most Athenian girls were married in their
teens; the chances of marrying beyond that age probably diminished
sharply.

604 *wreath*: wreaths (cf. e.g. *We.* 592, *AW* 538) and ribbons (*AW* 1032)
were standard funerary items; see n. on *AW* 1033.

619 *Hippias*: son of Peisistratos and tyrant of Athens 527–510; cf. 1153.
His brother Hipparchos was murdered in 514 by the so-called tyrannicides (note on 632). The old men's suspicions of tyranny (see
630–1) have a comically paranoiac tinge (cf. *W.* 487 ff.); but the
idea played a real part in the Athenian political atmosphere in this
period (Thucydides 6.53.3, 6.60.1, cf. 6.28.2).

625 *jury-pay*: a rate of two obols a day was introduced on Perikles' proposal, and raised to three obols on Kleon's (see *W.* 300, 525,
689–90, etc.); for Athenian currency, see n. on *B.* 18. Jury service
is associated in comedy especially with the elderly, who have the
leisure to give up the necessary time: see e.g. *We.* 277, 1166–7, and
W., passim. Payment for public office was something which concerned opponents of radical democracy: cf. Aristotle, *Constitution of
the Athenians* 33.1, referring to events in the same year as *L.*

629 *wolves*: see n. on 169.

632 '*wear . . . branch*': the men quote from a famous drinking-song which
celebrated the 'tyrannicides', Harmodios (see *AW* 682) and
Aristogeiton, killers of Hipparchos in 514 (n. on 619), and expressed
undying allegiance to the democratic cause.

641–7 *At seven . . . necklace*: a sequence of religious duties performed by
Athenian girls selected from prominent families. The first refers to
those (four girls, aged 7–10) involved in the weaving of the goddess'
robe for the Panathenaia, Athena's major festival (July/August), celebrated in a particularly grand form, the Great Panathenaia, every
fourth year (as pictured on the Parthenon frieze); cf. *AW* 730 ff. The
second is unknown. The third evokes the ritual in which every five
years girls dressed as bears to celebrate the cult of Artemis at
Brauron in east Attika. For basket-carriers, see n. on *B.* 1551; for
necklaces of food, cf. *We.* 765.

653 *Persian Wars*: the invasions of 490 (cf. 285) and 480–479 (see
1250–61), esp. the naval victory at Salamis.

669 *Leipsydrion*: after the murder of Hipparchos in 514, opponents of the
tyrant Hippias (n. on 619) were besieged in a fort at Leipsydrion in
north-west Attika (Herodotos 5.62); the men therefore are singing
once more (cf. 630–3) as allies of the tyrannicides, and their fictional

age has grown even greater (cf. n. on 285)! The point of 'white-footed' is not certain.

675 *Artemisia*: queen of Karia, who accompanied Xerxes on the Persian invasion of Greece in 480 which culminated in the sea battle of Salamis; see Herodotos 7.99, 8.68 ff.

678 *Amazons*: mythical Asiatic female warriors, noted for horseback archery; a common subject in Greek art, including more than one depiction by Mikon (fifth-century Athenian painter/sculptor) of their attack on Athens in the time of Theseus.

695 *Aesop's beetle*: the beetle, wronged by the eagle, pestered Zeus and made him knock the bird's eggs from his lap—moral: even Zeus cannot protect wrongdoers. Cf. *P.* 129–30.

697 *girl from Thebes*: the Boiotian of 85 ff.; 'Ismenia' is a token Theban name (cf. *A.* 691).

702 *eel*: see n. on 36.

722 *pulley*: building work was still in progress on the Akropolis.

751 *Athena's helmet*: from one of the goddess' statues on the Akropolis.

757 *family party*: an occasion, a few days after birth, when infants were carried round the hearth in the presence of relatives and friends.

759 *guardian snake*: religious legend told of a snake which guarded the Akropolis (see Herodotos 8.41.2).

760 *owls*: Athena's bird (*B.* 516), though no doubt there were plenty anyhow on the Akropolis.

770–1 *swallows . . . hoopoes*: the conjunction suggests the myth of Tereus and Prokne (see Index of Names).

785 *Melanion*: sometimes associated with the female hunter Atalanta, but here a solitary misogynist.

799 *lift your legs*: cf. 229 for the sexual allusion.

800 *pubic region*: comedy's phallic costume needs to be kept in mind here; see the general Introduction, 'Stage Directions'.

804 *Phormio*: a successful Athenian general and naval commander from the 440s and 430s; cf. *K.* 562, *P.* 348.

814 *And lived on mountain slopes*: these words are a conjectural supplement to the Greek text.

828 *use a lamp*: Greek women sometimes reduced and shaped their pubic hair by singeing; cf. *AW* 13, *WT* 238 ff., with n. on 89 above.

835 *Chloe*: a title of Demeter's (see Index of Names).

846 *the wheel*: such torture was used to extract legal evidence from slaves; cf. n. on *We.* 875–6.

852 *Paionidai*: in north-west Attika; it is chosen here for a pun on a Greek verb equivalent to the English use of 'bang' as sexual slang. The name Kinesias itself, though not uncommon (see Index of

Names for one real bearer), also carries overtones here of the verb *kinein*, to 'screw'.

856 *apple or an egg*: the Greeks made toasts with food as well as drink; apples, at least, also have erotic associations.

904 *lie down*: Kinesias' eagerness may have reminded Aristophanes' audience, somewhat ironically, of Zeus' impatient desire for Hera at *Iliad* 14.292 ff.

908 *Manes*: a common slave-name at Athens; cf. note on *B*. 1311.

944 *Rhodian scent*: if there is a special point to perfume from Rhodes, we cannot say what it is.

957 *Foxy*: lit. 'dog-fox', the nickname of a certain Philostratos, a pimp, real or alleged; cf. *K*. 1067–9.

980 HERALD: as bearers of official messages, heralds traditionally enjoyed privileged immunity from interference; they were sometimes the only channel of communication between states during war.

980 *Elders*: displaying ignorance of Athenian democracy, the Spartan uses a term, *Gerousia*, which in his own city referred to a council of thirty elders, including the two kings.

982 *or priapic god*: for this type of comic alternative, see e.g. *B*. 102.

991 *message-stick*: see n. on *B*. 1283.

1004 *bushy plants*: lit. 'myrtle', a euphemism for female genitalia; myrtles were sacred to Aphrodite.

1021 *before*: see 663.

1048 *present troubles*: too vague a remark to be a sure allusion to the events which led to an oligarchic *coup* in Athens just a few weeks after the performance. But these were tense days in the city, and the chorus' avoidance of the customary personal satire, of which *Lysistrata* generally has little, may reflect the nervous mood. Cf. my Introduction to the play.

1054 *If . . . the war is over*: for an instant the chorus sings with reference to the real world (where hopes of peace are low) not to the plot's comic fantasy; there is a comparable point at *A*. 651.

1072 *hairy faces*: see n. on *B*. 1282.

1094 *herm-defacers*: a reference to the scandalous defacement of the city's herms (icons, often phallic, of Hermes) on the eve of the Sicilian expedition in 415; see Thucydides 6.27–9, 60–1.

1114 *Reconciliation*: the same personification is mentioned at *A*. 989; cf. the two female Truces at *K*. 1389 ff.

1124 *'A woman . . . wits.'*: a quotation from Euripides' (lost) *Melanippe the Wise* (fr. 483, Nauck); parts of the following two lines may also contain tragic borrowings.

1131 *Olympia . . . Delphi*: Lysistrata appeals to a religiously based sense of Greek unity which finds expression at shared shrines/festivals (see

Index of Names). Cf. the reference to this aspect of Greek 'nation-hood' at Herodotos 8.144.

1133 *barbarian armies*: a vexed line, but the underlying point is certainly that Greeks should unite against the traditional enemy, Persia; there is an allusion to Spartan and/or Athenian use of Persian funding during the war (cf. esp. Thucydides 8.4, 45-8).

1135 *'That . . . complete.'*: a line from Euripides' (lost) *Erechtheus* (fr. 363, Nauck).

1139-44 *Perikleidas . . . territory*: Perikleidas is not named elsewhere; for the historical context in 463/462, when Messene (in south-west Peloponnese) rose up against Spartan rule, see my Introduction to the play: Lysistrata's claim that Kimon saved Sparta is a fundamental distortion of events.

1146 *ravage*: a reference to the Spartan fort at Dekeleia in north Attika; see my Introduction to the play.

1150-53 *Spartans . . . Hippias*: the Spartans played a crucial role in ejecting Hippias (n. on 619) from Athens in 510 (Herodotos 5.64-5, Thucydides 6.54-9); Lysistrata omits to mention (but how could the audience forget it? cf. 271-81) that they had earlier lent support to the tyranny. Hippias employed Thessalian cavalry to shore up his regime.

1156 *cloak of freedom*: cf. the similar motif at 586.

1169-70 *Echinous . . . Megara*: Echinous, in Thessaly and close to the Malian gulf, belonged to a region recently oppressed by the Spartans (Thucydides 8.3); the name conveys an allusion to Reconciliation's pubic region. Megara had long been a bone of contention between Athens and Sparta; 'legs' refers to the long walls which connected the city to the settlement of Nisaia (held by Athens).

1184 *baskets*: the Greek probably involves a piece of sexual innuendo.

1194 *basket-carrier*: see 646, with n. on *B.* 1551.

1202 *nothing left*: as with the earlier song, at 1043-71, the humour is deliberately bathetic, a kind of puerile frivolity; but there may here also be a glance at the theme of hypocrisy in social relations (cf. e.g. *AW* 746 ff. for its development).

1219 *stoop*: cf. 381 with n.

1230 *drunk*: cf. the praise of unmixed wine at *K.* 85-100.

1242 *blowers*: normally taken to be bagpipes carried by a musician accompanying the Spartans; but though the ancient world did know some bagpipe-type instruments, the reference may simply be to the theatrical piper and his instruments (cf. n. on *B.* 861).

1253 *won the day*: the Athenians supplied many of the ships for the Greek naval encounter with the Persians near Artemision (promontory on north Euboia) in 480; see Herodotos 7.175 ff.

1254–6 *Leonidas . . . tusks*: Leonidas, Spartan king, was commander of the Spartan 'three hundred' who resisted the Persians heroically at Thermopylai (see Index of Names) in 480; see Herodotos 7.204 ff., 219 ff.

1270 *wily foxes*: see n. on 169.

1274 *these women*: no Spartan wives were previously mentioned as in the Akropolis, only the female 'hostages' from Sparta's allies left by Lampito at 244. But this is surely a further instance of Aristophanic insouciance about factual consistency.

1283 *Nysa's god*: Dionysos (see Index of Names); the location of Nysa (cf. F. 215), associated with the god's birth, was not agreed.

1298 *Amyklai*: a township close to Sparta; site of a major sanctuary of Apollo.

1299 *Bronze-House shrine*: 'Bronze-House goddess' was Athena's cult-title at Sparta; cf. 1321.

1300–1 *Tyndaridai . . . Eurotas*: the Tyndaridai are Kastor (see Index of Names) and Polydeukes; Sparta lay on the west bank of the River Eurotas.

1313 *Bacchants*: ecstatic female devotees of the god Dionysos.

1314 *Leda's daughter*: Helen, who had the status of a goddess in Sparta.

ASSEMBLY-WOMEN

3 *like a god's*: Greek prayers/hymns often cited the birth of a deity, and important events in its life. Praxagora's lamp is partly a humble surrogate for the Sun-god himself, partly an accomplice to conspiracy.

13 *singe*: on female depilation, see n. at L. 89.

16 *blab*: Praxagora speaks as though accepting the (comic) stereotype of women as secret and compulsive consumers of food and drink; cf. 44–5, 132, 154–7, 226–7 below, with n. on L. 64.

22 *Phyromachos*: unidentifiable (though he may have been a minor politician or an actor), and no convincing explanation of the passage has yet been proposed.

31 *herald's voice*: announcing the imminent Assembly meeting; cf. the herald's role at A. 43 ff.

46 *thingummy's wife*: here, as also at 41–3, 49, 51, I have omitted proper names which are in the Greek; although these might conceivably be those of real Athenians, they are probably ficitional, and in any case it is the gossipy flavour that matters.

64 *get a tan*: because both social practice and (consequent) aesthetic taste made Athenian women typically paler than men, the wives have deliberately spent longer than usual in the sun: see nn. on 699, 878.

71 *Epikrates*: a contemporary politician, noted for a supposedly large beard.

78 *farting Lamia's*: the joke plays on the husband's name, Lamios, and that of Lamia, a disgusting bogey of folklore (cf. *W.* 1035, 1177).

80–1 *Argos . . . cowherd*: Argos, a multi-eyed giant of mythology, was set to guard Io after she had been turned into a cow by Zeus; cf. Aischylos, *Prometheus Bound* 677–9.

96–7 *hitched . . . Phormisios*: women sometimes hitched up their clothes for wool-working (cf. n. on *L.* 537); the hairiness of Phormisios (perhaps the same man as at *F.* 965) allows the substitution of his name for the female pudenda.

102 *Pronomos*: otherwise unknown; the implication may be that he had been the lover of Agyrrhios (see Index of Names).

109 *neither sails nor oars*: an expression of nautical origin for a hopeless or powerless condition.

110 '*But how . . . congregation*': a line in tragic style (adesp. 51, *TrGF* II).

112–13 *young men . . . politicians*: a piece of popular cynicism about homosexual availability as a route to political success for young males; cf. *K.* 424–6, 878–80, *C.* 1093–4.

127 *grilling*: cf. the women's attempt to tan themselves, 64.

128 *cat*: perhaps from ignorance, Praxagora substitutes a domestic pet for the pig which was used in purificatory ritual at the start of the Assembly; cf. *A.* 44 ff. for this and other aspects of Assembly procedure.

129 *Ariphrades*: for an earlier comic target called Ariphrades, see *K.* 1281, *W.* 1280, *P.* 883; we cannot say whether we have the same person here, or even a real person at all.

133 *garland*: Praxagora meant the garland as a practice sometimes used by public speakers in the Assembly (cf. *K.* 1227, *WT* 380), but Woman^A assumed—in bibulous fashion (cf. n. on 16)—that she had a symposium in mind.

137 *unmixed*: see n. on *L.* 197.

143 *archers*: Scythian slaves who helped the Prytaneis to keep order; see 258, *A.* 54, *K.* 665. 'Abuse' refers to the practices of political invective: see 248 ff.

155 *by the two goddesses*: this oath, by Demeter and Persephone, is characteristically female; cf. 532, and *L.* 112.

167 *Epigonos*: otherwise unknown, the butt of a standard comic slur on a man's masculinity; cf. n. on *We.* 800 for interplay with the audience.

188 *payment*: Assembly pay had been introduced originally by Agyrrhios (see Index of Names), somewhere around 400, at a rate of one obol (see 302); he subsequently proposed an increase from two to three

obols: see 292, 309, 380–93, 547–8, *We.* 171, 329–30. Three obols may have been about a third of the daily rate of wages for certain jobs by the early fourth century (cf. n. on *B.* 18).

190–1 *oath . . . Assembly*: the principle is the same as with an oath 'by the two goddesses', 155.

194 *this league*: probably the original anti-Spartan league of Athens and Thebes, formed in 396/395; we do not know who the proposer (195) was.

197–8 *Suppose . . . farmers*: the generalization implies that 'poor' urban citizens were the most likely to seek work as oarsmen in the navy (cf. n. on *We.* 172); the opposition of the rich would stem from their responsibility, under the system of liturgies (whereby the cost of certain civic requirements devolved upon rich individuals), for equipping triremes.

199–200 *at one time . . . credit*: the reference need not be specific, but it probably alludes to fluctuating relations in the years around 395–393.

201 '*Argives . . . shrewd*': the snippets of popular opinion may allude to Argive opposition to a peace with Sparta in 394–393, and perhaps the support of Hieronymos (otherwise unknown) for the same peace.

202–3 *We caught . . . required*: the allusion may be to events in the aftermath of the battle of Knidos, summer 394, when Athens's naval superiority might have allowed her to negotiate from a position of strength; Thrasyboulos (see Index of Names), like other leaders of the democracy, fluctuated in popular esteem.

208 *Aisimos*: probably a contemporary politician of this name; the point of the personal gibe can only be conjectured.

212 *purse strings*: see the similar reference to women's domestic financial responsibilities at *L.* 495.

220 *novel schemes*: Athenians may have thought of themselves, in their popular self-image, as given to innovations and inventiveness; Thucydides 1.70.2 and 1.102.3 suggest that others, at least, thought of them that way. Cf. 586–7.

243 *on the Pnyx*: we are probably meant to think of the later years of the Peloponnesian War, when the presence of a Spartan garrison at Dekeleia in north-west Attika from spring 413 led many Athenians with farms to move into the city. Praxagora took the opportunity (but is the suggestion absurd?) to eavesdrop on Assembly meetings.

247 *general*: cf. n. on 518.

248 *Kephalos*: an important democratic leader (see Demosthenes 18.219, 251), whose family presumably owned a pottery business (253).

265 *lifting . . . legs*: the same sexual position is mentioned at *L.* 229.

279 *sing*: cf. the old jurors' singing at *W.* 219–20.

284 *nothing . . . to show*: receipt of Assembly pay (n. on 188) depended on attendance at the start of the meeting; cf. 292.

291 *Archon*: Athens had nine major magistrates called Archons; six of them, *thesmothetai*, had responsibility for the daily running of law courts.

292 *pay*: see n. on 188.

296 *tickets*: those admitted at the start of the meeting received a ticket entitling them to pay (n. on 188); cf. the 'ticketing' system for the courts, *We.* 278.

302 *single obol*: see n. on 188

317 *knocking*: Blepyros refers to the exigent need of his bowels.

356 *blockade*: an unknown political incident or proposal relating to Athenian dealings with Sparta.

365 *Amynon*: otherwise unknown; he may have been a political figure, and thus the object of a standard sexual slur (see n. on 113).

366 *Antisthenes*: he too cannot be identified securely; cf. 806.

371 *chamber pot*: see *W.* 807 for such a prop.

379 *crimson rope*: a rope smeared with vermilion dye was once used to try to *make* people attend the Assembly (before payment was instituted); cf. *A.* 22. Here the same device appears to be used to keep people out when the meeting is full.

387 *white faces*: the women with their white complexions (n. on 64) are compared to cobblers because the latter too spent relatively little time exposed to the sun.

392–3 '*Antilochos . . . mine.*': a quotation from Aischylos *Myrmidons* (fr. 227, *TrGF* III); Achilles, speaking to Antilochos (cf. *Iliad* 18.2), is bewailing the loss of his friend Patroklos; 'three obols' bathetically replace the dead hero.

397 *preservation*: the Prytaneis (see Index of Names) had called for an urgent debate on the political state of affairs; for the theme of 'preservation' or 'salvation', cf. *L.* 30.

406 *smear it*: cf. the similarly stinging poultice at *We.* 716 ff; for a garlic poultice, see also *W.* 1172.

408 *Euaion*: not otherwise known; he is depicted as a demagogue who exploits his (supposedly) humble background to appeal to the poorest citizens.

426 *Nausikydes*: a prosperous grain merchant (cf. Xenophon, *Memories of Sokrates*, 2.6.7).

428 *white . . . Nikias*: for the significance of 'white', see nn. on 64, 699, 878; Nikias, possibly a nephew of the fifth-century general (see Index of Names), is cast as an effeminate.

432 *cobblers*: see 385.

439 *informer*: cf. 562, and see nn. on *B.* 1423, *We.* 918.

448 *Informally*: an intriguing glimpse, notwithstanding the comic context, of the kind of 'network' that might exist between women in different families; cf. Theophrastos, *Characters* 10.13.

471 *Compulsory sex*: cf. Lysistrata's sentiment at *L.* 162–3.

475 *for the best*: a piece of traditional Athenian folk psychology; cf. *C.*
587–9.

508 *'Unloose . . . tight.'*: a quasi-tragic line; perhaps a partial quotation.

518 *elected*: Praxagora speaks as though she had been voted into the
office of 'general' which the women had originally had in mind for
her (cf. 246, 491, 500); this is assumed later in the play, at 727,
835, 870.

525 *scent*: cf. the sexual humour at *L.* 938–47.

538 *wreath . . . flask*: see n. on 1033.

544 *muggers*: other comic references to the dangers of Athenian streets,
especially at night, occur at 565, 668, and e.g. *B.* 496–8.

553 *heard the decision*: with the implication of this question cf. the wives'
political interests posited by Lysistrata, *L.* 513–14.

556 *weave*: Praxagora disingenuously plays along with the existing idea
of a typical female activity (cf. *L.* 519); see 654.

563 *my living*: the joke depends on the implication that many Athenians
exploited the legal system maliciously for personal gain; cf. 439,
with the Informer scenes at *B.* 1410 ff., *We.* 850 ff.

571 *philosophical*: perhaps an allusion to the currents of intellectual speculation on which Aristophanes has drawn for Praxagora's commu-
nistic scheme; see my Introduction to the play.

587 *abandoning tradition*: cf. n. on 220.

590 *shared*: Praxagora proposes a radical communism, first economic
and then (613 ff.) sexual too; on the resemblance to Plato, *Republic*
book 5, see my Introduction to the play.

639 *throttle . . . fathers*: the comically cynical (and quasi-Oedipal) motif
of father-beating; cf. *B.* 1337 ff., *C.* 1321 ff.

644–5 *Epikouros . . . Leukolophos*: both unknown.

654 *weave you more*: despite the radicalism of her scheme, Praxagora
suggests that women will continue to fulfil their conventional roles
as makers of clothes (and food); cf. 556, and my Introduction to the
play.

677 *podium*: the platform from which litigants presented their case.

678–9 *boys . . . sing*: poetry was regularly performed at banquets; cf. the
(epic) poetry of heroism sung by the boys at *P.* 1265 ff.

681 *allotment racks*: devices—employing jurors' tickets (cf. *We.* 278) and
a system of black and white balls—for the random allocation of
jurors to particular courts.

682 *Harmodios*: with Aristogeiton one of the two 'tyrannicides' who

killed Hipparchos, brother of the tyrant Hippias, in 514 (see *L.* 619, 633, 1153); statues of the pair stood in the Athenian Agora.

685-6 *Royal . . . Stoa*: the Royal Portico or Stoa Basileios, which had administrative uses, stood in the north-west Agora; the location of the Barley-Market Stoa is not certain (cf. *A.* 548?). The Greek matches the initials of these stoas with the letters on the dining-tickets.

699 *white*: a white complexion, often heightened by cosmetics (n. on 878), was thought an ideal of female beauty.

724 *shaggy state*: i.e. slaves will not be allowed to practise genital depilation; see 12-13, with n. on *L.* 89.

729/30 *interlude*: at this juncture a choral interlude probably occurred in the original performance—a practice which later became the norm for act-dividing purposes in New Comedy's five-act structure. Cf. 876/7, and *We.* 626/7, 770/1, 801/2; *We.* 321/2 may also fall into this category.

730 *Panathenaic festival*: see n. on *L.* 641-7. For the humour of personified utensils, cf. the trial scene at *W.* 936-9.

732 *basket-carrier*: see n. on *B.* 1551.

734 *carry the stool*: see *B.* 1552.

738 *pitcher*: water pitchers were carried at the Panathenaia by the wives of metics.

739 *musician*: a cock (despite its gender)?

743 *honeycombs . . . olive-branches*: bowls of honeycombs were carried at the Panathenaia by metics, and olive branches by old men (cf. *W.* 542).

745 *riff-raff*: Chremes' household rubbish stands for the miscellaneous crowd following the official procession.

782-3 *hand . . . gift*: most surviving statues of deities do *not* have hands outstretched in this manner; but cf. *B.* 518 for a similar allusion.

791-2 *earthquake . . . lightning . . . cat*: three types of religious omen, though the last probably represents an excessively superstitious attitude (cf. Theophrastos, *Characters* 16.3).

798 *go back on*: for the idea of Athenians as prone to changes of mind, cf. *A.* 630-2.

806-8 *Antisthenes . . . shit*: see 366.

809-10 *Kallimachos . . . Kallias*: Kallimachos is unknown; the ironic contrast with Kallias (see Index of Names) points to a gibe at financial problems.

814 *price of salt*: we know nothing of this decree, which may have been related to imports of salt from Megara (cf. *A.* 521, 760).

818 *in my mouth*: for this Athenian habit, see n. on *B.* 503.

822 *silver now*: in the later fifth century the Athenians switched from

their traditional silver coinage to silver-plated bronze (probably what 'bronze' means in this passage); they apparently switched back to silver at some point in the 390s.

825 *Euripides*: otherwise unknown. We do not know the exact nature of his putative tax; if it was a property levy, the figure of 500 talents (1 talent = 6,000 drachmas: see n. on *B*. 18) is exorbitant: between 377 and 357 Athens raised only 300 talents in this way (Demosthenes 22.44); cf. the general figure at *W*. 660.

836–7 *lot . . . dining hall*: cf. 681 ff.

846–7 *Smoios . . . lips*: otherwise unknown; he is imagined as engaging in cunnilinctus (cf. *K*. 1284–6, *W*. 1283, *P*. 885).

848 *Geron*: unknown; there is a play on his name, meaning 'old man'.

876/7 *interlude*: see n. on 729/30.

878–9 *white . . . dress*: Greek women often applied white-lead cosmetic, to enhance a desirable paleness of complexion; cf. 929, 1072, *We*. 1064, with the note on 699. For the type of dress, dyed with saffron, see 332 and *L*. 47.

917 *solitary pleasure*: cf. the reference to dildoes at *L*. 108.

920 *Lesbian*: the modern meaning of the adjective is irrelevant here; see Index of Names, under 'Lesbos'.

983 *cases*: sarcastic use of legal language; 'sixties' and 'twenty' pun on the idea of court cases involving particular sums of money.

996 *white oil-flasks*: the Youth plays on the whiteness of complexion thought desirable in women; cf. 1101, with n. on 699.

1007 *property transfers*: the Youth may imply that nothing less than the compulsion of slavery would make him accede to the woman's sexual requests.

1011 *document*: we do not know how often individuals possessed copies of decrees; apart from the professional Decree-Seller of *B*. 1035 ff. (but a fictitious type?), *B*. 1288–9 apparently refers to stalls in the Agora where they could, like other goods, be bought.

1021 *Prokroustes*: legendary Athenian brigand who tortured his victims to fit a bed (cf. Eng. 'procrustean'); the preceding lines contain an untranslatable play on the verbal root of his name.

1023–4 *demesmen . . . bail me out*: 'demesmen' are members of the same official deme (see n. on *B*. 645).

1025 *sums of money*: an inversion of the normal Athenian legal situation, in which *women* were prohibited from entering into contracts of more than a specified, modest value.

1027 *exemption*: merchants enjoyed special privileges, including exemption from military service and access to special legal procedures; cf. *We*. 904.

1030–3 *lay . . . door*: the Youth imagines standard funerary practices—the strewing of dittany and vine-twigs; ribbons (*L.* 603); oil-flasks (538, 996), which would subsequently be placed as urns on the grave (1111); a water-jug outside the door of the house; and wreaths, whether of fresh flowers or wax imitations.

1042 *Oedipuses*: the allusion is to Oedipus' unwitting incest with his mother Jocasta.

1069 *Dioskouroi*: i.e. Kastor (see Index of Names) and Polydeukes (Pollux), twin sons of Zeus and Leda, brothers of Helen; for other names, see the Index of Names.

1072 *white cosmetics*: see n. on 878.

1089 *Kannonos' law*: a decree (date unknown) which stipulated that certain offenders against the Athenian people should defend themselves in chains before the Assembly.

1092 *onions*: like certain other bulbous plants, these were sometimes regarded as aphrodisiacs.

1101 *funeral urn*: cf. 996 with n.

1108–11 *monument . . . urn*: the Youth pictures the Hag as a large, quasi-sculptural urn (cf. n. on 1033) attached to a base by lead (a technique also used for statues).

1123 *neat*: see n. on *L.* 197.

1132 *thirty thousand*: a conventional figure for the size of the Athenian citizen body (adult males), but possibly a reasonable estimate for the early fourth century (though some historians would think twenty thousand nearer the truth).

1148 *back in their homes*: the (deliberately?) corny humour is from the same mould as the songs at *L.* 1043–71; but here it seems to indicate a fading-back into reality from the fantasy of the play.

1154 *judges*: there are other addresses to judges at *C.* 1115 ff., *B.* 1102 ff; on the system of judging, see n. on *B.* 445.

1158 *order of the plays*: the order of performance was determined by lot.

1166 *Cretan style*: probably a high-stepping processional dance, traditional on the island.

1168 *without . . . breath*: in Greek, what follows is run together as a single, gargantuan *word*; cf. n. on *B.* 491.

1171 *silphium*: see n. on *B.* 534.

1178 *porridge*: another moment of comic bathos; cf. 1148.

WEALTH

7 *full rights*: for most practical and legal purposes, slaves counted as material property of their owners.

9 '*Who . . . golden*': possibly a line from a lost tragedy (adesp. fr. 61,

TrGF II); Loxias is a title of the god Apollo, and the tripod is that of his priestess at Delphi.

21 *wreathed*: Karion and his master still wear the wreaths they put on for their visit to the Delphic oracle; Karion treats his, somewhat hopefully, as giving him religious protection.

39 *'What . . . wreaths?'*: a line in tragic style, possibly from a lost play by Euripides (= adesp. fr. 61a, *TrGF* II).

41-3 *He urged . . . home with me*: cf. the similar oracular motif at Euripides, *Ion* 534-6.

84 *Patrokles*: identification is uncertain; he may have been a tragic poet of this name, or conceivably the half-brother of Sokrates (Plato, *Euthydemos* 297e).

87 *Zeus's . . . malice*: cf. Zeus' resentment against mankind at Hesiod, *Works and Days* 47.

114 *may heaven assist my hope*: this phrase occurs at Euripides, *Medea* 625; there may be further tragic borrowings hereabouts.

148 *slave . . . debt*: enslavement for non-payment of debts seems not to have occurred at Athens during the classical period; the passage probably implies that Karion was once a citizen of another Greek state.

159 *vices . . . words*: Athenian attitudes to male homosexuality drew an important distinction, often blurred in practice (Karion's point), between acceptable gift-giving and unacceptable, indeed (for citizens) illegal, prostitution (which is probably meant at *F*. 148); cf. *B*. 705-7.

168 *adulterers*: a reference to their punishment by violent genital depilation (cf. *C*. 1083), which might be used to extract an offer of monetary compensation.

171 *Assembly*: on payment for attendance, see n. at *AW* 188.

172 *triremes*: paid rowers of Athenian warships (cf. *B*. 108) were often drawn from the poorer citizen classes (cf. *AW* 197-8, *K*. 1366-8, *W*. 909, and pseudo-Xenophon, *Constitution of the Athenians* I.13).

175 *needle-maker*: an unknown politician, identified for the audience by his family business (cf. e.g. *AW* 252-3).

176 *farts*: i.e. Agyrrhios is, in the Greek description of passive homosexuals, 'wide-arsed'; underlying the joke is the cynical assumption that would-be politicians advanced themselves by homosexual availability: see n. on *AW* 112-13.

177 *Philepsios*: probably the politician mentioned at Demosthenes 24.134 as having been imprisoned for debt; his 'fictions' would allude to a legal defence.

178 *Egypt*: Athens had recently made an alliance with the Pharaoh Acoris, who at this time was in revolt against the Persian empire;

this may have been linked to support for another rebel, Evagoras of Cyprus.

179 *Laïs . . . Philonides*: Laïs was the name of at least two famous courtesans, one of whom came from Korinth (cf. 303); Philonides (cf. 303), a target of other comedians as a boor or decadent, is satirized as desirable only for his money.

180 *Timotheos's tower*: Timotheos was a rich Athenian whose important military-political career was still in the future at this date; his tower is probably part of a large house.

189 *surfeit*: cf. Menelaos' sentiment at Homer, *Iliad* 13.636.

194-5 *thirteen . . . sixteen talents*: these sums would be plausible only for the very richest of Athenians (1 talent = 6,000 drachmas: cf. n. on B. 18).

210 *Lynkeus*: one of the Argonauts, famous for especially keen sight; see e.g. Apollonios Rhodios, *Argonautika* 1.153-5.

213 *'When . . . me.'*: possibly a borrowing from an unknown tragedy (adesp. fr. 61c, *TrGF* II).

228 *joint*: part of a sacrifice which Chremylos had made on his visit to Delphi.

254 *fellow-demesmen*: see n. on B. 645 for the Athenian system of demes.

267 *circumcised*: apparently here a comic hyperbole for physical decrepitude; elsewhere it sometimes denotes an erection (cf. 295). Cf. n. on B. 507.

278 *ticket*: at this date jurors were allotted to courts on a daily basis by tickets from an allotment machine (*AW* 681 ff.); cf. tickets for Assembly attendance, *AW* 296. Serving jurors received a daily payment (at this date, three obols, as for Assembly attendance: n. on *AW* 188); see *W.* 300, 525, 689-90, etc., and note on *L.* 625. For the sarcastic reference to Charon, cf. *L.* 606.

287 *Midases*: Midas, legendary king of Phrygia given the power to turn objects into gold by Dionysos, and given ass's ears by Apollo for voting against him in a musical contest.

290 *thrum-de-thrum*: Karion mimes the sound of a lyre; this is part of the parody of a contemporary dithyramb (see n. on B. 918-19) by the poet Philoxenos, in which the Cyclops (one-eyed, monstrous shepherd of Homer, *Odyssey* 9, etc.) played a lyre. Philoxenos' poem seems itself to have had burlesque qualities.

300-1 *wine . . . blind*: see *Odyssey* 9.345-96.

302 *Circe's role*: Karion now switches to a parody of Odysseus' encounter with Circe at *Odyssey* 10.210 ff., where the sorceress turns his companions into swine; Philonides (n. on 179), depicted as leader of a group of debauchees, is the burlesque surrogate for Odysseus.

321/2 *routine*: this may be parallel to other points in the play at which a choral interlude probably occurred; cf. 626/7, 770/1, 801/2, with my n. on *AW* 729/30.

329-30 *three obols . . . meeting*: another allusion to payment for attendance at the Assembly; cf. 171.

338 *barbers' shops*: see n. on *B*. 1440.

342 *not the normal practice*: a piece of popular Athenian cynicism about self-seeking behaviour; cf. 237-41, 829-37, and the scene with the Neighbour at *AW* 746 ff.

384 *wife and children*: in Athenian courts the convicted sometimes brought in their families to enhance their pleas for leniency. Cf. *W*. 975-8, and the famous passage at Plato, *Apology* 34c.

423-4 *Fury . . . tragic look*: a Fury, *Erinys*, was one of a group of fearsome spirits of vengeance, usually represented as snake-haired, torch-wielding women; especially associated with tragedy (e.g. Aischylos, *Eumenides*). Poverty may have been given a semi-tragic mask.

426-8 *hostel-keeper . . . voice*: see n. on *L*. 458.

431 *pit*: this place, outside the city proper, was where the bodies of executed, and possibly sometimes living, criminals were thrown; cf. 1109 and e.g. *K*. 1362, *F*. 574, 1448-9, with the famous passage at Plato, *Republic* 4.439e.

450-1 *breastplate . . . pawn*: taken literally, this would imply that the two men had once been well enough off to own some hoplite (infantry) armour, but had subsequently fallen on hard times.

487 HALF-AGON: note the lack of an introductory strophe, in keeping with the reduced choral element in the play. See the Introduction to the play, and the general Introduction under 'Formality and Performance'.

515 *and who . . . produce*: the line contains some elevated poetic diction.

520 *Thessalians*: central Greece may have been a kind of entrepôt in the slave trade, trafficking in slaves kidnapped from barbarian peoples to the north.

535 *bathhouse*: the poor frequented such places in winter to warm themselves at their fires; cf. 952-3.

550 *Dionysios . . . Thrasyboulos*: the conjunction piquantly pairs Dionysios I, tyrant of Syracuse and friend of Sparta, who by this date controlled much of Sicily, with a democratic politician (see Index of Names).

560-1 *bloated . . . waists*: cf. Plato, *Republic* 8.556d for a contrast between rich/obese and poor/trim in a hoplite battle-line.

601 *'O city . . . words!'*: a quotation from Euripides' (lost) *Telephos* (fr. 713, Nauck) which occurs also at *K*. 813; the exclamation (a hyperbolic call for witnesses) is an expression of outrage.

602 *Pauson*: this target of a gibe at (supposed) poverty is probably the

same person as at *A.* 854, *WT* 949; whether he is the painter of
Aristotle, *Poetics* 1448a6 is uncertain.

626/7 INTERLUDE: see n. on *AW* 729/30.

628 *Theseus' festival*: the Theseia, in honour of Athens's greatest hero,
supposedly included generous feasting on meat, as at other major
festivals; Karion implies that the elderly at least sometimes had to
make do with poor fare.

635-6 'His sight . . . *art.*': a quotation, at least in part, from Sophokles'
satyr-play, *Phineus* (fr. 710, *TrGF* IV).

645 *tipple*: for this stereotype of women, see 737, 972, and n. on *L.* 64.

653 *the shrine*: the context indicates that this is the shrine at Zea, near
the Peiraieus harbour.

661 *Hephaistos' flame*: the periphrasis, with its reference to the god of fire,
is redolent of tragic diction.

677-8 *pastries . . . table*: the offerings had been placed there, notionally for
the god, by visitors to the shrine.

690 *like snake's fangs*: Karion makes her think he is one of Asklepios'
sacred snakes (cf. 733-41).

701-2 *Iaso . . . Panakeia*: Iaso (lit. 'Healer') and Panakeia (lit. 'Healer of
all', cf. panacea) were daughters of Asklepios.

706 *eats shit*: the expression was used as a colloquial insult, normally to
denote shameless insensitivity.

717 *poultice*: cf. the comparable mixture suggested by Blepyros at *AW*
404-6; one of the ingredients, squill, was sometimes used for
apotropaic purposes (Theophrastos, *Characters* 16.15).

765-6 *neck . . . of loaves*: necklaces of food were worn in several celebratory and ritual contexts; cf. the figs at *L.* 647.

769 *new-purchased eyes*: a play on an adjective normally applied to
slaves; cf. *K.* 2.

770/1 INTERLUDE: see n. on *AW* 729/30.

772-3 *Pallas . . . Kekrops*: Pallas was an old title of Athena; Kekrops was
the legendary first king of Athens (cf. e.g. *C.* 301).

797-9 *director . . . laugh*: comic performances sometimes involved the
throwing of food to the audience; cf. *W.* 58-9, *P.* 962-6.

800 *Dexinikos*: an unknown individual; for such play with a member of
the audience, cf. *AW* 167, *W.* 74 ff., *P.* 883 ff.

801/2 INTERLUDE: see n. on *AW* 729/30.

845 *Greater Mysteries*: in honour of Demeter and Persephone, held at
Eleusis in north-west Attika (cf. 1013); initiates sometimes wore
rags (cf. *F.* 404-6) which they subsequently dedicated at the shrine.

850 INFORMER: for the type, see n. on *B.* 1423.

876 *the wheel*: the evidence of slaves was admissible in Athenian
courts only if extracted under torture; the 'wheel' was a rack-like

instrument on which slaves were stretched and whipped: cf. e.g. *F.* 616 ff., *P.* 452, with *L.* 846.

884 *Eudamos*: a well-known seller of amulets, charms, etc.; such things were widely used in antiquity, and were believed to protect against both physical and other harms. A drachma was a day's pay for some jobs (n. on *B.* 18).

886 *verbal abuse*: certain kinds of insult were actionable under the Athenian legal category of *hybris*.

904 *claim so*: in order to take advantage of merchants' legal privileges; cf. n. on *AW* 1027.

918 *Anyone who wants*: Athenian law lacked a prosecuting agent, and specified that criminal charges could be brought to court by any willing party; the idea is fundamentally democratic, but it leads to the suspicion that some people ('informers') abuse the system for personal gain.

943 *offerings*: religious dedications could be attached to many kinds of objects; Vergil, *Aeneid* 12.766-9 mentions survivors of shipwreck nailing clothes to an olive tree.

953 *warm yourself*: see n. on 535.

970 *another of those*: Chremylos speaks as though he knows about the preceding scene with the Informer.

972 *drink*: see n. on *L.* 64 for the female stereotype evoked here.

982-3 *twenty . . . eight*: the sums are substantial; for Athenian currency, see n. on *B.* 18.

1002 *'Long . . . brave.'*: a proverbial expression, ironically applied, implying that things are not what they used to be; possibly it involves an allusion to Miletos' leadership of, but eventual failure in, the Ionian revolt against Persia in 499-4.

1004 *lentil soup*: this proverbially plain fare is here a sexual euphemism.

1013-14 *Eleusis . . . wagon*: the implication *may* be that at the Greater Mysteries (n. on 845) the woman was taking part in a traditional form of indecent jesting which took place on wagons.

1017 *food*: cf. 1004.

1019 *twenty drachmas*: cf. 982.

1054 *olive branch*: such branches were hung outside houses to celebrate the harvest; cf. *K.* 729, *W.* 398.

1057 *'Guess the —— teeth'*: a variation on a game which involved guessing the number of nuts concealed in a person's hand.

1064 *white cosmetic*: see n. on *AW* 878.

1070 *in Hekate's name*: Chremylos' oath is doubly ironic; it is typically female, and it evokes Hekate's associations with death.

1083 *thirteen thousand*: the hyperbole, which happens to provide probably the most plausible classical estimate of the audience in the Theatre of Dionysos, implies that the woman is the most widely available of whores.

1093 *tarred . . . enough*: the metaphor, from the use of pitch to repair ships' hulls, involves obscene connotations; cf. the related imagery, referring to pubic hair, at *W.* 1374–5.

1109 *pit*: see n. on 431; for the culinary imagery of the previous line, cf. *P.* 228 ff.

1110 *the tongue*: for the religious practice alluded to, see n. on *B.* 1704–5; Karion thinks Hermes, herald of the gods, deserves reward for betraying Zeus.

1113–16 *For ever since . . . nothing at all*: the situation bears out what was said at 133–43. Cf. *B.* 1515–20 for a similar scenario; Hermes here, like Prometheus there, is a defector from the 'starving' gods.

1126 *fourth of the month*: the day was traditionally Hermes' birthday and a time for special celebrations; cf. Theophrastos, *Characters* 16.10.

1127 *'You pine . . . gone.'*: a line from an unknown tragedy (adesp. fr. 63, *TrGF* II), referring to Herakles' loss of his beloved boyfriend Hylas.

1151 *'One's . . . home.'*: the line is redolent of tragedy; but it may not be strictly a quotation.

1153 *'god of the hinge'*: most Greek gods had multiple titles, but Hermes' were particularly extensive (cf. *F.* 1141–6 for another joke on them); this and the following are all genuine.

1158 *'Our . . . honest.'*: another possible quotation from tragedy (adesp. fr. 63a, *TrGF* II).

1162–3 *Poetic . . . wealth*: the Greeks incorporated many activities, including poetry and athletics, in competitive festivals on which large amounts of money were expended. Aristophanes' own comedies were performed in competition at the Athenian dramatic festivals.

1167 *several lists*: the names of jurors were distributed into ten lists or sections (known by letters of the alphabet), which in turn were used for allotment to individual courts (see n. on 278); it was presumably known for some to try to increase their chances of active service, and thus of pay (n. on *L.* 625), by getting their names on more than one list.

1184 *defecate*: disrespectful use of temples as lavatories was presumably not unknown; cf. the gibe at Kinesias, *F.* 366, and the possibly more loaded accusation at *B.* 1054.

1193 *Athena's treasury*: on the Akropolis; cf. *L.* 174.

1198 *top of your head*: common practice; cf. *AW* 222.

1199 *bright enough*: the precise visual joke is irrecoverable, but there is an allusion to special finery worn by women in religious processions.

INDEX OF NAMES

Listed here are those proper names (excluding the purely fictional) of people, places, and institutions which are not explained in the Explanatory Notes. References are selective. An acute accent over a vowel or diphthong is used to mark the appropriate syllable for the main stress in English pronunciation. Capitals within entries indicate cross references. Play titles are abbreviated as in the Explanatory Notes.

in hope of cure (*We.* 659 ff., cf. *W.* 123), which might sometimes involve the god's sacred snakes

ASSEMBLY (*ekklesia*), sovereign popular institution of Athenian democracy, whose meetings, held roughly every ten days on the PNYX, were open in principle to all citizens (cf. 376 ff.); voting-forum, after public debate (*L.* 390 ff., *AW* 116 ff., 397 ff.), for state decrees (*L.* 513 ff., *AW* 813 ff.); from around 400 payment was made for attendance (n. on *AW* 188)

ATHENA, daughter of ZEUS, worshipped as Athena Polias (*B.* 828), patron-goddess of Athens, on the AKRÓPOLIS, where she had an ancient olive-wood statue (*L.* 262); various images, including Phidias' statue in the Parthenon, showed her in a warrior's helmet (*L.* 751 ff.); traditionally associated with craftsmen, including potters (*B.* 358); often depicted with an owl (*B.* 516)

ATTIKA (adj. Attic, *B.* 1704), geographical region of the Athenian polis, comprising both the city proper and the territory of the demes (*L.* 56)

BOIOTIA, region of south-central Greece, bordering ATTIKA to the north-west, including the city of Thebes (*L.* 697); notable for its plains (*L.* 88) and for the culinary delicacy of eels (*L.* 36, 702)

CHAIREPHON, associate of SOKRATES, nicknamed 'the bat' for his supposedly ghostly pallor (*B.* 1296, 1564); cf. *C.* 104, 144 ff., etc., *W.* 1408 ff

CHAOS, mythological entity (*B.* 691–3), representing a primordial vacuum before the emergence of EARTH, HEAVEN, etc.

CHARON, ferryman of souls on the river Styx in Hades (*L.* 606, *We.* 278; cf. *F.* 180 ff.)

CHIOS (adj. Chian), Greek island in east Aegean, member of Athenian empire (cf. *B.* 879–80); noted for its wines (*AW* 1139)

COUNCIL (*boulê*), of 500, drawn from the ten tribes of ATTIKA, responsible for day-to-day administration of the democracy (*L.* 1011, *We.* 949), including preparation of business for the ASSEMBLY; the PRÝTANEIS were its standing committee; Council members had special seats in the theatre (*B.* 794)

DELPHI, site of APOLLO's shrine in south central Greece, the most important oracle in the Greek world (*B.* 618, 716, *We.* 32 ff.)

DEMETER, daughter of ZEUS, a corn-goddess (*B.* 580, *We.* 515, 555) whose cults included the Greater Mysteries (*We.* 845) and the THESMOPHÓRIA; under the title of Chloe, 'green' goddess of new crops, she had a shrine near the west end of the AKRÓPOLIS (*L.* 835)

DIEITREPHES, a cavalry officer satirized as a parvenu and for a family business involving wicker jars (*B.* 798, 1442); in fact known to have belonged to a well-established Athenian family; cf. Thucydides 7.29, 8.64 for his military activity in 413–411

DIONYSOS, son of ZEUS and Semele (*B.* 558); god of wine, ecstasy, etc., enjoyed by his Bacchic/Bacchant followers (*L.* 1, 1284, 1312); associated with Mount Nysa (*L.* 1282)

DODÓNA, oracle of ZEUS in north-west Greece (*B.* 716), long established (Homer, *Iliad* 16.233–4)

EARTH (*Gê*), primordial mythological wife of HEAVEN and mother of various beings (*B.* 470, 694 ff.)

EILEITHÝA, goddess of childbirth (*AW* 369, *L.* 742)

ÉREBOS, primordial realm of darkness, associated with CHAOS and NIGHT (*B.* 691–4, 1193)

EROS, winged deity and symbol of sexual desire, sometimes (see *L.* 551) associated with, though not yet standardly counted as the son of, APHRODITE, but also regarded as a primeval cosmic force (*B.* 696 ff.)

EURIPIDES, major Athenian tragedian (*c.*480–406), source of paratragic material (*L.* 1124, *We.* 601), sometimes comically depicted as a misogynist (*L.* 283, 368–9); the Euripides of *AW* 825–9 is different

EXEKÉSTIDES, figure of supposedly dubious rights to Athenian citizenship, probably of topical note at the time of *Birds* (*B.* 11, 764, 1527)

GRACES, a trio of divine females, personifications of beauty, charm, etc., generally associated with amatory or sensual imagery (*B.* 1100, 1320, *AW* 973), and often linked with the MUSES and the attractions of music/dance (*B.* 782, *L.* 1279)

HEAVEN, Ouranos, primeval region of the cosmos, mythological husband of EARTH (*B.* 694–701)

HÉKATE, goddess of (often) dark significance, linked esp. with the Underworld and magic; she received monthly offerings at crossroads (*We.* 594–7); oaths by her are typically female (but cf. *We.* 1070); and her worship may have appealed to women (*L.* 700)

HELEN, daughter of ZEUS and Leda (*L.* 1314), wife of MENELAOS (*L.* 155); her seduction by Paris (*B.* 1104) caused the Trojan War

HERA, sister/wife of ZEUS (*B.* 1633, 1731 ff.), goddess of marriage, etc.

HERAKLES, son of ZEUS and Alkmene (*B.* 558, cf. 1652), accomplisher of heroic labours; subject of apotheosis; but also a notorious glutton in comedy (*B.* 567, 1583 ff., *L.* 928); his family, persecuted by the tyrant Eurystheus, took refuge in Athens (*We.* 385, cf. Euripides, *Herakleidai*)

HERMES, messenger of the gods, and god of merchandise, theft, etc. (*We.* 1099 ff.); capable of flight (*B.* 572), normally because of winged sandals

HOMER, supreme epic poet, *c.*700 BC, creator of *Iliad* and *Odyssey*

HYMEN, not so much god of marriage as quasi-divine personification of the wedding-hymn itself (*B.* 1736 ff., cf. *P.* 1332 ff.)

IONIA (adj. Ionian), eastern region of Aegean, now West Turkey; commonly associated (because of near-eastern influence) with ideas of luxury and decadence (*AW* 883, 918)

IRIS, goddess of the rainbow and winged messenger of the gods (*B.* 575, 1202 ff.)

KALLIAS, a member of one of the richest and most aristocratic of Athenian families, reputed for his patronage of intellectuals (cf. e.g. Plato's *Protagoras*, set in his house); he is ridiculed in comedy for a profligate, sexually scandalous life style (*B.* 284-6, cf. *F.* 428-30) which led to eventual financial difficulties (*AW* 810)

KARIA (adj. -ian), south-west region of Asia Minor, a source of Greek slaves (*B.* 764); its native peoples traditionally lived in hill-top villages (*B.* 292-3, where a pun on helmet-crests, which Karians were supposed to have invented, may be involved)

KARÝSTOS (adj. Karystian), town in south Euboia, an ally of Athens (*L.* 1058); its men may have been popularly thought of as highly sexed (*L.* 1181)

KASTOR, with his brother Polydeukes (Pollux) one of the twin Dioskouroi (*AW* 1069), sons of ZEUS and Leda, brothers of HELEN; also called Tyndaridai (*L.* 1301), sons of Tyndareus (their supposed human father); subject of a typically Spartan oath (*L.* 206, 988)

KINÉSIAS, contemporary lyric poet and chorus-trainer, particularly associated with dithyramb (*B.* 1385 n.); also known to have been politically active; mocked for gawkiness (*B.* 1378-9), and for allegedly loose bowels (*AW* 330, cf. *F.* 366); not to be identified with the fictional husband of this name in *L.*

KLEISTHENES, an Athenian, possibly of some political prominence, repeatedly satirized as a passive homosexual (*B.* 831, *L.* 621, 1092, cf. *A.* 118, *WT* 574 ff.)

KLEÓNYMOS, Athenian politician, probably an associate of Kleon's in the 420s (cf. *W.* 592); mocked for gluttony/obesity (*B.* 289, 1477, cf. *K.* 1293), malicious, informer-type use of the courts (*B.* 1479), and alleged cowardice in battle (*B.* 290, 1477-81, cf. *C.* 353)

KLEPSÝDRA, a spring and fountain house at the north-west corner of the AKRÓPOLIS (*L.* 913, n. on *B.* 1695)

KORINTH, major city at west end of isthmus between central Greece and the Peloponnese; traditional enemy of Athens, though intermittently an ally in early 4th cent. (*AW* 199); noted for mercenaries (*We.* 173) and prostitutes (*We.* 149)

KORYBANTICS, priests/worshippers of the goddess Kýbele (see *B.* 876), noted for their ecstatic rituals and trance-like states (*L.* 558, cf. *AW* 1069)

KYPROS (adj. Kyprian) [Cyprus], island noted for the birth of APHRODITE and for the goddess' shrine at Paphos (*L.* 833)

KYRÉNE, Greek colony in north Africa, famous for its silphium (see n. on *B.* 534), whose export was a source of its wealth (*We.* 925)

KYTHÉRA, island off south Peloponnese, site of a sanctuary of APHRODITE (*L.* 833)

LAMPON, Athenian religious expert on oracles and related matters; a target for popular cynicism about the integrity of such people (*B.* 521, cf. 988)

LESBOS (adj. Lesbian), Greek island in north-east Aegean; often used as byword for sexual licence (*AW* 920, cf. *W.* 1346, *F.* 1308), but not usually for 'Lesbian' activities in the modern sense

LYSÍKRATES, the target of a gibe of financial corruption at *B.* 513; possibly the same person mocked for an ugly nose (*AW* 630) and use of hair-dye (*AW* 736)

MARATHON, region of north ATTIKA, noted for its plain (*B.* 247), site of major Greek victory over PERSIANS in 490 (*L.* 285)

MELOS (adj. Melian), Greek island in south-west Aegean, besieged into submission by Athens in 416 (*B.* 186, see Thucydides 5.84 ff.); home of Diagoras (*B.* 1072)

MENELAOS, king of SPARTA, brother of AGAMEMNON, husband of HELEN

METON, Athenian astronomer and intellectual (*B.* 992 ff.), famous for the calendaric harmonizing of lunar and solar cycles ('the Metonic cycle', covering 235 lunar months)

MILETOS (adj. Milesian), major Greek city in Asia Minor, an ally of Athens until its revolt in 412 (*L.* 108, cf. Thucydides 8.17); reputed for its fine wool (*L.* 729) as well as more recherché products (cf. *L.* 108-10)

MUSES, daughters of ZEUS and Memory (*L.* 1248), nine goddesses of memory and poetic inspiration (*B.* 781, 924, *AW* 882)

MYRONIDES, successful Athenian general during period of the city's military expansionism in the mid-fifth century (*L.* 801, *AW* 304)

NEOKLEIDES, Athenian politician active in the 390s and 380s; accused of corruption (*We.* 666, 725); mocked for supposedly defective vision (*AW* 254, 398 ff., *We.* 665, 716 ff., 747)

NIGHT, primeval cosmic entity, mother of EROS at *B.* 693-6

NIKE, 'Victory', a (usually) winged goddess (*B.* 574), symbolic of success in war, athletics, etc., and sometimes associated with ATHENA (probably *L.* 317), who as Athena Nike had a small temple to the right of the Propylaia on the AKRÓPOLIS

NIKIAS, Athenian general, one of the leaders of the Sicilian expedition in 415-413 (*B.* 363), his reluctance for which (cf. Thucydides 6.8.4) encouraged a reputation for hesitation (*B.* 639); *AW* 428 may refer to his nephew

PROKNE, Athenian princess, wife of TEREUS, mother of Itys (*B.* 212), meta-morphosed into a nightingale (*B.* 203 ff., 665 ff.)

PROMETHEUS, a Titan (see n. on *B.* 469) who betrayed ZEUS and befriended men (*B.* 1545) by giving fire to the latter

PRÝTANEIS, standing committee of the COUNCIL, responsible for presiding at its meetings and at those of the ASSEMBLY; each Athenian tribe's fifty repre-sentatives served for a prytany (a tenth of the year)

PYLOS, in south-west Peloponnese, was captured by Athens in 425 (see *K.* 55 etc.) and held as a military base until 410 (*L.* 104, 1163)

SABAZIOS, a PHRYGIAN god (*B.* 875) whose cult, involving ecstatic rituals (*L.* 388) and perhaps trance-like states (*W.* 9–10), had been introduced into Athens

SALAMIS (adj. Salaminian), island off west coast of ATTIKA and belonging to Athens; a traditional source of Athenian sailors/rowers, hence the butt of sexually suggestive jokes (*AW* 37–8, *L.* 59–60, cf. *L.* 411)

SCYTHIANS, nomadic peoples north of the Black Sea (*B.* 941); source of Greek slaves (*L.* 184, 433 ff.)

SKIRA, an Athenian festival, in early summer, exclusively for women (*AW* 18, 59, cf. *WT* 834)

SOKRATES, Athenian philosopher (469–399), reputedly neglectful of bodily hygiene (*B.* 1282), and notable for a special, semi-mystical concern with the soul (cf. *B.* 1553 ff.); mentor of CHAIREPHON; central butt of Aristophanes' *Clouds*

SPARTA, leading city of Peloponnese and head of military league at war with the Athenian empire 431–404 (see esp. *L.*, *passim*); hence Athens's *bête noire* (*B.* 814–16) and supposedly perfidious (*L.* 169, 629); notorious for periodic 'expulsions of foreigners' (*B.* 1013, cf. Thucydides 1.144.2), and reputed for cultivation of physical toughness (n. on *B.* 1281–3); its people were sometimes called Lakedaimonians (*B.* 813)

TARTAROS, a primordial realm of darkness (*B.* 693–8), traditionally treated as part of the Underworld

TAÝGETOS, mountain overlooking SPARTA from thr south-west (*L.* 117, 1297)

TÉLEAS, a rich Athenian, active as a political official around the time of *Birds*, where he is mentioned as the proposer of an ASSEMBLY decree (*B.* 1025); cf. *B.* 168, *P.* 1008

TEREUS, mythological king of THRACE, husband of PROKNE, who killed their son Itys in revenge for Tereus' rape of her sister Philomela; metamorphosed into a hoopoe (*B.* 92 ff. and *passim*)

THASOS (adj. Thasian), north Aegean island, producer of one of the finer, more aromatic wines of the Greek world (*L.* 196 ff., *AW* 1119, *We.* 1021)

American Literature

British and Irish Literature

Children's Literature

Classics and Ancient Literature

Colonial Literature

Eastern Literature

European Literature

Gothic Literature

History

Medieval Literature

Oxford English Drama

Poetry

Philosophy

Politics

Religion

The Oxford Shakespeare

A complete list of Oxford World's Classics, including Authors in Context, Oxford English Drama, and the Oxford Shakespeare, is available in the UK from the Marketing Services Department, Oxford University Press, Great Clarendon Street, Oxford OX2 6DP, or visit the website at www.oup.com/uk/worldsclassics.

In the USA, visit www.oup.com/us/owc for a complete title list.

Oxford World's Classics are available from all good bookshops. In case of difficulty, customers in the UK should contact Oxford University Press Bookshop, 116 High Street, Oxford OX1 4BR.

A SELECTION OF   OXFORD WORLD'S CLASSICS